**Sebastian Smith** is a prize winning author and journalist. He has been a correspondent in Washington, Moscow and London for the English-language service of Agence France-Presse and is currently living and working in Georgia.

'Fluent and persuasive prose ... admirably clear,' *New Statesman*

'A moving example of how history can be written. Smith's account of the historical background to the conflict reads like a novel, but better, because it also has the intimacy and immediacy of an eyewitness account. He has given us a memorable, well-researched account of a peculiarly horrible war' *Literary Review*

'This is a riveting book, written with almost seamless elegance. But *Allah's Mountains* is not simply a reportage. In a commendable effort to go beyond the present facts, Smith has delved deeply into the broader Caucasian context, steeping himself in the knowledge of its myriad peoples, cultures and languages' *International Affairs*

'Sebastian Smith's *Allah's Mountains* is a riveting battle by battle account' *The Tablet*

'Excellent, readable, insightful' *Jane's Intelligence Review*

'Smith's book is exceptionally well written, alternating between hard reporting and more personal vignettes that give the flavour and emotional colouring of the area' *The Moscow Times*

'Heads of state and their foreign ministers should be forced to read and ponder this book' Professor George Hewitt

**Tauris Parke Paperbacks** is an imprint of I.B.Tauris. It is dedicated to publishing books in accessible paperback editions for the serious general reader within a wide range of categories, including biography, history, travel, art and the ancient world. The list includes select, critically acclaimed works of top quality writing by distinguished authors that continue to challenge, to inform and to inspire. These are books that possess those subtle but intrinsic elements that mark them out as something exceptional.

**The Colophon** of Tauris Parke Paperbacks is a representation of the ancient Egyptian ibis, sacred to the god Thoth, who was himself often depicted in the form of this most elegant of birds. Thoth was credited in antiquity as the scribe of the ancient Egyptian gods and as the inventor of writing and was associated with many aspects of wisdom and learning.

# ALLAH'S MOUNTAINS

## The Battle for Chechnya

SEBASTIAN SMITH

TPP

TAURIS PARKE
PAPERBACKS

Published in 2006 by Tauris Parke Paperbacks
An imprint of I.B.Tauris and Co Ltd
6 Salem Road, London W2 4BU
175 Fifth Avenue, New York NY 10010
www.ibtauris.com

In the United States of America and Canada distributed by
Palgrave Macmillan a division of St. Martin's Press
175 Fifth Avenue, New York NY 10010

First published in 1998 by I.B.Tauris & Co. Ltd
Copyright © 1998, 2001, 2006 Sebastian Smith

Cover image: Female Chechen rebel fighter © Heidi Bradner/Panos

ISBN 1 85043 979 6
EAN 978 1 85043 979 0

A full CIP record for this book is available from the British Library
A full CIP record is available from the Library of Congress

Library of Congress Catalog Card Number: available


Printed and bound in India by Replika Press Pvt. Ltd.

For my Father

# Contents

# Contents

# Maps

# Acknowledgements

The first people I owe thanks are those in Chechnya who risked their lives to protect mine, or to help me get the story for my news agency, usually for no reward. In true Caucasus style, many others ignored considerable hardships to house and feed me.

Some are named in this book, but many are not. A special thanks to Mussa Damayev of Shali, Salamu Turlayev of Novy Tsenteroi, Khanzad Batayev and Movladi Yermolayev of Bamut, Ali Atuyev of Stary Achkhoi, Islam Gunayev of Hadji Yurt, Yussup of Serzhen Yurt.

I am grateful to all those in other parts of the North Caucasus who displayed such magnicifent hospitality and also to the many academics and officials who gave me their time. Especially: in Dagestan, Sayid Khabetov of Novoselskoye, Natasha Stoyanova of Makhachkala and Gussein Gazimagomedov of Gimry; in Ingushetia, Boris Khaniyev; in North Ossetia, Anatoly Isayenko at Vladikavkaz University and Vladimir Shakbazidi at the Greek Society; in Kabardino-Balkaria, Kazir Dzhammal and his family in the mountains; in Karachai-Cherkessia, Karachai leader Kazbek Chomayev and mullah Kazbek Shamatayev, Rasul and friends; in Adygea, Khamzet Kazanov, Aslan, museum director Almir Abregov and national dance troupe director Amerbi Kulov; also the staff of the *Severny Kavkaz* newspaper, especially Tatyana Mamkhyagova in Cherkessk.

For their great help in knocking sense into my manuscript, I am forever grateful to Andrew Harding, James Meek, Carey Scott and Antony Smith. I also thank Anna-Maria Boura, Laurence Peter, Andrei Piontkovsky and Dmitri Trenin for their comments on the text, and Agence France-Presse and the Moscow Times for their archives, and the Centre for Global Energy Studies and Philip Armstrong for maps.

Also thanks to my AFP boss Paola Messana for giving me time off to write and an unlimited chance to work in Chechnya; to Natasha Fairweather for helping me find a publisher; to Marina Lapenkova and Valentina Blinova for teaching me to enjoy the Russian winter; to the late Peter Braestrup and to Jack Kneece Åsne Seierstad for their early encouragement; to fellow journalists in Chechnya, some of whom, but not all, are mentioned in this book, for their company and support; and finally to Anna Enayat at my publishers I.B.Tauris for taking on the book and being so patient at my rewrites and delays.

This book could not have been written without help from previously published works. They are listed in the bibliography, but I am particularly indebted to the various works of Alexandre Bennigsen and S. Enders Wimbush on Islam under the Soviet Union; to Robert Conquest for his definitive account of the deportations *The Nation Killers*; to Marie Bennigsen Broxup et al for *The North Caucasus Barrier* – a classic reference on the region – and to Moshe Gammer for his detailed history of Imam Shamil's reign in *Muslim Resistance to the Tsar*. For understanding the history of the 19th-century wars, there is still no better book than John F. Baddeley's 1908 work *The Russian Conquest of the Caucasus*. And for understanding the nature of the opposing sides, there are no more accurate accounts than those by Tolstoy in *Hadji Murat* and *The Cossacks*, and by Lermontov in *A Hero of Our Time*; for help in entering the world of Lermontov, I am grateful to Laurence Kelly for his *Lermontov. Tragedy in the Caucasus*.

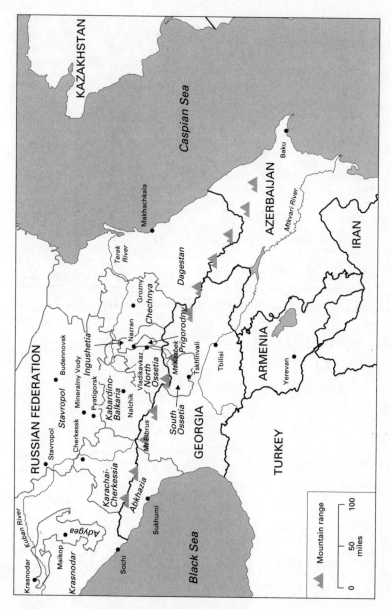

Map 1: Southern Russia and the Caucasus

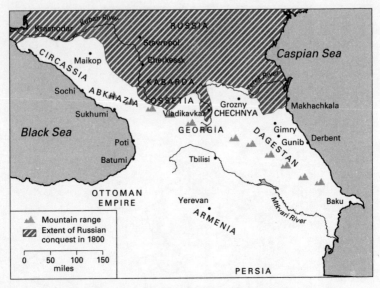

Map 2: Extent of Russian Conquest in Caucasus in 1800

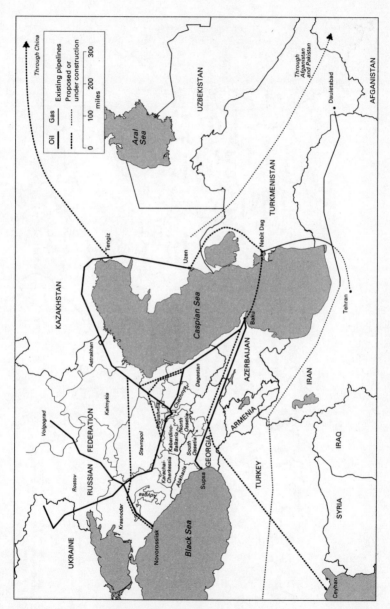

Map 3: Existing and Proposed Oil and Gas Pipelines

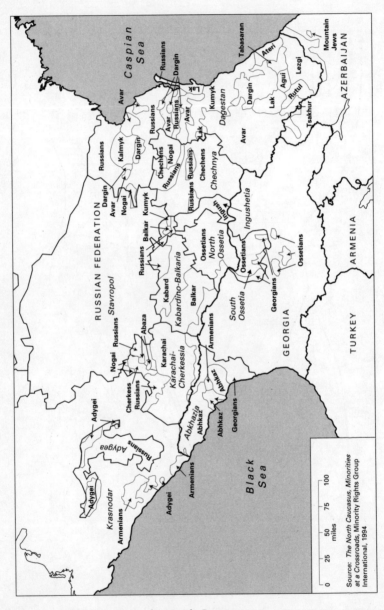

Map 4: Ethnic Groups in the North Caucasus

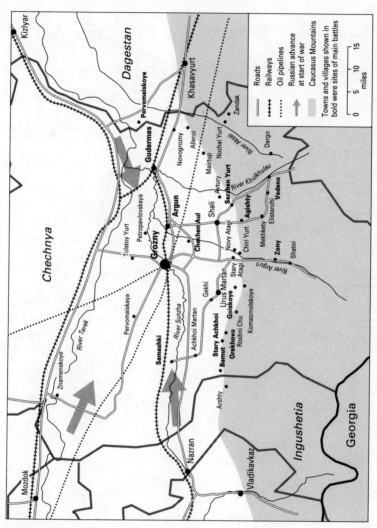

Map 5: Chechnya During 1994–96 War

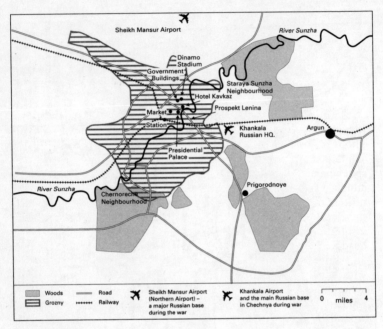

Map 6: Grozny

# Introduction

Just over 100 years ago, Leo Tolstoy described in the novella *Hadji Murat* a skirmish between Russian soldiers and Chechen guerrillas. The action begins when Russian troops stationed at the edge of a forest spot a handful of Chechen fighters on horseback. Shots are exchanged and the Chechens melt back into the trees. In the brief clash, which the officers treat as sport, a bullet fatally wounds one Russian conscript; the Chechens suffer no visible casualties. Militarily speaking, it is an insignificant engagement. Yet when the time comes to report to headquarters, wrote Tolstoy, the incident balloons into a heroic battle: an assault of 'considerable' Chechen forces, a Russian counterattack with bayonets and the routing of the enemy. 'In the course of this action two privates were slightly wounded and one killed,' reads the report. 'The highlanders' losses were about a hundred killed and wounded.'

Tolstoy, who'd served in the Caucasus, knew what he was writing about, and in *Hadji Murat*, set in the mid-nineteenth century, he portrayed the self-serving lies of an imperial army with memorable effect. So what would he have made of the gap between reality and the official version in the contemporary Chechen war?

More than a decade has passed since then president Boris Yeltsin ordered the Russian army to take control of Chechnya and 'restore constitutional order'. More than five years have passed since Vladimir Putin sent the army back to Chechnya with the aim of securing Russia from terrorism.

The so-called 'first' war (1994–96) and 'second' war (1999–to date) both had lofty official aims. The results, however, have brought about precisely the opposite. Rather than a place of constitutional, or any other order, Chechnya has for years been a lawless ghetto. Here, soldiers and policemen have been able to loot, rape and murder – almost certain of escaping punishment. Chechen rebel factions have blown up civilians who happen to be around military targets; increasingly they have dispensed with military targets altogether and simply aimed at civilians. Chechens in irregular, pro-Kremlin units torture and kidnap fellow Chechens – often former rebel comrades in arms.

As for protecting Russia from terrorism, President Putin's war has provoked an unprecedented wave of outrages: the downing of passenger planes, a mass hostage-taking at a Moscow theatre, an explosion in the Moscow metro and a bloodbath at a school in Beslan. If terrorism can be defined as violence against civilians in the name of politico-military goals, then much of what the Russian military has perpetrated in Chechnya should be added to this sinister list. A recent survey by the aid group *Médecins Sans Frontières* found that Chechens suffer some of the highest levels of psychological trauma in the world. 9 out of 10 people in the study had lost someone close to them in the war. 1 in 6 had witnessed the death of a close relative. 80 per cent had seen people wounded. Two thirds said they never felt safe and almost every single respondent had come under aerial bombardment or crossfire. Terror: the word is apt.

According to various reliable estimates, more than 100,000 Chechens have been killed in the last decade, and several hundred thousand others have at some point lost their homes or been forced to flee: that from a population of one million. Grozny, once a city of about 450,000 and one of the Soviet Union's major oil refining centres, is a gruesome ruin. Oil spills, radiation, landmines, unexploded ordnance, and destroyed forests scar and poison Chechnya's landscape. By sober unofficial estimates, more than 20,000 Russian soldiers have been killed.

Yet on Russian television screens, all now controlled by President Putin's Kremlin, Chechnya is at peace. There is rarely any mention of resistance to Russian forces, only a flow of Tolstoyan success stories about 'liquidated' bandits and foiled terrorist plots. Believe the Russian media and Chechnya has enthusiastically embraced the Russian state and President Putin himself. Accept this version and one believes official reports that Chechens voted unreservedly for a constitution cementing them within Russia. One believes they flocked to elect as president Akhmad Kadyrov, a former rebel mufti who went over to the Russians at the start of Vladimir Putin's war. (Kadyrov – who in fact was hated, feared or mistrusted by almost all sides in Chechnya – was assassinated in the summer of 2004.) Logically, one must also consider it normal that many of Kadyrov's powers were transferred to his son Ramzan, a boxing enthusiast accused by human rights specialists of being one of the republic's chief torturers.

As 2004 gave way to 2005, the official media portrayal of Chechen loyalty to – love for – the Russian Federation knew no bounds. The Russian-installed government in Chechnya was promising its sick, broken population not only peace, but a film industry, a football stadium and what the prime minister, Sergei Abramov, called

'Disneyland', apparently an aquatic fun park in the city of Gudermes. To mark the New Year, President Putin personally awarded Ramzan Kadyrov the Hero of Russia medal – the supreme decoration of the Russian state.

\* \* \*

At about this time, 10 years after the first tanks rolled toward Grozny, I made a visit to Chechnya. I had been there many times before. Its capital was a place I knew well and over the last decade I had observed several stages of its slow-motion catastrophe. Yet I found myself in a place I had difficulty recognising. Certainly Grozny was not the impoverished, but still functioning ex-Soviet regional centre I'd seen in 1994. But neither did it resemble the devilish battlefield I'd come to know later. Grozny had become a twilight zone – a place where the definitions of war and peace were blurred, all loyalties suspect and the aims of the combatants themselves unclear.

The fact of having made previous visits also did little to lessen the shock of witnessing the city's appalling condition. In the central square kilometre – an area once thick with institutional buildings, the university, large apartment blocks, major thoroughfares and parks – barely a stone is left. Flattened by bombs and shells, then bulldozed clean, the one-time heart of the city is a desert. And from this ground zero the destruction radiates for miles: through gutted factories and sprawling neighbourhoods of smashed houses, through disembowelled apartment complexes, through tangled, wild undergrowth that no one dares enter for fear of bombs and mines.

The only crowds you'll find are those in the Stalingrad-like centre. War never prevented the Chechens from trading and in a place where there have long been no shops, the open-air bazaar is a lifeline. But at dusk, even those crowds leave for the villages and Grozny becomes dark, quiet and dangerous. In my estimate – reached by driving at night and counting lighted windows – no more than a third of the population, or 150,000 people, permanently reside in what was once one of the most important cities in the Caucasus.

Official Moscow and its subordinates in Chechnya talk up their reconstruction programmes. But in reality these projects have in ten years accomplished almost nothing other than enrich those controlling the funds. In Grozny the restored or reconstructed buildings are in such small numbers that they are startling – far more so than the ruins. I counted only dozens and, bar a few exceptions, they were security forces barracks and offices, institutions serving the oil industry, or the electricity and gas companies that keep Chechens, however miserable, alive. Grozny is a monument not only to the Russian army's destructiveness, but the Russian state's inability to rebuild the peace.

Walking through this wasteland, I discovered the former site of the presidential palace and its rose garden. Across the way, there would have been the Hotel Kavkaz, an exotic, semi-Soviet, semi-Oriental building in which I stayed once before the war. There would have been the national bank, parliament and internal security ministry. Today, only mud on each side of the asphalt indicates where the road, the pavements, squares and buildings used to lie. A young girl passed. Did she remember the presidential palace? This had been the headquarters of Dzhokhar Dudayev and the original separatist government, as well as the scene of an epic battle early in the first war. 'No idea!' the girl said. She was sixteen, so only six when the wars began.

Nearby, I found a woman, one of these typically expressive and incalculably tough Chechen housewives. She was collecting water. This meant towing a trolley-load of bottles and urns to a broken pipe, then towing the trolley home, where she would boil the lot. Few parts of Chechnya have running water anymore. Taps, sinks and baths, like phones and rubbish bins, are relics of a forgotten civilisation. (Not that the lack of water is hindering the plan for an aqua fun park in Gudermes.)

This woman, however, possessed something valuable: memory. 'Over there,' she said, 'you had the jewellers. There was the music school. There was a college. There were apartment buildings...' All this time she pointed into space. The broken pipe gushing water marked the site of the Okean (meaning ocean) restaurant and fish shop, she said. I remembered the spot well: it was there that one of the first bombs dropped in 1994, killing two bystanders and drawing a crowd of bemused, outraged Grozny residents. None of them could have imagined what was yet to come. 'It's like a dream,' the woman said.

Think of the towns annihilated in the Boxing Day 2004 tsunami in the Indian Ocean and you have Grozny – the difference being that one disaster was delivered in minutes by nature, the other over 10 years, with great effort, planning and determination, by mankind.

* * *

Large-scale combat in the second war ended in 2000 after the capture of Grozny and the scattering of thousands of poorly supplied rebels to the mountain villages. Yet, as happened in Iraq after President George Bush's famous declaration of an end to major operations, the war was only entering the first of numerous new phases. Each of these has been more opaque than the last, reaching the point today when few in Russia or even Chechnya can fully define what the conflict is about anymore.

There is still open fighting in the mountains. Long range artillery salvos directed into the forests are audible from Grozny in the early hours. But the combat takes place far from most witnesses. It is up in the Nozhai Yurt, Vedeno and Shatoi regions that a new generation of commanders almost unknown to the outside world, continue to operate. Until his killing in March of 2005, the veteran leader and Chechnya's only freely elected president, Aslan Maskhadov, also remained active. He is survived by Shamil Basayev, another of the original commanders, and, for a long time now, the most extreme of them all. Their survival – in Maskhadov's case lasting five and a half years continuously on the run since 1999 – testifies partly to the inefficiency and corruption of the Russian forces, partly to the rebels' determination, robust intelligence gathering and a widespread network of civilian supporters. There is simply no other way that a guerrilla force could function so long in such a small place.

In the plains, insurgents wage a campaign of assassinations and small-scale ambushes. Russian forces and their Chechen irregular allies respond with equally ruthless counter-insurgency operations, ranging from raids on suspected hideouts to the kidnapping of rebels' relatives. But this is a low-level conflict. Even in Grozny, that great vortex of urban warfare, extended combat has become the exception. Every week, or every other week, guerrillas will gun down a pro-Russian official, or perhaps blow apart a jeep-load of police. Just as often, if not more, Russian and pro-Russian Chechen forces will corner and kill a suspected rebel, or group of rebels. However, larger-scale actions – such as the rebel takeover of much of the city for a few hours in the summer of 2004 – are infrequent. On a random visit to Grozny, one will probably hear nothing more than isolated bursts of rifle fire. There are no longer aerial attacks on the city, no shelling, or rocketing and almost never any battle involving more than a few houses or a single street. Nights, which for years were rocked by incessant firefights and guerrilla rocket attacks, are now eerily silent. The rebels have gone into deep cover, hiding, as they now must, not only from regular forces, but many of their own countrymen who have turned, or have been turned against them. One fighter I met, his 'disguise' consisting of a smart overcoat and polished shoes, told me that even the long-favourite tactic of laying roadside bombs against military traffic in the city had become ineffective. The security forces reacted too quickly; the waves of arrests were too difficult to escape. Besides, as this man put it, Russia has more armoured personnel carriers and jeeps than the Chechen rebels have men. 'They don't really care about an APC or two. We can't afford to keep losing a man for an operation like that.'

On their websites, the rebels have lost none of their old swagger and bellicosity. But evidence on the ground suggests that after all these years the assorted rebel forces are at least badly weakened. The Russian military's incomparably greater resources have squeezed the guerrillas, hampered their ability to regroup and reduced the territory in which they feel at home. An undeclared state of martial law, torture, and the use of informants (themselves, often previously victims of torture) have undercut the rebels' links to a society already bled by poverty and fatigue. Rebel access to funds has been slashed. And on a purely tactical level, years of practice have brought improvements to the performance of Russian units. Unlike their hapless predecessors in the early stages of the first war, they are often well-trained, experienced and know where they are going and what to expect when they get there.

However, to believe the rebels are broken would be simplistic and to say that the war is ending, or already has, would be wrong. The insurgents kill Russian soldiers on an almost daily basis and when cornered often fight to the death. The fact is that the resistance has fragmented to the point where it is almost impossible to defeat in the normal sense of the term. There is no Reichstag to capture in Chechnya and the death of Maskhadov – ultimately more a political, than military leader – means that many of his supporters will simply become more hardline.

The core resistance, which springs from the original nationalist rebellion of the first war, has adapted for a long game. For these fighters, resisting Russian troops is a calling: they have no interest in surrender. Another wing is composed of part-timers with grievances to avenge against the Russian authorities and soldiers. This potentially includes most Chechen men, although in practice only a small percentage take up arms. The other principal wing consists of Islamic ideologues, blinded by their revolutionary fervour into committing horrific terrorist acts. There is also a large pool of men who might be simultaneously bandits, guerrilla fighters and opportunists. Whether all these separate wings could ever again unite is questionable, but the fact is they have survived, and the result is stalemate: the rebels cannot drive out the Russian army, yet nor can the Russian army crush the rebels.

Bizarre as it appears, the impasse is one that suits powerful elements on each side. An unseasoned observer would naturally imagine that all the impressive Russian hardware, those helmeted soldiers, secret service operatives and loyal Chechen militiamen are moving irresistibly towards the day when they can clear the last cellar and forest of resistance. The goal, one would assume, is total victory. Yet closer inspection reveals something quite different: an army more interested in reaching accommodations than winning, and a war that is self-perpetuating, sustainable in the long term – a career. In the rebels' extremist wing, war has also become a way of life. War means power and war means recruits, mostly young people barely able to imagine anything else. There are those in Chechnya, and in Russia generally, for whom peace and order would spell catastrophe.

Not surprising, then, that the federal army resembles the enemy it was sent to fight. Just like textbook bandits, regular troops roam in unmarked vehicles. They wear the same masks worn by terrorists. They raid and loot private homes at night. They execute people without trial. They hold hostages, even dead bodies for ransom. They organise and provide cover for smuggling operations and for black market deals between lawless Chechnya and the neighbouring regions. Picture this conflict not just as a war, but an extreme version of a mafia turf struggle in which armed gangs chase money and power while trying to stay alive.

Indeed, anything, anybody can be sold and bought in Chechnya. The ruins are scavenged for their bricks and scrap metal; oil is stolen and driven into southern Russia; compensation money is pilfered, extorted and diverted. Killing has a price: Russian citizens sell the Chechens weapons and ammunition. (For sceptics: note that every bullet and grenade fired by the rebels is Russian-made; there are no arms factories in Chechnya; Russian territory surrounds Chechnya on 3 sides and the fourth frontier, Georgia, is impassable to anything but light foot traffic.) Peace, too, has its price. A senior officer within the pro-Russian Chechen forces told me that the Russians cut deals with the rebels on ceasefire zones in the mountains. So there may be fighting in one valley, but calm in the next, despite the presence of guerrillas.

Such deal-making – and blurring of lines – has its apex in the complex relationship between Russia's federal forces and their irregular Chechen allies. Many, perhaps a majority, of the local militia joining the Russians are themselves ex-guerrillas. Some enlist because they are sickened by rebel radicalisation, others because there is no other work. But for many, joining the Russians is a way to legalise what they were already doing: wielding a gun and ransacking what remains of Chechnya's resources. In their black uniforms, unmarked cars and with their reputation for abduction and torture, the irregular units are as disconcerting a presence to most Chechens as are the Russian soldiers. Many Chechen militiamen are thought to be double agents and their military contribution in the fight against the guerrillas shows mixed results. Indeed, rather than help Russia to end to the war, the pitting of

Chechens against Chechens has wreaked havoc in the clannish society, triggering innumerable blood feuds and a guarantee of many years more violence – something the profiteers on all sides must welcome.

Banditry has not been 'cleaned up' in Chechnya, as patriotic Russians might fancy. It has been expanded, diversified and nationalised.

*\*\*\**

Back in 1994, the idea of a serious war appeared absurd. It seemed impossible to outside observers that Russia, while lumbering towards democracy, could turn its vast army against what officials themselves described as a few hundred armed criminals. In a state stretching across eleven time zones, Chechnya was a pinprick, its entire population numbering less than the Russian armed forces alone. Some generals refused to take part in the so-called 'disarming of bandit formations'. One famously halted his column when a group of unarmed Chechen women blocked the road. For a few tense days, it seemed there might be enough sense left in Moscow and Grozny somehow to pull from the brink. There was still a sense of certain taboos – a taboo, for example, against airforce pilots bombing elderly people and children and any other bystanders who were supposedly citizens of their own country.

However, such scruples are only hard to break once and as soon as the first aerial bombs hit Grozny's crowded streets, anything became possible. Indeed, those first air raids seem almost innocent in retrospect – more like simple murder than the total abandonment of moral principles that soon came. Between the explosions, there remained time to experience shock. Then the bombs fell too fast and this luxury vanished. The impossible became normal and Chechnya slid into the abyss in which it has remained since.

So what was at the root of the Kremlin's obsession with Chechnya in 1994 and again in 1999? What was it about this remote corner that motivated Russia's leaders to stumble not once, but twice into a military and political quagmire? There are two answers in both cases – one related to broad national security and geo-strategic concerns, the other to narrow interests of internal Kremlin politics.

Chechnya and the Caucasus region around it have been strategically significant for centuries. Home to dozens of little-known ethnic groups, the Caucasus forms a crossroads between Asia and Europe that the regional rivals – Iran, Turkey and, especially, Russia – have always coveted. So although it is common to talk of the 'first' war in Chechnya in 1994–96 and the 'second' starting in 1999, the truth is that these are only the latest in a centuries-long string of conflicts throughout the region, including two centuries of Russian-Chechen bloodshed.

At the collapse of the USSR, these mostly dormant geo-strategic issues became newly relevant. With the independence of the south Caucasus states, the northern slopes of the mountains turned into Russia's most troubled frontier. On the northern, Russian side there was inter-ethnic tension and Chechnya's independence declaration. To the south, in Georgia, Armenia and Azerbaijan, Moscow faced growing diplomatic and economic competition from Western countries – particularly in relation to the Caspian Sea oil boom. For some, the intense diplomatic struggle to decide the pipeline routes from the Caspian was a key factor in starting the Chechen conflict. Originally, the principal export pipeline from Azerbaijan's big offshore fields ran through the North Caucasus.

The oil argument is essentially that Russia had to secure Chechnya from the separatists in order to secure the oil export route. But that has always been something of a red herring. The Russian pipeline (now eclipsed by the new, US-backed pipe going through Georgia to Turkey) was antiquated and in any case simple to re-route around unstable Chechnya. As for oil in Chechnya itself, there is very little, while the infrastructure, including the once mammoth refinery in Grozny, has been heavily and deliberately bombed.

Another strategic factor that some believe to be instrumental in the decision to go to war was fear in Moscow that Chechnya's separatist revolution would spread through the rest of the region, even to Tatarstan in the centre of Russia. However, although various degrees of unrest swept the seven tiny ethnic republics of the North Caucasus, only Chechnya sought independence, while Tatarstan was clearly content with autonomy.

So while there were valid areas for concern throughout the early 1990s, none presented overwhelming danger in late 1994, as Boris Yeltsin's Kremlin Security Council decided to send troops into the region.

In 1999, the situation was rather different. From a Russian viewpoint, the southern Caucasus was stabilising. But to the north, Chechnya was out of control. In ruins, full of unemployed, traumatised and armed men, and abandoned by the outside world, the republic was the model of a failed state. The elected president Aslan Maskhadov, who had negotiated the withdrawal of Russian troops, was unable to impose his authority. The traditional, decentralised rule of clan elders lay in tatters from the wartime upheavals. And amid all the disorder, only newly arrived, radical Islamic groups – groups that had both money and at least the illusion of discipline – seemed to gain in strength. Chechnya made headlines as kidnapping capital of the world. Journalists, businessmen, aid workers – all who entered the republic were at great risk. A handful of hostages were killed, the most gruesome cases being four telecom engineers, (three British, one a New Zealander) who were beheaded two months after being kidnapped in 1998.

In the summer of 1999, things suddenly got worse. Warlord Shamil Basayev led hundreds of Chechens into the neighbouring region of Dagestan, ostensibly to support an uprising of radical Islamic groups – so-called *Wahabbis*. Russia's people were in shock. For the first time in three years, their soldiers were being sent into pitched battles with the feared Chechens and there seemed to be no limit to how weak the country under Boris Yeltsin, by now in the last months of his presidency, could become. Then without warning in September a series of bombings ripped down blocks of apartments in Moscow and elsewhere, killing 294 people. No one claimed responsibility, no one was caught, no concrete evidence was produced, but the blame was decided at once: Chechen terrorism.

Of course, even at this stage, there were important arguments against sending in the army for another full-blown invasion. The experience of the first war, ended just three years earlier, did not recommend military solutions. The first war had failed militarily, weakened Russia's image abroad, scuttled reforms of the armed services, alienated Chechens of all stripes and stoked the fires of Islamic revolution. Yet despite these recent lessons, the Kremlin did not hesitate. Another war – destined to be as ruinous and unsuccessful as the first – was the only option considered.

Why? The simple answer, of course, is that the Kremlin blundered in 1994 and failed to learn its lessons for 1999. But there is another, more complex and far more important reason, and for this one must delve into the politics of the Kremlin itself.

Consider the first war. In the winter of 1994, Yeltsin was at almost the lowest ebb of a turbulent career. Disillusioned Russians no longer believed in his economic and political reforms – and with good reason. Just a year earlier, Yeltsin had used tanks to resolve his breakdown in relations with the opposition in parliament. Millions were subject to crushing poverty. Diminished by ill health and drink, Yeltsin himself barely appeared to be in control. At the same time, a shift was taking place inside the Kremlin, with the last of Yeltsin's politically liberal allies making way for a hawkish, unsavoury and unprofessional entourage including Yeltsin's bodyguard.

It was this new team that insisted on force to resolve Chechnya's nationalist revolt, which Moscow had largely ignored during the previous three years. There was little analysis of the situation, while the defence minister Pavel Grachev, who should have known better, was mired in corruption allegations and ready to go along with anything. All the evidence suggests that these men, headed by Yeltsin, believed they had hit on a good idea. Invading Chechnya would show the country that the Kremlin was still in charge and that Yeltsin, blamed by nostalgic patriots for losing the Soviet Union, would not 'lose' another centimetre of territory. Far from being a ludicrous concept, war in Chechnya – in the Yeltsin team's eyes – was inevitable.

Of course, things did not turn out as hoped. The victorious little expedition turned into a twenty one month guerrilla conflict that took tens of thousands of lives and ended in 1996 with a humiliating Russian pullout and de facto Chechen independence. Yet the war had done little real harm to its political and military authors back in Moscow, an astonishing fact helping to explain the willingness with which a second invasion was embraced just three years later.

This time, Yeltsin's Kremlin found itself in even more trouble than in 1994. Yeltsin in 1999 was ill (again) and barely in control of the presidency. His latest entourage was deeply unpopular. Only recently, the country had suffered the collapse of the rouble and the loss of millions of people's bank savings – one of the darkest periods in ten painful years of Russia's attempt to create a market economy. As if that were not enough, Russians had also endured the humiliation of watching NATO bomb their old ally Yugoslavia to eject Serb forces from Kosovo. In Moscow parliament was inching towards impeachment proceedings for, among other things, the first Chechen war. In New York and Geneva investigators were closing in on allegations of kickbacks, embezzlement, hidden bank accounts and the laundering of billions of dollars. Most seriously, legislative elections threatened the Kremlin and its allies in December 1999. In July 2000 there would be all-important presidential polls to replace Yeltsin.

With anger against Yeltsin mounting throughout the country, the entire Kremlin establishment that had dominated Russia and enriched itself from Russia over the last decade faced destruction. The most effective challenger, Moscow mayor Yury Luzhkov, looked increasingly likely to win any election, and there was for the first time real speculation that Yeltsin's people could end up in jail. The appointment in August of Vladimir Putin, a man with no political base, no economics experience, nor even charisma, as prime minister only seemed to confirm that Yeltsin had lost his grip. But then came the events in Dagestan and the apartment block bombings.

It was now that Vladimir Putin, the almost unknown ex-chief of the FSB, or secret services, suddenly came into his own. By taking personal responsibility for the military response in Dagestan, the decisive, strong-willed martial arts expert became man of the hour. By talking up Russia's military prowess, using crude, violent language and simply by looking and acting sober, Putin caught the mood of the nation. 'Wipe out the terrorists in the shithouse,' Putin declared in his celebrated phrase.

Scared, enraged and frustrated, Russians took little persuading that another merciless campaign was needed in Chechnya. Among the military, too, there was hunger for revenge. Russia had a great many problems in the late Yeltsin years – poverty, unbridled corruption, awesome environmental ills, a shambolic armed forces, declining birth rate – but Chechnya was seen as the sorest part of the whole sick body. Cure Chechnya, the idea went, and the rest could be cured too – even the country's chronic sense of impotence on the international stage. After all, what could those NATO countries that brushed aside Russian objections to bombing the sovereign state of Yugoslavia say when Moscow unleashed jets against Chechnya?

The risk posed by Chechnya in 1999 clearly required drastic action. Regardless of any political motives, the security argument for going to war was strong – infinitely more so than in 1994. Yet another total occupation was always going to be a disaster. Some cooler heads suggested attempting to seal off Chechnya. Others put forward the idea of partitioning the republic, with Russia occupying only the more easily controllable plains in the north. The beleaguered Aslan Maskhadov called desperately for negotiations, but was dismissed out of hand. Having been unable to control Shamil Basayev, Maskhadov was declared a spent force. However, many in Chechnya still supported him. At the very least they supported anyone who was not Basayev or one of the other radical warlords. The thought of more war was agony to the vast majority, who had not had time to recover morally and materially from the first. Yet no one in Moscow wanted to help Maskhadov or any moderate element. The war started with enthusiastic backing from the Russian public.

*\*\*\**

Questions over the extent of political ambitions in driving the start of the second Chechen war become more troubling on inspection of the outwardly solid *casus belli*: the Dagestan incursion, followed by the apartment block bombs.

Moscow's line was that the Dagestan incursion and the bombs were directly linked and that the decision to invade Chechnya was merely a response. However, Moscow had begun plans to attack Chechnya long before either of these events. That was stated by Sergei Stepashin, prime minister before Putin's surprise appointment in late summer of 1999.

According to his account, the original plan for moving into Chechnya had been drawn up in March, long before Dagestan or the apartment block bombs, and was to be executed that summer. In other words, the Chechen assault on Dagestan had forced a delay in the Russian invasion of several months.

Maybe the Chechen raiders, as Basayev boasted, did want to establish a fundamentalist Islamic state stretching to the Caspian Sea, and in so doing triggered Russian reprisal. On the other hand, Basayev the military man would have known very well that the bare, rocky slopes of Dagestan (as opposed to the forests of Chechnya) would make a poor place to defend against Russian helicopters and jets. So it is also possible that the whole Dagestan affair was really just a diversionary attack by the Chechens in order to win time before the long-planned Russian assault on their own territory.

The truth could easily lie between theories. Maybe Basayev planned to draw Russian forces away from Chechnya, while at the same time making a speculative attempt at destabilising Dagestan. Maybe, as has been rumoured in Russia, Basayev was himself tricked, with some apparently friendly force in Moscow encouraging, even funding the adventure with the idea that a flare up in Dagestan would better prepare the ground for a new war in Chechnya. After all, until then the Russians had ignored, even tolerated the presence of the radical Islamic groups in Dagestan's mountains and, although Basayev's incursion was especially large in scale, it was far from the first. Skirmishes had been taking place along the Chechen-Dagestan border ever since the end of the first war.

One of the many strange elements in this episode, according to the speaker of the upper house of the Russian parliament, was that border guards actually withdrew just ahead of Basayev's incursion. Equally odd are the many eyewitness accounts, including those from journalists, claiming that Russian military helicopters flew above the Chechen guerrillas during their retreat from Dagestan – not to attack, but to escort.

The official details of the apartment bombings are even less convincing. What made these attacks so shocking was their arbitrary and massive nature. Their scale alone, and the way they were expertly detonated in order to destroy buildings like houses of cards, was terrifying enough. Above all, these attacks happened right in the heart of Russia against blameless, sleeping citizens. Hysteria took over and once the authorities, led by Mayor Yury Luzhkov, announced on national television that Chechens were responsible, the reaction was predictable. In Moscow, latent hatred and mistrust of people from the Caucasus erupted and anyone from the region, particularly Chechens, faced detention and beating, or expulsion from the city. Almost overnight, the weariness and apathy afflicting Russian society was replaced by open racism and war fever.

Yet the police could produce no credible Chechen suspect and none came forward to claim responsibility. No one, in fact, attempted to extract gain – not publicly, that is. No demands were made and there were no threats of new bombs. Basayev, never shy about claiming terrorist attacks, including the Beslan school hostage-taking of 2004, denied involvement. In addition, the official investigation was perfunctory, with almost no time taken to comb the ruins for clues, or perform other basic detective work. That was unsurprising. The list of unsolved major crimes in Russia, including assassinations of leading journalists, politicians and businessmen, is long and growing. Few have faith in the police. But how, then, could the same police so rapidly deduce Chechen guilt?

Then something occurred in the city of Ryazan, which lent support to what until then had been only a wild conspiracy theory: that the FSB secret services were somehow linked to, or even at the origin of the whole terror campaign, their motive – to whip up support for a war only they needed.

The essentials of the Ryazan incident are these: a man returning to his apartment building late one evening found strangers placing large sacks in the basement. At once the man called the local police who discovered that the sacks contained explosive and a detonator set for 5:30 a.m. the next day. Those planting the sacks, it turned out, were from the FSB. Naturally, there was some confusion, but the FSB offered the explanation that the whole thing had been a misunderstanding, that the sacks were actually harmless and that they had been placed in the building as an exercise in civil defence. The local police repeated that what they'd found was not a dummy, but the real thing. The investigation never went further and neither version was publicly proved. Had that resident merely shown himself an alert citizen? Or, had he in fact prevented the secret services from carrying out another massacre? The question was never satisfactorily answered.

As so often in Russia, the truth could well lie in unexplored corners. Maybe Dagestanis or even Basayev were behind some of the bombs. The first bomb attack did not target civilian apartments within Russia proper, but military housing in Dagestan. This quite plausibly could have been the work of Dagestani or Chechen guerrillas. After all, they were fighting with Russian forces in that very region. Maybe these same guerrillas went on, anonymously, to bomb the apartment buildings, but it cannot be ruled out that the

FSB, or the Kremlin, had by then seen the potential and planted the bombs itself. We will probably never know the truth, nor, even as their tanks rolled into Chechnya, did Russian voters.

\* \* \*

What are very clear are the political benefits that this turmoil and the coming war brought Yeltsin and his protégé Putin.

Whether through chance, or plotting, the apartment bombings gave Yeltsin and his so-called 'family' of business cronies and relatives the national crisis they needed – not a full-blown state of emergency, but a *casus belli* against a hated minority group that distracted the country from other worries. Already by November 1999, with much blood under the bridge, Putin the nobody had become a hero, his popularity ratings up from 1 to 50 percent, and every day that Russian air and ground forces bombarded Chechnya, rising another notch. Yeltsin's surprise resignation announcement on New Year's Eve 1999 looked abrupt, but was perfectly timed. Putin automatically became acting president, with early elections set for March 2000. With the constitution demanding only three months before voting, rather than the much longer period that would have been required had Yeltsin held on until scheduled elections, Putin could avoid the uncertainties both of drawn-out campaigning and what might happen in Chechnya during the summer months, the best for guerrilla resistance. As Putin began his acting presidency by flying to a Russian base in Chechnya and handing out daggers, Yeltsin and the 'family' were able to sleep soundly.

That any government could organise bombings of apartment blocks for political gain seems absurd, but with such gaps in the official story, the possibility cannot be ignored. Certainly no one should rule out FSB involvement in the apartment bombs in the belief that Yeltsin's Kremlin was insufficiently ruthless. Consider the shelling of the Russian parliament in 1993 or, indeed, the first war in Chechnya. The Russian government wasn't capable of blowing up innocent people's homes? It already had – by the thousands in Chechnya during the first war, including many a Grozny apartment block full of defenceless ethnic Russians.

And if the bombings let Yeltsin off the hook, the subsequent war brought his successor no less a political windfall.

In the initial stages, the media loyally portrayed the invasion as a blitzkrieg, its glorious success reflecting new Russia and its young president. Of course, the propaganda was unable to keep up. The fighting turned out to be every bit as hard as during the first conflict and Grozny had to be encircled and bombed for weeks before the remnants of its three thousand or so defenders withdrew. Even then, the war was manifestly not going to end quickly: resistance flared up across Chechnya, increasing in the spring and continuing, in ever mutating forms, to this day.

Yet no setback could damage Putin's war dividend. The political and military ineptitude would in many countries have brought down the government. At the very least, as in the United States following the controversies over the Iraq war, society would be deeply split and the ruling party put on the defensive. But to the ever self-confident Putin, the damage – huge military and civilian casualties, terrorism, Islamic radicalism and international opprobrium – was outweighed by important, even historic opportunities as a ruler. The events of 1999 had put the security services and their figurehead, Putin, in power. They had saved the Yeltsin clan from further harassment. Now, war allowed Putin to set in motion the slide to authoritarianism. War justified the destruction of the independent media, the rolling back of electoral freedoms, censorship, and any other government aim that could be labelled as 'in the interests of security'. Chechnya's war made Putin and Putin used the war to remake Russia.

\*\*\*

Responsibility for the modern Chechen tragedy lies at the feet of many vain and incompetent men, including the independence leader Dzohkhar Dudayev. Yet Boris Yeltsin must take by far the greatest blame. That President Putin became architect of the second war is a phenomenon born directly from Yeltsin's misguided policies. Even if President Putin proved more ruthless than his predecessor, his instincts and policies are essentially the same. He simply tries harder.

Yet President Putin apparently is not a man who can end the war. The measure of his failure does not seem to enter his orderly, KGB-trained mind. On one of his fleeting, secretive visits to Chechnya, President Putin was quoted as saying that from a helicopter the ruins of Grozny looked 'horrible'. Generally President Putin does not like to discuss such matters. At his infrequent press conferences he tends either not to take questions on Chechnya, or, when he does, loses his otherwise implacable cool. This apparently heartfelt statement about Grozny was unusually frank, but inadequate, even naïve from a man in large part responsible for the destruction.

Ideally, President Putin would have somehow extended that brief glimpse of reality over Grozny, looking into his own army, into what is left of Chechen society, the hill villages, the homes of the bereaved, and the ranks of the guerrillas. If Putin could see all of Chechnya, not just one corner, he'd soon understand what had happened, even if the best he managed to come up with was 'horrible'. Even as it is, Putin has seen plenty. One could say that the ruins of Grozny mirror a decade of disastrous Kremlin policies. But this is a logic that the president seems unlikely to explore. For him, the war is over and reconstruction is underway. No other version is allowed.

In the absence of honest appraisals, an early peace probably remains out of reach. However, despite the killing of Maskhadov, the one player in all this drama who consistently called for negotiations, one should not write off Chechnya's tragedy as intractable. Minimal resources have been dedicated to finding peace there – far less, for example, than to the infinitely smaller scale conflict in Northern Ireland, let alone to those in the former Yugoslavia. There have been no joint ceasefires in the second war and, apart from a furtive contact early on, no attempt to negotiate with the armed resistance. For years the Kremlin said there was no one left to talk to, while simultaneously rebuffing, then killing Aslan Maskhadov.

What could be discussed? Most Chechens have stopped thinking of independence per se as a goal. They do not need symbols now and they stopped, long ago, believing in the separatist mythology. They need guarantees of survival and human rights. They want to be treated with respect. They need justice. They need huge assistance – medical, moral, financial and practical. They need help to achieve stability while they rebuild. It is improbable that many Chechen survivors of this decade, or their descendants, will ever proudly call themselves citizens of the Russian Federation. Yet Chechens have always been realistic about their geographical location and a compromise solution to the status issue could both satisfy honour and reflect the physical facts.

Russians' basic needs are remarkably similar. Polls consistently show that Russians have little interest in fighting Chechens for the sake of it. The patriotic blush is off this nasty war. What they do want is security: an end to the terrorist bombs and hostage-takings. The land of Chechnya itself has little meaning to most living outside. Yet Russians yearn for the sense of living in a strong, stable state. This second war seemed to promise that, but the promise was empty, and Russia – if you peer under the veneer created by Putin's authoritarianism – is in many ways as weak as under Yeltsin. The choice, Russians should realise, is attempting to build a strong peace, or succumbing to the chronic sickness of endless war.

Challenging goals, perhaps, but hardly unreachable.

\* \* \*

Of course, a huge obstacle to negotiations lies in the radicalisation of the warring parties, something exacerbated by Maskhadov's death. On the Russian side there are too many with vested interests in war. On the Chechen side there are growing numbers of extremists with whom no Russian government could agree to talk.

Indeed, the Kremlin claims to be fighting 'international terrorism' in Chechnya, rather than separatists or any other nationalist rebellion. This view is overblown and for a long time it failed to get much credence in the West, which rightly saw the war as home-grown, not some jihadist import. However, the almost total media blackout imposed from Moscow made the message easier to push and after 9/11 the US president, George Bush, gave his broadest endorsement yet. This was, of course, payback for Kremlin acquiescence in the deployment of US troops across former Soviet Central Asia and Afghanistan. But from that moment, world leaders, journalists and analysts – few, if any, of whom had been in Chechnya – began to nurture the erroneous theory of Chechnya as part of the al-Qaeda phenomenon.

What is the reality? On the one hand, Islamic radicals in Chechnya form the armed groups with the greatest support among the disillusioned younger generation. They also have the greatest access to foreign funding, which means power, and the greatest propensity to carry out terrorist attacks. On the other hand, the puritanical Islamicists have almost no support from Chechen society in general, which practises a localised Sufi tradition and has little time for outsiders. It is also seldom mentioned that in practical terms Chechnya is not a simple place for foreign mercenaries or volunteers to reach. There is no real equivalent of the Pakistani border with Afghanistan. The southern border with Georgia is only passable during a small part of the year and even then to no more than a trickle of insurgents. Once within Chechnya, the territory is too small and the need for local knowledge too great for a rebel force to be able to incorporate many foreigners. As for any significant Chechen involvement in fighting US forces in Afghanistan or Iraq, that has never once been backed up with independent evidence. For the record: of the eight Russian citizens held at Guantanamo Bay, not one is Chechen.

In practice, the lines between many of Chechnya's factions are blurred. A typical Islamic radical in Chechnya may simply be a person who during all his formative years has seen nothing but war. He has listened to the more moderate rebel leaders beg, without result, for Western help. He associates Russia with nothing but occupation. Poor, surrounded by violence and hopeless, he makes an easy convert to religious causes. But more likely than not, his root motives will be revenge, or nationalism, rather than religious fervour, let alone allegiance to a nebulous al-Qaeda agenda.

The terrible possibility, though, is that with the death of Maskhadov – figurehead of all Islamic moderates and secular nationalists – the radicals will completely take over the armed resistance. This would be a disaster for Russia and for Chechnya in particular. In 1994, the separatist leaders, like all Chechens, shared a recent Soviet existence with Russians. They spoke Russian well, knew Russian culture, had served with Russians in the Soviet army and even fought with Russians against fellow Muslims in Afghanistan. In the context of the Soviet collapse, miniscule Chechnya's aspirations were patently open to compromise. Today, the original leaders are dead, exiled or outlawed and their replacements are men forged in war, men for whom nothing is too extreme. Islamic terrorism looks increasingly to be one of the Kremlin's self-fulfilling prophecies.

Neither is such a danger confined to Chechnya. Brutal policing, corruption, lack of an independent justice system and the rolling back of democracy, is infecting the entire North Caucasus with what were once considered Chechnya-specific problems. Ingushetia, where the popular local president Ruslan Aushev was summarily forced out of office to make way for one of President Putin's secret service colleagues, is spiralling out of control. Firefights between soldiers and insurgents take place there every other week. The Beslan school hostage massacre reignited tensions between the North Ossetians and the Ingush, and shook the traditionally loyal Ossetians' faith in the state. In Kabardino-Balkaria the authorities are so worried about Islamic radicals that all but one mosque has been shut down. In Dagestan, politics and business has become ever more violent and corrupt, sometimes reducing the role of Russian federal laws to a sideshow. The activity of radical Islamic groups there is second only to that in Chechnya. Here is a region containing all the conditions for a rapid spread of religious and political extremism.

In the West, more realistic views about the growing cost of Chechnya may be emerging after Beslan. The horrific live coverage of the terrorists' school takeover and the subsequent rescue fiasco demonstrated to what depths this part of the world has sunk. No one gave much credit to President Putin's claims about international conspiracies. Reports about the presence of a large number of Arabs and even an African among the hostage-takers soon proved exaggerated. President Putin's apparent failure to see any link between the catastrophe and the mayhem these last 10 years in Chechnya provoked incredulity. The hostage-takers' demands – largely kept from the Russian public – had no 'jihadist' overtone, but called for a troop pullout from Chechnya. And when President Putin then reacted to the crisis by announcing an end to elections for regional governors and new restraints on parliament's already limited independence, the international community was aghast.

A growing number of observers now see President Putin's behaviour over Chechnya in the same light as that in other areas: the hounding of his potential rival, tycoon Mikhail Khodorkovsky; the shutdown of the free media; support for the vote-rigging government in Ukraine and for Belarussian dictator Alexander Lukashenko... But there should be less surprise. For years, Chechnya has been treated as an anomaly in Russia's search for stability and democracy. Yet Chechnya is at the heart, not at the margins of Russia's post-Soviet military, political and moral decline. It is because of Chechnya that Boris Yeltsin finally cut ties with the democratic reformers; that Russians came to elect the ex-KGB officer Vladimir Putin; that extreme nationalists and racists left the shadows for centre stage; that the armed forces failed to reform.

Russians badly want to believe that Chechnya is a fringe affair. This is made easier when the media hides what has happened. Yet, regardless, the ruins of Grozny and many Chechen villages are there. So are the graves of many tens of thousands of Russian citizens and Russian soldiers. Ultimately, these facts will have to be faced. Weary Russians often describe their sole ambition as being allowed to live in what they call a 'normal' country. But until they confront what has been done in their name, this modest desire will remain forever beyond reach.

\* \* \*

The real situation in Chechnya is all but impenetrable to ordinary Russians and to many foreigners today. Just a handful of foreign journalists still visit. Russian reporters, with one or two brave exceptions, go there to serve as government mouthpieces. Internet websites present all views, but few facts. The only way even to taste the truth is to travel inside Chechnya and speak to ordinary Chechens – but this is complicated, time-consuming and on occasion dangerous.

In such a climate, one could do far worse than to reopen Tolstoy, who a century ago absorbed a number of profound lessons about Russia and about Chechnya that are worth relearning.

The reader might turn to the famous scene in *Hadji Murat* in which Russian troops lay waste to a Chechen village.

The soldiers Tolstoy describes are not evil. Simply, they believe that the natives need to be punished. This is their job. Their attitude might be summed up in the colonialist maxim that the people being brought into the empire 'only understand force'. It is an age-old theory and one as fresh in Russian minds concerning Chechens today as it was to their predecessors in the nineteenth century.

In this particular episode, the protagonist is called Butler. He is a likeable young man for whom the Chechen war provides adventure and an escape from his debt-ridden life in Saint Petersburg. His participation in the operation to destroy the village provokes no moral questioning. His soldiers perform tasks as they might clear a wood or gather crops. They foul the well and mosque; bayonet a young boy; shoot livestock; destroy fruit trees and haystacks; and torch houses. These are not crimes in the Russians' mind. Their job that day is to persuade Chechens in the village to turn from the resistance leader Imam Shamil. The job is to ask Chechens to join the great Russian state.

It is a scene that has been (and continues to be) repeated countless times in Chechen villages and towns over the last decade – with the contemporary twists of Kalashnikovs and aircraft. And the job too is the same: to persuade Chechens that they are Russian citizens.

So the description of the Chechen villager's reaction after the troops depart should interest modern Russians. In reading this, they might understand why, ten years after Yeltsin first sent in the military, that the 'job' is unfinished – and probably doomed to remain so for good.

The passage is worth quoting in full:

> The village elders gathered in the square and squatted on their heels to discuss the situation. Nobody spoke a word of hatred for the Russians. The emotion felt by every Chechen, old and young alike, was stronger than hatred. It was not hatred, it was a refusal to recognise these Russian dogs as men at all, and a feeling of such disgust, revulsion and bewilderment at the senseless cruelty of these creatures that the urge to destroy them – like the urge to destroy rats, venomous spiders or wolves – was an instinct as natural as that of self-preservation.

> The villagers were faced with a choice: either to remain as before and by terrible exertions restore all that had been created with such labour and so easily and senselessly destroyed, while every minute expecting a repetition of the same thing, or they could act contrary to the law of their religion and, despite the revulsion and scorn they felt for the Russians, submit to them.

The old men prayed and resolved unanimously to send envoys to ask Shamil for help, and straightaway they set about rebuilding what had been destroyed.

Tbilisi. 2005.

# Prologue

## Dargo, Chechnya

*Shamil Basayev – Chechen hero, most wanted man in Russia – sits in front of me and lights a Marlboro. We are in a dusty courtyard at the edge of Dargo, a village lost in the jungle-like foothills of the Caucasus, far behind the frontlines, with only the speck of a war plane circling high overhead to remind us of the Russians.*

*Basayev wears a faded camouflage suit, sandals and a Moslem amulet on a thin black cord around his neck. A Russian special forces rifle topped by a silencer lies on his lap and he drinks heavily-sweetened black tea from a tin mug. Nearby sit bodyguards: tall men with carved, tanned and bearded faces – faces from another age, almost Biblical. Their chests are heavy with grenades, Kalashnikov ammunition clips and the long Caucasus dagger, the kinzhal.*

*A hush falls as soon as Basayev – thickly bearded, dark-eyed and surprisingly small – begins to speak. This is the man who two weeks ago shot his way into a hospital in the Russian town of Budennovsk, held 1,500 people hostage to force a ceasefire in Chechnya, and got away with it. He is the criminal whose barricades were made from living, innocent bodies, who turned a hospital into a battlefield. But he is also the man who fooled the mighty Russian army and made it halt its war. In Dargo, he is king.*

*'We showed them,' Basayev laughs and everyone laughs with him. Basayev plays the celebrity terrorist – flippant, unbalanced, spouting pretentious political statements one moment, crass boasts of war the next – but the bravado slowly cools. He stops talking about what he did in Budennovsk, or even about this brutal war. He goes back to his legendary namesake, Shamil, the Islamic warrior who led a 25-year struggle against the tsars' armies in the 19th century. He speaks of Communist repressions. He recalls, above all, that event which enveloped the entire Chechen people like a shroud: Stalin's genocidal deportation in 1944 of every man, woman and child to Central Asia, a repression that as many as one in three did not survive.*

*'When Stalin deported us,' Basayev begins, 'the Russians took over*

1

*our empty homes and they ripped the stones out of our graveyards, then they used them to make roads, bridges, pigsties.'* His voice is quiet, but filled with hatred. Of course. What could be more loathsome to a people who consider ancestors as important as the living, who still rise out of their car seats in respect as they drive past cemeteries? The Soviets tore out hundreds, perhaps thousands of tombstones, purely to insult and humiliate. Eventually, Stalin died and the Chechens returned to their homeland. As soon as they got the chance, they gathered all the stones up again and built a memorial, a garden of death, in the centre of Grozny. Dignity was restored.

Then this war. New blood, new fury. *'When the Russians stormed Grozny, they fired their tanks from the memorial,'* Basayev says. *'On the hill over Alkhan-Kala, the soldiers took stones from the graveyard there and built toilets for their camp.'*

Basayev stared at the ground a lot before, during the joking, but now, he's looking me right in the eye. *'They want to force the whole people on to its knees and turn us into their slaves, but we can't take these insults anymore. Our fathers and grandfathers fought and died for freedom, and we consider it a great honour to die for this too. It's an honour to continue the fight.'*

Under the spell of the Caucasus mountains, it is easy to forget the curse of history. The peaks are usually hidden away in the winter months, yet their presence looms unseen, like royalty, and one always hopes to catch a glimpse. One February day, after a two-week stint in Chechnya for my news agency, I drove out numb from an overdose of the mud, blood and cold of war. Near the border, the claustrophobic grey sky unexpectedly parted and the Caucasus erupted to our south. My Chechen driver pointed out Kazbek, the jagged, second highest peak in the chain and I laughed out, exhilarated. The summit of eternal snow floated massive but weightless, brilliantly white, and for one tantalising second, I felt such relief, almost giddiness, that the war seemed to have never happened. But this was only my third visit to Chechnya and I had that bitter lesson to learn: the Russian Caucasus may be a garden, but it is a poisoned garden.

The mountain range runs about the length of Cuba, 1,100 kilometres, halving the region between the Caspian Sea and the Black Sea diagonally, like a sword stroke. On the southern side lies the Transcaucasus, made up of the newly independent ex-Soviet republics of Armenia, Azerbaijan and Georgia. To the north are the seven autonomous Russian republics of the North Caucasus, probably the most ethnically diverse region on the planet.

A village in one of the autonomous republics like Dagestan or Ingushetia feels remote these days, but the North Caucasus has always been, and remains, the eye of a geopolitical storm. From earliest times to the Mongol era, a period spanning more than 2,000 years, Asiatic tribes used the Caucasus as a bridge from Asia to Europe. The mountains then became a strategic key in the struggle between the Russian, Persian and Ottoman empires. Today, the region is on the doorstep of the Caspian's vast oil reserves, one of the world's last great untapped sources, a possible Persian Gulf of the 21st century and the scene of intense international intrigue.

My first visit to the North Caucasus was in the summer of 1994 to Chechnya, which had declared unilateral independence. Few took the republic's separatist drive very seriously then – it seemed chaotic, criminal, the stuff of comic opera – although to my surprise I immediately felt I had indeed arrived in a foreign state, certainly not part of the same country as Saint Petersburg or Samara.

When war broke out that winter, the Russian army was expected to put a quick end to this people's rag-tag revolt. Instead, Chechen fighters gave the Russians a horrific mauling from the first day, worse many said than the Soviet experience in Afghanistan. The Russian response – bombing Grozny, a city of 400,000 people, to the ground, then doing the same thing to village after village – was sick beyond comprehension.

President Boris Yeltsin said he was just 'restoring constitutional order,' but a day in Grozny was enough to realise that something deep rooted was underway. Chechnya was where the curses of history and revenge raged out control. Battles were fought in exactly the same places, with the same tactics and the same slogans as 100, even 200 years before. Chechens had a phrase – 'every 50 years they try and crush us, but we'll fight to the end' – that was repeated so often it became a cliche. But it was eerily true. Every 50 years.

What about the rest of the North Caucasus? Although there were no other armed, separatist revolts, small Moslem nations such as the Adygei and Avars had much in common with the Chechens historically and politically. The same genocidal deportations were carried out by Stalin against the Ingush, Karachai and Balkars. These peoples' stories were virtually unknown both in Russia and abroad, and I wanted to compare their modern fates. Did they also consider themselves trapped in the wheel of history, or had their republics become integrated Russian provinces? Was Chechnya merely an aberration, a one-off blunder?

I drifted from the incredible ethnic mix of the Dagestani capital Makhachkala, to the mountains of Karachai-Cherkessia, to the fervor of Moslem dervish sects in Ingushetia and the tree gods of North Ossetia. At first only the diversity, the endless tribal and linguistic subdivisions and internal borders, seemed to stand out. Yet as I collected the pieces, a pattern emerged. The North Caucasus was not just another Russian region, it was the troubled remains of an empire. Obviously, much had changed since the time of the tsars, but the underlying dynamics – tiny ethnic groups everywhere struggling for cultural, even physical survival – had not. I was left with a final question: would the conflict ever end, would the North Caucasus and Russia meet on common ground?

Today, minarets of newly built mosques poke above the low roofs where the Soviets once thought they had eradicated religion. On calm summer evenings, the *muezzin's* sad voice calls in Arabic for the faithful to come to prayers. Old men with carved walking sticks and white beards come up the road. Behind them are young children in bright skull caps, already being instructed in the faith. Inside the mosque, hidden behind a curtain to separate them from the men, women in bright, patterned clothes and headscarfs kneel on prayer rugs. Not a word of Russian is spoken. Whichever autonomous republic you are in – from Dagestan, to Kabardino-Balkaria or Adygea – the scene is the same. The map says you are on the southern border of the Russian Federation, but this is in theory. In fact, you left Russia long ago and you have now entered the ancient, enduring and tragic world of Allah's mountains.

PART I

# The Jigsaw

*"Why should she be homesick? She saw the same mountains from the fort as she did from her village – and that's all these savages want."*

from *A Hero of Our Time*, by Mikhail Lermontov.

# 1. BADLANDS

## Vnukovo Airport, Moscow

*Vnukovo Airport, outside Moscow, is the gateway to the North Caucasus.
Planes to Grozny, Stavropol, Makhachkala, Vladikavkaz – they all leave
from here. The airport is a hive of vendors, travellers with vast quantities
of baggage, beggars, stray dogs and litter. Almost the only attempt at
decoration is a roughly painted mural in the men's toilets. The painting,
covering most of the wall next to the standups, shows several angry
dinosaurs against a backdrop of mountains and volcanoes. Overhead
flies a tiny airliner, with cosy yellow passenger windows, a fragile cocoon
of civilisation over a savage mountain world. For those in their last quiet
moments before leaving for the Caucasus, could this be a warning?*

*The women at the gate know me from previous trips to Chechnya
and we always chat. They are real Soviet creations, giving newcomers at
the shabby departure lounge (for foreigners only) the full treatment:
shrugged shoulders and rolled eyes at any request. But I rather like these
women. They are motherly, fuss over me having to go to Grozny, and
call me 'our poor boy.' They natter in sing-song voices from their great
double chins, let me use their telephone and are truly delighted if I give
them a small present like a chocolate bar.*

*Conversation is kept to banter. Above all, we avoid the subject of
Chechnya. Until one day, on about my sixth trip, I'm asked what I think
of the Chechens. I don't get a word in and don't really want to; there's
no point. Every time I open my mouth, my friend fires out another
sentence. I have the impression it's been pent up a very long time.*

*'The Chechens are lazy. That I can tell you for sure – they are lazy.
All they want is prestige, gold teeth, nice clothes, good cars, and lots and
lots of children. They know nothing except stealing and conning. The
only people who ever worked hard in Chechnya were the Russians. The
ones who built all the houses were Russians. All Chechens do is steal.
They're terrorists, they're criminals. The mafia there is also over here.
Simple honest people among the Chechens are a minority.'*

*'I see the criminals from the Caucasus come and go through this
airport all the time. They don't work and yet they live better than we
Russians do. How is that? We're workers, us Russians. All our lives, we
work for a few kopeks, yet Caucasians live better than we do. Chechens,
Armenians, Georgians, they're all the same. They take from us and
make nothing themselves. You should have seen in the old days how we
lived in Russia, under the Communists. There was nothing on the shelves.
You know why? Because it was all going to them, to the Caucasians.'*

On the surface, the North Caucasus looks like many other non-ethnic-Russian regions which have undergone decades of Russification. The major towns are off the Soviet production line – wide, treelined avenues, sombre blocks of flats around courtyards, desolate main squares named after Lenin and monstrous concrete administration headquarters. Russian is the *lingua franca*, while the schools and every other sphere of official life look, sound and smell Soviet. But Russification stops there, and the North Caucasus remains fiercely proud of its differences.

Maps of the region are a psychodelic quilt. Stretching down the slopes of the North Caucasus are seven tiny autonomous republics: Dagestan, Chechnya, Ingushetia, North Ossetia, Kabardino-Balkaria, Karachai-Cherkessia, and Adygea. Although they are on the southern side of the mountains, within Georgia, two more areas, South Ossetia and Abkhazia, are considered part of the North Caucasian world. No one can settle on exactly how many groups there really are among the region's 5.3 million people. Some say 40, others up to 100. In Dagestan alone, which is the size of a couple of English counties and has a population of just 1.8 million, there are officially 34 of these mini nations, most of them speaking languages incomprehensible to the others. But even that figure disguises the extent of the complexity because many groups are themselves broken down into subgroups, sometimes only in one village, speaking their own dialect. Of the Dagestani peoples, the Avar nation is the most populous, with 500,000 to 600,000 members, but they are further divided into 14 separate branches with their own names and dialects.

Travelling eastwards from the Black Sea to the Caspian Sea, you cut right through the jigsaw. The western end – Adygea, Karachai-Cherkessia, Kabardino-Balkaria and North Ossetia – is the more Russified. The proportion of ethnic-Russians is most dominant – 68 per cent in Adygea, which was abandoned by the majority of its people after the Russian conquest 130 years ago. In the other western republics, Russians make up about a third of the population. Further east – Ingushetia, Chechnya and Dagestan – the North Caucasian peoples overwhelmingly dominate. One can spend days without seeing a single Russian and Islam is perhaps more intense than in any other part of the former Soviet Union.

Legend has it that when God created the world, he sprinkled nations over the globe, but clumsily dropped his shaker over what ancient travellers called the 'mountain of languages'. Pliny wrote that ancient Greeks needed 300 interpreters to conduct business in the North Caucasus, while later, 'we Romans conducted our affairs there with the aid of 130 interpreters.' Today the mountains remain a living language laboratory. In Dagestan, one village may speak Avar, the next village Darghin, the next Lezghin. There are three main linguistic groups: Turkic, such as Karachai and Balkar; Indo-European, such as Ossetian, which is related to Persian; and the truly indigenous Caucasian tongues. The Caucasian languages, which are not found anywhere else in the world, are themselves divided into two branches: the eastern, such as Chechen, Ingush, and several Dagestani languages, and the western Adygei dialects, spoken by the Adygei, Cherkess, Kabards and Abkhaz.

The fact that these languages thrive after a century of Russification, and even though they may be useless an hour's drive from the home village or enclave, is the best indication of the North Caucasians' will to survive. The 1989 census showed that every group knew its native tongue, with most speaking Russian as a second language. Most loyal were the Chechens, 98 per cent of whom spoke their own language. The Ingush, Kabardians, Avars, Adygei, Karachai and others registered well over 90 per cent fluency in native tongues. The Ossetians, alone among the mountain peoples, are majority Christian, and this helped them adapt to Russian rule better than all the other nations. Yet a remarkable 87 per cent were still shown as speaking fluent Ossetian. Although these figures might be somewhat rosy – many North Caucasians speak a corrupted, Russified form of their language – the record, compared for example to Gaelic in Britain, is remarkable. That ancient nations such as the Rutuls, a Dagestani people who only number 20,000, still speak their languages and live in their mountain territory seems nothing less than a miracle.

In the past, tribes were divided by language and valley walls, but they had the same warrior culture and, in many cases, common cause against Russian colonisation. The costume of leather riding boots, a long narrow-waisted tunic called the Cherkesska, and shaggy sheepskin or tall lambskin *papakha* hat, was seen throughout the region. All men carried the *kinzhal*, the heavy, tapered blade, which varies between a short sword and a long dagger. As time went on, most in the region became Sunni Moslems (small numbers of Tats and Azeris in Dagestan are Shia), with only the Ossetians living in the mountains along the central Daryal Pass practising Christianity. In other words, the mountains which nurtured so many divisions became a melting pot. The mountains were a state of mind and the people who lived there were *gortsy* – the Russian word for highlanders.

Part of the *gortsy* bond uniting all seven autonomous republics were the mountains themselves.Today the majority of the population live in the plains, farming or in towns. Yet a connection to the mountains is still *gortsy* pedigree. All across the region, one meets citified, pot-bellied men who wouldn't dream of riding a horse or living in an isolated village, but will proudly talk about their relatives in the highlands. Even the Adygei people – who haven't lived in the mountains since the 19th century, when they were driven out onto the plains by the Russians – consider themselves highlanders.

The main range reaches an average height of 3,600 metres above sea level. At 5,642 metres, Mount Elbrus is not only the highest in the Caucasus, but considerably higher than the biggest mountain in the

European Alps, Mont Blanc (4,810 metres). In the summer the aggressive lushness of the wooded foothills, thick with the din of birds and whirring insects can feel like the tropics. Wolves, bear, wild boar, eagles, bison and wild cats can still be seen in some parts. Once I climbed a steep hill in Adygea and surprised a pair of wild goats – large, black creatures with swirling horns, which vanished over the rocks in a heartbeat. In Dagestan the dark foothills give way to moonscape cliffs and crags where only the wind seems to have life. Even here, the mountains surprise and charm. Microclimates bring warm breezes through cliff-walled valleys and a single river is enough to support graceful poplars and orchards.

*Gortsy* culture looks contradictory. There is still an almost medieval sense of honour, yet banditry is admired; lavish hospitality is sacred, yet blood feuds cannot be shirked. Consistent threads do run through this mixture of ideals. Most important is the worship of freedom – for the individual, his clan, his nation and all the North Caucasus peoples. Freedom is considered a birthright and every extreme, including murder and war, has been used in its defence. Primitive democracy has also existed for centuries. Chechens considered themselves 'free as wolves,' bound to no master except family and clan. This was unheard of in pre-revolutionary Russia. In other eastern areas there were hierarchal societies, but the leaders were often elected by the nobles and mullahs. In the western Adygei-Circassian tribes there was a strict set of classes headed by nobles, but slaves could voluntarily change masters and often lived with relative comfort and freedom of movement. According to James Bell – a Briton who spent long periods in Adygea during the 19th-century wars – serfs could buy their freedom with 30 oxen; on the death of their master, they won liberty.

To Russians, the Caucasus are the *enfant terrible* of an empire. The region may be beautiful, but the people are suspect. Conveniently for xenophobes, and Moscow's notorious police, most of the Caucasians are dark-haired and dark-eyed. Forget all the variety. To many Russians all Caucasians are simply *cheorny* – 'blacks.' A more clinical racist label is *litso kavkazkovo natsionalnosty*, or 'Caucasian national features.'

In Moscow, the Caucasians you're most likely to see are fruit sellers sitting behind huge piles of green, yellow and red fruits, the gift of their lush homeland. Invariably, these *cheorny* seem to have the edge on competitors – more stalls, more choice, lower prices – and that causes resentment among the Russians. The traders fuel the deep suspicion of wealth nurtured by Communist sermons about speculation and economic sabotage. Lumped straight in with the fruitsellers are the shady business-men who rip through Moscow in their BMWs and Mercedes. Their sullen faces and fantastic wealth seem to confirm all the worst fears of Muscovites. Of course there are also cohorts of young Russian *biznesmen*, with gold chains, black shirts, hourglass girls, and German-made cars.

But Caucasians carry that extra element of menace – whatever the map says, they're foreign, aliens. The racism cuts both ways. Caucasians may be back-stabbing, thieving and primitive, but Russians are cowardly, brutish, godless. Ask anyone. As one earnest Chechen said to me: 'The Russians, who are they? They're gypsies, nothing better. They have nothing of their own so they take from other people. Pushkin was from Africa, Lermontov was Scottish, and their whole ruling class used to speak French.'

Television news from the North Caucasus paints an unremitting scene of hostage-takings, bomb explosions and incomprehensible ethnic disputes. The other, acceptable side of the Caucasus which reaches Russian living rooms is folklore, such as the occasional performance on variety shows by child actors dressed up in fur hats, Cherkessk, and *kinzhal*. An annual TV fixture is the beloved Soviet slapstick film 'Caucasian Prisoner', where the exotic costumes and whacky Caucasus traditions of wife stealing and hospitality are given a hilarious sendup. One of the few attempts to make a serious film about the North Caucasus' conflict with Russia, also called 'Caucasian Prisoner' and modelled on a story by Tolstoy, was riddled with cliches about the mountain peoples. While beautifully shot in the Dagestani mountains and an Oscar nominee in 1997, 'Caucasian Prisoner' didn't move beyond the same old formula – bandits and folklore. It used local languages with Russian subtitles to appear authentic, but then cast a Georgian-speaking actor as a Dagestani. Few Russian film goers knew the difference – after all, to them the actors were speaking some foreign babble.

Blended in with the hate, sometimes indistinguishably, is a long, confused love affair. In the 19th century, Tsar Alexander II so admired the Chechens' struggle against his armies that he let their defeated leader Shamil live out his life under comfortable and honourable house arrest; a son of Shamil became a Russian general. Chechnya's modern independence leader Dzhokhar Dudayev was previously a trusted general in the Soviet air force, commanding a nuclear bomber base. Another Chechen, Ruslan Khasbulatov, became speaker of the Russian parliament. Even the tyrant Stalin was Georgian, a Caucasian.

The great 19th-century Russian poets and writers Lermontov, Tolstoy and Pushkin were fascinated by the mountains and their colourful, fierce tribes. Lermontov wrote, at the age of 10, that the Caucasus were 'sacred' to him and in 1841, at 26, he was killed in a duel in Pyatigorsk, a spa town within sight of his beloved mountains. To a rebel like Lermontov, author of the masterpiece *A Hero of Our Time*, the peoples of the North Caucasus and their defiance of Russia were the greatest inspiration he knew. Some of his writings, like this verse, were considered subversive. Freedom was a dangerous topic in a country where millions of people were born as enslaved serfs and a tiny elite fawned before the tsar.

*Farewell, unwashed Russia,*
*Land of slaves, land of lords,*
*And you blue uniforms*
*And submissive hordes.*
*Perhaps beyond Caucasian peaks*
*I'll find a peace from tears,*
*From Tsars' all-seeing eyes,*
*from their all-hearing ears.*

Leo Tolstoy was entranced by both the mountains and their inhabitants. In his story *The Cossacks*, the young Muscovite nobleman, Olenin, wakes up in his long-distance horse-drawn carriage after a night drive from Russia into Chechnya, sees the Caucasus for the first time and becomes obsessed.

He looked at the sky and thought of the mountains. He looked at himself or Vanyusha and still thought of the mountains. Two Cossacks rode by, their guns in their holsters swinging rhythmically behind their backs, the white and bay legs of their horses intermingling ... and the mountains.

Even then, the Russians saw the North Caucasians at best as noble savages, at worst as bandits. Lermontov's sing-song 'Cossack Lullaby' promises that babies will sleep safely, even though 'the wicked Chechen creeps/ and whets his dagger keen.' The Caucasus inspired some of these writers' most glorious works, but ultimately they were imperial servants, collectors of new countries. Willingly, they carried a pen in one hand, a sword in the other, fighting to subdue the people they admired so much. In his poem 'The Dispute', Lermontov prophesied that Russian conquest and loss of freedom for the highlanders was inevitable. 'Terrible, like gathering storm clouds, east, due east, they pour', he wrote of the Russian armies. Tolstoy believed in the colonial mission, even volunteering to take part in military operations in 1851. Pushkin, also in the army, had this advice for the people trying to oppose the invasion led by General Yermolov in the early 19th century: 'Humble thyselves, oh Caucasus, for Yermolov is coming.'

The muddled relationship with the highlanders is reflected in Russia's policies in the region and the apparently contradictory results. The peak of these contradictions is the system of autonomous republics built into the Soviet Union. Given the totalitarian nature of the Soviet government, Moscow might have been expected simply to declare the North Caucasus another part of the Russified superstate. Instead, the Communists allowed ethnic homelands with their own governments, symbols, borders and capitals. It is therefore tempting to think – and this is what the propagandists always said – that Soviet policy, and Russian rule in general, was benevolent, that the state had found a way of living alongside its minorities. But in fact, these autonomies demonstrated the opposite – the

Soviets' fundamental failure to dismantle imperial rule in the Caucasus, a failure whose after-effects are clear today.

True, Moscow showed generosity by acknowledging that there were minority peoples with separate, non-Slav identities and histories. But that generosity never went beyond a symbolic minimum, just enough to disguise a ruthless police state where the Communist Party ruled everything and non-Russians were rarely trusted 100 per cent. For example, although the USSR groomed elite classes within the ethnic minorities, allowing exceptions to Slav dominance, they were only exceptions. Yes, Dzhokhar Dudayev made Soviet general, but he was the first Chechen to do so.

The reality was that these ethnic homelands had no self-rule, while at the same time being classified as quasi-foreign entities. In other words they remained what they had been under the tsars: conquered territories ruled as colonies directly from Moscow, territories that had been swallowed, but not digested. The unintended bonus of the system – and this is why the autonomies system can be mistaken today as benelovent – was that these tiny nations were forced to close ranks and as a result preserved their identities and languages to a remarkable degree. The dark side of this legacy was that even after the collapse of the USSR in 1991, relations between Moscow and the locals were frozen in the past, more 19th than late 20th century. There had been no democratisation and no decolonisation. The old tsarist-communist cycle of resistance and repression was dormant, but intact, waiting to be given another, bloody spin.

## 2. REBELS

The hotel Nart in Nalchik, capital of Kabardino-Balkaria, is one of those Soviet dreams of modernity which turned to parody. Built as part of the mass tourism programme, the Nart is all glass and concrete, towering over the central park. You can almost hear the party official thinking, 'this will be just like in the West.' But a decade after *glasnost* and *perestroika*, the Nart is on hard times and unlikely to improve. The cramped, threadbare rooms with their fake-wood panelling, stained wall-to-wall carpeting, and temperamental televisions, are empty; some floors are simply shut down, as if they'd been the scene of a tragic death; the huge restaurant in the basement, designed for busloads of comrades, is padlocked, while up in the lobby not all the lights work and receptionists shiver in the emptiness. Yet I wanted to stay at the Nart, not only because the alternatives didn't look any more cockroach-free, but on a simple impulse – I was looking for Narts, the mythological giants who once roamed the North Caucasus as rebels, heroes and outlaws.

Even without Narts, the Caucasus is steeped in myth and legend. The Garden of Eden is said to have been in Abkhazia and Noah's dove rested on Mount Elbrus. The ancient Greek hero Prometheus was chained to the Caucasus – either Elbrus or Kazbek, according to different versions – after he stole fire from the gods, and Jason landed on the coast of Georgia in search of the Golden Fleece. But Narts are peculiarly Caucasian. They were North Caucasians at the beginning of time, close cousins of the Titans in Greek myth. The Narts' origin is obscure, but they're claimed by every nation now and, in a sense, they're a shared heritage, common forefathers. They live on in epic poems, shop names and the Nalchik hotel, but also in the North Caucasus psyche, the spirit of rebellion and heroism.

There was a Nart with one eye, the 'sun eye' in Chechen and some Dagestani legends, there was the Ossetian Nart who lived in an underwater palace, there was the Nart who climbed Mount Elbrus to understand the mystery of its twin peaks, and there were Narts who brought honour and Narts who brought ruin, then refused to repent. In one of the best known myths from Adygea, the giant was chained to a mountain by God for rebelling. A dog – or in other versions a pair of wolves – was placed on guard and every time the dog gnawed through the heavy links, the chain instantly became whole again and even thicker. Another story has it that the Adygei Nart was chained and attacked by a bird. Here, the Nart myth and its Greek counterpart – bound Prometheus having his liver pecked out for all eternity – are almost indistinguishable. Scholars today argue over which came first, even suggesting that the earliest Greeks may have first travelled from the North Caucasus to the Balkans.

In another version of the Nart's punishment, the chained anti-hero cries out in rage, setting off a storm of hail and thunder. Lightening rods shoot out when he beats his chains, and huge stones tumble down the mountainside. Local people become afraid they will also be hurt by God, so they appeal that he not be set free – they reject him. Could this legend then be the genesis of the *abreg*, that Caucasian fixture – the lone outlaw in the mountains, half-admired, half-feared?

*Abregs* were men who for one reason or another had left their villages for the hills; these were violent, cruel, possibly evil men, fugitives, full time raiders. Yet although they had to live as outsiders, real *abregs* were due at least grudging respect and sometimes were considered heroes. Yes they were bloody, yes they stole, but they were daring, desperate men. Though many *abregs* were criminals, an *abreg* could also be a man who had killed to defend his, or his family's honour and then fled to escape a vendetta. When the Russians invaded, there were rebels who continued to fight on alone in the mountain ravines and forests, becoming cult figures and symbols of freedom. They too were *abregs*. Such men could be cut-throats, but they could also be Robin Hood type folk heroes, defenders of the people. They were known as bandits of honour.

One of the most famous was Zelimkhan, who died in Chechnya early in the 20th century. A shrapnel-chipped statue of him with his horse stands today outside Serzhen Yurt, a village bombed flat in 1995 by Russian artillery and planes in the foothills of the Caucasus. Dakha Gaisultan, a local amateur historian who clearly liked his subject, told me that Zelimkhan's career started when a quarrel with the Russian-installed village head over a girl escalated into a blood feud.

> Zelimkhan and his father were arrested and taken to Grozny by the Russians. The rest got away. Zelimkhan managed to escape by digging out of the prison and, from then on, he lived in the mountains – he was an *abreg*. It was 1901. Everyone knew him and he could stay anywhere with friends, who would hide him and look after him. He started to fight against Russian soldiers, who were seen as invaders and Christian infidels, and whenever he needed men, he could find them.
>
> One day he sent a note to the colonel at the Russian fort in Kizlyar and said 'don't hide like a woman, come and meet me in Kizlyar.' The Russians laughed and said 'how could he ever get into Kizlyar, a fort?' So Zelimkhan took 60 men and they dressed up as Cossacks and rode right into Kizlyar and robbed the bank. Before leaving, Zelimkhan left a note to the colonel saying 'I waited for you. Where were you?' That was in 1907. He got back to the mountains and handed the money out to his people and some to the orphans. When he was still young, in his 40s, he became ill and had to see his relatives in Shali. It was there that one of his own relatives – on his mother's side – sold him out and he was killed fighting.

Zelimkhan was a classic: anti-Russian, bank-robber, good shot, apparently invincible, and finally brought down by treachery. But defining the *abreg* is not always easy and probably depends what side of the gun you're on, an ambiguity repeated in general attitudes to banditry and stealing. A convenient myth exists that when God dished out riches throughout the world, he forgot the Caucasus, and realising his error, allowed the peoples there to go to their neighbours and take what they needed. Lermontov said in *A Hero of Our Time*: 'These Circassians (North Caucasians) have got thieving in their blood. They'll steal anything, given the chance. Even things they don't want, they'll take them just the same.' It is true that stealing was a fact of life in the 19th-century North Caucasus. But this was not petty, ordinary burglary, this was the *nabeg*, the full-blown raid. In 19th-century society, attacking Russians or your rival ethnic group's villages and carrying off livestock and human hostages not only brought in the goods you couldn't get any other way, but raised your personal stock. A family whose men were brave during raids and successful at stealing horses, sheep and other riches under fire, was a family with honour. The more daring the exploit, the more profit, but also the more honour. A family without fighting men lost prestige and was itself vulnerable.

Like Narts and lone wolves, North Caucasian rebels of myth and fact tend to end up on their own. It's part of the *abreg's* aura. The last anti-Soviet Chechen *abreg* died in 1976. Legend has it that he came down from the mountains where he'd lived for decades to the village graveyard in Komsomolskoye and prepared to die. He was already in his 70s, alone, ill and weighing just 38 kilogrammes. He was recognised and reported to the Soviet authorities who surrounded him in the graveyard and shot him down – but not before he managed to pick off the hated KGB official and a few others. When nine *abregs* in Tolstoy's *The Cossacks* are surrounded by Russian troops, they also decide to fight to the death. 'To avoid any temptation to run, they had strapped themselves together, knee to knee, had their guns ready and were singing their death song.'

*Abregs* are far from extinct, particularly in Chechnya, a place where the chaos of the early 1990s has been a heyday for outlaws. One was Alaudi Khamzatov, a handsome racketeer who reputedly put his dirty money into buying weapons to mount a legendary defence of the town of Argun against the Russians at the start of the war in 1994. Like most *abregs* Alaudi lived, and also died, by the sword – killed in a blood feud started by his murder of an old man.

Another Chechen who some considered an *abreg* was Ruslan Labazanov, an imposing thug whose private army travelled in fleets of BMWs and Japanese-made jeeps. He fell out with Dzhokhar Dudayev after Dudayev became the separatist president of Chechnya in 1991, and ended up working for the Russian invasion forces. But whatever the truth about Labazanov – and all the evidence indicates the truth is nasty – he played up his *abreg* role, even handing out cash to poverty stricken members of his home village of Tolstoy Yurt in northern Chechnya. His house was built in the shape of a tiny castle, with a concrete tower and ramparts where his faithful bodyguards kept watch behind a machine-gun. When we met in 1995, Labazanov wore enormous gold rings and bracelets and kept two pistols, a *kinzhal* dagger, an automatic rifle, an Uzi sub-machine-gun and a machine-gun at his desk. He also possessed a room full of hifi and video equipment, a slender wife whose face was heavily painted in white makeup, and perhaps the only airconditioning unit in all of Chechnya. When I asked him which faction in Chechnya he supported, he answered: 'I'm on the side of the poor.' Violence also caught up with Labazanov, considered a traitor by the independence fighters, and he was gunned down in 1996, apparently by one of his own men at point-blank range in the castle at Tolstoy Yurt.

Thanks to their experience from *nabegs*, North Caucasians were able to raise some of the deadliest light cavalry in history. James Bell described in the 1830s how one grizzled old Adygei warrior's *nabegs* had turned into a family passion.

> Nor are his exploits merely predatory; for he goes to the wars accompanied by his five sons (he lost another one recently in the expedition across the Kuban), the eldest of whom he obliged the other day to *train* himself by attacking alone two out-posted Cossacks. The young man slew one and captured the other.

Quite apart from *nabegs*, the North Caucasus has always had a deep-rooted martial culture. Until the Bolshevik revolution, every man kept a firearm at home and boys were brought up knowing and loving weapons. No North Caucasian went anywhere unarmed. The *kinzhal* was known as the 'court of last appeal' and poems were written in its honour. Today the old passions survive, even if in diluted form.

High up in the mountains of Dagestan, in Gunib, an old man asked me to lunch at his home down an alley from the tiny Imam Shamil Street. Saidputin was 77, a World War II hero, and also a born and bred Soviet citizen. He still used the term *tovarish*, or comrade, and thought the collapse of the USSR was a disaster. In fact, he had very little bad to say about Soviet rule – not the religious repression, not the deportations of his fellow Moslem highlanders, or the bloody Soviet suppression of the North Caucasus' attempts to win independence after the Bolshevik revolution. He was a loyal Soviet man rather than Dagestani. Just before leaving, I asked him if he had a *kinzhal*. Because he was old, I thought he might have an interesting antique. Finally, accidentally, I hit a nerve: Caucasians love their weapons. 'Oh, that's gone,' he said. 'They took it. The Soviets. They took everything, left us nothing – not *kinzhals*, not rifles, not even shotguns. It's a pity that, *tovarish*.'

Despite what Saidputin said, there's no shortage of guns today in Dagestan. You can buy almost any infantry weapon in the Russian arsenal on the black market. In neighbouring Chechnya, even before the latest war, every household had a gun of some sort. Few males have not learned to shoot and clean a rifle, while often the first thing a proud father shows his guests is a display of his boys' karate skills. One man I met, a fighter in the independence forces, collected knives and even made his own. They were heavy and gleaming, their blades inscribed with phrases from the Koran. His neighbour had been a martial arts expert and had a two-handed sword so sharp it could shave the hair off your arm.

If men of the past had wickedly fast horses and could ride like gods (the Russians reckoned the Kabard horses among the best in the world), today they have cars – as many and as fast as they can afford. The sooner the ubiquitous Lada and other Soviet matchbox cars can be ditched, the better. You could say that the old totems of *kinzhals* and horses have been replaced by Kalashnikovs and BMWs.

In Chechnya I have seen a Rolls Royce, a Porsche, a black US limousine and – most incredible of all – a bona fide American police car, complete with stripes and lights, swerving around the potholes and stray cattle. The leader of Ingushetia has a US army Humvee jeep. Another impressive sight was the motorcade of Dagestani ethnic leaders – about 20, each representing different Dagestani nations – that crossed into Chechnya for talks on a hostage crisis in 1996. The line of Mercedes, BMWs, Cadillacs and Japanese jeeps swept through the row of muddy farms and village houses, horns blaring, lights blazing. Bodyguards with snub-nosed sub-machine guns jumped out almost before the cars had stopped moving, and the delegates emerged in a sea of lambskin hats and elegant overcoats. These men were plumper and richer than their 19th-century ancestors, but they would have had little difficulty recognising each other.

A 24-year-old *biznesman* in the Dagestani capital Makhachkala got onto the subject of his cars all of two minutes after we'd met. 'I have a BMW seven series in Moscow and here in Makhachkala I keep a Toyota Landcruiser,' he said, describing the BMW as 'umm, the real thing.' An enormous young man, his fingers, wrists and neck glittered with gold, the fruits of what he described as a 'bit of trading, here and there.' But, rather touchingly I thought, he had one other status symbol: the mountains. 'My parents live high, high up in the mountains. You wouldn't believe how beautiful it is up there, the nature. In Soviet times, Americans used to come there and pay thousands of dollars a day to shoot animals. On your first day up there your head hurts. Then you get used to it and you feel like God. Once a car stopped a kilometre from where I was and I could smell the exhaust within seconds, it's that clean. Actually, I hardly ever go. I've only been back once since I left home. There's nothing to do up there. It's all old people. They live till they're 120.'

Even in the most apparently modern settings, the warrior instinct lies unexpectedly close to the surface. One evening in the Karachai mountain town of Karachayevsk, some Russian soldiers from the local garrison crossed the street in front of our car. I was with three Karachai men, one a 23-year-old farmer called Murad. 'Oh look, there they go. They'll be getting really drunk tonight,' he said, as the off-duty soldiers, berets pushed back, sauntered into the market place. 'You can always hear shooting on nights when they're let out. Thank God they haven't started shooting at us yet,' he said. 'But you know, if they do, we could get rid of that rabble in a night and take their guns. We don't have a lot of weapons, but we have got knives and we'd do a lot of cutting,' he added, grinning. I thought Murad was showing off – you often think that in the Caucasus, where you hear much big talk and meet a lot of weekend warriors. But later I watched Murad throwing knives in an orchard. From ten paces he could hit a small apple tree every time, the knife blade quivering in the trunk.

In his poem 'Ismail Bey,' Lermontov wrote that in the Caucasus 'they render good for good, evil for ill, and hate with them is limitless as love.' Most tsarist Russian generals, who had just defeated Napoleon and were building an empire from Poland to the Pacific, expected the Caucasians to cower before their might, not mount some of the most ferocious guerrilla wars in history. Before the war in Chechnya started in 1994, people thought the same thing: that the Chechens' big talk about resistance was bluff. But fighting and weapons handling run in the makeup of people like Murad. It's in the blood. Deep in the blood.

### Hadji Yurt, Chechnya

*'The Russians, the only thing they have ever taught us, is how to fight,' Vizit says through the darkness. The young Chechen fighter is sitting on a hillside near the Moslem holy place of Hadji Yurt, in the beautiful rolling foothills of the Caucasus called the Black Mountains.*

*The war is in its sixth month, mid 1995, and the Chechens are being driven back. We're in one of the last rebel-held areas. The starry night is quiet, except for the dull roar of Russian planes, dropping giant magnesium illumination flares that hang beautifully, like chandeliers over the smooth silhouettes of the hills.*

*'At the beginning of this war, we didn't know much about fighting. But just like our forefathers, we learnt quickly and they've paid for it,' Vizit says. 'They'll never take this valley, not our village, not the holy hill. At least not while I live.'*

*He pulls out a foot-long kinzhal. I walked with him to this spot and don't remember his carrying it. But here it is. Must have been in his jacket. 'Look at this kinzhal. A friend of mine from Avtury gave it to me at the start of the war. It belonged to his grandfather, who was an abreg. You know what an abreg is? A bandit. It's a beautiful thing this kinzhal.' The knife feels solid, well-weighted, cold, sharp and smooth. I don't suppose Vizit uses it much, but a lot of these guerrillas like to wear a kinzhal along with their grenades, Kalashnikov ammunition clips and pistols. It's a way of saying that they're continuing the fight of their forefathers.*

*Vizit is the genuine article, a mountain man who thinks plains dwellers are soft, who keeps home-made anti-tank rockets in his barn and has six children. Vizit says he loves freedom and weapons. To him, they're inseparable.*

*After putting the kinzhal back in its sheath, he pulls out a shiny revolver. Damned if I know where that's from; he just produces it, like a conjuror. He spins the chamber, making a clean, smooth clicking sound in the night air. 'This revolver here is an antique. My grandfather gave it to me. It was made during Tsar Nicholas's time near Moscow. You could play roulette with it,' he laughs, spinning the chamber. 'Weapons are our weakness.'*

*A year later the Russians capture Hadji Yurt. I hear that Vizit was killed by an artillery shell.*

## 3. VILLAGES

*The women whom we met seldom covered their faces, but merely turned them to one side. They generally were good looking. The skin beneath the eye was usually dyed dark; their nails had received a reddish hue. They were dressed in most gaudy colours – red blue and yellow. The men had a most determined and warlike appearance; they were invariably armed, and their long flowing beards frequently were dyed bright red.*

Lieut. Gen Sir Arthur Thurlow Cunynghame, *Travels in the Eastern Caucasus*, 1871.

We were driving through Adygea, when police stopped me at a roadblock and questioned me for half an hour. My ordinary tourist map of the area was scanned for coded plans of a terrorist attack and my passport and press card caused confusion. They said I was the first foreigner to pass through in a long time. The last had been a Chinese man.

The roadblock seemed to symbolise the main faultline of the North Caucasus – where Russification stops and indigenous life begins. Roadblocks are studded across the region outside every major town. Sometimes an armoured personnel carrier is parked at the post – little use against ordinary criminals, or even terrorists, but a symbol of Russia's power. The police, a mixture of ethnic-Russians and Caucasians, sit in massively built concrete pill boxes, emerging to inspect drivers' documents. Often they wear flack jackets and carry Kalashnikov automatic rifles. The mixture of bureaucracy, brutality and paranoia, not to mention the inevitable bribes, can be infuriating.

Then come the villages, the *auls*, as they're called in the North Caucasus. Road block or not, you cross a psychological border every time you enter an *aul*. It is another country, a place where the patriarchal family matters more than the state, the mosque more than the police, and hospitality is given without question.

From the Caspian Sea to the Black Sea, life is essentially rural. Settlements may have more than 30,000 people but they still call themselves – and feel like – villages. Many look poor, with dirt roads which turn to rivers of mud in winter, a lack of gas or even electricity supplies, animals loose in the streets, no central sewer system, and even no running water, except the village tap.

As in much of the ex-Soviet Union, the formal economies of the North

Caucasian autonomous republics are in ruins and massively dependent on subsidies from Moscow. Yet villages have an undeniable vibrancy often missing in their Russian equivalents, where collective farms are bankrupt, their workers sinking into alcoholism and despair. The North Caucasus villages are growing and their primitive aspects are gradually being replaced by new houses, new gas lines. Census figures show that while the region's ethnic Russian population shrinks, both through declining birth rates and emmigration to other parts of Russia, the highlander peoples are growing – an average of 16.3 per cent from 1979 to 1989. By comparison the overall rate was 9.1 per cent, with the local Slav population actually dropping by 3.1 per cent.

The poor live in small but usually adequate cottages. Squalor is rare, even among the very poor. The newly rich love extravagance, but often don't abandon their village, preferring to build a palace on top of their old cottage. They live in anything from sprawling one-floor compounds to towering, castle-like buildings with high brick walls and gates. The interior of the courtyard is often decorated with elaborate wood work. Inside, men's and women's quarters are often separated. Rugs are hung on the walls and, when affordable, the decoration tends to be fancy – Caucasians love to show off. But rich or poor, the toilets are squatters, almost invariably evil smelling outdoor sentry boxes over a pit in the ground. In Ingushetia, I stayed at a huge place that looked like a mixture of Santa Barbara and 1001 Nights, a confusion of mirrors, gold paint, varnished woodwork, purple draperies and white chandeliers. Not only was the toilet far out in the yard, it had no door and a bull had been tied to a post five metres away. I've rarely felt more vulnerable.

This modest but comfortable lifestyle has nothing to do with the much talked-about Caucasian mafia, but the social structure. Extended families and traditions of mutual-help provide free labour, setting them apart from many of their Russian counterparts. A Caucasian may not be rich but will still live in a handsome house, because relatives help him build it, in return, of course, for his help on their houses. Family help is particularly important in the agricultural sector. With perfect summers and rich earth for growing all the food they need, North Caucasian families cooperate to produce a surplus to sell on the market. It is not uncommon for families to have four or more children, all of whom are expected to work at an early age.

Even in the cities, North Caucasians often grow vegetables and keep animals. Houses are built around courtyards, with enough space for small plots, bee hives and rows of grapevines forming a living roof. For Russians, with their smaller families, anything more than small-scale production for their own kitchen is usually impossible. A Russian family I met in the Stavropol region, which borders on the North Caucasus, made a delicious dry white wine. When, after a few sips, I enthusiastically began plotting their expansion into the drinks industry, they laughed and shook their heads. The children were grown up and refused to do agricultural labour. They couldn't afford to hire help – so only enough wine was made for their own dinner table. For Caucasian families, the opposite is often true. They seem to have the knack of business, and were at the forefront of the boom in small-time traders under Gorbachev's *perestroika* in the late 1980s. A Chechen family I met in the village of Avtury made extra money, despite the war, by sewing dresses. Their simple house had been turned into a mini-factory. Several women sat in front of sewing machines all day turning piles of cloth into summer dresses. Another relative would then drive the goods up into southern Russia and sell them to a dealer, for a nice profit.

Natasha, a Bulgarian woman married to a Dargin in the Dagestani capital Makhachkala, said the small business revolution there had started with people going to Mecca to perform the *hadj* and discovering the more earthly delights of the Saudi marketplaces. 'People started getting in trouble because they were trading, not praying – selling Korans and so on. Then the idea of travelling and buying goods to sell back here really caught on. People started going to China. Amazingly for our repressed women here, it was the women who started trading with China, then Turkey, then Poland. Now everyone goes to the United Arab Emirates. When they travel, they take 10,000 dollars and invest it in a week. A friend of mine goes to Greece in winter, gets furs and makes 1,000 dollars on each. She's managed to redo her entire apartment. That's our women! Our men are not so flexible – they go to Moscow and join mafia groups.'

The mafia, in its Russian context, is a highly flexible term. In the Caucasus these small traders may be a world away from the organised crime groups which work throughout Russia's cities, but there's no doubt that many take an edge by dealing behind the backs of the authorities. Sometimes they almost relish skirting what they consider anti-enterprise laws – rules take away freedom and must be bent. 'Personal independence was carried to such a pitch that sons were not supposed even to obey their parents,' an English traveller wrote in the 1880s after visiting the Adygei tribes, or what remained of them following their recent conquest by the Russians.

An Adygei told me how he used his tough Russian Niva jeep to navigate dirt roads where there are no police posts and trade small goods such as vodka and video cassettes from the provinces to the big centres of Stavropol and Krasnodar. Apparently his advantage over conventional traders was simply not registering, avoiding taxes and having to pay bribes to the police, and not having to say where he got the goods from. He was not by any means rich, but he was noticeably better off than his Russian neighbours, something that he said caused friction.

Even at the height of the war in Chechnya, outdoor market places thrived behind the lines. Wall Street was the Saturday market in the eastern village of Kurchaloi. Here, Audis, BMWs, all the Russian cars, rows of sacks of grain, flour, nuts, fruit and honey, spare parts, plumbing and furniture were spread over a ragged field. Riders cantered up and down, testing horses in front of a crowd of sunburnt men in faded black trilbies. Tucked away next to the washing powder saleswomen were knots of men with hard faces, crew cuts, and more than a few broken noses – the arms dealers. Even though Russian troops were deployed a few kilometres away, Chechens could buy a Kalashnikov rifle for $100 or an anti-tank grenade launcher for $200. The guns were openly displayed and a wild-faced character who had a sawn-off shotgun in his belt and a foot-long black beard claimed he could procure me a tank. 'Anything you want, we can get it!'

Probably the region's most extraordinary entrepreneurial project was in Ingushetia, a tiny, rural republic with just 300,000 native Ingush and a handful of Russians, which set up an offshore tax zone in a bid to become the Jersey Island of the Caucasus. The project looked crazy, except that it was up and running for several years, with the *offshornaya zona* funding a series of developments, starting with the hotel Assa in the capital Nazran. Tired travellers may have thought they were hallucinating, but there, rising out of a field was a modern hotel with marble floors, hot showers, clean rooms, bar, friendly staff, televisions in the rooms. Unique in the North Caucasus, it made the usual dour staff, teacloth-sized towels, stained beds and murky bathrooms, seem thankfully distant.

Although the *offshornya zona* was sanctioned by the Russian government in 1994, the project was tinged with ambiguity – much like other business in the North Caucasus and the new Russia in general – and in 1997, Moscow shut the tax haven down. A tell-tale item in the development of Ingushetia was a new (the only) jewellery shop in Nazran. It was just around the corner from a delapidated, empty Soviet-era general store and from its mirror windows you looked out onto a potholed street where monstrous Japanese and US jeeps battled with humble Russian Ladas. Officially, this shop was just another sign of Ingush recovery, but if you believed the Russian interior ministry, Ingushetia has long and shady links to the underground gold trade. Nazran has even been dubbed the 'Russian Klondike,' with three families allegedly smuggling tonnes of gold from the Russian far east. In the same way, North Ossetia became famous as a centre of bootleg vodka, and Dagestan for black market caviar taken from the Caspian Sea.

It seems contradictory, but the anarchic love of freedom coexists with strictly observed social laws. North Caucasians traditionally belong to a patriarchal pyramid of families, clans and tribes, headed by councils of male elders – either in the family home, or in the village as a whole. The system was battered by the Soviet revolution, but lives on in a modified form, particularly in the eastern end of the region. In Dagestan, most nations are subdivided into *tukhums*, or extended family clans, which traditionally did not intermarry and often fought long blood feuds. The *tukhum* managed the village affairs and laws. Today, the *tukhum* still functions as a unit, but to greatly varying degrees among different ethnic groups of the mountain land. In Chechnya and Ingushetia, large clans called *teips* exercise considerable control, often over several villages at once, and even speak their own dialects. Members are all interrelated and answer to councils of elders. They also follow vendettas, hospitality and marriage laws as a clan.

In the western republics the Karachai and Balkar nations still have *tukhums*, but the Adygei-Circassian tribes, spread out across three different autonomous republics, have a much less well-defined clan system. The centuries-old Adygei social structure, which was hierarchal and aristocratic, vanished after the Russian conquest. What does remain, as everywhere else, is the patriarchal element.

The very old are automatically respected. Gatherings of village elders at important meetings usually include a few white bearded relics, hobbling along on walking sticks, but often they also include relatively fit men in their 60s. Respect, popularity and education, as well as age, are what give a man the right to call himself an elder and don the tall grey, or brown Astrakhan lambskin hat of the Caucasus, the *papakha*. Village elders often include holy men, such as people who have made the pilgrimage to Mecca, or people who know Arabic.

Men are expected to rise out of their seats for elders and in many cases smoking or drinking in front of them, even if they are simply older brothers, is strictly forbidden. In Adygea, however, when there was drinking to be done and the elder of the family approved, then it was he who made the first toast and led the charge. Everyone followed with relish, released from the usual ban.

Chechen elders have great influence, often acting as intermediaries between feuding families or between villages and beseiging Russian troops during the war, sometimes even deciding whether their village would fight or not. At the other end of the scale, an elder may have authority only within his own extended family, deciding on marriages, presiding over funerals and other internal matters. This is largely the case among the Kabards in the central republic of Kabardino-Balkaria, where the elders' role in public life shrank under Communist rule. Even so, elders throughout the region play a vital role in ensuring the preservation of traditional rules within the family and, by extension, in society.

Given the mix of machoism, Islam and the institutionalised respect for old men, women in some areas face dire existences. Not that women are made to wear the chadoor or go veiled, but they are expected to dress conservatively, wearing a headscarf for example, and their careers are essentially devoted to serving men. In even mildly traditional households throughout the North Caucasus, women never eat at the same time as men and during visits you begin to wonder when the women eat at all, not to mention sleep or go the toilet. They seem to exist to serve. When I asked a man in Karachai-Cherkessia when the women of his household ate, he joked: 'What, do you think they actually eat?'

The separation of sexes extends to the street. When two young beauties from the Chechen mountain village of Dargo came down to the village spring and saw a half dozen guerrillas washing the mud off their boots, they automatically held back 50 yards from the spring until the fighters had finished. When the guerrillas walked past, the young women turned their heads to the side, a graceful, yet tantalising gesture often seen in the mountains. But although modesty and gentle femininity are expected, so is a strong arm. Milking the cow, gardening, household repairs, bringing in the wood for the fire – these are women's duties. Fetching buckets or churns of water from the well or spring is back-breaking. I don't know how many times I've watched women in their spotted headscarfs dragging churns home through the mud on trolleys, while the men squat Arab fashion, smoking, picking at sunflower seeds or simply spitting.

Fittingly enough, the wedding ceremony is the climax of machismo and female humility. According to James Bell, men from the Adygei tribes in the 19th century would start their wedding nights by ripping open their wife's corset with a *kinzhal*, the ultimate blend of violence and passion. In Chechnya, the bride is traditionally picked up from her house for the wedding by gun-toting friends of the groom who drive a convoy of cars, horns blaring and gunfire roaring out of open windows. Even in quieter parts of the North Caucasus, the bride's relatives are not allowed to the ceremony, which takes place after elders from the two families have agreed on bride money. In rare cases, men simply 'steal' their brides, either because they can't be bothered to go through the usual course of negotiations or because their love is unrequited. When a girl is kidnapped, the elders again have to negotiate and try to come to a deal, or in a few cases her relatives try to rescue her by force. A Chechen guerrilla told me in 1996, shortly after the war ended, how one of his young comrades in arms, Alikhan, had recently tried to 'steal' a girl. 'We drove up to where she lives and Alikhan jumped out to get her. When she saw him, she screamed and the parents came out of the house. He got scared and we drove away. So we really make fun of Alikhan now – nothing in the war scared him, but the girl did.'

## Hadji Yurt

*'Sebastian – over here.'*

*It's pitch black outside Islam's house in the Chechen mountains, near Vedeno. I can't see him, but I sense his bulk, for he's a big man.*

*'Over here.'*

*I move further out into the yard and see Islam standing near the vegetable patch.*

*'Come on, let's smoke.'*

*'Here you go.'*

*I give him a cig in the darkness, carefully shielding the flame of the lighter. When we smoke, we cup the burning end in the palms of our hands and whisper. It's like being back at school.*

*'I don't want my uncle to see. It's just wouldn't be right in front of him,' says Islam, father, houseowner and Chechen war veteran.*

Hospitality is another constant of the North Caucasus. Kazbek, mullah in Karachayevsk, invited me to be his guest at his house next to the mosque ten minutes after we met. A few hours later, he killed a sheep in my honour and cooked it in a cauldron over an open fire in the orchard. Overhead, the moon was a sharp white crescent, accompanied by a sole star to its right, exactly like the Islamic symbol. Jagged black outlines of nearby cliffs were just visible. Inside, several women, who had not said a word the whole time I'd been there, then brought us plate after plate of mutton, broth, fried potatoes, cucumber salad, tea, and a yoghurt drink called *ayran* which we drank straight from a huge, common bowl.

Hospitality is more than generosity – it's at the root of the high-landers' psychology. Opening doors to strangers is part of the brother-hood between all Moslem *gortsy*. You are hospitable because all are equal – equal under Allah and the mountains. The guest is sacred, 'a son of the family', as one Adygei woman put it to me, and the son must be pampered and protected. James Bell wrote in the 1830s how, in Adygea

> a murderer can seek sanctuary in another brotherhood's area. (The murderer) now enjoys sanctuary at the hamlet of a respected armourer at Subesh; and that which shows the complete recognition of the principle is, that this armourer incurs no danger whatever in visiting the neighbourhood where the murder was committed.

In fact hospitality is so ritualised and important that it can become embarrassingly overdone. In Chechnya I've had to have 'tea,' actually a large lunch, three times in a matter of hours simply because I needed to talk to three different people. Even Kazbek, the Karachai mullah who entertained me so royally, could become exasperatingly overattentive. Once, he sprayed himself with cologne, then thinking that I was being neglected, came over to me and began squirting me too, backing me up against the wall and refusing to listen to my protests. In more liberal places of the North Caucasus, being a guest means lots of warm, neat vodka drunk in shots after long toasts. Saying no can go down badly.

On Uraza Bayram, celebrating the end of the month-long fast of Ramadan, I was invited to festivities in the Adygei village of Blechipsin. The day began with a dawn *namaz* at the mosque, then the whole male population walked up to the cemetery to pay respects to family plots, the gravestones decorated with Moslem crescents, Soviet-style portraits, and ancient Adygei hierogliphics, denoting tribe. All this time, the women had been cooking the third and most important stage of the day – the feast. Each year the routine is the same: every house prepares a meal and each head of household invites all his male relatives, then they move on to the next. That way every man can show off his hospitality, his house and the hard work of his womenfolk, who hover proudly in the background.

At the first stop, the long table was heaped with lamb, chicken, salads and a dozen other dishes. The graveyard and mosque were draining and having had no breakfast, it was good to eat. Someone produced a bottle of vodka. It seemed a bit eccentric at this time and on a Moslem holiday, but I gave it a go. Everyone pronounced toasts. Already feeling light-headed, I looked at my watch: 9:45 a.m. 'Don't try and keep up with the old folks on the drink. They're used to it. Just have as much as you feel like,' someone warned me. But it was too late. Didn't he know that the guest of honour is forbidden from refusing hospitality?

We went to another house for another feast, then the next. Sometimes driving, sometimes walking. I lost count, but guessed that by 3:00 p.m. we'd hit half a dozen houses, meeting up with the same dozen middle-aged men in each one. At every stop there were prayers and then (never mind the Koran) hard drinking – a church service and pub crawl rolled into one. Outside, the master of one of the houses saw me patting his huge, over-energetic dog and drunkenly insisted I keep it. I had to protest for several minutes to avoid taking the dog with me back to Moscow. The host looked offended. 'Everything for the guest. If you like something and you're a guest, we have to give it to you. I saw you liked the dog. That's the way of the Adygei.'

How do you repay them? What can you give in return to someone who has given you, a stranger, his time, trust, best room and food? Offering money actually causes offense and is refused anyway. F. C. Grove, author of *The Frosty Caucasus*, wrote after leaving one hospitable village in 1875: 'We wished to recompense them so that they might lose nothing by their kindness, but they were greater men than any who had yet entertained us, and how to make a payment troubled us sore.' When Grove tried to give his hosts money, in addition to some gifts, he was told: 'We had rather not take the money. It is not our custom to receive payment from our friends.'

I once stayed several nights on the floor of a school room in Ingushetia with a family of Chechen refugees whose entire village, Bamut, had been destroyed. When I tried to give them $100 before leaving they firmly refused. 'It's not done here,' Movladi said. This was a man whose house and belongings had been burnt to the ground, whose brother had been killed by a helicopter rocket, and who had escaped with nothing but his family, a few bundles of clothing and his tractor. Each day he made sure that I was fed and had a space to sleep and work. Only on my last day did I notice the blue and white tin cans that said 'Humanitarian Aid - Corned Beef.' Chechens are a proud people. For a Chechen to give his guest humanitarian aid from a tin, he had to be really, really poor. So when he refused the money, I wrapped a $100 bill into a note saying: 'I'm sorry if it offends you, but I insist.' I planned to slip the letter and the money onto the table just before I left, so they'd find it later. But there were so many people in that room that I never found the moment and had to leave without giving them the money. That always made me feel like hell.

Of all the unwritten mountain laws, one is supreme: the vendetta. This is where Russia never seems further away, its own law code forgotten, replaced by more ancient rules. There are regular occurrences of vendetta killings, at least in parts of Dagestan and across Chechnya and Ingushetia. The feud could be in revenge for an earlier murder, or a family might kill a girl who got pregnant before marriage, and, of course, her lover, but this dark law more often than not acts as a vicious deterrent. During the upheaval of war in Chechnya, your chances of getting killed and robbed by bandits increased. A lot of people were hungry, a lot of people were armed. Of course, I was outside the vendetta circle, but I had Chechen friends who considered me their guest – a valuable status. I soon made the habit – when travelling alone with complete strangers or guides, as I often had to – of stopping at my friends' houses and introducing my companions, before going on. I'd say I just wanted to say hello, but everyone knew what this was about: now that my friends knew whom I was with and had seen their faces and car, I was covered. Because they are outside this homegrown social safety net, it is invariably Russians who become crime victims in Chechnya. For similar reasons, nearly the only beggars are ethnic-Russians, since a Caucasian family would do anything to prevent one of its own ending up on the street and bringing dishonour to the family name.

Last-minute reprieves are not unheard of. Up in Vedeno, in the Chechen mountains, I came across the 'trial' of a young man who had killed another in a car accident, and now faced – along with his entire family – the vendetta. That morning, the main street filled with several hundred men led by elders – men with beards, carved walking sticks and Astrakhan hats. Some wore Cherkesska tunics passed down from their forefathers. They prayed, waving their sticks like swords, and marched up the street, with the great snow-covered peaks of the Caucasus looming on the horizon. Once they reached the main square the men stopped and joined a waiting circle of more elders. Then the accused, his face covered by a hood, was brought before the elders by the guerrilla commander of the village, Shervani Basayev. Mass prayers began, all the men with their palms up, lips moving in a murmur under the clear autumn sky. Then the wait for the elders' decision. Not guilty. All tension evaporated. There would be reconciliation, not vengeance. Men prayed again to praise God.

## Shali, Chechnya

*We're eating watermelon in a garden in southern Chechnya. There's a summer lull in the war. The guns are silent here now and after capturing the town, most Russian troops have pulled out, leaving the area in peace for the first time in half a year. People are looking for work, rebuilding houses, getting married. My friend offers more tea. He's a civilised man, educated. But earlier this summer, Russian soldiers beat, murdered and robbed a cousin and two of his best friends. Now he has a blood feud and as long as the vendetta goes on, so does the war.*

'They disappeared in May. We looked everywhere: here, in southern Russia, at the Russian headquarters. Then we decided we had to search here from the bottom. We knew what area they'd gone missing in and so we started taking soldiers from the unit there. One, then another, then another, and a fourth. We got them, I mean we took them by force, kidnapped them. We were paying Chechens who worked with the Russians, in the FSB (the secret services) – $1,000 for each of these boys and then we kept them for questioning.

'This is a really dirty business, really dirty. One we kept three days, another a week. If they didn't know anything, we'd hand them back. We'd turn them back in as liberated prisoners of war and the Russians asked no questions. It was a bonus for them – they could say these soldiers had been recovered from the guerrillas and could pretend these gifts we made them were the result of work.

'Then the fourth. He'd seen everything with his own eyes. He'd been there and he told us everything. Our three lads had been in a new Zhiguli (car) when they were stopped by Russians near the old psychiatric hospital. Then they were put into a pit. The Zhiguli was driven into another pit, flattened by an armoured car, and buried. My cousin and friends were then shot – they were beaten up first – and then their pit was covered over and a track was made right over the top of it, where vehicles would drive every day.

'This soldier we were keeping prisoner took us to the spot. You never would have guessed it had once been dug up. It was right in the middle of where the tents had been. Vehicles had been driving all over it. We found our boys and also two other bodies buried there.

'I don't know if this soldier had participated. He said he hadn't, but I wouldn't blame him anyway. These conscripts are like animals. They know nothing. He told us that his officers had made him shoot at dead bodies to get used to shooting humans. The conscripts are blameless, barely human – they have no documents, nothing, just metal dog tags. They're not even told where they're going when they get sent to Chechnya in the first place.

'The men who organised these murders were a first lieutentant and two others. I told our contacts to give me that lieutenant or I'll search for him the world over. We know who they are, we have their names. They permanently patrolled and when there were few people around, they'd stop cars, put the people in an armoured car, rob them, strip the car, crush it like a pancake, sell the parts and kill the people, shooting them at night when there was a lot of firing anyway.

'These men could be handed over to us dead, but we need them alive, and that's what costs a lot of money, a lot. I want them alive, I want to look into their eyes. It doesn't matter if they leave here. They can't go too far from us.

'We're not going to kill them. They will live. But we're going to do something to them so that they never forget Chechnya to the end of their days. They're going to be able to eat, but they'll never feed themselves or their families again.

'You understand, my cousin and the other two, they were crystal clear. They weren't politicians or anything, they were crystal clear, the best. They were robbed for a bit of money and killed like dogs.

'We were all raised together and they were called the three musketeers. When the war started, their parents forbade them from joining the fighters. So they left and came back when they thought the war was over. This was what they got. They were all in their twenties. Shamkhan, he was the strongest and healthiest of all of them. He had his fingers cut off and his ribs broken before being shot. Another had a hole in his head. The other had a broken leg.

'The Russians, they think it's all over here. They take control of this hill or that hill, but then they find they have to keep running backwards and forwards. They'll never live quietly here. Never. They forget we have the blood feud here and that this is a frightening business. We're going to take revenge and we're going to stay alive.'

# PART 2

# Fires of Liberty

*This simple hut that cheered their humble ease*
*Burns high – fire of Circassian liberties.*

Lermontov.

## 1. THE PEOPLE OF THE MOUNDS

*The Russians always present their conquest of the Caucasus as a good
thing, a gift to the people here. They say they brought us civilisation. But
they ignore that we already had our own customs, our own life, our own
culture.*

Aslan Tov, head archeologist at the history museum in the Adygei capital
Maikop.

Up in the wooded hills of Adygea, beyond the village of Khamyshky,
there's a prehistoric tomb that looks like a cross between a bus stop and
Stonehenge. Massive slabs of moss-covered grey stone are propped up
against each other to form a single, four-walled chamber. The front of
the tomb is a single slab about two metres tall and one and a half
across, with a perfectly round, head-sized hole carved through at ground
level, like a ship's porthole. The fading sign for tourists says only that
the stones are 3,000–3,500 years old, and none of the locals, Russians,
know what the mysterious tomb, a *dolmen*, is all about.

Everyone in the North Caucasus has a theory – usually the most
exotic possible – on where his people came from, but few can be
conclusively proven. The Chechens have a myth of how 'we were born
when the she-wolf gave birth.' Imam Shamil, an Avar from Dagestan
who led the biggest of the 19th century wars against the Russians, said
Alexander the Great had exiled all his empire's criminals to the Caucasus,
thus creating the amazing ethnic mix. The Ossetians claim direct
descendency from the great Scythian and Sarmatian hordes, others from
Ghengis Khan, or Tamerlane. Sometimes the theories are ludicrous, such
as a claim I heard from a drunk Chechen that his people are descended
from a lost Roman army.

The tangle will probably never be unwound. Forming a land bridge
between Asia and Europe, the plains of the North Caucasus hosted one
invader or trader after the other – Persian, Greek, Roman, Goth, Arab,
Mongol, Jew, Turk, Slav. In this cultural whirlwind, languages and ethnic
types merged, appeared and disappeared, creating today's jigsaw. Likewise
religion. Christianity reached the pagan North Caucasus in the 4th
century AD, followed by Islam, which established firm roots in Dagestan
by 733 AD.

Symbolising the mystery are the *dolmens*. They have been dated to
before 2000 bc and appear to be the work of newcomers to the North
Caucasus, even closely resembling constructions in Europe. But like
Stonehenge, in the English plains of Salisbury, no one knows where the
*dolmens* came from, who built them, or even for sure how they were
used. Much better understood is a huge archipelago of underground
burial mounds called *kurgans* which dots the Black Sea area of the
North Caucasus.

The *kurgan* culture, in which the dead were buried on their backs, with their knees up, covered in ochre, and often accompanied by their possessions and wives, is dated to the third and second millenia bc. One of the oldest and most famous *kurgans* is the barrow complex at Maikop, capital of today's Adygea. Dated to around 2200 BC, and discovered only at the end of the 19th century, the barrow contained a trove of 17 fabulous gold, silver and stone vessels, weapons apparently imported from across the mountains in Georgia, or from Mesopotamia, and beads of lapis and turquoise that suggested links to Persia and Afghanistan. Only riches in Greece at that time could compare. Many of the burial sites have long since been looted, but much of their golden contents has also found its way into Russian museums. The Maikop treasures are at the Hermitage museum in Saint Petersburg.

The great sparks for the development of the North Caucasus were the growth of the Greek empire and the arrival of migrating Asian hordes who'd already occupied the southern Russian steppe. The Scythians, who spoke an Indo-Iranian language, were one of the most important newcomers, sweeping into the Black Sea region on horseback in about 850 BC. Shortly after, Greek colonists began settling on the Black Sea around the Crimean peninsula and the straits of the Azov Sea. Both groups began mixing with the indigenous Caucasians, such as the Maeotians, forerunners of the modern Adygei or Circassian people.

The colourful 5th-century bc Greek historian Herodotus thought the Scythians – fabled to have descended from a union between Heracles and a snake-legged woman – especially fierce. Warriors, he said, drank the blood of their enemy and always beheaded the dead to claim bounties from their leaders. Human scalps were hung 'from his bridle rein; the greater number of such napkins that a man can show, the more highly he is esteemed among them. Many make themselves cloaks, like the capotes of our peasants, by sewing a quantity of these scalps together.'

According to Herodotus, the fabled women warriors, the Amazons, also originated in a Scythian offshoot, the Sauromatians. His accounts were long dismissed but archeological evidence has fleshed out the myth of sword-wielding women in the steppes of what is now southern Russia. Yet the Scythians, and the later Sarmatians, who were related but would push the Scythians out of the North Caucasus, were also lovers of beauty and mystery. The Amazons not only had swords, but perfume bottles and amulets. Greek artisans worked constantly to fill orders for gold plates, jewellry and ornaments from their barbarian clients across the Black Sea.

Scythian–Sarmatian burials were horrible but spectacular. A royal would be buried in a *kurgan* alongside piles of gold, weapons, horses, and, Herodotus writes, 'various members of his household: one of his concubines, his butler, his cook, his groom, his steward, and his chamberlain – all of them strangled.' A year later, 50 fine horses and 50 young men would be strangled, gutted, stuffed with chaff, sewn up, then impaled and stuck around the *kurgan* to mount a ghoulish guard for their departed king.

The second half of the first millenium bc was a golden age for the North Caucasus, during which proto-Adygei Maeotians, Thracians, Greeks, Scythians and then Sarmatians peacefully coexisted in what was called the Bosphoran Kingdom. Stretching from the Crimean peninsula to the lands of the proto-Adygei on the northeast coast of the Black Sea, the kingdom began as a Greek colony. From about 480 bc, it consolidated into a wealthy, independent state, booming under a new dynasty started by a Thracian called Spartok in 438 bc.

The Bosphoran Kingdom was a remarkable fusion of cultures: the trading Greeks, the steppe-roving Scythians, the more settled, agricultural Maeotians. Politically, the state found strength in flexibility. There was a central king, but the growing cast of warrior nobles among the Scythians and Maeotians retained their autonomy. Trade was what held them together. They had their own merchant guilds and coined currency. They controlled nearly all the business in the Azov and Black seas, dealing with the Greeks in honey, wood, furs, leathers, grain, fish, wine, olive oil and bricks. Huge quantities of fish were exported from the main ports – Panticapaeum (modern day Kerch) and Phanagoria – facing each other across the narrow straits where the Azov Sea meets the Black Sea. From the steppes, the Scythian-Sarmatian herdsmen sent meat and cereals, making the Bosphoran Kingdom the bread basket of Athens.

In the first century bc, the Bosphoran Kingdom moved into the sphere of the Roman Empire and began a slow decline, racked by political turmoil, wars, invasion, then destruction by the Huns in the 4th century ad. Today only Black Sea ruins mark the site of the Bosphoran Kingdom, yet the legacies of that early state and its peoples live on. Descendants of the Sarmatians survive in Ossetia, where the language, music and pagan religion distantly echo the ancient era. Symbolically, North Ossetians officially renamed their republic Alania after the Alans, a major Sarmatian tribe, when the Soviet Union collapsed. The Alans left other footprints across Europe, where they fought both for and against the Romans. Several towns in France, such as Alencon, may bear their mark, and more than 5,000 Sarmatian cavalry troops who guarded Hadrian's Wall between England and Scotland ended up moving to the village of Ribchester, Lancashire, in the 3rd century ad. Credited with the introduction of armoured cavalry to the Romans, the Sarmatians may well have been the precursors of a much later phenomenon – the European knight. Perhaps chivalry itself, that knightly culture of war and honour, also began in the Caucasus, where gallantry is still part of the highlander identity.

There are also tangible reflections of the past in the hundreds of mysterious heraldic designs called *tamgas*, elegant, simple designs that look something like the brands used on Spanish bulls. Dated to the first century AD, *tamgas* are still used to represent Adygei surnames and can be seen etched on gravestones in the Adygei cemeteries. The lost kingdom also lives on in the echoes of classical Greece: the Nart version of the Prometheus myth, the Greek belief in the sacred duties of hospitality, the surviving deities of the ancient pantheon in today's Ossetian and Adygei pagan religions. But perhaps the most intriguing time traveller is the Greek stabbing sword. Go to a museum and look on a 2,500-year-old weapon, with its tapered blade and knob-ended handle. Then you realise: this is surely nothing but a rusty ancestor of the *kinzhal*.

The cycle of great invasions sped up after the disintegration of the Bosphoran Kingdom. Following the Baltic Goths in 240 AD, came the Asian Huns in 370 AD, then the Avars, then the Khazars, a Turkic people whose North Caucasus empire, which adopted Judaism, lasted from the 8th to 11th centuries.

From the 10th to 13th centuries, the Circassians, who had been exposed to early Christianity, expanded in the western Black Sea region under the rule of highly autonomous feudal princes. Their failure to transform considerable cultural unity into a centralised political system would cost the Adygei-Circassians dearly later but, at the time, the wealth of trading links with the outside world was all that mattered. Dealing with Christian Byzantium and the Italians of Genoa and Venice, the Adygei became famous for the beauty of their gold-woven clothes and quality weapons, and also for the export of their people – men as mercenaries, women as concubines. Circassian soldiers founded and dominated the Mameluke dynasty which ruled Egypt from the 13th to 19th centuries, and even now ethnic-Circassians are well represented in the security forces of several Middle Eastern countries.

During the first half of the 13th century a new, until then unimagineably powerful Mongol horde sent by Genghis Khan swept aside all resistance to capture Central Asia, southern Russia, much of Europe and the North Caucasus. At the end of the 14th century, it was the turn of Tamerlane to conquer Asia and the Caucasus, bringing Circassian prosperity to a halt, and driving the Sarmatian-Alans and other tribes into the impregnable safety, but total isolation of the mountains. Of course, like every horde before them, the Mongols dispersed and disintegrated. But a new invasion of the Caucasus soon got underway. As before, these conquerors rode horses and had endless military supplies. But there were differences: for the first time, they came from the north, not the east; they were Christian; their invasion would stick. These were the Russians.

## 2. HOLY WAR

*This small Christian clan, stranded in a tiny corner of the earth, surrounded by half-savage Mohammedan tribes and Russian soldiers, considers itself highly advanced, acknowledges none but Cossacks as human beings and despises everyone else.*

Leo Tolstoy's description of the Cossacks.

As the dust of the Middle Ages settled in the 16th century, following the Mongols' definitive defeat in 1480, the North Caucasus found itself on the horns of two great powers with competing religions – Christian Russia and the Moslem Ottomans.

By 1556, the expanding Russian state was in control of the well-positioned Caspian Sea port of Astrakhan. Shortly after, it had pushed forward inland beyond the Volga, as far as the Terek River, which bordered the territory of the Ossetians, Chechens and Ingush. Moscow had allies south of the mountains in Christian Georgia and Armenia, who wanted help against the Moslem Persians – the region's third empire, but by then the weakest. In the Black Sea, Turkey had strategically-placed allies in the remains of the Mongol peoples living in the Crimean peninsula, under a khan.

The Adygei-Circassian tribes occupied the whole western half of the North Caucasus and both Turkey and Russia made special efforts to win their loyalty. Moscow made early inroads with these nominally Christian peoples, such as its signing of a treaty with princes from the Kabard tribe in 1557 and the marriage of Tsar Ivan to the daughter of a Kabard chieftan called Temruk in 1561. But these alliances, despite being portrayed by Soviet historians as the official date of the North Caucasus' entry into Russia, were superficial, with no meaning to the throng of competing princes and Circassian potentates. Between the late 16th and early 18th centuries, as it became increasingly clear that Russia aimed to conquer their lands, the Kabards and other Adygei-Circassian tribes in fact moved decisively away from Russia and embraced the Ottoman world. Already by 1580, Islam had become the region's dominant religion.

The ultimate goal was strategic control over the link between Asia and Europe. For the Turks, the Caucasus were a way to outflank Persia, control the Black Sea and keep the growing Russian empire at bay. For Moscow, the Caucasus meant a warm-water opening in the Black Sea and eventually a path to Persia, Turkey and even India. Persia had roots in the Caucasus stretching back to the ancient world, but it was now the loser, weakened by its rivalry with the Ottomans, then driven south by the Russians, and pushed out of the Transcaucasus by the early 19th century.

The vanguard of the Russian march south were the Cossacks, a human colonising machine, fire against fire. Like their opponents in the struggle for the Caucasus, they have mysterious origins. Some Cossacks claim their Slav ancestors mixed with Scythians, Sarmatians or Khazars to create a unique race. Most believe the Cossacks started off as Slav adventurers and escaped Russian serfs in the Middle Ages who formed bands of marauders, free from any state or laws, roaming southern Russia on horseback. Gradually, the Cossacks consolidated on the Don, Volga and Dnieper rivers, creating a separate identity, with a love of independence and a unique, communal way of rural life. Although the fierce Dnieper group only came under the control of the Russian state in the late 18th century, the bulk of Cossacks agreed to serve Russia, with considerable autonomy, in 1654. In the Caucasus there were two main groups, one in the west along the Kuban river, the other in the east along the Terek river, occupying the black earth zone – the richest agricultural lands in the growing Russian empire.

The Cossacks were adaptable, tough and perfectly suited to war. Living in self-ruled villages called *stanitsas*, the Cossacks were free from serfdom, but each male was pledged to serve 25 years in the army. In some respects, they were an earlier version of the American cowboy – brilliant horsemen, independently minded and, most important of all, settlers. Instead of relying on homesick armies to garrison the Caucasus, Moscow was always able to settle its new lands with Cossacks. They made each conquest permanent.

Though loyal servants of the tsar and the Christian cross, the Cossacks developed a love-hate relationship with their Moslem enemy. They copied the North Caucasians' dashing clothes and weapons, revered horseman-ship and emulated the tribesmen's raiding tactics, constantly attacking native villages. Sometimes they even intermarried, creating what many thought was a particularly beautiful ethnic mix.

Alexander Dumas, author of *The Count of Monte Cristo*, *The Three Musketeers* and a string of hair-raising travel books, wrote in his *Adventures in the Caucasus* that the Cossacks were themselves divided into the rearguard settlers on the river Don, and the pioneers who lived on the frontier, the 'line'.

> A Cossack of the Line, born within sight of the enemy he has to fight and familiar with danger from his earliest childhood, is a soldier upon reaching the age of twelve. ... The Cossack of the Don, on the other hand, comes of agricultural stock and spends his childhood on the peaceful plains of that serene, majestic river.

In *The Cossacks*, Tolstoy portrayed a vigorous, brave people who understood the region better than arrogant Russian officers down for a bit of sport and medals. Even so, the Cossacks too were essentially outsiders, invaders of another's home and emnity between them and the Moslems is deeply felt to this day. Nineteenth-century travellers and writers, including Tolstoy, sensed this – that although the Cossacks outwardly had the qualities of the Caucasians, they always seemed to be one step behind, not riding quite as well, not shooting quite as straight. After all, there was one vital difference: the Caucasians were fighting to defend what had been their homeland since the beginning of recorded history.

In *The Cossacks*, Tolstoy describes an incident when a young Cossack, who is part of a night-time patrol, ambushes and shoots dead a Chechen fighter sneaking across the river for a raid. There's an initial euphoria as the Cossacks outwit the Chechen and get their man, but then there's a slight feeling of shame – as if it hadn't been a fair match.

'He, too, were a man,' he muttered, evidently admiring the corpse.

'Aye, if he'd a caught you, you wouldn't have stood much chance,' said one of the Cossacks.

The old *stanitsas* still exist in the line across the region, places with names like Pravoberezhnoye, or 'right hand side of the bank' of the Terek river in northern Chechnya – the friendly, non-Chechen side in those days. The Cossacks themselves deteriorated a great deal under Soviet rule. But they remain very much aware of their curious historical position, both as guardians of Russian interests in the North Caucasus and the ones who understand the local Moslem peoples best.

----

*Born to tread the Moscoff's pride*
*Down to the lowly dust,*
*He fought, he conquered, near and wide,*
*That northern race accursed.*

Tatar ballad about Sheikh Mansur.

In 1785, a Chechen holy man called Mansur had a vision of the prophet Mohammed in which he was instructed to declare holy war – *ghazawat* – against the encroaching Russians. No one is really sure who this revolutionary was. Some say he was a true visionary, others a renegade Italian monk and adventurer. Even his real name is in doubt. But the origins of Mansur are almost irrelevant now. Like any mystic, his real life dated from the time he saw the light and although he was in his late thirties at the time, and died less than 10 years later, it was that brief, intense final period that mattered.

The most reliable version is that he was a Chechen originally named Ushurma from the village of Aldy. Ushurma was a holy man, an adherent to the mystical Islamic tradition of Sufism, following the *tariqat*, or path, called Naqshabandi. This had been practised for centuries in the central Asian city of Bukhara, but was new to the North Caucasus, so it is unclear how Ushurma became a disciple. After his vision he changed his name to Mansur, which means Victor in Arabic, and took the title sheikh. Launching a long tradition of Chechen holy warriors, he was also a born soldier. 'He even slept in his coat fully armed. He would explain this strange habit by saying that it was shameful for an honourable Chechen to sleep undressed since in his opinion a Chechen must always be prepared for every eventuality and must never become accustomed to comfort,' an anonymous early 20th-century biographer wrote.

By the time Sheikh Mansur appeared, the Russian conquest had been creeping forward, slowly, but steadily for generations, going into high gear in the 1760s. There had been major setbacks, such as in 1605 when an army of 10,000 was surrounded and much of it massacred by Dagestani mountain men helping the Turks. That slowed the conquest, but did not mean it would be abandoned. Even after that early disaster, how could Tsar Boris Godunov have known that this pitting of clumsy, big modern armies against ferocious guerrilla warriors in complicated terrain, would be repeated countlessly in the future? Would he have believed that it would take another 250 years before Russia mastered the North Caucasus?

In 1772, Peter the Great captured the Caspian Sea city of Derbent, in Dagestan, then Baku, further down the coast in Azerbaijan, a year later. A decade after, the Russians scored their most significant breakthrough yet, winning the Crimean peninsula from the Tatar-Mongol remnants and their Ottoman protectors. The way was open to the Black Sea, whetting the appetite of the Saint Petersburg dreamers who wanted to go all the way to Istanbul, or Constantinople as the Christians still saw it, and eventually to India. Another milestone was the building, in 1784, of the fort of Vladikavkaz – Russian for Master of the Caucasus – to control the main north-south link across the mountains – the Georgian Military Highway through the Daryal Pass into Christian Georgia. The combination of the fort and peace deals with the local Ossets and Kabards drove a wedge between the Moslem tribes in the east and west. Meanwhile, the Russian 'line,' that great wall of forts and Cossack settlements, inched forward.

Mansur's six-year campaign started with a famous victory in 1785 over Russian forces on the river Sunzha in Chechnya. Empress Catherine II's troops had stormed his home village Aldy, but when they left the ruins, they were surrounded in the forest and ambushed. In all, about 600 soldiers and officers died. Mansur aimed to unite the scattered peoples of the North Caucasus and at one point he may have had as many as 20,000 men under arms from Dagestan to the Kuban river in the west. However, most of the major battles at this time were military failures, nothing like that first bloodbath in the Chechen forest. Mansur's men were untrained and faced disciplined, well-armed Russian regulars, as well as Cossacks.

From Chechnya, Mansur took his holy war into Dagestan, attacking, but failing to overrun the Russian fort in Kizlyar. Later, he moved into today's Kabardino-Balkaria but was again driven out and, taking advantage of Russia's simultaneous war with Turkey, exported his fight to the Adygei-Circassian tribes.

In the end, Mansur was a victim of pure bad luck. He was in the Turkish fort of Anapa on the Black Sea coast when the Russians attacked and seized the important fortress, taking him prisoner. The Turks got their fortress back not long after by treaty, but the capture of Mansur made the battle worthwhile for the Russians. He was brought before Catherine II, then imprisoned.

Though he died not long after, still only in his forties, the legacy of Mansur's mystic Sufi teachings and *ghazawat* outlasted Catherine and everyone else alive at the time. The Sufi *tariqat,* or religious path, that he spread was destined for the North Caucasus – it is the ideal form of religion for facing outside cultural and military pressure. Sufism has no need for formal buildings such as mosques, and its undocumented but fanatically loyal members can easily go underground or surface whenever they choose. In addition to the Naqshabandi *tariqat* popularised by Mansur, another prophet – Kunta Hadji – introduced the even more passionate Qadiriya *tariqat* in the 1850s. The central group prayer ritual of Sufism is the *zikr,* a series of litanies which deliver a powerful spiritual high. Its form varies greatly. Among the Naqshabandi, the *zikr* is performed discreetly and quietly, but Qadiriya adherents go into frenzies, with small groups running and dancing in circles, jumping up and down on the spot, or beating drums, depending on the particular sect. The *zikr* can last for hours.

Recognising the power of the Sufi orders, the Russians tried banning the *zikr* in the late 1860s, while the Soviet authorities used more drastic tactics – rounding up and killing the spiritual leaders and closing mosques. However both *tariqa* not only survived the persecutions, they thrived even in the Soviet era, unseen and underground, in Dagestan, Chechnya and Ingushetia. The *zikr* ritual formed an unbreakable shield around these peoples' sense of identity and self-confidence. The tightly knit groups which gathered everywhere, and still gather, to perform the *zikr* simultaneously reinforced the disciples' feelings of ethnic brotherhood and religious purity. Psychologically, the Sufi disciples practising the *zikr* were perfectly equipped for battle. Many were unafraid to die, because they felt close to Allah, and their training in the brotherhood had prepared them to act as a group, with the discipline vital to fighting. This was true when Mansur launched the Naqshabandi *tariqat,* inspiring his rag-tag armies to heroic feats, and it was true in the 1990s conflict in Chechnya, where fighters often came straight from these brotherhoods and found constant sustenance in the *zikr*.

*Gekhi, Chechnya*

*Fifteen men in a circle. A prayer at the start of the zikr rings out in a high, slow, sad voice against a background harmony and rhythmic clapping. 'La ilaha ill allah, la ilaha ill allah!' – 'there is no god but Allah!' – goes the chorus. The prayer song becomes louder and faster until the leader is red-faced, eyes fixed on the sky over the blue-walled courtyard.*

*The men stand within inches of each other, clapping hard, and singing. The leader cups his hands over his ears and the others gather momentum, clapping, shifting from foot to foot, then stamping, and raising the constant cry: 'there is no god but Allaaah!' Some of the men reach the ecstasy they all seek from the zikr. You spot them at once: the ones with sweat pouring down their faces, shirts wet in the great heat, the ones whose eyes are glazed, the ones who clap and stamp with violence, but feel nothing. Every now and then these break the harmony and cry out prayers of their own in uncontrolled voices, or give whoops of energy, of unashamed pashion and joy.*

*Suddenly the circle breaks into a slow, anti-clockwise trot, still singing, picking up pace, then spinning, a whirl of shirts and prayer caps. The men drag their outside feet and stamp with the inside. Women standing by toss water to keep the dust down, but it soon dries and the men's boots pound up an ankle-high cloud across the courtyard. Frenzy. Just as suddenly, the 15 stop and turn inwards again, perfectly synchronised.*

*The leader's new, long cry to God signals a calm after the spinning. But the clapping and stamping picks up again, so hard that the ground shakes several metres away. A long, high-pitched cry of 'Allaah!' again switches the tempo, jerking the 15 to a slower beat, until once again the fever starts and they begin spinning in a circle. Just then, a Russian bomber jet buzzes the village, screaming low over the rooftops and disappearing out into the countryside. No one even looks up. The whooping grows louder.*

## 3. THE LION OF DAGESTAN

*Make bare the sword, oh people!*
*Come to our help:*
*Bid goodbye to sleep and quiet,*
*I call you in the name of God.*

Imam Shamil's battle hymn.

All life in Gimry, deep in the Dagestani mountains, is squeezed from the stones. The earth is so hard that the inhabitants, from the Avar nation, have invented a hoe unique to their village. It's hand-made and hand-held. You hold a wishbone-shaped shaft, place your feet on special struts, like a po-go stick, and jam the blade into the stony, dry earth. In Gimry the air may be unexpectedly mild because of a valley microclimate, but earth that will actually yield life is so scarce that houses are piled up on each other like honeycomb. When villagers find a place they can irrigate and plant peaches or vines, they use every inch of soil; they then hack into the hillsides with shovels and build tiny terraces to get a few metres more. On every side of the village valley are towering, almost sheer hills and crags of rock. Beyond those cliffs, as far as the eye can see, are more mountains of dry, hard, stony earth.

This was the birthplace, in 1796, of Shamil the Avar. He was not a healthy infant, but Shamil not only recovered, he became as hard as his inhospitable land. Then he spent three decades of his life defending it, spearheading the fight against up to half a million Russian soldiers in one of the most remarkable struggles between guerrillas and a superpower in history.

By Shamil's adolescence, the Russians had pushed deep into the fertile plains of the North Caucasus, advancing their line from sea to sea. The Russian colonial campaigns wreaked havoc in the social structure, introducing hard drinking to the Moslems, pushing panicked natives back into the hills and upsetting the ages-old balance of power between village kingdoms, local tyrants and the clans. The campaigns of Russian General Yermolov, from 1816 to 1826, brought much worse. A bear-like man with a heavy face and swooping grey hair, Yermolov made sport of human life. Atrocities were policy, and Yermolov moved his army around like a giant fist. 'I desire that the terror of my name should guard our frontiers, ... that my word should be for the natives a law more inevitable than death.' In this nightmare, villagers were either 'pacified', in other words made to surrender, or annihilated. Villages were burned down and their inhabitants slaughtered in 'punitive raids' retaliating for attacks by the tribesmen on Russian forts or Cossack units. Artillery butchered the North Caucasians who charged forts on horseback.

In 1818 Yermolov built a big fort in the lowlands of Chechnya and called it Grozny, which means 'menacing.' The way he saw it, the natives were savage and understood only force. He hoped to wrap up the 'pacification' in Dagestan and Chechnya by 1820, then take his talents to those other troublesome tribes in Kabardia and Circassia in the west. The man breathed arrogance: 'Out of pure humanity I am inexorably severe. One execution saves hundreds of Russians from destruction.' The same campaigns of fire and sword swept the Adygei-Circassian lands, in the fertile zones south of the Kuban river. 'Yesterday and today we destroyed the grain of the Abazas and the Kalmyks and trod it under the horses' hooves. Whatever remained I told the master first major and the campaign chief Yanov to burn,' a Brigadier Knorring wrote in his report in 1786.

In these times the Chechens and some of the Dagestani nations still lived as free men, bound to no authority except that of the clan and village. This part of the North Caucasus was largely isolated from the outside world, with no military allies or political sponsors. Besides, not only did the highlander peoples have few inter-tribal alliances, they often couldn't understand each other's languages. Towards the west, mountain society was very different, but no more ready to withstand the Russian invasion. The Circassian tribes had considerable wealth – gold, slaves and livestock, particularly the brilliant Kabardian horses – with society rigidly stratified into classes of nobles and landowners, free peasants and serfs. But although they had a common language, culture, and increasingly a common Moslem religion, the Circassians were unable to unite their various fiefdoms. The Kabards in the centre were always more willing to cut deals with the Russians, while tribes nearer the Black Sea, like the Shapsugs, resisted any encroachment by the northeners at all. Although the Circassians had trading, religious and political ties to the Ottoman empire, they were discovering how little difference the loose alliance actually made.

The man who stepped into this void was Shamil. Unlike Mansur, he was well known. When Shamil was declared Imam – or religious leader – of Dagestan in 1834, the groundwork for a lengthy *ghazawat* had already been laid by his two immediate predecessors, the first and second Imams. The first Imam was Ghazi Mohammed, Shamil's close friend from the house next door in Gimry. In 1829 Ghazi Mohammed gathered the growing Naqshabandi Sufi *murids*, or disciples, and formed the basis of an army to fight the holy war. He launched a series of lightning strikes on the Russians, and his men learned fast. Because they were all expert swordsmen, rifle shots, riders and knew their country by heart, it took only the single-mindedness and fundamentalism of the Naqshabandi teachings to turn these simple people into soldiers. Their spartan, fanatical and heroic movement became known as *muridism*.

The *murids* struck far beyond the black cliffs of upper Dagestan, attacking Russian forces to the west in Ingushetia, to the north in Kizlyar, and to the east at the Caspian Sea fort of Derbent. Perhaps lapsing into his weakness for exaggeration, Alexander Dumas wrote, during a later trip to the North Caucasus, that 6,000 heads were severed during the devastation of Kizlyar. By 1831 the Russians had a force of 20,000 bayonets hunting Ghazi Mohammed and, a year later, his men were cornered in a ravine near Gimry. Of the 50, including the Imam, who barricaded themselves up in a small stone house under the cliffside, surrounded by troops, only two men got out alive. One was Shamil.

Shamil's breakout through the surrounding Russian soldiers is still famous. It's said he came out the door of the house, jumped over the heads of the first line, then hacked his way through the rest, and disappeared into the night, blood gushing from bayonet and sword wounds. One can see the spot today: a narrow, lifeless canyon giving access to Gimry. A sign marks where Shamil landed after jumping over the heads of the soldiers. It's ridiculously far away – one can imagine proud locals moving it a little further each year – but however far the young Shamil really leapt, his escape was miraculous. It took another two years – an interim period when Hamza Bek, the second Imam, led the rebellion – before Shamil took over and became third Imam. But that leap to freedom was the moment that launched the legend: saint to his people, devil to the Russians, and to the exotica-loving 19th-century English 'Shamil, the Lion of Dagestan.'

## Gimry, Dagestan

*There's nothing very old in Gimry – it was destroyed during the war against Shamil and again by the Communists. But any place hacked out of a stone landscape instantly looks ancient. The streets are cobbled, steep and very narrow. The houses are small and jostled together, with flat roofs, which double as terraces. In places, you could almost lean out the window and touch hands with someone across the street. The interiors – more spacious than you'd believe from the outside – have tiny courtyards opening onto basements, rooms inside rooms, verandas and rooftops. The flat roofs are strung with grapevines and some houses have enclosed balconies jutting out over the cobbles, measured to be high enough for a horseman to ride underneath without having to duck.*

*In my notebook I've scribbled four words to remind me of sights I had no time to note down at the time: 'fountains, blood, no booze'. Somehow they sum up the otherworldliness of Gimry.*

*The fountains: this is where the women meet to draw water from the neighbourhood spring taps and gossip. Young and old gather at the trough, most wearing black headscarfs and dresses which contrast with the polished water vessels, their long spouts glinting silver in the sunlight. Some of the young are stunning. They turn their heads away as I walk by. The old pause in their conversations and watch me, poker faced.*

*Blood: they slaughter a sheep at the main square and a small river of blood runs down the steep cobbles. The bright red is exhilarating in such a bleak environment.*

*No booze: as you enter the cliff-walled valley of Gimry, the sign on the road makes it clear. 'Dear traveller! You are entering the territory of Gimry village, home of the Imams. To protect the purity of the Imams' heritage, we ask you not to bring alcoholic drinks to this holy ground.'*

*Shamil's original house is long gone. Another has been built on exactly the same site, totally closed off by courtyard walls and a large studded wooden door from the street. The inside is cramped and, at the same time, full of unexpected openings and space – like the two levels of flat roof tops where I sit in the sun and look up at the cliffs on every side. Khussein Khazimagomedov, a distant descendant of Shamil, brings me tea and we talk about Caucasian relations with Russia. 'They can't buy our friendship. You can't buy spirit,' he says. 'All they can do is buy our leaders – that's been done.'*

*There are few cars in Gimry, but our street would be too narrow anyway. Donkeys and cows occasionally wander up, guided by old women wearing black from head to toe, or children with dark eyes and hair. Just up the street is the mosque. From the minaret we look down into courtyards all over the village. A whole world opens. Every space is used – this corner for the cow, that for the chickens, others for vegetables and places where the washing dries. Children and women are busy on the rooftops and in the courtyards; the men, as usual in the North Caucasus, are nowhere to be seen.*

*Ghazi Mohammed, the first Imam, is buried in the graveyard at the edge of the village. His tomb, inside a simple cottage-type building which serves as a mausoleum, is a pilgrimage site for Sufi worshipers and, like his death place in the ravine, it is draped with hundreds of coloured handkerchiefs. They blow, red, white and green against the golden grass which grows long and peacefully between the gravestones.*

*The village has a bloody past, but there's been no war here for 70 years, and now that Communism has gone, the mosque is open. Many of the old furies have subsided. I look around at the black cliffs and the jagged river cutting down the valley and tell Khussein how surprised I am that the reality actually does match the romantic 19th-century paintings done by Russian officers. The compliment doesn't go down well. 'Never mind the Russian officers,' he says. 'They destroyed Gimry three times during Shamil's time, you know. I couldn't tell you how many times they destroyed our crops so we couldn't eat.' In such a setting, the past may be impossible to forget.*

Shamil's rule is still remembered with enormous pride among North Caucasians. Unlike previous leaders, he not only defied the Russians, but held the resistance together for almost three decades of unbroken warfare against the army which had defeated Napoleon. Far more than a military genius, he was a religious leader who used Islam, and a personal ruthlessness, to reach across the deep tribal divides and create an alliance of Moslem highlanders. The alliance's horsemen, cannons and swords were eventually ground to pieces by the relentless Russian military machine, but the psychology of that *gortsy* alliance survives to this day. That is Shamil's greatest legacy.

He offered a stern life – strict *shariat* Islamic law, and war against the mighty invader, whatever the consequences. But Shamil both forced and earned respect from the mountaineers, terrifying the uncommitted and offering protection to any villages threatened by the Russians. The imam could be viciously cruel, publically displaying the severed heads of traitors as examples, or, in one case, cutting a would-be assassin to pieces and burning his family alive. The Russians attempted to exploit discontent and in 1851 managed to secure the defection of one of Shamil's top commanders, Hadji Murat, a figure immortalized by Tolstoy. But ultimately Shamil's bloody rule was mild compared to the mayhem inflicted by the Russians, who destroyed families and villages not in revenge, but as policy. As so often happens in guerrilla wars, civilians preferred the brutality of one of their own to that of the foreign invader.

Shamil was also an inventive and energetic administrator. There were taxes, fines, ways of sorting out the eternal problem of blood feuds and a full militarisation of society. Out of the raw material of thousands of well-trained but poorly organised fighters, Shamil forged an elite of devout, fearless *naibs*, and then a larger regular force made from *murtaziqs*, a man drawn from one in ten houses in every village for the standing army. The other nine houses looked after the *murtaziq's* upkeep.

In battle Shamil was able to outwit and outfight one Russian general after another, while his troops, when they could fight man-to-man, were unparalleled. One of the more successful 19th-century Russian generals, Velyaminov, wrote:

> the mounted natives are very superior in many ways both to our regular cavalry and the Cossacks. They are all but born on horseback and being used to riding from their earliest years, become extremely expert in this art. ... Success in military undertakings is a matter of necessity for the native. Without it he will find amongst his own compatriots neither friendship, nor confidence nor respect. He becomes a laughing stock and an object of contempt even for the women.

Shamil's forces were almost exclusively cavalry, or infantry which got to and from the battlefield on horseback, with few heavy weapons. Cannons, the core of the Russian military machine, as they would be in Chechnya's modern war, had to be captured from the enemy, to supplement primitive homemade pieces – something also true in the latest conflict. As long as the North Caucasians were on their own territory, above all in the highlands of Dagestan and the forests of Chechnya, they had the advantage. 'I'm just an ordinary mountain man,' the wry Shamil said. 'But my woods and mountains make me more powerful than many monarchs. I must crown my ravines because they help a lot in the fight for Dagestani freedom.'

Ambushes and surprise raids were the core of the mountaineers' tactics, and even the best Russian soldiers, compelled to strike out into enemy territory, were at enormous risk. With the cavalry sabre and the *kinzhal*, the North Caucasians were ferocious. The unofficial museum in Gimry, a simple but proudly kept room of artefacts in an old man's house, has a couple of 19th-century sabres. They're gently curved, long and still sharp. Though surprisingly light, the blades of Shamil's swords are said to have been so strong they could be bent into a circle without snapping. 'A Chechen, a Lesghian or a Cherkess may be literally in rags, but his sword, dagger and gun are of the finest quality,' Alexander Dumas wrote. 'Some mountaineers still own swords that once belonged to the crusaders. Some still wear coats of mail and breastplates emblazoned with a red cross, quite unaware that these are relics from the conquest of Jerusalem or Constantinople. All they know is that these blades are still razor sharp.'

The Russians could capture any objective, given enough guns and men. But as their successors discovered in the modern Chechen war, controlling an objective did not mean controlling the people or the surrounding area. Worse, the deeper the army pushed, the more exposed it became to the kinds of ambushes that Shamil revelled in. The most notorious and bloody of these expeditions was Count Vorontsov's 1845 mission to capture Shamil's headquarters in Dargo. Vorontsov, the new and respected viceroy in Chechnya, headed an army of 21,000 when he advanced, with little opposition, into the foothills. On July 18, 1845, he led a force of 11,500 men into Dargo, a miserable little village which armchair strategists in Saint Petersburg had imagined to be a major base.

The expedition had gone well and Vorontsov was warmly praised by Tsar Nicholas I. But Shamil hadn't been defeated, he'd simply made a strategic retreat, the recoil a snake makes before striking. Now, only when the Russians were beyond the point of no return, did the seriousness of their position become clear, with every minor operation, such as chasing off harrassing Chechens in the surrounding forests, costing lives. The enemy, sniping and ambushing from the trees, was hardly ever seen. Shamil's trap was closing.

The bloodbath began when the Dargo occupiers started to run out of supplies. Part of the force was dispatched down to a waiting supply column but fell into a horrendous forest ambush, with 556 men killed and 858 wounded, and left the corps up in Dargo with almost no food and ammunition. On 25 July Vorontsov began a total retreat to the plains. But the nightmare was far from over. As the weary, cut-off army retreated, now burdened by huge numbers of wounded, Shamil kept springing ambushes, one after the other. Scores of men died daily, baggage was discarded in the panic, cannons were lost and generals found themselves sword in hand, fighting alongside their men. By the end of the month, when the force finally reached a rendezvous with reinforcements and then a secure village, losses from the Dargo expedition totalled 984 killed, including three generals, 2,753 wounded and 179 missing. Nothing had been achieved.

The British consul in Odessa, James Yeames, summed up in his report on the disaster the amazing difference in morale between the two sides, given that the war between an imperial army and Shamil's guerrilla force – fighting without any help from the outside world – had already been going on for 10 years. 'The (Russian) troops, at first animated by the presence of a new commander of high character, are said to have now relapsed into a state of great moral depression,' Yeames wrote. 'While Shamil, and the free tribes of the Caucasus, are, it is feared, elated to a degree dangerous to all future plans of pacification.'

―――――

*Young men of Circassia, rush forth to the battle,*
*For brave youths always love war.*
*If ye fall, ye become martyrs, and if ye survive, ye have half that glory!*

19th-century Circassian war song.

In the west, nearer the Black Sea, the Circassians, or Adygei, did not sign on to the spartan state of Shamil. Although Ottoman missionaries were succeeding in replacing the remnants of Christianity and paganism with Islam, the Adygei were not interested in *muridism* or Naqshabandi Sufism. Yet despite these religious differences, they fought a parallel war against the same enemy, with many of the same tactics.

One of the most convincing eyewitness accounts of the Circassian fighting was by James Bell, one of a handful of Britons who played unofficial roles behind-the-scenes, encouraging the rebels, but all the evidence suggests, bringing little concrete help from London. In his *Residence in Circassia – 1837, 1838, 1839*, Bell described the carnival atmosphere as a large group of fighters, numbering about 1,500, prepared one of their raids inside Russian-held territory. As usual, to guard against spies, the target of the raid was only given out at the last moment and strict discipline was enforced. 'The spectacle was equally novel, exciting and picturesque,' Bell wrote. 'A mass of rugged mountaineers, men and boys, horse and foot, mingled promiscuously, with the flags of cognizance of their respective chiefs fluttering over them – volunteering invasion of a great empire to seek revenge for the ravaged home of their countrymen.'

A major difference in the warfare at this end of the Caucasus was that much of it took place along the Black Sea coast and involved bombardments from Russian naval ships. Like Shamil's men facing artillery from forts, the Circassians were at their weakest when under fire from the big guns. They were only really effective in close-quarter fighting – then they were deadly. 'Makhmet only replied by a challenge to land and fight,' Bell wrote.

The ships cannonaded for some time and two battalions of about 3,000 men and two pieces of cannon were landed at a corner of the bay under cover of their own fire. The suddenness of the attack had not given time for the assemblage of any considerable Circassian force; but the immediate neighbourhood furnished about 1,000 warriors who remained in groups behind such cover as the sides of the valley afforded, until the Russian infantry began to advance through the grove. A very sanguinary struggle then ensued, terminating, as already mentioned, in the repulse of the Russians who had not been able to advance more than half way towards the hamlet, the destruction of which was, no doubt, the purpose.

The Circassians and Shamil were in frequent contact and encouraged each other with news of their latest successes, but the tribes never managed to unite. A daring, large-scale attempt by Shamil to carry the war to the crucial central section – Kabarda and much of modern-day Ossetia – failed in 1846 due to a mixture of bad luck, clever Russian manoeuvers and fatal hesitation on the part of the Kabards. With hindsight, it's clear the Kabarda campaign – demonstrating the limits of his long-distance offensive capabilities – was the high tide for Shamil. Amazingly, resistance continued from one end of the mountains to the other for another generation, but it was now a defensive war against an attacker with almost unlimited resources – and therefore a doomed war.

Shamil's unsuccessful offensive also coincided with the start of Viceroy Vorontsov's leadership. Although most famous for the Dargo catastrophe, it was actually Vorontsov who finally managed to implement an earlier plan for the slow, patient strangulation of any resistance. The author of the plan, Velyaminov, had written back in 1828 that

> the Caucasus may be likened to a mighty fortress, marvellously strong by nature, artificially protected by military works, and defended by a numerous garrison. Only a thoughtless man would attempt to escalate such a stronghold. A wise commander would see the necessity of having recourse to military art; would lay his parallels; advance by gap and mine and so master the place.

Stage by stage, 500,000 Russian soldiers were deployed in the region and the fighters were marginalised, cut off from their popular support. The exhausted civilians were herded into the plains, where they could be controlled more easily. Bribes and positions of power were handed out to local leaders willing to cooperate. Denying the militants the chance to fight on their own terms was particularly difficult to ensure in Chechnya, where thick forests made almost everywhere a potential ambush point. So the Russians responded by fighting the trees, rather than the enemy. Swathes of woodland were hacked or burnt away, never to be replaced, to deprive Shamil's men of cover. When the ancient trees were too big to axe, they were blown up.

The highlanders' only real chance lay in foreign intervention. They could fight on for years, but they could never drive the Russians back. Only Turkish or British help could force that. There was reason to hope. After all, other outnumbered peoples, like the Greeks, had won international support for their independence struggles in the 19th century. Shamil in particular believed that help would come from Britain, then Russia's greatest superpower rival.

There were popular support groups in England, and the newspapers were full of the highlanders' exploits. 'Shamil, Imam of Dagestan, is believed to be still holding out in the hills north of Khunzak,' *The Times* reported in 1846. 'A force of of some 4,000 Russian regulars and Cossack cavalry, under command of General Gurko, are closing in, but rebel reinforcements led by the chiefs Tenguz the Wolf, and the Lion of Shepsuk, are flocking down from the mountains to harass the Russian lines.' Shamil had other backers. Russia and Britain were then playing what was called the 'great game,' a spy struggle for influence in Central Asia and, ultimately, power over India, Britain's most prized colony. Some feared Russia, using the Caucasus as the gateway to Asia, would try to invade India and that for this reason Shamil must be helped to block the Russians' advance. But these cold warriors of the day never quite won the debate and although Shamil wrote polite appeals for help in letters to Queen Victoria, the answers he wanted never came.

> For years, Oh honoured Queen, we have been at war against Russia, our invader,' Shamil wrote. 'Every year we must defend ourselves against the invader's fresh armies which pour into our valleys. Our resistance is stubborn, altogether we are obliged, in winter, to send our wives and children far away, to seek safety in the forests, where they have nothing, no food, no refuge against the severe cold. Yet we are resigned. It is Allah's will. ... We beseech you, we urge you, Oh Queen, to bring us aid.

The Circassians had a far more real chance of finding help. Their war was already mixed up in the power struggle between Russia and Turkey for control over the Black Sea and the European powers' desire to prevent Russia killing off the hapless Ottoman Empire. In London, Paris, Istanbul and Moscow, strategists watched with interest the Circassians' resistance along the Kuban river, the Caucasus foothills and the Black Sea coast.

The greatest opportunity was the Crimean War, when Britain, France and Turkey drove the Russians from the Crimean port of Sevastopol in 1855, and thus out of the Black Sea. Turkish military commander Omer Pasha tried to seize the moment and land ground troops in the Caucasus in order to push the Russians north. But his large army and the North Caucasus leaders failed to coordinate, and the winter was a poor time for the operation, so the Turks lost momentum and, in 1856, withdrew again from the region. Only British help might have saved the expedition, but having just won the unpopular Crimean War at such great cost, London was understandably reluctant to fight an obscure and fierce conflict alongside the Turks.

The 1856 Treaty of Paris, settling the Crimean War, was the final nail in the North Caucasians' coffin. Although the Black Sea was demilitarised, ending Russian naval operations, Russia was given back the Crimean peninsula and Turkey relinquished its claims to the Black Sea coast – effectively abandoning the Circassians. Russia, with its forces freed up from Crimea, could turn its full attention to the North Caucasus. The end was near.

In 1859, 40,000 soldiers led by Prince Baryatinsky were sent to finish off Shamil. The Lion of Dagestan was cornered in the Dagestani mountain village of Gunib. He had only 400 men left, having by then been largely abandoned by his people, who were tired of war and bloodshed. Surrounded by a vast army, he had a clear choice: either to surrender or send his last men to their destruction. Shamil recognised his fate and gave himself up with full military honours. Legend has it that a handful of Chechens in his group managed to break out and fight on for another year. But it was at Gunib that Shamil's epic, quarter-century war ended, and with it his imamate and the terrifying, passionate movement of *muridism*.

Baryatinsky, who had replaced Vorontsov as viceroy of the Caucasus, was a colourful, aristocratic figure and a talented general. In contrast to Yermolov he bribed rather than burnt the Moslem villages. He also perfected the military strategy of besieging the mountains and destroying the woods. His capture of Shamil at Gunib, an Avar village perched on a mountain cliff, was a perfect display of overwhelming force used in a calm, methodical manner.

The original Gunib lies in barely recognisable ruins, with the modern village rebuilt further down the mountainside. The place where the surrender took place is a shady opening in some trees by a dirt track. A white stone gazebo used to mark the spot, but it was blown up a couple years ago – by Avar nationalists, according to locals – and all that remains is the heap of gleaming stones. Nearby, coloured ribbons left by Sufi pilgrims decorate the cherry trees growing around the ruins of the mosque where Shamil used to pray. Lower down the hill is a barracks of Russian soldiers stationed there when President Boris Yeltsin launched the war against Chechnya. Their camp is just beyond old stone fortifications, lined with fire slits, that their predecessors built a century and a half earlier.

Shamil's surrender continues to be a burning controversy in the North Caucasus. After handing over his curved sabre, he was taken into Russia, where he underwent a bizarre change. He began with a visit to Saint Petersburg, then lived as an honoured house prisoner in Kaluga, not far from Moscow, made friends with Tsar Alexander II and buried himself in religious studies. One of his sons became a Russian general, another a Turkish general. Shamil's great grandson returned to the Caucasus and fought the Russians in Dagestan in the 1920s.

Shamil died in 1871 in Medina after finally being allowed by the tsar to carry out his greatest wish – a pilgrimage to Mecca. It was a strange end. The lion became a lamb – the holy warrior, a holy man. But perhaps the imam's final days would have been less surprising to those who knew him. There were many hints of his pacifism, or at least his ordinary humanity, even in the darkest hours of his struggle with the Russian Empire.

In 1839, during one of the most terrible battles, the seige of Akhulgo in Dagestan, Russian soldiers kidnapped Shamil's seven-year-old son Dzhemal-Eddin. The boy was taken to Saint Petersburg and brought up personally by Tsar Nicholas I, becoming almost entirely Russified and forgetting his mountain roots. Shamil, however, neither forgot his boy nor forgave the kidnap. In 1854, his men seized a Georgian princess, Annette Chavchavadze, and Shamil was finally able to bargain back his son. Shamil, the hardest of the hard, is said to have cried. But the tragedy only deepened. After growing up at the tsar's court, Dzhemal-Eddin was lost to his father. A creature from an alien land unable to stand the rough life of the mountains, he pined for the only world he knew – that of the enemy – and died within a few months.

After her release, Princess Chavchavadze gave unique outsider's testimony to the character of Shamil. This glamorous woman, who had been lucky to survive her ordeal, praised the warrior-priest. She said he was honest, ascetic, wise, and had a great love for cats.

'Some say he was wrong to surrender, that he should have fought to the last man,' said his descendant Khussein Khazimagomedov.

> But I think he did the wise thing. Yes, he could have said 'let's all die,' but he didn't. Instead he offered himself as a sacrifice to save all the others – he was sure they would behead him or hang him when he surrendered. He knew if they fought on they would eventually be wiped out and he knew what would happen to the village afterwards. People say he was frightened, but that's ridiculous. This is a man who had been in every terrifying situation and wounded a dozen times. Instead, he showed his dignity, that he was not just a warrior, but a politician. He understood that the people were tired of war.

The end of Shamil meant the Circassians, whose resistance had sputtered on as long as Shamil's, couldn't last much longer. Back in the 1830s an elderly Circassian chieftan had told James Bell that:

> the Russians cannot conquer this country. They may, by means of their ships and cannon, possess themselves of some more points on our coast; but granting they could gain the whole of it, that shall make no difference in our determination to resist to the last; for if they gain these hills we will retire to these snowy mountains and fight them.

Now in the time of reckoning, the Circassians kept their word, battling on for a full five years after Shamil's defeat, until they too were wiped out in a four-day last stand at Aibga, in the hills, in May 1864.

Unlike inhospitable Dagestan, the Circassians inhabited rich agricultural land. They also had the idyllic and strategic Black Sea coast. The inhabitants were the only obstacle standing between Russia and a first-class land grab. So when military resistance finally collapsed, Russian forces turned their attention to organised ethnic cleansing. Troops, frustrated by 35 years opposition from these simple, poorly armed people, went on a rampage of burning and looting. The mountains – that 'mighty fortress' – were emptied of their inhabitants.

'Break the resistance of the mountaineers. Take them out of the mountains to the plains and put Cossacks and Russians in captured places,' Baryatinsky wrote in 1860. An estimated 400,000 to 500,000 Circassians were driven in terror to the coast where they took whatever ships available, including vessels thoughtfully provided by the Russians, to Turkey, abandoning what had been their homeland since the beginning of time. Thousands died of disease and starvation in the humiliating panic to escape. There are stories of defeated Circassian chiefs who rode their horses, weighed down with weapons, into the sea rather than face the shame.

Any Adygei who remained were split up and put into special areas where they could be kept under control. Finally the Cossacks moved in along with other Slavic settlers and the land was declared an integral part of Russia. Today the Circassian tribes are divided into three separate, autonomous republics – Adygea, Karachai-Cherkessia and Kabardino-Balkaria. On the once hotly contested Black Sea coast of the North Caucasus there are almost no Adygei at all, just a handful of Shapsugs, and the Ubykh's coastal settlement of Sochi is the summer playground of Russia's rich. Even in the Adygea republic itself, the ethnic-Adygei – descendants of the Maeotians of the Bosphoran Kingdom – are a minority, the rest being Slavs. On the coast south of the mountains, within Georgia, the expulsions also reduced the related Abkhaz tribe to a minority. 'In America you have Indians and reservations – well that's what they've done to us here,' said a doctor in Maikop, the capital of Adygea.

In addition to the Circassians, numerous Chechens, Ingush, Dagestanis and Moslem Ossetians were made to leave their homes. The exact numbers of North Caucasians driven away will never be known, because no records were kept. Who cared enough to count? Estimated totals run as high as 1.2 million people – more than a quarter of the region's population at the time. Today, the descendants of the exiled Circassians and other North Caucasians number between one and 3.5 million according to different estimates, living in Turkey, Jordan, Syria, Israel and even the United States. Whole peoples were scattered into the wind.

And although no one could have known it during those days of total defeat, the tragedy of the Adygei ethnic cleansing was to be repeated on an even grander scale just 80 years later – this time not by a tsar, but by a man who called himself Josef Stalin.

## Novosvobodnaya, Adygea

*'Today they claim that these have always been Russian lands,' says Khamzet Kazanov, a white-haired Adygei history professor who takes me to the Cossack village of Novosvobodnaya, deep in the Caucasus foothills.'Not long ago, they wanted to celebrate the 150th anniversary of the so-called founding of Sochi – but our people were there millenia ago.'*

*We walk up to the ruins of a church. This is the spot where, in 1861, Alexander II met with Circassian chieftans and offered a last chance of surrender. They refused and within three years were annihilated. The Cossacks felt victorious when they moved in and built this church in honour of the tsar's visit, but today it is a deeply lonely place. The big arched doorway stands, but as no walls remain, it leads on only to more grass growing over rubble. There used to be a monument with a bust of the tsar, but that disappeared too – destroyed, locals say, in the Communist revolution. 'I just wish they'd admit they had to fight us for all this,' Kazanov says, 'that they took it from us in war, that this was where our forefathers lived'.*

## 4. BETRAYAL

*People of Europe! Learn to fight for freedom and independence from the heroic example of the Caucasian highlanders.*

From *The Communist Manifesto.*

When the 1917 Bolshevik revolution overturned Tsar Nicholas II and civil war erupted across Russia, the North Caucasus peoples thought their chance for freedom had come. There were still many people alive who remembered Imam Shamil. Sporadic revolts and repressions had continued ever since the end of the 19th-century conquest, such as a rebellion in much of the region coordinated with Turkish troops during the Ottoman-Russian war of 1877–1878. So Lenin's calls for freedom, human rights and an end to the hated tsar's regime struck a chord with the highlanders, who he said were 'until recently methodically dispossessed of their best lands by Russian colonists. Driven gradually into sterile deserts, these people were devoted to certain death.'

Taking advantage of the collapse in central power, a string of attempts were made to unite the North Caucasus into a single, self-ruling state. Like Mansur and Shamil before them, nationalist leaders thought that their only hope lay in unity between the small nations. Besides, at this time the general *gortsy* identity was at least as strong as the identities held by individual ethnic groups, adding to the feasiblity of some kind of union. As early as May 1917, before the Bolshevik victory in October, a United Highlanders organisation brought together representatives from parts of today's Dagestan, Chechnya, Ingushetia, North Ossetia and Kabardino-Balkaria. Only the crushed Adygei-Circassian tribes to the west were not included. The organisation united with Cossack groups in October, but then ground to a halt because of the revolution. In December, a successor was declared, the temporary Terek-Dagestan government, but it fell apart within six weeks. Muddying the waters, a pro-Communist Terek Republic was set up in March 1918, claiming authority across much of the same territory as the previous entities.

The most serious attempt by nationalists to unite against Russian rule and the anarchy of the Red-White civil war came in May 1918, with the creation of the Republic of the North Caucasus Mountains. The new entity, really a successor of the United Highlanders, again claimed control over most of the eastern part of the North Caucasus. On May 11 it declared independence, signed a friendship treaty with Turkey, and was promised support by Britain and the other European powers backing the tsarist armies in their struggle against the Bolsheviks.

In the minds of the Mountain Republic's leaders, the North Caucasus had never been closer to winning freedom. The foreign minister, Haidar Bammate, wrote later from exile that the declaration of independence 'was the logical consequence of and gave official sanction to the historical process which began with the century long fight for independence by the peoples of the North Caucasus against the Russian Empire – a period of cruel servitude punctuated by revolts, insurrections, the exile to Siberia of entire villages.' There were even plans to create a confederation of the whole Caucasus, uniting the North and the three southern Transcaucasus states – Armenia, Azerbaijan and Georgia – which declared independence just after the Mountain Republic.

But the Mountain Republic proved another illusion. The declaration of independence immediately sparked fighting between highlanders and local Cossacks, ending a brief period of cooperation between the historic enemies. Internally, the republic's government was divided on whether or not to support the White general, Anton Denikin, in his losing struggle against the Bolsheviks. There had been indications that Denikin would recognise the Mountain Republic in return for help against the Reds, but aided by Cossacks he set about taking control of the region. The Ingush put up desperate resistance in a week-long battle, but were doomed when the Mountain Republic failed to mobilise support. Similar inaction opened Chechnya and Dagestan to conquest by Denikin. By May 1919 the republic ceased to function and its leaders fled.

Out of the ashes rose an even more ephemeral, radical confederation bent on driving out the Russians at any cost – the North Caucasian Emirate. Created in 1919 by Uzun Hadji, a 90-year-old Naqshabandi Chechen sheikh, this theoretically covered the same territory as the original Mountain Republic, but it was planned as an ultra-Islamic state linked to Turkey and governed exclusively by *shariat* law. The Bolsheviks, in a clever piece of opportunism, now promised the highlanders that their autonomy and religious freedoms would be respected in return for help defeating Denikin. By February 1920, the combined Red army and North Caucasian independence movements had driven the White army from the region. The Soviets were greeted as a liberators. But North Caucasian hopes were again betrayed, as the Communists rapidly set about occupying the entire Caucasus, north and south. The Emirate and remains of the Mountain Republic were banned and many of the people who had helped the Reds expel Denikin were executed or imprisoned.

Dreams of independence were dead, but faced with the prospect of continuing to live under Russian, anti-Islamic rule, the hard core element – as usual in the mountains of Dagestan and Chechnya – didn't hesitate. They declared *ghazawat* – holy war. The 1920–21 uprising was as suicidal as every other North Caucasus rebellion. The rebels could only muster an estimated 10,000 men armed with antiquated rifles, swords and 40 machine guns. This peasant force faced a battle-hardened Soviet army of 40,000 men, equipped with heavy weapons and by now even aircraft. But the Dagestanis and Chechens had the support of their people and the fanatical bravery and dedication that Sufi mysticism can bring. In the end, the Soviets won the way the Russian empire had won in the 19th century – by strangling the rebellion valley by valley, and deporting, or massacring civilian supporters – but the resistance was epic. The final stand at Gidatl, in southern Dagestan, was in true North Caucasus style. No more than 300 rebels with four machine guns were pitted against six infantry regiments and four cavalry squadrons. The rebels fought to the end and there were virtually no survivors.

---

*– Long life to you, beloved Stalin!*
*Such is our hope and prayer for you.*
*... The Caucasus, its youth restored,*
*Comes to you, its people sing:*
*The name Stalin gleams like a star!*
*You, our father and our brother,*
*Gave us happiness and opened*

*Wide gates to future joy.*
*– Long life to you, beloved Stalin!*
*Such is our hope and prayer for you.*
From the Chechen song of Stalin in Chechen-Ingush Folklore, 1940.

Communism did indeed bring electricity, literacy, hospitals and roads – even to the high mountain villages, where people lived in medieval conditions. Salaries, living space, holidays and a role in society were handed out to each comrade, standard issue and non-negotiable, like rations. In some ways, the Communist dream makers even exceeded expectations – not only was the North Caucasus declared a paradise, it became one, a prime tourist haven for the Soviet masses. *Turbazes*, or tourist facilities sprang up, including dozens of centres for taking water cures. The Communist Party elite bathed in Sochi and kept exclusive hunting lodges in the mountains of Karachai, while factory workers from all over the huge Union arrived on party-sponsored tour packages. Once a place of bitter conflict, the Caucasus became a place for sun, mineral water, skiing, forest walks and high-rise Intourist hotels.

Soviet rule began with a remarkably flexible policy – a Soviet Mountain Republic, which again united most of the highlander peoples, allowed *shariat* law and autonomy. But this only lasted briefly and between 1921 and 1924 Moscow gradually broke off each group into smaller, more controllable units – either a Soviet Socialist Autonomous Republic (ASSR by the Russian acronym) or the lower-status Autonomous Region (AO).

The ASSRs and AOs were separate ethnic homelands only in name. The ASSR governments answered directly to Moscow, much in the same way as regions, but they were dominated by ethnic-Russians, with only the most carefully vetted indigenous people allowed to participate. The AOs were even less meaningful. These were ethnic-minority enclaves subordinate either to Stavropol or Krasnodar Russian regions with almost no say over their own affairs. The ASSR and AO map went through repeated convulsions as Soviet planners drew and redrew the internal dividing lines. The final design of 1936 was a maze of artificially created entities lumping together unrelated, even competing ethnic groups, and thus ensuring that Soviet authority remained the only unifying force – the old imperial principle of divide and rule.

The Avars and Chechens, closely allied in the wars against the Russians, were split, the Avars going into Dagestan ASSR, the Chechens into a joint Chechnya-Ingushetia ASSR. The North Ossetians were given their own ASSR, but separated from the South Ossetians, across the mountains, who were put into an AO district subordinate to the Soviet republic of Georgia. The Circassian peoples suffered a particularly complex fate. The Adygei proper were shunted off into an AO subordinate to Krasnodar region. The Cherkess were lumped with the Turkic-speaking Karachai into an AO called Karachai-Cherkessia under the jurisdiction of Stavropol region. The Kabards were put with the Turkic-speaking Balkars into the ASSR of Kabardino-Balkaria. In a single move, this policy split up not only the Circassian groups, but the related Karachai and Balkars.

The North Caucasians had expected freedom at the end of the tsarist era. Instead they got Communist atheism, Russian language, Russian officials and brutal land collectivisation. Mosques were shut down or destroyed, and the mullahs arrested or shot. Even after the 1920–21 war rebellions kept coming, in every generation and area, right up to the Soviet Union's entry into World War II. There were uprisings against religious repression in Dagestan in 1927 and against land collectivisation from Dagestan to the Karachai in 1929–1930, including major battles against regular army troops in Chechnya. In the summer of 1937 alone, 14,000 leading figures of Chechnya-Ingushetia were arrested, thousands in a single July night. Even then, the 'reactionary' Moslems kept preaching resistance, the highlanders clung to their way of life and up in the high mountains, armed resistance flickered on.


## 5. PUNISHMENT

*I can't tell you all that happened, there's not room in your book. Just God grant it won't happen again.*

Karachai man remembering Stalin's 1943 deportation of his entire people.

World War II pushed the North Caucasians back into the whirlwind of history. Germany, chasing the Baku oil resources, invaded and briefly occupied much of the region in 1942–43, although they never made it into the Transcaucasus. When the Nazis were driven out, the war seemed to be over for the Caucasus and the region faded from the world's view. But for the highlanders, the nightmare was only beginning. Stalin accused, with no evidence, four North Caucasian nations of mass collaboration with the Nazis. His sentence: *likvidatsia* – 'liquidation.'

In chillingly efficient operations that took no more than a couple of days, the secret police herded the entire Karachai, Chechen, Ingush and Balkar nations, down to the last person, onto cattle trains and dumped the survivors in the wastelands of Central Asia. Of course Stalin was already an accomplished organiser of concentration camps, death marches, purges and deportations. But this was genocide – whole nations vanishing into the void, people killed purely on the basis of their ethnic group. And nobody, not in the USSR, not abroad, even knew.

The North Caucasus deportees totalled at least 618,000, going by the 1939 Soviet census. The 76,000 Karachai vanished in October–November

1943; then 408,000 Chechens and 92,000 Ingush in February 1944; a month later the 43,000 Balkars. An unknown number of Avars, Adygei and Moslem Ossetians were also uprooted. As Robert Conquest points out in *The Nation Killers*, these numbers are probably low, given the likely population increase in the years between the census and the genocide.

Elsewhere the liquidators were busy sweeping the Kalmyks, Greeks, Volga Germans, the Tatars in the Crimean peninsula, and even the people of remote, tiny Meskhetia under the giant Central Asian and Siberian rugs. That is not to mention the mass, but not total, deportations of Balts, Ukrainians and others in the same period. Only a generation later, in 1956, Nikita Khrushchev acknowledged the crimes for the first time, and a year later the so-called 'punished peoples' were allowed to return to the homelands they thought they'd never see again.

## Karachayevsk, Karachai-Cherkessia

*Mukhidin, 68, was one of the Karachai serving on the Ukrainian front in the Soviet army. He survived the fighting but instead of being treated as a hero, discovered that his family, his entire people, had vanished.*

*The rage he feels all these years later makes it impossible for Mukhidin to spell out what happened. His story is incoherent, caught in the whirlwind of human suffering. Wearing a Moslem prayer cap and an old suit jacket, he stands before me, shaking.*

*All I understand is this: he was taken from the battle front to work in a forced labour camp at a lumber yard, then to an armaments factory; he had no idea where the Karachai people had gone; he eventually tracked them down in Kazakhstan and then found the remains of his family. 'My father had died of hunger. Four of my sisters' children also died,' he yells at the top of his broken, old voice.*

The highlanders were rounded up by troops who had been billeted in their houses in advance, ostensibly for rest or for wartime deployment. They were given between 15 minutes and two hours to get ready and took only what they could carry. The stage between the villages and the train stations in the towns was often by truck – American Studebaker trucks on lease to the Soviet Union. It's a detail everyone remembers. 'They came for us and wanted to load us up into these American trucks, but they wouldn't fit into our narrow streets,' Taukau Makayev, a Balkar, said with a bitter smile. 'But it was very well planned. Nothing was left to chance. They only gave us 15 minutes to gather a few belongings and we didn't even know what was going on. It was only when they put us in the train wagons that we realised we were going far away.'

The train journey in the cruel Siberian winter killed the weak within days. When guards found corpses in the unheated, unventiltated goods wagons they threw them out the doors. 'I remember, the trains would stop for 15 minutes and we'd try to build fires in the snow,' Taukau said. 'Once a woman had died in the wagon and her son tried to bury her by the rails. The ground was frozen hard but he found a hole and covered her up. That's where he left her.'

There are no hard figures for how many people died. There were no journalists, no human rights activists, no independent courts. Reliable estimates are that at least 20 to 30 per cent of deportees – especially the elderly and young who could not withstand the cold, starvation and diease – perished. Hundreds, maybe thousands, were simply shot; again, no one will ever know how many. Population figures analysed in *The Nation Killers* tell their own story. In the 13-year period between 1926-39, (hardly a peaceful time, including thousands of executions and arrests by the Soviets), the Chechens grew 28 per cent, the Balkars 28 per cent, the Karachai 37 per cent, the Ingush 24 per cent. Compare this to the 13 years of forced exile: the Chechens grew 2.5 per cent; the Balkars didn't grow at all; the Karachai grew at eight per cent; the Ingush grew at 15 per cent. These were ravaged, emasculated nations.

The scar is deep, not only on the generation which survived the train journey and the generation born in exile, but on their descendants. Because this was punishment based on race, the deportations have become part of the national identity of the Chechens, Ingush, Karachai and Balkars. Like Jewish Holocaust surivors, it is an event which quietly dominates both individuals' lives and the nation as a whole. Everyone without exception is a victim. Even for those born after, the tragedy is impossible to put aside, since their parents, relatives, village and entire people suffered – punished simply because of their race.

Tamara, a big, dark-eyed Chechen grandmother in a spotted-red headscarf, cried as soon as she retold the story. Although she was only eight when the troops sent her to Kazakhstan, she lived in daily fear that it might happen again, that her nation might inexplicably be swept up into the void.

First, soldiers came to live in our houses and we put them up like guests. Lots of them came to every house. They ate with us, dumped all their gear everywhere. We had about 30 in our place and they were there for more than a month.

One day, we were told there would be a very important meeting and all the men were taken away. I had three sisters and we were put on a train wagon together. My brother was born on the train. It was so cold. It was a cattle train and there were no windows, just darkness. They never told us a thing, didn't tell us where we were going.

Some people were in other villages at the time, so when we were deported they were split up from their families and it took years and years before they ever found their relatives again. In the train, we would shout from carriage to carriage, trying to see if there were relatives. Oh God, I can't forget this for more than an hour, even today.

Sofia Makhadelova, a fiesty 103-year-old Karachai mountain woman, was already 40 when they came for her. 'It was early morning and these soldiers who had been billeted in our house, just as they had been in every house in the village, suddenly told us that we had two hours to get things ready for a journey. We had no idea where we were going, or what they wanted.'

> We were put into goods wagons at the train station. It was cold and pitch black dark and everybody was shouting and crying because they couldn't see or find a place to sit. We didn't know where we were going, we had no idea. There was a Russian woman who had married a Karachai and she was also thrown in with us. She was the one who told us – 'Don't worry, we're going to Central Asia. It's a good place, we'll be all right.' That was the first time I'd heard of it.
>
> This went on for 20 days. Near my corner, there were an old man and boy. They both died from the cold and we kept them secretly among us so that the guards wouldn't just throw them out of the train. They were throwing bodies out like rubbish. We wanted to keep them and bury them later.

Exile was mostly in Kazakhstan or Kyrgzstan. The North Caucasians were contained in special settlement areas and ordinary villages under what amounted to mass house arrest. They were banned from leaving their villages without special permission, and restricted in the use of their own languages. Slowly the deportees began rebuilding their lives from scratch, working at collective farms, labour camps or factories. 'We lived like sheep in Kazakhstan – whole families in one room,' a Karachai woman said over tea and *ayran* yogurt. 'But when the Kazakhs saw we were not bandits but hard working people, they began to help us. They saw how hard we worked on the collective farms and how bit by bit we started to build our own houses. The Kazakhs turned to us and by the end, the Communist authorities asked us not to go home. Of course, when the permission came, we all left. But I married a Kazakh. They're the best Moslems of all,' she said smiling.

Behind the deportees were swathes of empty land, deserted villages, and a handful of men who managed to escape into the mountains, chased by units of Soviet soldiers. The names of the liquidated republics were removed from maps, any signs of their culture, including graveyards and mosques, were destroyed. Thousands of Russians, Ukrainains, Georgians and also North Caucasians, such as Avars, Laks and Ossetians, were then forcibly moved into the banished peoples' houses – an ethnic time bomb that would tick away ignored until the breakup of the Soviet Union in 1991.

At the time, the world never even noticed, and the Communist authorities kept silent. The fact of the Ingush and Chechen deportations was admitted in 1946, but the other nations vanished without trace – George Orwell's 'unpersons.' If anyone had carefully analysed reference materials of the time, as Conquest does in *The Nation Killers*, he would have found sinister half-clues to what had happened. In the first edition of the Large Soviet Encyclopedia, which was completed in 1948, Kabardino-Balkaria had simply become Kabardine, while Chechnya-Ingushetia was renamed Grozny Province. There was no explanation or further comment. The Karachai were not mentioned.

*Article I:*
*The contracting parties confirm that genocide, whether committed in time of peace or in time of war, is a crime under international law which they undertake to prevent and punish.*

*Article II:*
*In the present Convention genocide means any of the following acts committed with intent to destroy, in whole or in part, a national, ethnical, racial or religious group, as such:*
*(a) Killing members of the group;*
*(b) Causing grievous bodily or mental harm to members of the group;*
*(c) Deliberately inflicting on the group conditions of life calculated to bring about its physical destruction in whole or in part;*
*(d) Imposing measures intended to prevent births within the group;*
*(e) Forcibly transferring children of the group to another group.*

*– from the United Nations Convention on Prevention and Punishment of the Crime of Genocide, adopted in 1948, in effect from 1950, ratified by the USSR in 1954.*

The logic of the operation remains something of a mystery, as is often the case in repressions of such massive cruelty. Exactly why were the North Caucasians punished?

The Germans, whose main target was Azerbaijan's oil industry, briefly occupied the region before being driven out. No one disputes that the Nazis could, or at least planned, to form local, anti-Soviet units, just as they did in other fringes of the USSR. Given the brutal history of the North Caucasus, it is hardly surprising that the Germans would find collaborators. The average Chechen or Balkar was hardly going to feel loyal to a government that had outlawed his culture, taken his lands and sent the NKVD secret police to repress his leaders. Many ordinary people were no doubt secretly pleased to see the Germans, or anyone else, attack the Soviets.

Neither is it disputed that some in the North Caucasus, quite independently of the Germans, took advantage of the upheaval to attack the Soviet authorities in the same way their forefathers had attacked the

Russians for generations. For example, a major insurrection was launched in the mountains of Chechnya in 1940. It was suppressed, as usual, with considerable violence including aerial bombing. But this was long before fascist soldiers came anywhere near the Caucasus and, it must be stressed – German soldiers never set foot in Chechnya.

An old Chechen man told me about a strange incident that highlights the atmosphere of distrust, fear and ignorance in those wartime days, with NKVD spies everywhere, German troops advancing, and ordinary people basically too concerned about their own survival to plot any grand schemes. 'Some Soviet paratroopers landed up in the mountains. God knows what they were doing. Probably training or something. Up there in those days, people didn't know what was going on. They were very poor and they lived cut-off from everything. When they saw these men come out of the sky, they surrounded them and killed them. They made clothes out of the parachutes.' Who knows exactly what happened that day when the fierce Chechen farmers met the soldiers. But maybe incidents like these were used to justify the accusation that all of Chechnya was actively working for the Germans.

'We only had the Germans around where we lived for a few months,' Sofia Makhadelova, the Karachai woman, said. 'We did nothing wrong. They took all our animals while they were here, I remember that. There were only a few who even saw the Germans. There should have been an investigation to see whom to blame. Instead, they took everyone – even the children whose fathers were fighting at the front.'

Beyond this rag-tag collection of incidents, little different from the rebellious pattern of the past, there was nothing to indict the highlanders. The timing alone – troops had already left the region when the deportations took place – contradicts the claim that this was to prevent unloyal populations from aiding the enemy.

North Caucasians serving in the Red Army and in partisan units fought the Germans, often heroically, as would be expected from peoples with such a martial tradition. The list of Heroes of the Soviet Union from the North Caucasus is disproportionately long for these ethnic groups' tiny numbers. The Chechens and Ingush, whose population was only half a million at the start of World War II, officially won 56 Hero of the Soviet Union medals in the Red Army – more members of their race were decorated, but hid their ethnic identity from the authorities. Even today, few Russians are aware that more than 300 of the men who perished during the suicidal defence of the fortress in Brest, Belarus, a battle of almost legendary symbolism in Soviet patriotic lore, were Chechens and Ingush. Likewise, there were 14 Karachai Heroes of the Soviet Union, from a population of just 76,000, although none lived to see their medals. Meanwhile, back home, their cities, like Grozny and Nalchik, were being bombed by German aircraft or attacked by Nazi troops.

Right up until the deportations Soviet propaganda lauded the North Caucasians' contribution to the war effort, saying the Chechens, Ingush, Karachai and Balkars were model Soviet citizens. Just two years before, Kalinin, chairman of the presidium of the Supreme Soviet, said that 'the Caucasus is the most enlightening demonstration of the reforming beneficial effect of the Soviet system on the psychology and character of people. The Caucasians have become a socialist people. ... The whole Soviet land, from border to border, has become their beloved home.'

Most likely the deportations were the result of different forces converging – some practical, some psychological. One of the more plausible theories is that Stalin wanted to finish off the perpetually rebellious Chechens and that he instinctively mistrusted the Karachai, Balkars and Meskhetians because they are ethnically Turkic, Russia's great rival. Impossible to prove today is a theory that Stalin, usually portrayed as a Georgian, actually had an Ossetian father and suffered from an inferiority complex about belonging to one of what Russians call the 'small peoples.' He pretended to be fully Georgian by Georgianising his Ossetian surname to Dzhugashvili and then, so the theory goes, turned his twisted self-hatred by becoming a historic Russian tyrant. This is disputed territory, but as the experience of Hitler showed, the paranoias and psychoses of tyrants can have catastrophic effects.

## Grozny, Chechnya

*'Things were quite different back then,' says Natasha. She's 70 years old, the descendant of a Cossack family that has lived in Chechnya for three generations. She's seen a lot and remembers the day the Chechens were deported well. It was another era before the war and a lot of things had hardly changed from the 19th century.*

*'The Chechen women then, they wore long dresses with cut-off leggings. They had headscarves wrapped around like that. And the men, ooh, they wore Cherkessk tunics, with pouches for bullets. Until the deportations, they always carried kinzhals and had sashes. Of course, the kinzhals were polished and they'd show off to the girls and dance. Then they had these amazing papakhas (tall, lambskin hats). The Chechens would come down to Grozny – almost only Russians lived there then – from the mountains and sell butter and eggs. What butter! Oh, and great sacks of nuts. The men were not like our Russian men. Their wives walked behind them and did what they said. Not like our men, who always obey the wife! I remember one elder in Yermolovka. He was 92 and had three wives. One on each side and a nice young one behind him.'*

*'There's nothing they could have done. I mean what could they have done to resist? Nowadays, these (Chechen rebel) fighters look on themselves as supermen, but back then there were no real guerrillas, just*

*a few bandits. All they had were hunting guns and what good were those against troops? What could they do against something like this? You know what Beria (the NKVD chief) said? He said it wasn't enough to send them to Kazakhstan, that they all should have been dropped into the middle of the Caspian Sea.*

'*All this was because of a few abregs, a few bandits. There was no organised resistance against the Soviets, just a few bandits who fired on the troops and shouted they would help the Germans and kill all Russians. Most people lived quietly, looking after cows and chickens. Because of a few bad people, a whole nation suffered.*'

*The day of the deportations, Natasha woke up to find her Chechen neighbours had vanished. '*My mother got up in the morning and said 'What's happened? Where are they?' We got to the train station and the wagons were already closed. People were crying out and weeping. A lot of people were from the mountains and couldn't speak a word of Russian and they cried out in Chechen from the wagons. The NKVD said they would take people out of wagons and shoot them.*'*

*Had Natasha been scared that she too might be swept up in the great persecution, even by mistake?*

'*The soldiers never even knocked on our door. They knew we were Russian, of course they did – they knew everything.*'

Stalin died in March 1953, but it was not until February 1956 that Khrushchev denounced him in a secret speech to the 20th Communist Party Congress, finally opening the way for salvation of the exiles. 'Comrades, let us reach for some facts,' Khrushchev said.

> The Soviet Union is justly considered as a model of a multinational state because we have in practice assured the equality and friendship of all nations who live in our great fatherland. All the more monstrous are the acts whose initiator was Stalin and which are crude violations of the basic Leninist principles of the nationality policy of the Soviet State. We refer to the mass deportations from their native places of whole nations, together with Communists and Komsomols without any exception; this deportation action was not dictated by any military consideration.

Khrushchev's 1956 speech shattered the official silence, but it took another year before action was taken to liberate the deported peoples. Decrees on rehabilitation of the North Caucasian peoples were issued in January 1957. The punished peoples packed up everything they'd built over almost 15 years and began the great return. An entire generation had been born in exile and grown up in Kazakhstan or Kyrgyzstan, but the young had always waited for the day they could return to a home they'd never seen. Another generation had grown old, but they also went – 'to die at home,' as an Ingush woman told me. Some dug up their dead for the journey.

When the North Caucasians returned, they discovered that much had changed in their beloved mountains. Not only were their houses occupied, but mosques had been demolished and the graveyards in many villages ripped up, their stones used as building materials, in a deliberate policy of destroying the highlanders' 'punished' culture. In the cemetery at the Karachai village of Kammenomost, unmarked burial mounds still undulate across the field. By the time the Karachai returned, too many families had been destroyed and too much time had passed for more than a few of the graves to be identified and given new stones. The forgotten dead haunt the Caucasus.

'When we came back home, all the mosques had been destroyed. We went to our old house and there were Russians living in it,' Tamara, the Chechen, said. 'They refused to leave and said 'we're not afraid of you, go away'. We had some money left so we went and bought another house.'

'My father's family had nine people in it when they sent us away. Only my father survived – his parents, sister, brothers, they all died,' said Magomed, a Balkar. 'As soon as we were allowed, we came back to our village, but we found out that our house had been burned down. Just the walls were standing. So we started to rebuild it. Now we live in the same house as always, even if it's changed shape,' he said proudly. 'The other houses in the village had been occupied by Russians, Kabards and some Georgians. A lot of people had no choice but to pay, to use the money they'd saved and buy back their own houses. My aunt though was very fierce and said to the people in her house: 'If you don't get out, I'll kill you tomorrow, I'll cut your heads off.' They left. Many of us gave ultimatums like that – we're a warlike people, you see.'

North Caucasians joke that they are such good builders because the Russians keep destroying their homes. There's some truth in this. Kazir Dzhamal, a magnicifently robust 75-year-old Balkar, famed as a mountain huntsman, was 19 when he was deported from the village of Verkhny Balkar. In Kazakhstan, his people built their own houses. On return, they found their ancient village was a deserted ruin, so they built an entire new village a little lower down the valley.

'It was beautiful,' Kazir said, taking me up to the ruined foundations of the original village, which still juts out on terraces from a steep hillside. He pointed out the remains of the house he had grown up in. 'The streets were tiny and all the houses were built close to each other. Once a Russian engineer, a real city slicker, visited us and he couldn't believe it. The joke went that when he saw our houses all stacked up like that on the hillside he thought it was one huge house and said: 'Even in Moscow we don't have buildings with that many floors.'

The legacy of Stalin was only partially cleared by Khrushchev's speech. The perpetrators of the genocide were never punished and the denunciation itself was padded with excuses. According to Khrushchev, Stalin was 'convinced that this was necessary for the defence of the interests of the working classes against the plotting of enemies and against the attack of the imperialist camp.' The deportations were not 'the deeds of a giddy despot. He considered that this should be done in the interest of the party.' Khrushchev's lament that Stalin deported even 'Communists and Komsomols' verged on black humour.

The Khrushchev thaw also did little to change the colonial-style policies of Russian rule in the North Caucasus, where all the keys to nationhood were undermined. The deportations were considered non-events. No memorial monuments were erected and there was certainly no mention of what happened in the cheerful guide books printed for all those newly arrived Soviet holiday makers staying at the *turbazes*. The punished peoples carried their pain in silence. Even a guide book on Karachai-Cherkessia published in 1992, a year after the collapse of the Soviet Union, failed to mention the wiping out of the Karachai. 'In January, 1943 our area was liberated. ... All Soviet peoples rose up against facism. In our area, 13 partisan groups were formed. Women of Karachai-Cherkessia were killed defending their homeland.'

More distant history, rather than simply denied, was distorted to suit the political agenda. Shamil was posthumously tried and retried by ideologues, who presented him first as an anti-tsarist people's hero, then as a figure who was better than the tsar but no more, and finally, after the deportations, as a straightforward reactionary cleric and bandit.

Culture was served up in official dance troupes wearing extinct national costumes, while the meat of Caucasus society – the mosques, the weddings, burials and councils of elders – was condemned as reactionary and primitive. Linguistic Russification took on new intensity during the Khrushchev and Brezhnev years, lasting from the 1950s to 1980s. Non-Slavs were officially said to have an 'inner need' for the Russian langauge and the region's long and scholarly association with Arabic, particularly in Dagestan, was ended. In the 1940s the Russian Cyrillic alphabet became standard. In 1958–59 the right to schooling in one's mother tongue was abolished, and between 1961 and 1982, 31 languages were dropped from schools, including Adygei, Balkar, Karachai, and Chechen-Ingush. As for national literature, such as the coffee-table-book sized 'Heroic-epic songs of the Chechen and Ingush,' it was in Russian and crammed with propaganda. The first two entries in my 'Heroic-epic songs' book, printed in 1979 in Russian, are called 'Song to Lenin.'

The last decades of the USSR were peaceful in the North Caucasus. There were no uprisings or wars and the Soviets believed their dream of creating a happy Russified 'family of nations' was coming true. But the silence was deceptive. Under the surface of this brave new world, the passions and terrors of the old lay deep and fermenting.

## Grozny

After half a year of war in Chechnya, I look through the little packet of postcards a Chechen fighter had given me when the Russian tanks were first approaching Grozny. 'Keep them so you can remember what a beautiful city we once had,' the guerrilla said, taking the 17 faded pictures out of his camouflage smock breast pocket.

The postcards were printed in 1988 when there was still the Soviet Union. But after six months of combat in Chechnya, there's not much left: the Lenin statue – pulled down by the Chechens; the circus – hit by Russian air force bombs; the parliament building – destroyed by bombs; a bridge over the river Sunzha – now a tangle of concrete slabs and steel rods; the oil institute – gutted by fire; Minutka traffic circle – pitted and blackened by bomb and shell craters; the Chernoreche suburb, where the Chechens made a last stand – hit by thousands of Russian artillery shells.

'Welcome to Grozny,' the blurb on the Soviet postcards packet says. 'Every year Grozny grows and improves. Wide avenues go through new residential complexes, modern multi-storey buildings have been built.'

# PART 3

# The Jigsaw in Pieces

*Russia is not going to be able to handle this. There are just too many peoples who have tasted freedom.*

Almir Abregov, director of the Adygei history museum in Maikop.

# 1. THE NEW FRONTIER

*In 1936 the Fuhrer delivered himself of the following: 'If the Urals and the Caucasus, with their incalculable wealth of raw materials, the rich forests of Siberia, and the unending cornfields of Ukraine, were within the command of Germany under the Nationalist Socialist leadership, the country (Germany) would swim in fat.'*

From *The Soviet Caucasus*, by David Tutaeff.

Russian power is like one of those matrioshka dolls hawked to Moscow tourists alongside the fur hats and lacquered boxes. Each time a layer is removed, the same doll appears underneath, only smaller. The tsarist state gave way to the geographically similar empire of the USSR. When that collapsed in December, 1991, many of the colonies fell away, with 14 ex-Soviet republics, from Estonia to Kyrgyzstan, becoming independent. Yet inside was one more incarnation of the original matrioshka doll: the 89 regions and autonomous republics of the Russian Federation.

A political backwater during Soviet times, the North Caucasus suddenly became Russia's new frontier facing independent Georgia, Armenia and Azerbaijan, NATO-member and Moslem Turkey, and Moslem Iran. For Moscow, the initial focus was on the Transcaucasus, where the humiliation of lost influence was heightened by a renewal of the age-old anxiety about Islamic and Turkic expansion along the strategic southern flank. There were visions of Turkey, which held an inaugural Turcophone summit in Ankara in 1992, rebuilding links with the belt of 120 million Moslem Turkic-speakers, including the Azeris, who live from Istanbul to Almaty.

The loss of the Transcaucasus dealt Moscow serious economic blows. Soviet planning had stranded many production facilities far beyond Russia's borders, including vital oil drilling equipment facilities in Azerbaijan and the Sukhoi-25 warplane factory in Georgia. Most galling was the loss of the Caspian Sea oil fields, once part of the Soviet treasure chest, now lying in the waters off the coast of Azerbaijan and exclusively claimed by the government in Baku. There were also huge oil and natural gas fields in newly independent Kazakhstan and Turkmenistan on the other side of the Caspian.

At first there was no policy. Moscow rushed its troops or diplomats like firemen from one crisis to the other in a bid to maintain calm and, thereby, its own influence. In 1993, the chaotic and sometimes bloody search for strategy hardened into a more coordinated, aggressive foreign policy. Russia's sense of being a great power, or *velikaya derzhava*, had reawakened and Moscow's pro-western democratic reformers gave way to a revamped old regime made up of neo-imperialists and realpolitik proponents. True the army was in tatters, the police state gone and overnight Moscow had lost control of unimagineably vast territories, from Estonia to Kyrgyzstan. But the old imperial dream survived the confidence crisis of the early 1990s, in the same way that red stars still topped the Kremlin towers, winking at the new gold double-headed imperial eagle hung on the government building across town.

That year, the Kremlin reestablished part of its lost clout in the Transcaucasus, with all three newly independent countries signed into the Russian-dominated Commonwealth of Independent States. Georgia was brought to heel after internal rebellions and Russian-backed separatist wars by the Abkhaz and South Ossetian minorities so weakened the Georgian leader, ex-Soviet foreign minister Eduard Shevardnadze, that in the end he had no choice but to turn to Moscow for help. There was suspected foul play in Azerbaijan, where the hand of Moscow was seen in the 1993 coup d'etat replacing the nationalist president, Abulfaz Elchibey, with the more amenable, at least temporarily, Geydar Aliyev, a relic of Brezhnev's Politburo. Russia also reclaimed its power-broker role during the 1988–1994 war between Azerbaijan and Armenian separatists living in the enclave of Nagorno-Karabakh. Not only did Moscow generally – if unofficially – back the Christian Armenians, it firmly kept Turkey out of the game, warning in 1992 of a world war should Ankara intervene on behalf of the hard-pressed Azeris. Russia also markedly improved relations with Iran, the third former empire in the region, which shared Moscow's goal of minimising US influence in the Caspian.

The backdrop in this power struggle was the oil – a lot of oil. There are widely varying estimates – between 25 billion to well over 100 billion barrels – of total recoverable reserves, but the region is certainly an important future source of world energy. The western oil giants, with their financial and technical clout, lined up in the 1990s for the chance to transform the decrepit Soviet infrastructure, and the enraged Russian government was forced to scramble just to join the queue.

Russia disputed Azerbaijan's claim to sovereignty over its offshore fields, arguing that the Caspian was a lake, not a sea, and therefore that all five countries with coastlines should share the resources. Azerbaijan, knowing that possession was nine-tenths of the law, dug its heels in and, in the short term, there was little Moscow could do.

Finally in September 1994 a consortium of nine major oil players signed an eight-billion dollar 'deal of the century' to invest in and exploit three Azeri oil fields estimated to hold 3.8 billion barrels of crude. The consortium, the Azerbaijan International Operating Company (AIOC), in which US companies held more than a third of the interests, hoped to extract low-volume 'early' oil by 1997, then build up to 700,000 barrels a day of 'main' oil by 2010. Moscow was helped by the departure of Elcibey, who'd been markedly pro-Turk, and his replacement by Aliyev. Although far from a yes-man, Aliyev was under pressure due to the

Nagorno-Karabakh war, and Russia's LUKoil duly won a 10-per cent stake in the AIOC. Soon the consortium grew to 12 members, with its main share holders British Petroleum and Amoco holding 17.1 and 17 per cent each, and its investment treasure chest expanding all the time. Several more deals by the AIOC and by new consortiums to develop additional offshore fields around the Caspian were struck in 1996 and 1997.

A key chance for Russia to stay in the oil rush and remain a major strategic player in the Transcaucasus was possession of the only currently viable pipeline to transport the oil out of Azerbaijan to world markets. Likewise, it had the best route for piping oil out of northern Kazakhstan's vast Tengiz fields. However, this liquid caravan road, snaking across the North Caucasus and southern Russia to the Black Sea port of Novorossiisk, soon suffered stiff competition. Georgia wanted to upgrade an existing pipeline going straight from Baku to the Black Sea terminal of Supsa. Other ideas were for the pipeline to go straight through Azerbaijan and Armenia into Turkey, or to cut through northern Iran and then into Turkey. All the alternatives were shorter than the meandering Russian line, although, conviently for Moscow, they all had flaws: the Abkhazia war in Georgia; the Nagorno-Karabakh war in Azerbaijan; US economic sanctions against Iran.

The pipeline route debate was suspended in 1995 with a temporary compromise: both the Russian Novorossiisk option and the line through Georgia to the port of Supsa would be used for the 'early' oil. Oil men made it clear that long-term they favoured the big flow of oil in the next century going via Georgia then to Ceyhan on Turkey's southern coast, an option which could potentially free Azerbaijan from dependence on Russia. There were also ambitious ideas to link Tengiz directly to Baku across the Caspian Sea, meaning even Central Asia would circumvent Russia.

However, most pipelines bypassing Russia remain at the drawing board stage, and Moscow has shown it is determined to play hard. Several attempts have been made to undermine Geidar Aliyev – the Azeris blamed these intrigues on Russia – and because he was already in his seventies when he became president, there are serious questions over what will happen when he goes. Aliyev's death could spark a new round of fighting over Nagorno-Karabakh or political instability inside Azerbaijan – again, giving Moscow an excuse to meddle. Then hanging over the entire 'deal of the century' like an unwelcome guest is Moscow's menacing, if so far powerless, claim to joint ownership of the Caspian Sea. Clearly, as long as the diplomatic battle for the oil export route is not over, the Caucasus will be threatened by more shooting wars.

Focus inevitably shifted north of the mountains. Thrust on centre stage, because of the pipeline and because it was now a frontier zone, the North Caucasus first rattled, then started to disintegrate. Chechnya shocked Moscow in 1991 by declaring independence, North Ossetia and the Ingush fought a war over a narrow strip of land in 1992, and a dozen other peoples demanded greater autonomy and the ripping up of Stalin's map. The situation was dangerous. If the ethnic house of cards collapsed in Karachai-Cherkessia and Kabardino-Balkaria, or if Ingushetia joined Chechnya's separatist rebellion, the entire region might Balkanise into unmanageable conflicts. After all, the oil pipeline crossed Dagestan, Chechnya, Ingushetia, North Ossetia, Kabardino-Balkaria and Karachai Cherkessia. Even the Krasnodar and Stavropol bread baskets, the famous black earth provinces of southern Russia, might come under threat. And if Russia could not be master north of the mountains, its influence and economic links with the Transcaucasus would also shrivel. The North Caucasus was one layer of the matrioshka doll that Russia did not intend to shed – whatever the cost.

## Pyatigorsk, Stavropol region

*In the North Caucasus you have only to say 'nefteprovod', or 'the oil pipeline', and everyone knows what you mean. Not many people have ever seen it or really know exactly where it is, but there's no mistaking what pipeline you're talking about. The Baku-Novorossiisk pipeline has its own presence, like the mountains, and when people look at the war in Chechnya, they think of the pipeline.*

*I'm determined to visit the pipeline. I've thought about it a lot while in Chechnya, where the columns of smoke from bombed-out oil facilities stretch miles across the horizon, sometimes blocking the sun. In Chechnya, ordinary people don't talk about black gold, deals of the century, or oil fever.*

*A decrepit Lada taxi takes me out of the spa town of Pyatigorsk into the countryside, where fog and snow lie over the black Stavropol earth. There's no sign of the pipeline and I check my map for the tenth time. By now, we're bumping along a partially frozen mud track, then suddenly, a white sign with red and black writing: 'ATTENTION! Oil pipeline. High tension. Protected zone.'*

*'Stop!' This is it. Under my feet lies the pipeline, east to west. This is the gold thread which runs through the tattered fabric of Russia's southern flank. This is the blessing and the curse.*

*Nearby is an isolated collective farm. It looks deserted, except for a pack of hungry, snapping dogs and some rusty equipment. I find an old man inside a one-room cabin keeping watch. Here is a man who lives almost on top of one of the great strategic interests of the new Russia, one of the reasons for the war in Chechnya, for the deaths of tens of thousands of people. Somehow I expect a kind of oracle, an old man living alone at the source, a simple man who understands great truths.*

*Even as we speak in his warm cabin, the war rages about 200 kilometres to the east. I ask his opinion.*

*It turns out the old man isn't even aware he works near the pipeline and he clearly doesn't understand why a foreigner has suddenly dropped in. 'I don't know about politics and all that', he says. 'I don't want to be in any newspaper.' I press him, he must have an opinion on Chechnya. And yes he does. 'First Stalin deported them down to the last man. Then that Krushchev, he let them all go. And now look.'*

## 2. PRAYING

*God preserve us from backsliding.*
*On, fellow fighters in the cause of God!*

From Imam Shamil's hymn.

The North Caucasus in the early 1990s became synonymous with nationalist politicians, generals and guerrillas. But long before the ideologues and fighters, a revolution got underway among ordinary people – people who had been Soviet and now, as if looking in the mirror for the first time, were discovering their true identities. For some, it was an exhilarating shock of recognition; others found the mirror dirty, the light inconsistent, and could only slowly piece the picture together. From these individuals, the process rippled out to their communities, then to the entire region, as it reclaimed its religion, culture and, to varying degrees, its historic struggle with Russia.

The most visible face of this rebirth in the North Caucasus were the mosques. There were few old mosques. Most had been destroyed by the Soviets, along with many of the Christian churches, but new ones sprang up under Soviet President Mikhail Gorbachev's *glasnost* thaw in 1987. By the 1990s new mosques, or *mechety* as they're called in Russian, were everywhere. Red brick minarets towered over muddy village streets; miniature travellers' mosques sat open and unattended by roads; huge polished-steel domes glinted in the distance under sunlight. A new one was built at the main Dagestani airport outside Makhachkala on the Caspian Sea and in Makhachkala itself a cathedral mosque was under construction with the help of Turkey. One of my favourites was in southwestern Chechnya. The main building, a handsome brick hall, was finished, but work had to stop because of the war and the only part of the minaret which went up was the iron, spiral staircase, rising high into the empty sky.

Along with the mosques came Islamic schools, or *medressehs*, and a renewal of Arabic studies. There was a steady flow of pilgrimages to Mecca – at first flying out of Moscow and then on flights direct from the

North Caucasus airhub of Mineralny Vody. Where there used to be anti-Islamic and atheist propaganda in the newspapers, there were now regular deliveries through the North Caucasus airports of Russian-language Korans sent from the Middle East and how-to pamphlets, like 'Lets get to know Islam', which describes itself as 'a gift from your brother believers' in the World Assembly of Moslem Youth.

Many people across the region were so ignorant about Islam that this was often less a revival than a rediscovery. The middle aged had grown up in an atheist state, while their children were just as likely to be inspired by the thought of making money and becoming post-Soviet consumers as they were by the mosque. This was very much the case in Adygea, where the less than 125,000 native people spent the Communist years buried as a tiny ethnic enclave within Stavropol district, losing much of their identity and culture. 'Of course, before the Communist revolution, more of us believed,' said Mohammed Khafitsev, a village mullah in Adygea, who said he was self-taught.

> Right up until 1991 we were not allowed to observe our faith. Fifty metres from here there used to be a big mosque. There were four others in the village. On Fridays there would be mass prayer at the big one and on other days people went to their neighbourhood mosque. First the main mosque was turned into a school and then 10 years ago it was knocked down. For 75 years we had no religion. One mosque was left, but no one went. Adults still find it uncomfortable to stand and pray to God, but now it's coming back, especially among the children.

In Maikop, the Adygei capital, the mufti, or Islamic lawyer, had been born in Syria, a member of the Adygei diaspora. He spoke Adygei, which had been handed down through the generations since the 19th century, but no Russian. 'I came here in 1990 from Syria. I consider this my motherland', said the mufti, Sagid Khuaka. 'It's easier to live there, but this is our land, this is where our hearts are.'

I asked him whether he was shocked by the level of knowledge about Islam in Adygea, having come from the Middle East. 'People want to return to their faith', he said. 'Now the burials are all done properly, for example. But in the current situation it can't be fully restored. People don't have the time or money to concentrate and accept Islam. They're thinking about other things.' There were also problems with getting the funds for a big mosque in Maikop and the building site lay abandoned outside Sagid's small office. However seven mosques had been built in the outlying villages in six years, he said.

There were similar problems among the Karachai, whose culture was badly shaken during the deportations, and some of whom still didn't seem to believe they could pray freely. The elderly were afraid of the secret police and everyone was horrified by the war in Chechnya, which they saw as a war against the Chechens' own reassertion of Islam. Kazbek

Shamatayev, the hospitable mullah of the mountain town of Karachayevsk,
said mosques only began reopening around 1992.

> The very young are the ones who are interested. The elderly have not managed
> to overcome their fears. In those days, they were arrested for praying. They
> had to do it secretly and they haven't got over it. Not long ago, a sheikh from
> Damascus came to visit us. But the elders here even had doubts about him.
> Was he a real sheikh, was he a Communist, had he been sent by someone?
>    For a lot of people, Islam still doesn't mean much. After the (Soviet)
> revolution they gathered all our books, Korans and manuscripts and burned
> them. They told us, 'see, you have no literature'. Then they shot any intel-
> lectuals. So we have no learning left. I think it was a Russian plan to take
> away the *shariat* law from us and make money by selling us vodka.

But again, some of the young are catching on, suggesting that the
Islamic revival has depth. In Karachai-Cherkessia's capital Cherkessk, an
Islamic institute has been opened and every year, groups of young make
the *hadj* pilgrimage to Mecca. At a makeshift mosque in an old
fairground in Karachayevsk, all the men praying were either in their late
teens or early twenties.

Kazbek himself was young and self taught, the product of a true
vocation. 'When I was little, I saw my grandmother praying and being
afraid that someone would see her. That moved me', he said. 'I grew up
an atheist but somehow that moment stayed with me. One day I got ill
and went to hospital for several months. Next to me there was an elder
who was dying and I saw him write something down in Arabic and
begin praying. I asked him what he was doing and he said, 'praying to
Allah'. He told me to remember these prayers and that they would
protect me from evil. I remembered those two verses and I started
learning Arabic bit by bit. When it became allowed a few years ago, I
found a Russian translation of the Koran.'

The scenario was repeated in Kabardino-Balkaria, the neighbouring
republic. 'The young are going to Turkey and places to learn the Koran',
said Nasar, a middle-aged man, who clearly felt the Islamic revival had
come too late for him. 'I'm 44 already and don't know the Koran. I never
learnt it. I do believe in Allah, but I don't know how to pray. Ninety per
cent of my friends don't pray either – this was the Soviet Union, you
understand. I remember my grandmother praying, but in schools we had
no Turkish or Arabic or anything. There was no religion in society. Now
these youngsters who are going to Turkey and places and bringing back
the knowledge – they seem to be everywhere. In the old days, mullahs
would be men in their fifties, now they're 25-year-old youngsters.'

As so often in the past, it was the eastern part of the region –
Chechnya, Dagestan and Ingushetia – which led the way. These were the
republics where the Sufi *tariqa*, or brotherhoods, which had the organisational ability and devotion to withstand the decades of Communism

intact, were most influential. The western half – Kabardino-Balkaria, Karachai-Cherkessia and Adygea – where Islam was never as deep-rooted, was most vulnerable to Communist influence. In the eastern republics, Islam was more overtly part of the national life. More women covered their heads, although not their faces, and many men wore prayer caps. It was not uncommon to see men praying by the roadside, or wherever they happened to be, at the hours of prayers, or *namaz*. Fundamentalist teachers from Saudi Arabia and elsewhere in the Middle East gravitated to the region, entering universities and other parts of public life and in parts of Chechnya there was an open revival of *shariat* law.

The power and speed of the Islamic revival was surprising, but not inexplicable, since it had long been thriving underground. Keeping the religion was crucial during the deportations, since in the North Caucasus Islam is interwoven inextricably with ethnic identity. To lose the faith was to lose everything; to keep it was to survive as a nation. 'We were all Moslems and we helped each other out', said an elderly Balkar who survived the deportations. 'If we did the *namaz*, we did it secretly. We'd close all the windows and doors. Some of our mullahs were arrested, but most people kept their traditions and faith this way.'

The Chechens and Ingush in particular were able to survive by re-treating into the inner world of the Sufi brotherhoods – the same secretive, sometimes fanatical organisations which led resistance to the tsarist armies and then the Bolsheviks. On the deportees' return to their homelands in the late 1950s and early 1960s, what became known as 'parallel Islam' – Sufi worship by close-knit groups in secret – thrived in private houses across Chechnya, Ingushetia and also in the mountains of Dagestan.

Soviet planners were frustrated and mystified by these 'transgressions', as they were called. The North Caucasians, who by now were meant to be model Soviet citizens, were resisting marriage among other religions, or even other ethnic groups. They were carrying out Moslem burials and making pilgrammages to Sufi holy places, mostly the graves of *murids*, the anti-Russian or anti-Soviet fighters. Robert Conquest, in *The Nation Killers*, cites a 1973 commentary in the newspaper *Sovietsky Dagestan*, which reflected Communist outrage:

> In recent years, the imperialists have been trying to introduce into the Soviet Union a fashionable little theory proclaiming the necessity of rejecting uniformity. This petty bourgeois, anarchic concept ... proclaims the supremacy of individual freedom. ... According to this theory, a believer is responsible to God alone and because the government – the Soviet government, not a bourgeois power – does not come from God, because it limits God's will, it must not be obeyed. This theory is propagated by some radical *murid* elements in Dagestan and Chechnya.

Despite the holy wars, the North Caucasus peoples have traditionally been remarkably tolerant of others' religions, but there were alarming signs in the 1990s that the vigour, and at times extremism, of the religious revival might put this quality under threat. In 1997 in the Dagestani town of Buinaksk, two local Adventist converts, a man and a woman, were burned alive in the main square by a cheering Moslem crowd. The mob accused the two of kidnapping children to sell their organs, but the Adventist church put the summary executions down to anti-Christian fanaticism, saying that the woman in the couple had already been disowned by her family.

Another sign of trouble was the spread of fundamentalist *Wahhabism*, the state religion of Saudi Arabia. The *Wahhabists* won a great deal of influence during the Chechnya war when their groups provided everything from financial help for refugees, to fighters and ideological indoctrination. After the war the *Wahhabists* did not go away, and their presence became resented by the local Sufis who saw the imported, ultra-pure brand of Islam as a threat to their proud and highly idiosynchratic mix of religious and non-religious laws, such as veneration of elders. In 1997 the split between *Wahhabist* converts and their countrymen was blamed for the murder of a Sufi mullah in Chechnya and armed clashes between hundreds of supporters from the two sides in Kara-Makhi, a village in the mountains of Dagestan.

### Surkhokhi, Ingushetia

*The Sufis are underground. They were banned by the tsarist authorities and mercilessly hunted by the Soviets and they could still be seen as the enemy – after all, they're behind much of the resistance in Chechnya. In Chechnya, you see the dervish prayer ritual, the zikr, all the time now. But that's because of the war and when there's war, an anti-Russian war, the Sufis materialise – armed.*

*In Ingushetia, it's different. You sense the Sufis, but no more. They're everywhere and they're nowhere. Start asking questions and you get puzzled looks or some guarded answer which discourages any other questions. Are they ignorant or are they just not talking? You never answer that either. This is part of the Sufi wall which kept out the KGB, the wall which protected the believers during the deportations to Central Asia. This is the wall around the North Caucasians' inner nation, the one which survives after the exterior nation has been destroyed.*

*One of Ingushetia's best-known Sufi groups is the Batal Hadji. I have an intriguing hardback copy of* Mystics and Commissars, Sufism in the Soviet Union, *by Alexandre Bennigsen and S. Enders Wimbush. The Batal Hadji are 'the most puritan and most militant of all Sufi tariqa'. They are led by the Belkhoroyev family in the Ingush village of Surkhokhi. They have a fierce reputation. Batal, who got to Mecca and thus became 'Hadji', founded the branch in 1867 and devoted himself to fighting the*

*Russian infidel. So did everyone else in his family, and dozens were killed either by the Russians or the Soviets.*

Surkhokhi turns out to be a maze of well-built brick houses and farmyards on a lush rolling hillside. There's no sign of fanatical warriors, or anti-western mobs. In fact, the place looks decidedly friendly and prosperous. 'Can you show us where the Belkhoroyevs live?' my Ingush driver and I ask the first villager. 'Up there', he points. 'Up there' means a winding dirt street leading deeper into the maze. Once there, we have to ask again. 'That way'. We enter even smaller streets, but nothing to indicate we've arrived. I'm starting to get nervous again. It's the same old question – do they just not know the exact directions or are they not talking? We ask again and we're told: 'wait here'.

Before long, a small boy with a shaved head appears and says 'this way'. He runs down the muddy alley and we follow slowly in the car to a large, typical North Caucasus courtyard. I remove my shoes and go in, where a woman sits me down in a high-ceilinged room with a carpet hanging from one wall and a vast photograph of Mecca covering another.

When Akhmed Belkhoroyev, hereditary leader of the Batal Hadji sect, comes in, his first act is to fulfil the role of host, asking if I want to eat or drink tea. Next, he wants to know how I found him. Clearly, he doesn't believe that I simply took his name out of a western book on Sufism. Of course, I don't have the book with me and I can't prove it.

Belkhoroyev is old, but his hands are compact and strong. He talks in circles, rarely answering my questions, but says a lot and I don't interrupt. He scorns Americans, Jews, Russians and especially Ossetians, who, he says, are traitors to the Caucasus for embracing Christianity and Russia. He is fanatically proud of the Ingush. 'We were the first people on Earth'. When he sees I'm still taking notes, he warms up, and asks if I can come back the next day. Only then, I notice he has a dock leaf sticking out flat from under the back of his prayer cap – a traditional remedy for pain. 'I've got a headache', he says.

The next day, Belkhoroyev is waiting and, as soon as we're settled, he tells me about his god, his hatred and his holy ancestor Batal Hadji, shown in an old photograph with a black Cherkessk tunic and a smooth, beautiful, slightly cruel face.

'When they started to crush us, our religion made us strong, it bound us into one people. We broke bread between each other. In Kazakhstan, if we knew one village was starving, we would sneak out at night past the guards and bring food. Allah strengthened us.'

'In the Koran, it says that if the infidel come to your land and destroy your people, you must declare ghazawat, holy war. That's what's happened in Chechnya and here. During our deportation, the Russians came with bulldozers and destroyed all our graveyards and ancient monuments. They wanted to take away all our culture. But we came back and we rebuilt *everything. Now they're destroying Chechnya again. But the Chechens and Ingush cannot be put down. They always recover and take their revenge.'*

'Listen, right outside this house, Batal Hadji fought the tsarist soldiers for three days. At least 40 of his sons and cousins have been killed since then. My father was killed by the Communists, and I was imprisoned, six and a half years in the tundra in Norilsk', he says.

Norilsk – above the Arctic Circle, permanently below freezing – takes no explaining. To Russians, the name is synonymous with the gulag hell. 'They left me for 29 days on a concrete floor in the middle of winter to die. But I survived. At one time, there were a lot of us Ingush together and we performed the zikr in prison. I simply told the guards then to stay away. This was our business, you understand.'

'In 1974 I did the hadj to Mecca. I was the first of the Chechens or Ingush to do it. Then I persuaded them to let me take others. In 1975 I persuaded them to open mosques, one in each region. Then gradually we started opening them in every village, and Islamic institutes, and medresshes. Islam was reborn. But I didn't bring back Islam – it was already here. It was here, in secret, all the time.'

Belkhoroyev has married three times. His first two wives were childless, the third produced six children. The Batal Hadji don't give up easily. In the village, he shows me his mosque. One of the minarets dates from Batal Hadji's time, the rest was rebuilt under his care. Rugs, all of different colours, line the floor inside. An upper floor, where children pray, runs like a balcony overhead, some 50 metres of polished, carved wood, again new. In the courtyard, there's a medresseh, or religious school. It's full of small boys in white shirts, learning Arabic from a teenager, also in white. They all rise to their feet as we enter.

We go up to the graveyard on a hilltop outside Surkhokhi. At the entrance there's a small, recently built mosque for pilgrims and the door is kept shut by a small boulder. Batal Hadji is buried at the far end of the cemetery. His gravestone, covered in Arabic script, is painted green and topped by a polished, gold-coloured metal cap. Alongside are his wife and three of his sons.

As we leave the village we stop by a large pile of carved stones just off the road. These are the pieces of Ingush gravestones smashed during the deportations. I ask Belkhoroyev if the grave of Batal Hadji was also desecrated. 'Nothing could harm those stones', he answers. 'Whoever tried would fall over, as if he had been struck over the head. Their families would get sick.'

North Ossetia, despite being the most Russified of autonomous republics, was very much part of the region's religious renewal in the late 1980s and early 1990s, but with a difference: the Ossetians, at heart, are pagans.

Although commonly described as Christians, Ossetians are in fact a bewildering mixture of Christians, Moslems and fervent worshippers of pre-Christian gods and trees.

The most popular element of the animist-pagan tradition is the cult of Wasterzhi and his sacred grove about 30 kilometres from the capital Vladikavkaz. Part protector of warriors and travellers, part phallic symbol, Wasterzhi is a mysterious character whose origins have been linked to Indo-Iranian sun worship, star worship, war gods and the ancient Nart heroes of the Caucasus. A painting often seen reproduced on posters depicts him as a medieval knight with a long beard on a white stallion with sizeable testicles.

Hoping to fully convert the Ossetians, the Russian Orthodox church encouraged Christian saints as replacements for Wasterzhi and the rest of the extensive pagan pantheon, headed by Khusaw, the Almighty. But instead of abandoning their gods, the Ossetians fused them with the saints, creating hybrid deities subservient to Khusaw and Christianity's God. Wasterzhi's alter ego was Saint George, and Wasilla, the god of harvests and thunder, became interchangeable with Saint Ilya.

No priests are required in the popular Ossetian faith. Against a background of heavy feasting and many religious vodka toasts, Ossetian families and villages will sacrifice sheep and bulls to these lesser divinities and implore their help. The first toast is always to the head god – Khusaw, the Christian God, or in the case of the minority Moslems, Allah – the second to one of the local gods, who have varying specialities, ranging from bringing good luck to helping with rain, safe travels and protection from enemies. There is even Shaubarak, 'the force of darkness', and 'only popular with thieves', as a disapproving atheist ethnographist in Vladikavkaz put it to me.

No god gets quite as much attention as Wasterzhi. The legend behind the sacred grove outside Vladikavkaz is that a certain Hetag was fleeing his enemies in the 14th to 16th centuries when Wasterzhi called out from the mountain forest and told him to shelter there. Exhausted, Hetag collapsed on the plains, saying he could not go on, whereupon a clump of trees (today's wood) miraculously came down and hid him. One version I heard was that Hetag was a Kabard who had taken up Christianity and was fleeing his Moslem relatives; another is that he was an *abreg* on the run. Ever since, the grove has been a living cathedral for Wasterzhi, a memorial to Hetag, and an open-air chapel for Saint George.

Incredibly, the cult survived both the ban on religion under the Soviet Union and the considerable assimilation of the Ossetians. Since 1991 there have been several claims of visitations by Wasterzhi to villages, while the wood, best known as Hetag's Grove, is deeply venerated. It is largely made up of ashes and beeches, covering just under 13 hectares in a roughly triangular shape. A temple with a large wooden totem pole has been built nearby, alongside a Beowolf-like banquet hall for the yearly festivals, where each village is assigned its own tree and clearing.

I visited shortly after one of these feasts and there were still hundreds of vodka bottles and other party debris lying in piles on the ground. But despite the lack of dustbins, Ossetians really do treat this grove with religious respect. At the temple near the wood, I found two middle-aged men standing in front of the obviously phallic totem pole, their arms in the air. After, they put money in a collection box under a huge painting of Wasterzhi. Believers who pass the grove along the main road, about a kilometre away, rise out of their seats and mumble a few prayers to Wasterzhi, while once in the wood it is forbidden to break off even a single branch. Holy trees are decorated with ribbons and portraits of Saint George and the dragon. And because of his fertility powers, women are forbidden from saying either Hetag or the W word. I caused a ripple of embarrassed giggles in an Ossetian Orthhodox church in Vladikavkaz when I asked a nun – I was quite innocent of the rule – if she could explain Wasterzhi. 'It's forbidden for me to say his name, God forgive me', the nun said, shifting her head scarf nervously.

'When atheism was in force, there was a real barrier to local traditions', a young historian in Vladikavkaz said. 'The first secretary of our Communist Party for Ossetia was a Russian. But now it's all coming back. Our (North Ossetian) president says he's Christian, but he also participates in the Wasterzhi festival. Before Wasterzhi was very important. My grandmother, for example, said she'd see Heaven's door open and he'd be standing there. From time to time villages still see him. He's coming back; in fact he never really left. During Soviet times, the head of household would still gather his family and pray to him and drink a toast.'

It was really the ultimate joke on the Soviets and the Russians before them. Here were the supposedly loyal North Ossetians, the bulwark against the Moslem revolutionaries on either side, busily praying to trees and raising their vodka glasses to a man who appeared from the clouds on a white stallion.

### Vladikavkaz, North Ossetia

*I stop by a Russian Orthodox church in Vladikavkaz and ask to see the priest. He emerges, a frail blonde man with watery blue eyes and a black cassock. I ask him what he thinks about Wasterzhi's rather unorthodox pairing with Saint George. The priest, immediately defensive, answers in a bureaucratese that I hardly expected.*

'There are legends, but no confirmation. We don't see it from the same angle. We consider that praying to him is forbidden because there is no real proof about it', he says.

*I ask why the Ossetians declined to swap Wasterzhi for Saint George.
'Among simple people there're a lot of beliefs like that, even if they
aren't logical. You get strange things and fanaticisms like that. We pray
to Saint George', the priest says. 'But not that man on the white horse.
He's nothing to do with us.'*

## 3. REINVENTION AND REHABILITATION

*The Tartar thistle bush consisted of three shoots. One had been broken off
and the remnant of stalk stuck out like a severed arm. There was a flower on
each of the other two. The flowers had once been red, but were now black.
One stalk was broken and its upper half with the soiled flower at the end
hung down; the other, though caked with black mud, still stood erect. ... It
was like having part of its body torn away, its innards turned inside out, an
arm pulled off, and an eye plucked out. But still it was standing and would
not surrender to man who had destroyed all its brethren around.*

From Tolstoy's *Hadji Murat.*

In the same way that mosques mushroomed in places where religion had
been banned, the North Caucasus' ethnic groups emerged, one after the
other, to assert their separate identities. The shallowness of Soviet
homogeneity was exposed almost overnight. For two minorities – the
Mountain Jews and ethnic-Greeks – this voyage of rediscovery was
spectacular. The Mountain Jews, or Tats as they are properly known, are
one of the smallest groups, with just 18,000 people, but incredibly they
have retained Judaism and the Farsi dialect they picked up more than
1,000 years ago in Persia. The end of Soviet restrictions on culture and
religion meant the Tats, clustered around Derbent in Dagestan and Nalchik
in Kabardino-Balkaria, could again open cultural centres and start a
newspaper. But their real recovery of identity required a far greater step
– leaving the North Caucasus and emigrating to Israel to reinvent
themselves as Hebrew-speaking Israeli citizens, something they did in
droves. Out of about 12,000 Mountain Jews in Nalchik in the 1970s,
there were just 4,000 when I visited in 1996. It was as if the Mountain
Jews had simply been waiting to go home those thousand years.

Plunging down the same path were the region's ethnic-Greeks, the
Pontics – descendants of classical Greeks who settled Anatolia in what is
now Turkey, the Crimean peninsula and the Caucasus coast some 3,000
years ago. These had been traders, soldiers and settlers, whose ruined
theatres, temples and fortresses still lie around the Black Sea. The Greeks
survived one age after the other, until the horrors of the 20th century –
mass expulsion in 1923 of all Pontics from Turkey (all Turks were likewise
expelled from Greece), followed by repressions and deportations under

Stalin in the 1930s and 1940s. Even then, the Pontics of the Soviet Union maintained a Greek identity, despite never having been to Greece and their archaic dialect being incomprehensible to modern Greeks.

*Glasnost* opened the Pontics' next chapter – the right of 'return' to Greece, return to the Aegean to close a historic circle. In the first seven years of emigration, starting in about 1989, some 90,000 Pontics made the journey, which was given a special word in Greek – *palinostisy*. Like the Mountain Jews, the Pontics entered a completely strange country, where in practice they felt like foreigners and were often treated as such. The 'dumb Pontic' joke is standard. Most ironic of all, and sad, was that their dialect, after miraculously surviving all these ages, was in danger of finally dying as the new arrivals hurried to assimilate.

For Chechens, Balkars, Adygei and other highlanders, the process of regeneration did not require travelling, but in some senses it was even more fraught. The homelands – now called plain 'republics' not ASSRs or AOs – finally had true, not phony, autonomy. But nationalist leaders, with broad support, sought to go further. They wanted to break up the divide-and-rule republics in which unrelated groups were made to share and to return lands to groups dispossessed during the deportations. They wanted even greater political autonomy or, in some cases, to cut ties with Russia altogether. The word that always came up was *reabilitatsiya* – rehabilitation after the crimes of the tsars, of Stalin, and, above all, of the deportations.

Ethnic self-determination: this sounded worthy, but almost immediately anyone could see that in a place as complex as the North Caucasus, one group's demands automatically infringed on the rights of another. This was the timebomb hidden in Stalin's map. Defusing the charges and building a democratic Russian Federation would take the most minute cooperation between the central authorities and the highlanders, but Moscow, itself convulsed by political upheaval, stood to the side. Maybe this was because the North Caucasus looked easier to ignore than to fix, maybe because Russia was still wavering between a totalitarian past and a democratic future. This failure of the centre would have tragic consequences.

Dagestan, its two million people divided into 34 nations – unofficial estimates put the number at over 100 – was considered the republic to watch. The 'land of mountains' lay on the path of the Azeri oil, train and road routes, while the capital Makhachkala was now Russia's last all-year warm-water port on the Caspian. The internal situation looked explosive. Not only did all the main ethnic groups have political or territorial grudges, they had ethnically based national fronts with their own politicians, business interests and, sometimes, paramilitaries. Thirty four nations and all in an area smaller than Scotland. The largest group, the Avars, had an organisation called the National Front in the Name of Imam Shamil, which Russian reports said could raise 10,000 armed supporters.

Like everywhere else, Dagestan was riddled with the after-effects of Stalin's social engineering. When the Chechens living in Dagestan were rooted out and deported *en masse* along with the rest of their nation in 1944, other groups, especially the Laks, were shunted down from their mountain areas and made to take over the empty Chechen villages in the lowlands. They had no choice. The Kremlin could move nations the way croupiers move chips on the gambling table.

When the Chechens were allowed back, they tried to beg or buy their old homes. Often they had to build entirely new villages, but they never forgot their original territories and houses. Murad, a 44-year-old, living in Novoselskoye, a village built in the plains north of Khasavyurt, said his parents had lived in Kalenin Aul when they were deported. 'They were made to leave on foot and walk to the railways to be deported. By the time they got in the wagons, their homes had already been occupied by Avars.' But that house, a house he'd never lived in, still haunted Murad. 'We all know which house it is. I've been up there and looked. We haven't forgotten – my grandfather buried his personal weapons there.'

A decision by the Dagestani government in 1992 to return the 57,000 local Chechens their territory near the Dagestani-Chechen border and resettle the Laks in housing on the plains nearer Makhachkala caused outrage among a third group, the Kumyks. The Kumyks, a Turkic-speaking people, considered these steppe lands where the Laks were to be moved their own territory. For years Kumyk influence there had been steadily eroded, first by the arrival of Avars, who were forced down from the mountains under Communism, and now the Laks. The Kumyks were a minority in what they considered their own patch.

A national Kumyk front called Tenglik, formed in 1989, demanded a separate Kumyk autonomous statelet on the Caspian Sea and threatened to use force to resist the influx of Laks. This deepened already uneasy relations between the Kumyks and Avars, who threatened to call out their Imam Shamil Front. Here was a clear example of the simultaneous, but contradictory rights of several units: the perceived right of a 'nation' to dominate in its own territory; the right of other ethnic groups to resettle freely; the right of Dagestan's government to consider the republic's general interests ahead of any one ethnic group's.

A potentially even more explosive problem developed at the southern end of Dagestan, where the rights of the Lezghin nation, of Dagestan, and Azerbaijan were all at odds. The Lezghins, who officially number a total of 466,000, but could be well over a million according to unofficial figures, live in the extreme southern end of Dagestan and the north east of Azerbaijan. When the USSR collapsed, this people was severed by a new border between Russia and independent Azerbaijan, suddenly making it difficult for them to visit each other, trade or make other contacts. Bribe-taking and smuggling was so rampant at the border that the main Russian crossing was dubbed the 'golden bridge'. For the 175,000 (official figure) Lezghins in Azerbaijan, there was the added problem that they were Sunni Moslems and now found themselves isolated among the Azeri Shia majority.

In response, the Lezghin national front Sadval campaigned for reuniting Lezghins on both sides of the border in a self-rule area subordinate to Dagestan, which itself would be revamped as a federation of autonomous mini-republics within Russia. The Lezghin claim therefore threatened not only Dagestan's territorial integrity, but that of sovereign Azerbaijan, which was firmly opposed to any such initiative. Moscow, worried by its lack of control over cross-border weapons and contraband smuggling, also prefered the status quo, and so the problem smouldered on, unresolved.

Dagestan might have been expected to turn into a dozen miniature Yugoslavias. Paradoxically, however, the complexity of the ethnic map actually long helped prevent a crisis. No single group was big enough to dominate and territorial or political demands by one group invariably impacted too many others to get out of hand. The republic was run by a national council of 14 members, each representing one of the main ethnic groups. To prevent one group becoming the elite, the peoples of Dagestan voted overwhelmingly in 1992 both against private land ownership and having a single president. But perhaps the most important factors calming Dagestan were widely shared *gortsy* culture and Moslem religion.

A handful of groups inevitably rose to the top of public life by force or guile. The main political power and the biggest slices of economic resources were held by the most populous groups. In the early 1990s the chairman of the ruling council was Magomed Ali Magomedov, the canny, Soviet-era leader and an ethnic-Dargin (280,000 people). The prime minister, Abdurazan Mirzabekov, was a Kumyk (232,000). Dargins were also in charge of the lucrative customs operations. The Avars (496,000) however were in charge of the Dagestani oil company and the all-important police and secret service forces. The fisheries committee, ensuring a say in the Caspian Sea caviar business, was headed by ex-European karate champion Magomed Khachilayev, a Lak (92,000); Khachilayev's younger brother, Nadir, was chairman of the Union of Russian Moslems.

Moscow trod carefully in Dagestan. Policy was based on heavy subsidisation of the economy and a *laissez-faire* attitude to the dubious business and political activities in the autonomous republic. In return, local authorities were loyal to Kremlin policies and maintained a comfortable stability. The Dagestani government proved how well it could deliver in the 1996 Russian presidential elections. In the first round the mostly rural Dagestanis predictably voted overwhelmingly for President

Boris Yeltsin's Communist challenger. In the second round run-off, Yeltsin needed every last vote and when the count came in from Dagestan, it showed almost a reversal of the first-round figures – a surprise only to those who did not know the way the region worked.

Whether this fragile status quo could last was uncertain. The ethnic rivalries created a system of checks and balances, but at the same time, these so-far benign struggles were in danger of spinning out of control. Within a few years of the collapse of Soviet authority, Dagestan had become a seriously violent place, the leading region in Russia, bar Chechnya, for political killings and kidnappings. Terrorism had become standard business practice.

Take the case of Gamid Gamidov. He was a shady but popular Dargin businessman from a highly traditional clan who built up so much political support that he threatened to break the grip on power held by Magomed Ali Magomedov and the rest of the ex-Communist elite heading the national council. In 1994, his people placed a surprise third in elections to the local parliament. Then in August 1996 Gamidov, whose popularity and influence had kept rising over the previous two years, was standing in the centre of Makhachkala when a car bomb went off, killing him and three other people and wounding 20 more. Of course, as with most of the dozens of political killings in Dagestan, no one was convicted. But Gamidov's supporters threatened armed vengeance and this being the Caucasus, it seemed inconceivable that accounts would not eventually be settled.

The ruthlessness of the crime gangs was again tragically illustrated in 1996 when an expertly placed bomb demolished an entire apartment building in the Caspian coastal town of Kaspysk. The building housed border guards officers and their families and 67 people, including 21 children, were killed. The blast was so terrible that at first people assumed it must be connected to the war in Chechnya, or perhaps a freak accident. But later it was unofficially acknowledged that it was part of a mafia struggle, a lesson to the Russian federal border guards for a major anti-smuggling crackdown that year. Given the location of the attack and the fact that the border guards also patrol the Caspian Sea, the most likely culprits were undoubtedly connected to the caviar mafia. Of course, despite loud bluster in Moscow and Makhachkala, no one was caught.

Another longterm cancer eating into the stability of Dagestan were the republic's tense borders. A serious knock-on effect could be expected from neighbouring Chechnya's anarchic de facto independence, both in terms of criminal gangs using Dagestan as a route into Russia, and the spread of separatist ideals. Cross-border links between Chechens proper and Chechens living within Dagestan threatened to further undermine the republic's territorial integrity. To the south, the problem of the divided Lezghin nation smouldered on. The longer this people was broken into

Dagestani and Azeri sections, separated by corrupt border guards, the more the Lezghins were likely to support the idea of creating a unified, separatist Lezghinistan. That could lead to the unravelling of Dagestan. Again, Moscow appeared to have little idea of how to respond.

'It's as if everything is being done to set off an explosion', Russian General Lev Rokhlin said of policy in Dagestan. 'Who will allow the fires of war to burn again in the Caucasus? ... In its current conditions in Dagestan, it's simply a surprise that the republic has not yet exploded.' The Dagestani clock kept ticking.

*... seldom does a night pass without someone being carried off for ransom.*

Alexander Dumas in the Dagestani town of Khasavyurt in 1858.

———

In Dagestan, any realist could see that partition would lead to disaster. However, in Karachai-Cherkessia and Kabardino-Balkaria, another two republics where unrelated ethnic groups were forced to share, there were fewer players, and dismantling Stalin's map looked deceptively feasible.

The Karachai, who number about 150,000 and live in the southern, more mountainous end of Karachai-Cherkessia, were one of the first peoples to demand redrawing of borders and other measures to ensure their recovery. In the 1990s they were finally allowed to erect monuments to the deportations in their main town, Karachayevsk, 50 years after the genocide took place. Just outside the town, there's a statue of a woman and child, wrapped up to make the often fatal journey to Central Asia. Behind is a sweeping mural to the Karachai men who died in the Red Army fighting the Nazis, when Stalin said they were collaborating. The monument was in itself a victory over the past, but weeds grew through the cracks of nearby paving stones and the monument seemed unvisited. I wondered if the Karachai had grown so used to keeping the pain inside themselves that the monument simply came too late to mean much.

In 1991, Moscow allowed Karachai-Cherkessia to leave the jurisdiction of Stavropol region and become a full autonomous republic – able to run its own budget, local laws, constitution and government. This was an improvement for the people of the republic, but the Karachai, led by a radical movement called Dzhamagat, had been pressing since 1988 to go a step further and split off to form their own separate autonomous area up in the mountains. This is what they had had prior to the deportations in 1943 – it was only on the Karachai's return from exile 14 years later that they'd been forced to live in the newly created Karachai-Cherkessia entity, along with the Cherkess and the Russians. Being returned their old status, argued Karachai leaders, would be like drawing a line under the past. *Reabilitatsiya.*

But although there are only 415,000 people in Karachai-Cherkessia, its ethnic make-up is horrendously complex. According to the 1989 census, the Russians were the majority at 42 per cent, followed by the Karachai with 31, the Cherkess at nine per cent and the Abaza, another group closely related to the Adygei family, at seven per cent. There was also a minority of Nogais, Asiatic-featured descendants of the Mongols. Following the usual pattern, the Karachai and Cherkess were overwhelmingly rural, while Russians and Cossacks lived around the capital Cherkessk and dominated the government power posts. In this context, the Karachai's demand to separate was playing with fire. No sooner did Dzhamagat and its Islamic allies get serious, than a chain reaction of demands by the other groups threatened to break the already small Karachai-Cherkessia into as many as five micro ethnic-homelands. The Cherkess wanted autonomy and even the Russians and Cossacks were in favour of breaking off and joining their areas to the Krasnodar region of southern Russia.

In March 1992, 79 per cent of voters opted in a referendum to keep Karachai-Cherkessia a single unit. A mixture of fatigue from the passions of those early days and careful steering by the republic's pro-Moscow president, himself a Karachai, seemed to have at least temporarily defused the crisis. As part of an attempt to keep the lid on the disintegration threat, the authorities tried to give equal play to all five ethnic groups' languages, making the signs outside government buildings somewhat wordy.

All this was a bitter disappointment to the Karachai nationalists. When I met one of the leaders of the now disbanded Dzhamagat movement, Kazbek Chomayev, in Cherkessk in 1996, I expected a firebrand; after all, this was an organisation which had been actively supported by the radical Chechen independence leader Dzhokhar Dudayev. Instead, I found him rumpled and thoughtful, resigned to initial failure, but confident the debate was not over. Although even nationalists admit that subdividing the republic into four or five ethnic components would make communications and economic matters a nightmare, Chomayev still thought the idea worthy.

We really needed to break off and we could have done it. You see, in 1943 we were deported and underwent 14 years of genocide. Half of our people died. Then we came back and they took away the autonomous area we'd had prior to the deportations and they put us in Stavropol region so that all our leaders would be Russian. For 33 years we were under the thumb of the party officials. They wanted our mountain areas for tourism and for their government dachas, but they didn't want us. They even considered a second deportation in the late 1970s.

When the Soviet Union collapsed, we realised that in order to be rehabilitated we needed our own area, but legally, as part of the process of democratisation. We didn't want to take up arms, or be separatists or anything. That's all we wanted – rehabilitation. Now, after the poll, they say it's all quiet, everthing's OK. But we'll see. The very complicated issues underlying what happened are still there. The Karachai would still like to break off. So would the others. Just in March 1994 the Cossacks voted again to break their territories off so they can reunite with the Russians.

They say that people have become tired and they have. But people will never give up these issues until there is some resolution. For 50 years there was an official silence, no one talked about the problems. Now, they're here in the open again.

Just to the east in Kabardino-Balkaria, the approximately 80,000 Balkars remained poor and resentful after a similar failure to win separate autonomy. Like the Karachai, the basis of the Balkar movement was a quest for *reabilitatsiya* from the deportations. The Balkar leaders pointed out that the 391,000 Kabards dominated power in the supposedly shared republic and said that Russian federal funds intended to help develop their community were stolen. A sharp edge to the dispute was the demand by the Balkars for the return of lands taken away during their deportation and handed over to the Kabards.

When Balkar nationalists pointed to 1944 maps showing their now missing territory, Kabard nationalists brought out maps from 1863 which showed the Balkars living even higher up in the mountains with no plains territory at all. It was another North Caucasus case of each nation reinventing the past to suit present needs. Nevertheless, in 1991, amid great tension over the land dispute, both nations' representatives voted to break-up Kabardino-Balkaria into separate autonomies. A Balkar referendum on creating a separate statelet received huge – 95 per cent – support. Mirroring the scenario in Karachai-Cherkessia, the republic hung on the edge of chaos. Emotion was all it took to turn a minor incident, like the knifing by a drunk Balkar of his Kabard drinking partner, into a standoff verging on serious ethnic confrontation.

But eventually the unresolved territorial dispute made the proposed split-up impossible. Then nationalist momentum died out. In a republic-wide referendum held in 1994, as war clouds gathered over nearby Chechnya, the majority voted to keep Kabardino-Balkaria whole. But under the calm surface, the disputes continued to seethe and two years later, in November 1996, the Balkar Congress made another, but more half-hearted attempt to separate. With demographics against them, the Balkars seemed condemned to further powerlessness. They only formed 11 per cent of the republic, where the Kabards were 49 per cent and the Russians 32 per cent.

A Balkar couple I met in the village of Babugent, in the high foothills of the Caucasus, said they had been struggling to keep head above water since their family returned from the deportations at the end of the 1950s and were forced to build a new village lower down than their now ruined village in the highlands. 'We had to rebuild from scratch with almost no help from the government. We worked like slaves. We're mountain people and our only grazing lands down in the plains were given to the Kabards and now we don't have much left – just these woods and rocks. The Kabards have got the good land, the steppe,' said a 65-year-old man in his cluttered farm yard. I asked if he believed in the referendum on keeping Kabardino-Balkaria together. 'We wanted to break away and they didn't allow it,' he answered. In the North Caucasus, 'they' always means the Russians.

While much of the aggressive nationalism in the North Caucasus was caused by the frustration of deported peoples who were never properly rehabilitated, no one could really understand how to change borders and ethnic patterns laid down half a century ago. Ethnic cleansing is carried out during wars or dictatorships and reversing it in peacetime or under democracy is the hardest trick of all.

Moscow, engulfed in the political upheavals of the early 1990s, made one clumsy attempt with an April 1991 law, passed by what was then the Russian Soviet parliament, on rehabilitation of repressed peoples including a return to original borders. The law, later suspended, simultaneously promised the right of repressed peoples to 'return' to their 'traditional homeland,' but ordered that 'people currently living on the repressed peoples' territory' should not have their rights infringed. At best it was contradictory, at worst a Pandora's Box which could only fuel border disputes.

Chomayev, the former Karachai leader, blamed Russia's neo-imperial mentality, accusing Moscow of refusing to take the tiny nations seriously and still considering them tainted by their punishment under Stalin. To Chomayev, and other nationalist ideologues of the North Caucasus, the 1991 rehabilitation law didn't go far enough.

It was too general, it didn't go into specifics or make concrete proposals. It's not like in the United States where the Japanese-Americans who were put in camps during World War II were apologized to and given financial compensation. Or look at the Germans, the way they have apologized to the Jews and banned anything anti-Jewish.

Instead, our repressed peoples came back in the late 1950s either to have their oil exploited in the case of the Chechens, their best lands taken away in the case of the Ingush, their autonomous status removed in the case of the Karachai and, again, a loss of territory in the case of the Balkars. Now we realise this won't be solved today because the old imperial attitudes are still there. The people in power, Yeltsin and so on, still think in the old way. It's the ashes of an empire.

If rehabilitation of repressed peoples was solved, I don't think anything bad would happen in the North Caucasus. For this to be achieved, we need democracy, but our leaders are steeped in Soviet mentality. They wouldn't know democracy if they saw it. Russia is a prisoner of its own imperial past.

*They say they want a federation, a sort of United States. But how can you when there is a 5,000-year-old culture here, another there, and then the Russians? How can you take them and squash them into one?*

Ruslan Khanakha, Adygei historian.

One evening in the capital of Adygea, Maikop, I sat with an old man called Askar, who simultaneously opened a bottle of vodka, his heart and his list of national grievances. The Russian conquest and Soviet occupation were top of his agenda. 'Marx was the one who wrote that the world should learn about freedom by our example,' Askar said. 'But look what the Russians brought us – vodka. We never used to drink that stuff, we were Moslems.'

The Adygei were also fighting for *reabilitatsiya*, although this time less from Communist crimes, than the colonisation of a century before. They were in a perilous position. Ever since the tsarist conquest, they'd been widely scattered, with a large foreign diaspora. The Soviet system only reinforced the dispersal, putting the Adygei proper, the Cherkess, the Abaza, Abkhaz, Shapsugs and closely related Kabards into different regions and republics. There were warnings of the Adygei peoples disappearing through assimiliation.

Askar's ethnic pride – perhaps because it was under siege – was almost frantic. Driving through the centre of town to visit a friend, we stopped at the marketplace to buy some chicken. It was dark. Stray dogs and litter cluttered the ground between tattered vending stalls, the typical post-Soviet messy street scene. No sooner had the car stopped than three Russian women in head scarves bounded over, elbowing and pushing each other, thrusting out handfuls of chicken and sausage and pleading for custom. It was an ugly scene and Askar's pride hit new highs. 'Did you see that?' he asked triumphantly as we drove off again. 'Those were Russians. Now we have to sell in the market too, but we never sink to that kind of behaviour. We Adygei were aristocrats.'

Askar admitted that his Adygei was rusty and many other Adygei I talked to said they had difficulty making their children practise the language. In their own autonomous republic, the ethnic-Adygei, 125,000 people, made up only 22 per cent of the population, the rest being Slavs. Almost seven out of 10 people were native Russian speakers. 'Keeping our national memory is very difficult,' said an archeologist in Adygea, where the original inhabitants cohabited with the ancient Greeks. 'We've lost a lot and we have to prove what we used to be. They always told us we had no civilisation. But look, we had a life, our own customs, our own world,' he said, pushing a pile of archive photographs of classical pottery, rusty medieval swords and golden drinking vessels at me.

Yet the Adygei national movement – perhaps because it represented so few people and was not seen as a strategic threat, since Adygea was surrounded firmly by ethnic-Russian territory – proved one of the success stories in stemming the tide of assimilation. Despite resistance from the local majority Russians, who did not want to be shunted into a new entity where the minority would be the titular nation, Adygea was upgraded from an AO to a full republic in 1991. After much debate, and more opposition from the Russians, a constitution was approved in 1995, effectively guaranteeing the Adygei a substantial say in the running of affairs.

The days when a dance group or two was the extent of this ancient people's rights were apparently over. Voter districts were drawn along ethnic lines to ensure that the Adygei got a substantial number of deputies in the 45-seat parliament; in 1996 there were 18 ethnic Adygei deputies, far above their proportion of the population. Although the Russians retained a majority, enough for most parliamentary votes, they did not have the two-thirds needed to override presidential vetos or to impeach the president. Candidates for president had to speak both Adygei and Russian, a law which effectively ensured an Adygei president, since the Adygei are bilingual, while almost no Russians have mastered Adygei, a notoriously complex language. The arrangement, ironically, ended up almost the opposite of Soviet practice where the top leaders in ethnic republics were nearly always Russians, whatever the population proportions. This was a victory for the Adygei, but who knows, perhaps another ticking bomb if the local Russian majority ever decided to actively challenge the status quo.

The inland Adygei were luckier than the remnants of the once powerful Black Sea Adygei-Circassian tribe called the Shapsug. They were virtually wiped out in the 19th century and lived on in handfuls mostly around the Black Sea towns of Sochi and Tuapse, part of the Krasnodar region. Attempts by the Shapsug to win some kind of autonomy, or to link up with the Adygea republic, were rebuffed by the Krasnodar authorities who cited the danger of other minorities following suit. However the Shapsugs did get the right to teach the Adygei langauge in schools serving their villages.

Aslanbek Kerashev, formerly an Adygei Communist Party official, was one of the first to lobby for an Adygei republic, heading what was known as the 'Committee of 40,' a group of intellectuals. He said the Adygei movements were a direct attempt to roll back the legacy of the 19th-century wars.

We were accused of nationalism and separatism, but this was not our goal. We just wanted to ensure that one ethnic group should not have automatic rule over the other, as it always had been,' he said. 'We were destroyed in the last century and we suffered collectivisation and all these other experiments which reduced our gene pool. We decided it was enough and we should have some guarantees at last. Before, they never taught Adygei history or language, now we do. And we have Adygei language programmes on television and newspapers and a faculty in the university.

At the new Adygei representation in Moscow, where big leather chairs squat on Adygei-produced white marble floors, the envoy, a sort of internal ambassador, did not mince his words. 'In the 19th century, when there were the Caucasian wars and the Turkish–Russian wars, the Cossacks didn't come at will – they were pushed in by the tsars. They were paid and forced to grab our land. It's too much to blame their descendants and say 'you stole,' but at the same time we want our status to be recognised, that we are the titular nation.'

In 1990 the scattered ethnic-Adygei in the North Caucasus, from the Kabards to the Cherkess to the Shapsugs, founded a common organisation called Adygei Khase. It aimed to reunite the ethnic-Adygei still in Russia, help the return of the diaspora from Turkey, the Middle East and the United States, and win rehabilitation from the 19th-century conquest. There was mixed success. Adygei Khase did provide a united platform for the scattered Circassian tribes of old. But hopes for a mass return of the diaspora were likely to be disappointed for many years. Persuading people to come and live in Russia in the 1990s, particularly when they didn't speak Russian, took more than appeals to ethnic pride. Despite the bonds of language, which many of the diaspora keep up abroad, the Adgyei peoples had undergone profound Russification and probably had as many differences as they had things in common with their overseas cousins.

One story I heard – recounted by Tatyana Mamkhyagova, the Cherkessk correspondent of the regional *Severny Kavkaz* newspaper – was of a Jordanian Cherkess who came back to work as a mullah and attended a funeral where one of his Cherkess counterparts, who had only rudimentary Arabic, unwittingly read out an Arabic love poem instead of the required holy verses. Another diaspora returnee apparently settled down in a specially provided house in Karachai-Cherkessia and took over a collective farm. He began preaching Islamic diligence and hard work to his employees, but discovered they had long since opted for the latter-Soviet ambitions of doing as little work and getting home as early as possible. 'There had been a big welcome for him,' Tatyana said. 'But they came to hate him. A whole lot of special houses had been built for returnees. But no other families came. No one wants to come here. If anything, they'd like to leave.'

In 1996 Adygei Khase held its third congress in Cherkessk. It was attended by the prince of Jordan, in whose country many of the diaspora live, and Adygei representatives from dozens of states around the world. The hall where the congress was held was packed with all the incarnations of the Adygei – old men in traditional costume; diaspora representatives from New Jersey; long-legged, oval-eyed girls; tanned peasants in their worn black suits; and enormous new-Russian style bodyguards in slightly baggy designer suits, black silk shirts and skinheads.

Adgyei Khasse was doing its job of promoting contacts between the diaspora and homelands, but I couldn't help the feeling that the movement, like so many national organisations in the North Caucasus, had run out of the clout and energy it had had in those passionate years after the collapse of Soviet power. Once the initial fight for more autonomy was over, and largely won, in the early 1990s, going further meant radicalising, pushing for independence or redrawing disputed borders. In most places, no one was ready for this. Chechnya was an exception and it paid dearly when the Russians struck back in 1994.

The Jordanian prince was the star guest, a coup for the organisers and he was feted with full Caucasian hospitality. The young prince, who spoke English with a thick American accent and had his remarks badly translated into Russian, got a delirious standing ovation from the packed hall of Adygei, but his words were empty, almost Michael-Jacksonesque. 'The world owes the Adygei a favour. Wherever they have lived they have always done their utmost,' the prince said in his soft voice. 'You have a beautiful culture and you are a beautiful people.' It was as if the Adygei were clapping just to prove to themselves that they were still there.

### Budennovsk, Stavropol region

*The Cossacks, wearing blue and red cloaks and fur hats, line up in two rows facing each other and let out a cry of 'lyuba!', which roughly translates as 'hurrah!' President Boris Yeltsin, campaigning hard against the stolid Communist Gennady Zyuganov in the 1996 presidential elections, steps out of his Zil limousine and makes straight for them.*

*The meeting goes well. Yeltsin is given a thoroughbred horse and in return he gives a flattering speech. It is like some fantasy fusion of male bonding and Russian monarchism – the armed Cossacks and the big, hard-drinking president, more tsar-like than ever, rubbing shoulders here in Budennovsk, in the depths of the Stavropol region, on the fringe of the North Caucasus.*

*'You put the Chechens to panic,' Yeltsin says to cheers. 'They understand that no one messes with the Cossacks!' Yeltsin tells the Cossacks they are the 'fortress of the Russian state' and promises to help them 'restore the traditional way of life.' Then he says he will send them several billion rubles for schools. They cheer again. He gets back into the Zil and vanishes.*

For ethnic-Russians, these years of turmoil were especially disturbing. As the former dominant people, they had fallen furthest and hardest. Before, the Caucasus had been a place of resorts, mountaineering holidays and long summers. Now the entire Soviet empire was in ruins and even here at the doorstep of the Russian heartland, once-quiet minorities were asserting separate rights. Everywhere there was poverty caused by the post-Soviet economic breakdown, compounded by a sense of powerlessness and danger. Russians began to feel like strangers in their own homes, tens of thousands of them leaving from Chechnya alone.

For the Cossacks, however, the strategic shake-up in the Caucasus was a new lease on life. Maps took on a look eerily similar to the military campaigns of the 19th century: nationalist highlanders agitating along the mountains, ethnic-Russians fleeing the turmoil north into the Krasnodar and Stavropol regions, and the Cossack villages, or *stanitsas*, which had sunk into poverty and obscurity during the Soviet era, suddenly back on the frontier. The cross and crescent once again faced off.

The Cossacks brought out old uniforms and photographs, polished their swords and pinned on their grandfathers' medals. They lobbied for restoration of their old social status as armed farmers with their own administrations and local laws, demanding land and the right to form Cossack units within the Russian army, preferably for border guard service.

A combination of sympathetic coverage in the Russian media and enough sets of red-striped trousers and 19th-century jackets took the Cossacks – who number an estimated five million around Russia, including some 600,000 in the North Caucasus – a long way. They received powerful backing from the Orthodox Church, Yeltsin and a whole range of Russian nationalists in Moscow. A right-wing shift across Russian politics from 1993 only brought more encouragement. But there were major obstacles to really restoring *kozachestvo*, or Cossackry.

Apart from the results of their physical decimation under Communist rule, the modern Cossacks suffered two major problems in restoring their society. The first was simple: they were being exploited, as well as helped by Moscow. Much of Yeltsin's support, aimed solely at playing the neo-imperialist gallery, was illusory. His decrees gave the Cossacks some privileges, such as being classified as a repressed people, and he strongly hinted at the Cossacks regaining some kind of official military status, but he took little concrete action.

The second and biggest problem was less tangible: the Cossacks' difficulty in finding a *raison d'être*. As long as the empire existed, the Cossacks' role was colonisation. They lived only where they conquered – by definition their home was always someone else's first, even if centuries ago – and they were always ready to push on to new territory, serving the state. Like sharks, they had to remain in motion. In the later years of the Russian monarchy, with the empire already carved, they took on a new job – suppressing Jews, revolutionaries and others who stepped out of line. But then the arrival of the Bolsheviks put an abrupt and bloody end to their adventures and the Yeltsin era fell short of giving them a new role.

The result was that Cossacks today more often than not end up looking like American Civil War or battle of Waterloo re-enactment clubs, where middle-aged men dress up, fire blanks and lie down after someone on the other side pretends to shoot them. The honour guard wheeled out for Yeltsin in Budennovsk during his re-election campaign had this image problem, with its mixture of gangly youths and paunchy fathers in ill-fitting costumes, medals that belonged in museums and barely coordinated yelps of *'lyuba!'*

Nevertheless, Cossack leaders see a concrete role within the army as the only way forward. All-Cossack units struck agreements in the mid-1990s to guard borders between Siberia and Mongolia and they took up positions on the border with Kazakhstan, to the alarm of the Kazakh government. Unofficial units participated as mercenaries or volunteers in several post-Soviet wars, including in Chechnya, Abkhazia and in Moldova on the border with Romania. Cossack chiefs in the North Caucasus made the grandiose claim they could raise an army of 100,000 men and their shopping list for weapons expanded from sabres and rifles in the early years to tanks, planes and artillery.

Despite the Kremlin's flirtation with the idea of full fledged Cossack divisions, few concrete steps were taken in this direction. Besides, whatever Yeltsin claimed about Chechens fleeing in panic, the war there underlined that unlike their forefathers a century ago, modern Cossacks had no special talents to bring to the battlefield. Once their 19th-century medals came off they were no more invincible than anyone else. Two hundred Cossacks who volunteered to fight under the system of professional short-term contracts gave up, packed their kit bags and went home after just two weeks at war in southern Chechnya. Another all-Cossack unit was reported to have lost 22 men and 150 wounded in three weeks. As for the Cossack population living in Chechnya, mostly in Grozny and in a string of *stanitsas* along the River Terek in the north, they were in no position to defend themselves and little by little they vanished into the safety of southern Russia.

As for resurrecting colonial-era *stanitsas,* that would risk catapulting the Cossacks' already tense relations with highlanders in several republics into open conflict. As one Kabard put it: 'Restoring the military power of the Cossacks in the Caucasus would be about as tactful as putting up monuments in Russia to the Mongol hordes.' In Adygea, ethnic-Adygei villages are invariably sandwiched between Cossack villages, which, accidentally or not, gave the Adgygei a feeling that they were surrounded. 'They're reactionaries, warlike and it seems that Yeltsin's government is pushing them forward. I don't like their passion for fighting,' said Adygei history professor Khamzet Kazanov. 'At the start, I thought they were a bit of a joke, but now their culture is being restored. They make us very uncomfortable here.'

One of the Adygei peoples' most cherished demands – that Moscow recognise 21 May, the anniversary of the official end to the 19th-century conquest, as a day of remembrance for the victims of Circassia – was not granted largely because of Cossack opposition. 'In Moscow, they're worried about angering the Cossacks', one Adygei government official told me. 'At the same time, our (Adygei) president has asked the Cossacks not to wear their uniforms in public, saying this would help keep relations calm. Otherwise, the Adygei might be provoked into going out into the street wearing their Cherkessks and *kinzhals*. Of course he was joking a bit, but such steps really are necessary to prevent disputes flaring up, you see.'

On the eve of Yeltsin's visit to Budennovsk I sat with local Cossacks in a run-down shed serving as their headquarters. There was an elderly man in an alarmingly fascist-looking black uniform, a few youths in a bedraggled mixture of army camouflage and jeans, and the rest, mostly big, middle-aged men, in ordinary clothes. Oddly, several of the Cossacks, who began gathering around to look at me, were cross-eyed. On the wall hung a large Russian tricolour with an imperial double-headed eagle at the end of the pole.

'The process of restoring ourselves is going to take a very long time. After having had our lives taken away, we need to be born again. We will work on our children from the time they can walk,' said Alexander Mayevsky, the 38-year-old *ataman*, or elected Cossack chief. He said Russia needed a professional army, something few would argue with, and that the Cossacks should be at the forefront of changes.

I asked whether he didn't think that the North Caucasus, ruined by the war in Chechnya, the war between the Ingush and Ossetians and several other disputes, could do without yet another militarised ethnic group. 'All we want is to reclaim our customs', he answered.

Yes, but wouldn't that mean conflict? 'No, we just want our sense of honour restored. We get on well with all peoples. It's not as if we've been in the Caucasus for 10 years – we've been here for hundreds. We just want to give help. There should be order. All of this mess, Chechnya and so on, comes from a lack of order.'

In the settlement of Novosvobodnaya in the foothills of Adygea, the Cossacks were less enthusiastic about their role in keeping order. Their village had been founded after the Adygei were driven out in 1864. But this former outpost of empire was crumbling and deserted – more a victim of the Soviet economic collapse than beneficiary of the heralded Cossack revival. 'You can live well here. But you have to work and love the land. Now the young don't love the land, they run away from it,' said Pyotr Romanyenko, a sturdy old Cossack, born there in 1923.

He lived in a cottage next to the village cemetery. Although his yard was still tidy, cackling with geese and sheep, I feared that once he moved across the track into that graveyard, his farm would disappear, yet another blank on the Cossack list. In the village centre, a knot of young men in leather jackets and city shoes sat drinking beer in the sun.

## Pyatigorsk

*Pyatigorsk wears its bygone imperial glory like a faded, splendid old coat. There are long boulevards, turn-of-the-century buildings with exotic gables, arches and lots of glass. But inside, many of the buildings have been Sovietized, covered in brown wall paper and made to smell like bus stops. There's nothing much to do. The famous old spas, which are dotted all over Marshuk hill, are almost deserted. Cavernous restaurants with red-backed chairs, red carpets, chandeliers and white table cloths lack only customers. I'm told people stopped coming to Pyatigorsk when the war in Chechnya started, although it looks as if the decay started long before then. They still love their water though. There are special taps where you can fill bottles for free and although the minerals stink, people keep drinking the stuff.*

*The little cottages and yard where Lermontov lived with his army friends and wrote* A Hero of Our Time *are still there. An obelisk marks the spot on Marshuk hill where he was killed in a duel, aged 26, now a popular place for newly weds to get their picture taken.*

*The days of balls, intrigue and love matches between exiled poet officers and Muscovite princesses coming for the mountain air are long gone. Today it's like this: an advertisement in the local newspaper: 'Three girls looking for marriage with officers.' Or it's in the Intourist hotel, where the lounge lizards are playing 'Lady in Red' under three-colour disco lights and easy girls seem to outnumber the guests. Up in a grotto overlooking the whole city, where Pechorin might have secretly met Princess Mary in* A Hero of Our Time, *I find half a dozen youths coughing on cigarettes and playing a rap song on a tape recorder that goes: 'I want to hurt you, hurt you.'*

*Not all has changed. When Lermontov lived here, 150 years ago, Russia was trying to conquer Chechnya and the rest of the Caucasus. Today, Pyatigorsk is still full of resting Russian officers, and heavily armed police outside the city guard against infiltration by Chechen guerrillas. With the end of decades of Communist suppression, the descendants of the Cossacks who caught Lermontov's imagination are again allowed to put on their old uniforms and gather.*

*There are many ghosts. As we drive into Pyatigorsk at night in the fog, a horseman suddenly flashes across the main road, caught in our headlights for a second, before disappearing into the rocky countryside to our left. The driver hits the brakes, but I'm left wondering whether what we saw was real or not.*

## 4. DREAMS OF UNITY

When we met in 1996 in Nalchik, Mussa Shanibov had the haunted look of a man who's getting old and knows he's failed. But just a few years before, he'd been at the helm of an extraordinary attempt to fulfil the centuries-old dream of uniting the highlanders under one political roof. This was the ambition of North Caucasus leaders from Sheikh Mansur to the doomed confederations that flitted in and out of history during the Bolshevik revolution. If the unruly scattering of nations, often numbering well under 100,000 people, joined forces they would number several million and the balance of power in the region would dramatically change; Russia would meet its match.

Shanibov, a Kabard, had the backing of the most radical nationalists in the region when he created the Confederation of Peoples of the Caucasus. From small beginnings, the Confederation developed grandiose aims of replacing Russian rule in the North Caucasus and, at one point, boasted members from 16 of the tiny nations, its own parliament and paramilitary forces. However, by 1994, along with many other nationalist movements, the Confederation had lost cohesion and Shanibov stepped down, the loser in a complex battle with Russia for influence. North Caucasus unity had again been proved a myth.

When we met, Shanibov, 59, wore a traditional *papakha* Astrakhan hat and long black leather coat. After disappearing from the headlines, he was clearly pleased to see a journalist. We talked in a room at an office building with a long table but no distinguishing marks, no paper, no signs, nothing.

The organisation was founded in August 1989 in Sukhumi, capital of Akbhazia, an idyllic Black Sea area within Georgia, directly south of the mountain chain from Adygea. The original title was Assembly of Mountain Peoples of the Caucasus. Chechen, Ingush, Adygei, Kabard, Cherkess, Abazin, Shapsug, Abkhaz and Avar representatives – all indigenous Caucasian mountain peoples – signed on. Shanibov was chairman.

At the outset the focus was on the fate of the Abkhaz, a people related to the Adygei-Circassian tribes of the North Caucasus. A mixed Moslem, Christian and pagan people, the Abkhaz were likewise expelled en masse in the 19th century and became a minority – less than 20 per cent of a population of 537,000 – on their own historic lands. About 45 per cent of the modern population in Abkhazia were Georgians, and the rest were Russians and Armenians.

Mirroring what was happening north of the mountains, the Abkhaz agitated for greater autonomy, then demanded to leave Georgia's jurisdiction and form a separate republic. The Abkhaz nationalist leaders, headed by the dapper oriental scholar Vladislav Ardzinba, looked on the Georgians as occupiers, in the same way that nationalists in the North

Caucasus looked on the Russians. The Georgians, in the throes of trying to gain independence from the Soviet Union, which they achieved in 1991, saw the growing Abkhaz revolt as a deliberate piece of trouble-making inspired by Moscow to keep Georgia weak internally. Besides, argued the Georgians, how could the Abkhaz secede when they were were in such a minority? It was the old problem at the heart of much of the turmoil to the north.

As the conflict between the Abkhaz and Georgia grew, so did Shanibov's organisation. In November, 1991 another congress was held and the newly-renamed Confederation expanded to include the North Ossetians and several more nations from Dagestan. The organisation was declared the 'legitimate heir of the independent (1918) North Caucasian Republic' – in other words a self-declared independent state reaching from the Caspian to the Black Sea. 'I saw that we were too small individually to have any chances, that we had to unite', Shanibov said. 'Then, I thought, we could win political and economic power. We wanted it to be a federation, but for each of the republics to have real statehood, with UN membership.'

By the end of 1991 – against the background of the Communist hardliners' failed putsch in Moscow in August and the approaching collapse of the Soviet Union – the situation in Abkhazia reached boiling point. Georgia, with a population of about 5.4 million, already had its hands full trying to suppress a revolt by the South Ossetian minority, who wanted to leave Georgian jurisdiction and link up with North Ossetia on the Russian side of the mountains.

Then in August 1992, forces nominally loyal to Georgia's new leader, ex-Soviet foreign minister Eduard Shevardnadze, stormed into Abkhazia and took control of the capital Sukhumi. Although more a chaotic mixture of badly trained militias than an army, the force was expected to deal quickly with the Abkhaz separatists, who fled north, closer to the border with Russia.

Instead, the Abkhaz, secretly backed by elements of the Russian military and the Supreme Soviet (parliament) in Moscow, fought back, launching a savage war in which Abkhaz and Georgian civilians who had been neighbours now killed each other. Both sides, particularly the Georgians, blamed the other for unspeakable atrocities. The Abkhaz were accused of ethnically cleansing areas by burning civilians alive and pillaging villages. The Georgians were accused of starting the cycle of hatred by trying to wipe out Abkhaz identity and torching the national archives, almost the sole repository of Abkhazia's written past.

The war was what the ambitious Mussa Shanibov had been waiting for. The Confederation's armed supporters had already been prevented from crossing the mountains to back up the South Ossetians, but this time, neither the Russians nor the pro-Moscow North Caucasus political establishment could risk standing in Shanibov's way. 'Abkhazia battalions' of Chechen, Adygei, Kabard and Dagestani volunteers trekked over to fight on the side of the Abkhaz insurgents.

Estimates of how many fighters came in from the North Caucasus ranged from 500 to well over 1,000. In either case their help, along with that of the Russians' heavy weapons, such as Sukhoi ground attack planes and Grad multiple rocket systems, was crucial to the Abkhaz. Thirteen months after the war began, in September 1993, the Abkhaz routed the Georgians and recaptured Sukhumi. Almost all ethnic-Georgians, about 250,000 of them, abandoned their homes and fled into Georgia proper.

The Confederation and nationalists in the North Caucasus in general saw the war and establishment of Abkhazia's *de facto* independence as their defining chapter – a victory for the 'small nations'. In Shanibov's view, the Abkhazia episode proved for the first time since 1918 that the mountain peoples could act politically and militarily as a unified force. The reality, given the major role of the Russians, was more complex.

Exactly what Moscow's involvement was remains murky. Russia had no coordinated strategy for the Caucasus until 1993–94, and that policy vacuum was never plainer than in Abkhazia where, although Russia was officially neutral, local base commanders became deeply involved in the war. Moreover, Russian commanders were so lacking in guidance from the centre, that those in Georgia proper and those in Abkhazia operated independently of each other, even against each other. So while Russian planes bombed the Georgians on behalf of the Abkhaz, Russian officers inside Georgia supplied Georgian forces with equipment to be used against the Abkhaz. Moscow military sources say that Russian tank crews even took part on the side of the Georgians, facing their comrades helping the Abkhaz. Of course, base commanders in Sukhumi may not have had much choice about helping the Abkhaz because they were caught in the crossfire. Given the corruption in the armed forces, it is also perfectly feasible that the cooperation of the local Russian commanders was simply bought.

The Russian government consistently refused to admit involvement, even as the Abkhaz irregulars mysteriously deployed sophisticated weaponry. When the Georgian government complained about what were clearly Russian air strikes, Russian Defence Minister Pavel Grachev baldly denied any involvement. Then he claimed the Georgians were bombing themselves (incidentally, the same pattern of lies would be used later in Chechnya) and then admitted the truth. Finally, a Russian plane was shot down.

Given the confusion, it is also hard to define how close the link was between Moscow and the Confederation. Not only regular Russian troops helped the Abkhaz, but units of Russian rightwing mercenaries, Cossacks, and, according to the Georgians, undercover Russian secret service agents. Together with the North Caucasian nationalists, they made strange bedfellows, but also a perfect cross section of the passionate, chaotic forces sweeping the ex-Soviet empire.

Some in Russia and the Caucasus believe that the Confederation was set up and run by the Russian secret services, with Shanibov's participation, as part of a plan to undermine Georgia. Shevardnadze said Russia was 'at war' with Georgia. According to some analysts, Shamil Basayev, the young Chechen who commanded the North Caucasians, was trained for Abkhazia by none other than Russia's Main Intelligence Directorate, the GRU. However, it is unlikely that Moscow had the ideological or physical will to run such complex cloak-and-dagger conspiracies in the late 1980s and early 1990s. Probably, the military was simply trying to exploit the Confederation and the war as best it could, and vice versa. Although the Confederation may well have been infiltrated by Russian agents, it also included large numbers of radically anti-Russian nationalists, hardly supporters of Moscow's agenda. Beyond Abkhazia, the Confederation was agitating for independence in all the North Caucasus and was increasingly involved with the Chechen separatist leader Dzhokhar Dudayev. Certainly, the Russians would regret the day they heard of Basayev, for he and his Abkhaz Batallion were to become the scourge of Russian troops in Chechnya just two years on.

In her heavily pro-Georgian book on Abkhazia, *Conflict in the Caucasus*, Svetlana Chervonnaya said that the Confederation was a Russian brainchild that got out of hand, like 'the djinn freed from the bottle'. The organisation 'proved to be an uncontrollable force. The fierce anarchic love of freedom of the mountain peoples, and their reluctance to live either in the Russian or Soviet empire, made it very difficult to direct this force only against democratic Georgia.'

The Abkhaz war was the final blow in a string of setbacks to Shevardnadze's attempts to steer Georgia out of the Russian sphere. The earlier war in South Ossetia had ended with a Russian mediation plan in which the Georgians failed to regain proper control over the territory. Then while Shevardnadze's army was being defeated by the Abkhaz in September 1993, the rebel Georgian ex-president Zviad Gamsakhurdia took advantage of the chaos to step up his own insurgency. That left Shevardnadze in Tbilisi on his knees and with only one way out – Russian help. Moscow promised to comply, but at a price: Shevardnadze would have to sign Georgia into the Commonwealth of Independent States and agree to the basing of 20,000 Russian troops. On October 8, the humiliated Georgian leader joined the CIS. It was too late to reverse the situation in Abkhazia, but intervention by Russian marines did allow Shevardnadze to use his forces to defeat Gamsakhurdia within days and so retain power.

Russia was thus able to turn the extraordinary mess to its advantage and gain new dominance over Georgia. This had long been considered necessary for control over the Caucasus in general. Not only did Christian Georgia, with its long Black Sea coast, provide an important foothold in the Transcaucasus, but it bordered all seven autonomous republics in the North Caucasus. Without Georgia, Russia's southern underbelly would be more vulnerable than ever to internal separatist unrest and external threats from Turkey.

The episode was sweet revenge for the Russian military and other forces pining for the Soviet empire, who still blamed Shevardnadze for the dismantlement of the Soviet presence in eastern Europe when he was Gorbachev's foreign minister. But it remained to be seen whether the strong-arm tactics would work in the long term, since appalled Georgians were left only more keen to build links with the West and with Ukraine across the Black Sea, bypassing their northern neighbour.

Abkhazia, like South Ossetia, won only a pyrrhic victory. The fate of the mass of Georgian refugees remained unchanged and more than three years after the end of the war Abkhazia was poverty-stricken, half empty and with no diplomatic recognition. Stationed along the Georgian-Abkhaz border, were 3,000 (later 1,600) Russian troops, ostensibly peacekeepers, but effectively guaranteeing Abkhazia's uneasy semi-independence. Shevardnadze continued bitterly to insist that the conflict had been manipulated, but there was little he could do about this. Although there were growing Georgian calls for the 'peacekeepers' to be removed, everyone feared what that could mean – another Georgian attempt to recapture its province and more death among the citrus groves and vineyards, with no certainty of victory.

Meeting Shanibov I thought of him as a rather deluded figure. I think he had seriously believed that the North Caucasus could challenge Russian dominance and that the Confederation could be more successful than its even shorter-lived predecessor in 1918. But the war in Abkhazia was a chimera of success. Not only had the highlanders' victory been questionable – after all, they helped Russia divide and rule Georgia – but they proved unable to maintain their cooperation where it really mattered, back on the north side of the mountains.

The internal contradictions of 16 highlander nations tore away at the Confederation. The Adygei peoples and Chechens were divided. The Balkars and Karachai, at odds with the Adygei peoples, did not even want to join. Not everyone was happy at the growing influence of Chechnya's President Dudayev. There were also splits between the hardliners who wanted to confront Russian authority and the moderates, as well as a divide between Islamic radicals and those trying to keep religion out of the agenda.

The Confederation always insisted it was more a regional peacemaker than a warrior organisation and, at the end of 1992, it had a chance to exercise its influence in a tailor made case: territorial conflict between

Russian-backed Ossetians and the Ingush. But the Confederation was helpless, standing by as a border dispute turned into war and the Russians proved themselves the only regional power. By the time the crackdown on Chechnya began, in 1994, faith in the mountain republic as a political force had died.

### Nalchik, Kabardino-Balkaria

*Shanibov used to be called Yury. Very Russian. So when he entered nationalist politics he changed his first name to the Moslem Mussa. That kind of pride, almost vanity, is still there. When I ask to photograph him outside his apartment building in Nalchik, he steps around me so that the background will show the trees on the pavement, not his run-down, Soviet housing estate entrance, which would be more interesting. I don't object.*

*The Confederation was a failure, and now Shanibov plays the role of the prophet ignored. He says he's being investigated and that he frequently changes office. 'They're hounding us. We're getting kicked out of this place,' he says, pointing around the bare office. 'Before, we got kicked out of another. Many of our people work from their apartments.'*

*I wonder if he really still has many other 'people' or even if he is in touch with politics himself. He is full of frustration and anger and the more we talk, the more apocalyptic his views become.*

*'When they've finished with the Chechens – and that will take a very long time – they'll go on. They'll involve Dagestan and Ingushetia. The Ossetians will be sucked in. A lot of people in the Caucasus want just to reach a settlement with Russia. But Russia wouldn't stop there –their goal is to destroy the Caucasus.*

*'Right now in Chechnya, Yeltsin is preparing his two million soldiers to fight in any Russian city in case he loses the elections. There's going to be civil war in Russia, no question. And soon, all these western countries which stood by while Chechnya was destroyed will also be faced by the monstrous Russian army with atomic weapons. This will be no Germany, this will be worse – Hitler with atomic weapons. And then the western leaders will see.'*

*Then: 'People have been taught a lesson for now. But it's not in the Caucasus character to remain quiet for too long. Russia will pay. They'll suffer a Dostoyevskan punishment.'*

## 5. FIRST BLOOD

*In the Caucasus, the only thing that cannot be forgiven is blood.*

Anatoly Isayenko, Vladikavkaz University history professor.

The North Ossetians stand out. With their neighbours speaking either indigenous Caucasian languages or Turkic dialects, the Ossetians are alone in using a Persian dialect distantly related to the tongue of their Sarmatian forefathers. The Ossetians also seem to have been fated to help the Russian conquest. Their homeland straddles both sides of the main strategic pass in the Caucasus chain, the pass where the Russians built the spectacular Georgian Military Highway. Furthermore, a majority of Ossetians were at least nominally Christian and, as their neighbours' acceptance of Islam rose throughout the 19th century, the Ossetians, naturally, grew closer to Orthodox Russia.

When the Soviet Union collapsed and the North Ossetians rummaged around for their ethnic identity, they became newly aware of their special position in the Caucasus jigsaw. There were two especially pressing issues, both of them adding to an existing fear of overpopulation in the republic of 632,000 people. There was the war in South Ossetia across the mountains, and the resulting flood of refugees – up to 100,000 according to some estimates. And there was the still more serious problem of a dispute with the Ingush over lands just on the North Ossetian side of the border, an area to the east of Vladikavkaz called Prigorodny. This territory had been Ingush prior to the deportations and the Ingush wanted it back under their jurisdiction. On the face of it, this was another of those rows which had boiled, then dropped to a simmer across the North Caucasus without major confrontation. But this time, there would be the feared explosion. Highlander would fight highlander and the historic split between Ossetians and their Moslem neighbours would widen even further.

More urbanised than other North Caucasus peoples, the Ossetians often see themselves as a slightly higher breed to the other *gortsy*. Many look with horror on the deep attachment to Islam in parts of the region and consider the clan-based societies from Dagestan to Ingushetia nothing short of primitive. As for their own mix of Christianity, Islam and paganism, the Ossetians see this as a blessing. There's even an internal pecking order, with North Ossetians considering themselves a step above their South Ossetian cousins.

The centre of Vladikavkaz does have a relatively cosmopolitan feel to it. The tall, often strikingly beautiful young women wear stylish clothes with little of the modesty among the more devout Moslem republics; men and women eat out together at restaurants, something you almost never see elsewhere. The centre, with its trams, enclosed balconies and mock towers has real charm. In the summer, men and women even strip down to bathing suits around a brackish pond near the River Terek and after the foreignness of the rest of the North Caucasus, I found the sight of women in bikinis very refreshing. I felt I was back in Russia.

Where the North Ossetians are no different from their neighbours is their obsession with the past and ethnicity. These were certainly the favourite topics of Bugi, a taxi driver. He was in good form, not only happy to be getting a good fare to go out to the pagan wood outside Vladikavkaz, but to have a captive audience for his theories on why Ossetians are special.

A gnarled amateur wrestler, Bugi shouted as if we were in an open-top car going well over the speed limit, not in his sedate Volga taxi. 'You know why there are so few of us? Because we fought all over the world. We were called Alans and we fought everybody everywhere, like mercenaries. We were strong. I'm not speaking for myself of course, I don't want to kill anyone, I'm a Christian, I'm tolerant – we all are. Take my wife, she's a Moslem, pure Moslem actually.'

Bugi went on: 'you know who the greatest Ossetian of all was? Stalin. He wasn't Georgian, he was Ossetian. And don't believe anyone who says he was bad. He was the great leader. People of every age wept when he died; we only get people that clever once a century.'

I mentioned the deportations and the repressions, but Bugi was not listening. 'Stalin was clever. He specially didn't let the Baltics and those traitors write poems in their own languages because he knew where it would all lead to. And he was right: as soon as the Baltics got independence, the whole Soviet Union collapsed.'

One night at an outdoor cafe in Vladikavkaz, Anatoly Isayenko, an ebullient history professor from the city's university, picked up on a more learned note where Bugi had left off. We talked long about the Sarmatians and the military expeditions they made across Europe, and the earlier Scythians. A tape of haunting, cadenced traditional Ossetian music blasted from speakers hidden somewhere in the vines of the cafe walls. 'Listen!' Anatoly said excitedly. 'That's Scythian music you're listening to. That's music from millennia ago. It's all around you, Scythian culture. You are sitting among Scythian people. Look at what you're eating (a sort of Ossetian pizza filled with cheese), that's Scythian. That's a symbol of the sun that they used to worship. Look at the way I cut it, eight ways – the rays of the sun, that's a solar symbol.'

Anatoly, a charming man who was part Cossack, part Ossetian, said the Ossetians believed they were 'a sort of higher people. They don't care so much about the land, the way the Ingush and the Chechens do. To them the land is unimportant – they care instead about the spirit, friends, customs. They have a history that surely only the Jews can match.' When you first travel in the North Caucasus, this kind of stuff sounds extravagant, purple. Eventually you get used to it, and then it all starts sounding quite reasonable.

Across the border in Ingushetia, land certainly does count for a lot – it often does to repressed peoples. When the Ingush were deported by Stalin, they thought only about coming home. Their culture and gene pool were under assault, but the land was something firm and indestructible. Even though they officially no longer existed, erased from encyclopedias and their territory given out to other nations, the deportees knew where their forefathers were buried and that to them was vital proof of their own continued identity. So the discovery that their rich agricultural territory of Prigorodny was now closed off by a border and inhabited by Ossetians came, understandably, as a blow.

Under post-deportation Soviet rule, the Ingush shared a joint republic with the Chechens. When the Chechens declared independence from Russia in 1991, the Ingush decided, overwhelmingly, not to follow, and instead got Moscow's blessing to set up an autonomous republic of their own within the Russian Federation. The new Ingush republic, which came into legal existence in December 1992, had no city or much else to show for itself. An overgrown village called Nazran was the capital and the president, ex-Soviet army general Ruslan Aushev, had to swerve around cattle when his cortege swept through town. For the 270,000 Ingush, recovering control of their Prigorodny lands over the border in North Ossetia was now more important than ever.

Remaining loyal to Moscow seemed like a good first step, and President Yeltsin responded favourably – promising the Ingush during his 1991 presidential campaign that their problems would be resolved by the end of the year. They were also encouraged by the troubled 1991 law on rehabilitation of repressed peoples and by the fact that the speaker of the Russian parliament, Ruslan Khasbulatov, was a Chechen. Meanwhile, with or without permission, the Ingush were reclaiming their lands. By 1992, 30,000 had moved back to Prigorodny, according to official figures, although the real figure, including people who dodged the Ossetian residency permits system, was closer to 60,000. In addition to pressure for the territory to come officially within Ingushetia, some Ingush made a more provocative claim on the entire northeastern side of the city of Vladikavkaz – everything up to the right bank of the Terek, which included the industrial zone. This part of Vladikavkaz had also been Ingush territory in 1924, in the early days of the Soviet Union, with the Ossetians controlling the left bank. But the maps had been withdrawn in 1934, well before the deportations, and Vladikavkaz then decreed part of North Ossetia.

Tension grew throughout 1991. Ossetian thugs harassed the Ingush in Prigorodny, and a slow exodus of refugees began across the border into Ingushetia. Many Ingush refused to buckle. Throughout November of that year there were noisy demonstrations in Nazran, where the hot-heads received inspiration from the brazen rebellion of Chechnya. Both sides began to arm. For the Ingush, there was the Chechen arms market, but they amassed nothing like the force put together in Vladikavkaz. North Ossetia was the only autonomous republic in Russia allowed to create an official National Guard, essentially an armed force. In addition, the republic became the new base for some of the troops withdrawn from areas of the ex-Soviet Union and eastern Europe, including East Germany. With them came the usual mix of official and black market arms deals. Another source of weapons was the war in South Ossetia and the ex-combatants flowing into North Ossetia.

It is unclear who fired the first shot. In late October 1992 a North Ossetian armoured personnel carrier ran over an Ingush child in one of the Prigorodny villages. This provoked clashes between Ingush crowds and Ossetian police, with several people killed on both sides. On 24 October, the Ingush leaders ordered their villages to set up barricades and prepare for defence. On 30 October, the Ossetians began shelling Ingush parts of villages. So the next day the Ingush drove out the Ossetian police from the village of Chermen, captured weapons and rampaged through Ossetian areas until the Prigorodny region was in their hands. With heavy fighting underway, President Boris Yeltsin declared a state of emergency in the region on 2 November and ordered 3,000 Russian Interior Ministry soldiers and paratrooper units to intervene.

The battle ended in a disaster for the massively outgunned Ingush, who were burned and driven from their homes until there were none left in Prigorodny. Russian officials registered 65,000 refugees from North Ossetia into Ingushetia. Officially, 419 Ingush, 171 Ossetians and 60 others were killed. Other figures gave death tolls as high as 750 and 500 wounded. In all, 3,000 Ingush houses were burned.

The Ossetians said the Ingush were to blame, that they provoked a justifiably furious response by launching an assault on Vladikavkaz. The story you heard everywhere, always the same but impossible to prove, was that Ingush civilians in North Ossetia knew in advance that there would be a big Ingush assault to capture Prigorodny and Vladikavkaz. Secretly, they sneaked away before their fighters struck, leaving their former Ossetian neighbours and friends no warning of the attack. 'Vladikavkaz is to the Ingush what Rome was to the barbarians,' one Ossetian told me.

The Ingush were not blameless. Nationalists were agitating for the division of Vladikavkaz, and Ingush fighters were likely as much to blame as their young Ossetian counterparts in provoking the fatal first incidents. But there was no 'assault' on Vladikavkaz. The fighting was in Prigorodny. The story of Ingush inhabitants commiting a premeditated, mass betrayal of their Ossetian neighbours seems ludicrous. Many Ingush were them-selves caught unawares by the sudden start of war and had to flee North

Ossetia in desperate, often fatal, circumstances only after the fighting got underway.

The actual fighting was so one-sided that it was more a pogrom than battle. First the villages came under artillery fire, while helicopters either fired or directed fire. Then the settlements were attacked by troops equipped with armoured personnel carriers and no Ingush was safe. Many Ingush houses were set ablaze by arsonists, not as a result of fighting. You could see that in the ruins years later. The Ingush accused Russian troops in the area of directly supporting the Ossetians to commit ethnic cleansing in Prigorodny, and their case was not without basis. The heavy weapons and helicopters, and presumably the crews, could only have been supplied by the Russian armed forces. Two damning facts are sure. First, the Russian force did not intervene as it should have to prevent the massacre of civilians. Second, the end result of the war – even if this was not the aim, as the Ossetians insist – was ethnic cleansing. The Ingush fled *en masse*.

I went to Prigorodny in February 1996. It was a depressing sight. More than three years on and despite promises of action in Moscow and Vladikavkaz, only a trickle of Ingush had been able to return. Abandoned shells of houses lined the roads of the Prigorodny villages while just over the border inside Ingushetia, thousands of people still lived in refugee camps by the side of the road.

The few Ingush brave enough to come back to Prigorodny – and able to get the necessary Ossetian documentation – either lived in builders' cabins, called *vagonchiks*, or slowly tried to reconstruct their homes. Apart from these officially approved cases, no Ingush openly put foot on Ossetian soil and vice versa. The border was sealed by a security zone and Russian interior ministry checkpoints, but violence continued: just in the first year after the war ended, cross border raiders from both sides were reported to have blown up 167 Ingush houses and 107 Ossetian houses. Meanwhile, South Ossetian refugees were moving into many of the empty Ingush homes in Prigorodny. The South Ossetians were both hated by the Ingush and increasingly resented as a burden by the North Ossetians, but they too had nowhere to go, their homes in Georgia having been destroyed.

In the abandoned Prigorodny village of Dachnoye, just one of 13 villages which suffered a similar fate, only about 40 of the 400 original Ingush houses were being rebuilt. Beyond the ruins was a street of homes untouched by violence and still inhabited – Ossetian houses. Ingush who had returned were tormented by fear of being beaten up or shot, and the constant humiliation of being hated rejects on the patch of land where they were born. Radimkha, a 32-year-old woman who had gone back to try and rebuild her house in Dachnoye, still remembered the first hours of the war perfectly. 'It started overnight Friday-Saturday', she said. 'On

Sunday we heard it announced that the Russian troops were coming and we thought 'thank God, it will end.' We didn't have a cellar in our house, so there was no protection if we were hit. But it didn't stop, it got worse. By the time we left, people were being killed everywhere and houses were burning. All the time there were helicopters flying over our heads.'

Radimkha lived with two female relatives – they were three generations – in one *vagonchik* parked in the muddy lane near the ruins of their old house. An apartment building about a kilometre away had been taken over by South Ossetian refugees. 'We have to have our bread trucked specially from Ingushetia each day because we can't go to the shop at the apartment block. The children there throw stones at us', Radimkha said. I found her difficult to believe. But as I walked up to the shop, the daily bread truck rolled by and, sure enough, little South Ossetian children ran out into the street yelling, although they didn't throw stones. Inside the shop, the South Ossetian had all the conviction of Israeli settlers in the West Bank: 'We want no contact with those Ingush – they killed Ossetians, how can we live with the enemy? These are Ossetian lands, everybody knows that, it's clear.'

To my surprise the men working on one of the Ingush ruins were not Ingush at all but Ossetians. Was this a touching example of reconciliation? I asked the builders why they had taken this job. 'We have no work, so we're building for them, no not for them, but to make money for ourselves,' said one, correcting himself mid-sentence.

I asked how they got on with the Ingush.

'How would you get on with an enemy?' said one. 'That's right, they started the war. They asked for it and they got it', said another. 'They're responsible – they blew up their own houses.'

There were no cars on the mud-puddled road when I tried to hitch back to Vladikavkaz in the afternoon. I could hear the distant sound of cannon fire. 'Training for Chechnya', a passerby told me. Several policemen stood by the grey river bank. I went down to look. A woman had drowned and she lay bloated, pink and almost naked, while the police smoked in the drizzle. Finally, a bus rattled along, carrying a few Ossetian workmen and we drove from Prigorodny to Vladikavkaz in total silence.

To feel the pain caused by the conflict, and the hatred, you only need to visit the Ingush history museum in Nazran. A single room is devoted to the war and to the Stalin deportations – for the Ingush, they're part of the same thing. There are catalogues of gory photographs of Ingush incinerated in Prigorodny, Ingush with their throats slit, often women. A board is covered with school yearbook type photographs of smiling men, young and old, who died fighting, and of children who perished.

A painting shows Russian tanks rolling across fields, homes burning, an Ingush tied to a burning stake, an Ossetian knifing a woman, and two grotesque pigs tearing a Moslem Ingush baby apart. Another painting has the horror of Hieronimos Bosch: crazy dismembered bodies, troops in Soviet uniforms, helicopters and fire filling the sky, and a tiny Boris Yeltsin coming out of a windmill. The next painting depicts the ultimate symbol of the deportations – frozen, discarded bodies lying next to empty train tracks.

The Ingush suffered most of the carnage and they lost their homes. But in North Ossetia the war has also seared an indelible mark into the national consciousness. Despite their claims to higher civilisation, the Ossetians' hatred of the Ingush is now reflexive. Everybody, from government officials to taxi drivers, says that the Ingush should not be allowed to come back, that the two people simply cannot live next to each other. A renewed fear and distrust of Moslems is part of this hatred, as if North Ossetia's role as Christian bastion in a Moslem region was a self-fulfilling prophecy.

'In their Koran, they have written that every Moslem should kill at least 20 non-believers – especially us Orthodox Christians', said Zaira, a gentle 60-year-old woman in one of Vladikavkaz's bookshops. 'My husband is a doctor and you know what the little Ingush boys were saying in hospital when they were ill? 'We have to get better because we still haven't killed an Ossetian."

I decided to look in on the beautiful Vladikavkaz mosque. It was built next to the Terek in the 19th century and, amazingly, survived the Communist period, even though there was no one to pray in it. With the Prigorodny Ingush gone, the only worshippers were the handful of practising North Ossetian Moslems.

One of them, Yury, said he had only recently discovered his inherited faith and that he now came regularly to the mosque, although being an open Moslem in North Ossetia had become increasingly hard since the war. In 1995 a bomb blew a hole in the south wall of the building and it had to be put under permanent police guard. Nevertheless, ethnic ties were still stronger than the Moslem brotherhood Yury might have felt for the Ingush. 'No, I feel a great hatred for them and I was ready to fight if necessary. They lived well, they had great houses. What more did they want?'

### Ingush–North Ossetian border

*Magomed and Elbrus, both in their early twenties, sit together on the grass and share a pizza and glass of vodka. They laugh like schoolboys smoking in the woods, but their dare was much more dangerous.*

*Magomed is Ingush and Elbrus North Ossetian. They were friends and neighbours before the war, when Magomed lived in Vladikavkaz. Almost four years of peace were needed for them to make contact and Magomed was brave enough to come across the border hidden in a car with darkened windows. Now they are back at the main checkpoint on the Ingush-Northern Ossetian border preparing to say goodbye again.*

'*It was scary,*' Magomed says. '*I had to get around all my family in Ingushetia and not tell them where I was going. It would have been dangerous if our car had been stopped by Ossetian police. But once we got into Vladikavkaz, it was OK. We went to my old flat and there were South Ossetian refugees in it. There wasn't much I could tell them, except that they should go back to their own homes. My old neighbours – they all cried and laughed.*'

## 6. CLIMBING DOWN

In 1993, a series of body blows hit Russia's affair with Western-style democracy and with it the search for new freedoms in the North Caucasus. In Moscow President Yeltsin faced an implacable challenge from his parliament, the Supreme Soviet, which was dominated by Communist die-hards and nationalists. On one level, Yeltsin represented the forces dismantling the Soviet legacy and opening Russia to the West, while the Supreme Soviet fought to halt economic liberalisation. On another level, the ideological lines were increasingly blurred and power was the overriding goal. On a third level, the struggle took on a bitter personal nature, pitting Yeltsin against his one-time allies – parliament Speaker Ruslan Khasbulatov and Vice President Alexander Rutskoi.

The standoff finally deteriorated into a physical struggle, with the disbanded parliament barricading itself into its huge white building on the banks of the Moscow River. On 3 October supporters of the insurrection attempted to storm the Ostankino television tower and were repelled with considerable bloodshed, including many civilians caught in the crossfire. The next day Yeltsin called in the army and after tanks opened fire on the parliament from almost point-blank range, the rebel MPs surrendered.

The ugly episode formally ushered in an era of disillusion, as Russians, exhausted by liberal economic shock therapy, turned to neo-Communist, nationalist or authoritarian alternatives. The remarkable scenes of Muscovites calmly walking their dogs on Kutuzovsky Prospekt across the river from the parliament as tanks blasted the building, seemed to symbolise the desire for law and order, whatever the cost. As for Yeltsin, he had come out victorious, but not the same man, the hero of democracy, who three years earlier defended that parliament building against Soviet troops and brought the USSR crashing down.

One of the first peoples to feel the new chill were Caucasians. Mistrust and dislike of Caucasians had been building since they took advantage of Gorbachev's economic freedoms to sell their agricultural products in

Moscow and developed into one of the most conspicuous economic success groups. In an immediate post-rebellion security crackdown organised by the Moscow mayor, Yury Luzhkov, thousands of Caucasians were expelled from the capital. What made the mass round-ups especially significant was that Luzkhkov was not just a nationalist, he was a nationalist in close touch with the wishes of his electorate.

New parliamentary elections took place in December that year. The pro-Yeltsin, pro-reform Russia's Choice party had been expected to do well, but it was the racist and neo-imperialist Liberal Democratic Party led by Vladimir Zhirinovsky which flourished, with a fifth of the party list vote, albeit less in the constituency vote. Before long, the Zhirinovsky factor rippled through the Yeltsin government, with even the West's former liberal darling Foreign Minister Andrei Kozyrev beginning to toe a hard line. Neo-imperialism had come out of the closet. The legal underpinning of this shift was a new military doctrine adopted that November, which emphasised control over what Russians call 'the near abroad' – in other words the former Soviet territories – and internal, rather than external, enemies. Significantly for the North Caucasus, the doctrine paved the way for using the army in domestic conflicts, stressing the main threats to Russia as 'armed conflicts engendered by aggressive nationalism and religious intolerance'. Rapidly, the North Caucasus frontier became one of the most heavily militarised regions in the Russian Federation, breaking limits imposed by the Conventional Forces in Europe arms limitation treaty.

Under pressure, the anti-Russian nationalist movements began to peter out. Ordinary people, put off by the violence, dropped politics to concentrate on scraping a living in the chaos of economic reforms. Changing history was dangerous. 'People here became cynical', said Oleg Guseinov, a Kabard and deputy editor of the *Severny Kavkaz* newspaper. 'At first they believed that forcing out the Communists would end our problems, but then the nationalist movements also lost credibility. People understood that in fact all our crises were linked to Moscow. These nationalist movements had no real programme, they were fuelled on pure emotion, on anti-Russian feelings.'

Khassan Dumanov, head of the Kabardino-Balkaria government committee on ethnic relations, can remember the moment that national-ism in the republics peaked. It was in September 1992. Major nationalist demonstrations were being held on the central square of Nalchik, outside the Kabardino-Balkaria government building. The immediate cause of the unrest was the brief detention of Mussa Shanibov by the Russian police, but people were also demanding the resignation of the Soviet-era local authorities and more autonomy for the Kabards. The mood was angry, on the edge of mayhem, and a state of emergency was declared. Inside the government building, elite Russian interior ministry troops were called in to reinforce the local security forces. There were even the classic sparks: a soldier stabbed, a woman shot dead (apparently accidentally) and an attempt by demonstrators to storm the television centre and seize an armoured car. In Caucasus style, the fact that many of the riot police were local men and knew the demonstrators may have been the main reason that the violence didn't spin out of control.

The protestors were not a mob; they were ordinary people and also intellectuals who saw the North Caucasus reviving and wanted to challenge the status quo. But now the violence, and the fanaticism of leaders like Shanibov, divided the grass roots supporters into a radical minority and a majority which saw that a nationalist movement led to physical clashes with police and troops. The demonstrations receded and with them much of the nationalist energy.

'The people out there demonstrating in the square didn't really understand what they were asking for. It could have developed into a demand for full independence,' Dumanov said. 'Then Russia would have simply blockaded us. We would have been like mice. What happened here in 1992 was a dangerous moment. People now pray to give thanks it ended when it did.' One of Shanibov's fellow university professors said the demonstrations had been attractive, but that people in Kabardino-Balkaria were able to rein themselves in just in time. 'Crowds always believe in these types like Shanibov at difficult times. And all people have moments of madness and I think that was ours.'

If any further warning was needed, the Ingush-Ossetian conflict broke out shortly after. When it became apparent that Russian forces had armed and possibly helped the North Ossetians, many people in the North Caucasus republics felt their longtime suspicion – that Moscow wouldn't hesitate to use force to strengthen its grip over the region – had been confirmed. They saw the war as Moscow's way of proving itself the only real arbiter, just as it had done in Abkhazia. The Ingush president, Ruslan Aushev, said the war was an attempt to provoke the Chechens into helping the Ingush, giving Russian forces a *casus belli* to deal with Dzhokhar Dudayev. Whatever the case, the war succeeded in demonstrating the dangers of nationalism and in dividing the North Caucasus into its historical camps – Russian-backed Ossetians and punished Moslems. Divide and rule.

'This was not about ethnic hatred between the Ingush and Ossetians, this was politics,' Aushev told me. 'The people sorting this problem out are more interested in maintaining an imperial Russia. In the Caucasus they have always liked creating peoples they like and don't like, that are trustworthy and not trustworthy. They always look for trustworthy republics which will safeguard Moscow's interests. Chechnya, Ingushetia, Kabardino-Balkaria and some of the Dagestanis are not considered trustworthy and therefore need to be divided and ruled. Ossetia, however, has always been seen as a bastion for Russia.'

Moscow reasserted itself by providing support for loyal political forces. In January 1993, Moscow organised the first round table meeting of pro-democracy organisations from around the region in Pyatigorsk. The meeting wasn't supported by the Confederation of Peoples of the Caucasus or other powerful nationalist movements, but it did help establish links between the centre and the republics, signalling that Moscow wanted to put its regional policy on a more consistent course.

Another factor leading to the new stability was Moscow's control of the federal purse. Moscow supplied well over half the budget funds for all the autonomous republics in the region, for example 88 per cent of Dagestan's budget in 1994. Simultaneously, Moscow worked closely with the entrenched, ex-Communist partocrats. The men who had been first secretaries or party chairmen in their Soviet AOs and ASSRs, still ruled in Adygea, Kabardino-Balkaria, North Ossetia and Dagestan. In Karachai-Cherkessia, a constitutional power struggle paralysed politics until Moscow mediated a solution: the republic's leader would be picked by the Kremlin. These were all men used to taking Moscow's interests into account, preventing dissention and maintaining the status quo.

'The partocrats who always had been in power were able to stay there because they knew how to rule. They held the financial strings and the staff. The nationalist movements did not have the people, the professional technocrats of the old Communists. The old local Communist leaders are predators, but they're pragmatic', said Vladmir Degoyev, a history professor at Vladikavkaz University. He explained that the power of the ex-Communists had deep economic roots – not only were they backed by Moscow, but also by the mafia, which sprang up during the enormous black markets of the Gorbachev years. 'They rub each other's backs. The functionary needs education, marriage and pocket money, so he takes in one of these 'dealers' and makes sure he's left in peace by the tax authorities and so on.'

By 1994, apart from the extreme case of Chechnya, where Dzhokhar Dudayev's radical nationalists had their backs against the wall, there was only Ingushetia to be brought into line. This presented a unique problem to the central authorities. Unlike the other republics, Ingushetia had no ready-made loyal leadership left over from Soviet days. Instead, there was the independent-minded Aushev, at the head of a resentful, war-bloodied population, and he was demanding a high price for stability – Ingushetia had to be taken seriously. The republic wouldn't take Chechnya's separatist path, but it wanted true political and economic autonomy; it wouldn't attack North Ossetia, but it wanted a new capital city of its own; it wouldn't promote radical nationalism, but it wanted full rehabilitation, to put its history of war and deportation behind. Moscow essentially agreed to the lot.

The deal between Moscow and the Ingush was unique in the North

Caucasus. The Russian parliament authorised the funding of a new capital called Magas – or Sun City – just below the foothills of the Caucasus and, during 1994–1997, the government allowed Ingushetia to set up an off-shore tax haven as a way of bringing in funding for economic development. The sleepy republic enthusiastically set about transforming itself into what Aushev, a decorated Afghanistan veteran, promised would be 'a luxury, well-built, interesting republic – like Hong Kong, Singapore, Malta.'

The idea of Magas was so ambitious it was bizarre – a town was to sprout from empty fields near the archeological site of an ancient Alan settlement also called Magas. Instead of holding audiences in his provincial town hall in Nazran, Aushev would be housed in a handsome presidential palace surrounded by government office buildings. An artist's impression showed a collage of crescents, squares, shady areas and pleasant residential blocks modelled more on Western suburbia than the Soviet look. This was rehabilitation not through reinvention, but straight-forward invention.

When I visited in 1996, the sole visible sign of Magas was a stone marker inscribed with the words: 'Here the capital of the republic of Ingushetia will be built'. Beyond, there were only empty fields and the mountain chain to the south. But work had begun on the infrastructure and the Ingush really seemed to believe the project would take off. 'By the year 2000, we'll have nine neighbourhoods – that's 10,000 people', said Boris Khaniyev, the deputy director of the building project. 'By 2010, there'll be 30,000 people. There'll be hospitals, a sports complex, a river-front park, a concert hall.'

About 5,000 firms registered in the off-shore zone, which gave sub-stantial tax breaks, bringing in $100 million in investments after 18 months of operation, according to one report. The money was poured into Aushev's dream and the republic began crawling with a strange collection of Turkish, Slovak and even Scottish builders flown in to work on Magas and a variety of other projects. There was the Assa hotel in Nazran, schools, streets of western-style semi-detached houses, petrol stations, two factories, three electricity stations and a bigger airport. People came from neighbouring regions simply to gawk.

Such largesse was criticised in Moscow as spoiling Ingushetia, allowing them to create a legal black hole and drain the Russian tax coffers, which in turn meant pensions and salaries couldn't be paid across the country. Under pressure to tighten the budget purse strings, the Kremlin eventually annulled the off-shore zone. There had been some truth to the accusations, given the near-bankrupt conditions of the Russian state, but critics missed the point that the republic's particular circumstances required a highly unusual solution. In fact, Moscow showed rare skill in dealing with the Ingush; here was an example of how a minority could be integrated into a new type of Russian Federation.

The Ingush did Moscow a huge favour by not declaring independence along with the Chechens in 1991 and, in 1994, with Russian troops soon to move in against Chechnya, their loyalty would be needed more than ever before. The Ingush of course deny that they were bought off. It is true, that Magas only received Russian parliamentary approval in December 1995, a year after the Chechnya war began. But the project first received the blessing of President Boris Yeltsin as early as April 1994, well before the war and just as the situation was really deteriorating. The off-shore zone was approved in June 1994. Once the troops went in, many Ingush volunteered to fight alongside the Chechens and one of the first armoured columns to advance on Chechnya was ambushed while still inside Ingushetia. But in general Ingushetia remained quiet. Aushev, while an outspoken opponent to Moscow's invasion, worked hard to keep his republic from being sucked into the conflict – any support for the Chechens was given on a strictly unofficial level. For Ingushetia, the deal brought some of the rehabilitation it needed after Communism. For Moscow, it was money well spent.

## Nazran, Ingushetia

*Aushev has charisma and he knows it – fixing you with his brilliant blue-green eyes, wearing his Soviet general's uniform in Ingushetia and a suit when in Moscow. He may always travel the republic in a fleet of foreign cars, but he has the common touch, often attending football matches at Nazran's dusty little stadium, separated from the sunflower-seed spitting crowd by a rustic, but dignified box in the stands. When the loud speaker announces that the president is attending, people clap.*

*Aushev's presence is also strong in Moscow. The population of Ingushetia is little over 250,000, smaller than many cities, yet Aushev's ideas are big and win respect because he is a new type of Caucasus leader – neither the rifle-waving nationalist, nor the functionary of old who will do anything to curry favour.*

*A full-length portrait of a tall, fierce-looking man, one of the builders of the mysterious Ingush castles high in the Caucasus, hangs in his office. That's how Aushev sees himself – a builder, breaking with the Soviet era, returning to old Caucasian values, and forging an entirely new type of partnership with the Russian Federation. Back to the future.*

*His enthusiasm and ambitions are infectious, sometimes incredible.*

*'There's no danger of us going independent. We don't see that as a cure-all. The ordinary man on the street couldn't give a damn about independence', he says.*

*'What we want is for Magas to be one of the most beautiful cities in the Russian Federation in 20 years. It will certainly be the newest. No one has done this before, started from scratch – only Peter the Great when he*

*built Saint Petersburg. We want to have a world-standard republic, to have a market economy. Tourists will come to our beautiful mountains. Our republic may be small, but it will be known around the world.'*

Aushev aims beyond Magas and the hotels and factories. This is the real challenge and opportunity of his Ingushetia: 'We want to break the cycle of tragedy that has always surrounded us and the Chechens. Correcting those historical mistakes – that's the most important.'

# PART 4

# The Chechen Wolf

*Only one nation refused to submit to the psychology of submission ... the Chechens. The strange thing was that everybody feared them and no one prevented them from living as they liked. The authorities who had owned the country for 30 years could not force them to respect their laws. ... No Chechen ever tried to be of service or to please the authorities. Their attitude towards them was proud and hostile.*

Alexander Solzhenitsyn on the Chechens during the deportations.

## 1. REVOLUTION

*Grozny*

*At dusk, life fades from the Chechen capital. Dzhokhar Dudayev's regime is shaky, and armoured cars and men with automatic rifles guard the entrances to the presidential palace square. Trickles of people still go out to buy cigarettes at kiosks or get something to eat at the market place which flickers with the light of oil lamps and candles. Knots of men talk in low voices in the shadow of doorways, or squat unseen against the wall. No one spends longer than necessary outside. At the great concrete hulk of the presidential palace, there's still a light burning in President Dudayev's office on the ninth floor. Maybe it's for propaganda purposes. Or perhaps he really is working, building his dream of an independent state, stamping decrees with the lone-wolf symbol of the Republic of Chechnya-Ichkeria.*

*At dark, young Chechen blades appear for another night of revving their fancy cars and racing down the deserted avenues. This is night life, Grozny style. Flush with the foreign currency earnings of a hundred dubious deals, the youths treat their BMWs badly, just to show how little they care. I'm told there's even a competition where drivers speed up a ramp and try to jump a deep 20-metre gap in the Minutka traffic circle just down from the centre. Bets are laid in thousands of dollars; bodies, vehicles are broken.*

*Tonight it's handbrake turns. I join the guards at one of the barricades near the presidential palace, facing Prospekt Lenina. Just down the avenue the lads are revving their engines and shouting through the windows at each other in gutteral Chechen. There's a roar and the cars take it in turns to race up the avenue towards us. About 50 metres short they hit the handbrake and skid in a rough 180-degree turn, then burn back up to the starting point in a howl of tyres.*

*Down the street behind us, there's a burst of automatic rifle fire. I start, but the guards pay no attention. Then I hear shouting, laughter and more shots. A red military signal flare sails over the presidential palace square behind us and a dog begins to bark, setting off a mad chain reaction of barking. I ask the guard if everything is OK.*

*'Quiet night tonight,' he says.*

In the autumn of 1994 the Chechen revolution of General Dzokhar Dudayev was near meltdown. Three years from independence day, the Soviet state had vanished. Lenin's statue had been ripped down, leaving only his iron feet sticking from the top of the pedestal. The Chechen green-red-white flag, with a black wolf lying under the full moon, was all that told you a new state had been created. That and the day of rest on Friday, the Moslem sabbath. In a city built for 400,000 people, there was a giant bazaar well stocked with everything from assault rifles to silk dresses – all unaccounted for and untaxed – but not much else. I counted one bookshop, two restaurants and one empty department store. There were few working telephones and almost everyone was unemployed. To enter Chechnya you had to drive through Russian troops mounting a blockade on the border, accentuating the feeling you'd left Russia far behind.

Everywhere, there were signs of a revolution which had collapsed half way up the slope. The police directing traffic were Dudayev police, Chechens, not Russian or Soviet. Yet, slightly unnervingly, they still wore the blue uniform of the Soviet road cops, the same as in Moscow or Vladivostok. Dudayev's Chechnya had changed timezone. Clocks were given a twist one hour behind Moscow, breaking the tyranny of the Russian capital's standard time, but only independence supporters had their watches on 'Dudayev time', with the rest still on Moscow time, where it had been all their lives. Down at Minutka traffic circle a huge Soviet-style banner proclaimed 'Freedom – 1991' over the painting of a wolf. 'What freedom are they talking about? Freedom is when you've got a bit of money in your pocket and we haven't had that for years now', grumbled my driver.

The enthusiasts gossipped and whiled away the time in the main square outside the 11-storey presidential palace, a grim concrete affair built by the Soviets. The elders, in high Astrakhan hats, baggy jodhpurs and leather riding boots sat on benches among the rose beds and discussed the uncertain future with young men wearing sharp suits, camouflage or the black jeans and jacket of the presidential guard. Both generations carried rifles. Inside the palace were guards wearing something between an admiral's and a bellboy's uniform. They slouched against the wall or squatted on the floor chatting and eating sunflower seeds. Only their loaded automatics looked serious. I caught one guard, a curly forelock poking from his beret, sniffing a red rose plucked from one of the large flowerbeds in the main square. He wanted to go to America.

There were a lot of Dudayev opponents outside Grozny, but at the main square, you would not hear a word breathed against the revolution or Dzhokhar, as they called him. 'For 70 years, we didn't see the light, the meaning of life', murmured Mohammed, a young man who gave me a lift in his brand new Volvo on my first day. 'Now we've had three years of independence and we've never been better off. The Russians just want our oil. But we've decided we want it too, and we want to be able to sell it to whomever we want – Russia, Britain, whomever.' The black gold, which had disappeared into Moscow's coffers under Soviet rule, was important to the revolution. Reserves were meagre, but there was the huge business of refining other people's crude.

When I asked Economy Minister Taimaz Abubakarov why independent Chechnya was in ruins if it could now sell the oil anywhere, he calmly said he could answer me in five points. But people were high-strung in Chechnya in September 1994. The Russian blockade had little physical effect, but it caused psychological damage, a siege mentality. So Abubakarov, sitting under a portrait of Mikhail Gorbachev, the man who had made so many revolutions possible, expanded to some 10 points. He never did answer the question.

'If you look at who supports us you see it's the people without money. Those against us are the people who always had money, they're the people who 10 years ago lived well because they were in the KGB or the special services working for the Russians. Our opponents are ready to sign any document that the Russians give them on the status of Chechnya and this is what they're paid for. We don't need money, we need independence.'

It was true that many Chechens looked as if they really didn't need money. Despite the blockade there was meat and fruit in the markets, and in the villages people lived in far more solid and spacious houses than their peers in the alcohol-and-poverty-wracked Russian countryside. But later I found that, in most cases, this wealth was deceptive. The majority of ordinary people earned extra money in the late 1980s by roaming Russia and Central Asia doing seasonal work as builders and lorry drivers. The gruelling work brought in cash and then the men and their familes would build a handsome house with their own hands. The whole process could take years, up to a decade. Ordinary Chechens lived well, in solid, private homes, but they were not rich – there was a difference.

So when the economics minister talked about not needing money, he could only have been referring to the men inside the brick palaces and castillos rising out of corn fields around Grozny, the men gliding around potholes and stray animals in German import cars and even the odd Rolls Royce or Ferrari Testarossa. This was the new class of super rich, mainly counterfeit money men, oil mafiosi and the more successful 'shuttle traders' – Chechens who flew abroad, bought bulk electronic goods or clothing and sold them at considerable profits back in Russia. These were men who really didn't need more money and for whom the revolution, and the freedom to sell oil anywhere, had been a roaring success.

At the same time there were cholera scares, and hospitals in Dudayev-controlled territory were running out of everything from aspirin to anaesthetic. Often the water or electricity was cut off and hospitals would temporarily shut down. The only schools functioning were those where the parents chipped in or the teachers didn't mind working for nothing. At the First Republican Hospital in central Grozny they had no supplies and the head doctor refused to talk to me. As I left, a nurse explained the situation in a whisper, then burst into tears and begged me not to publish her name. Up in the northwest of Chechnya, Dudayev's gunmen threatened to shoot me and my driver, an opposition supporter, when we tried to visit several village schools and hospitals. 'Provocateurs' they called us.

---

*Chechnya is not a subject of Russia, it is a subject of Allah*

Chechen independence slogan.

The Chechens' overthrow of the local Communists and subsequent declaration of independence from the USSR on November 1 1991 seems extraordinary now, a wild mistake for which hundreds of thousands of people were made to pay. But there was also something inevitable about it. In 1990 the Chechens were on a roller coaster. As president of the Russian Federation within the Soviet Union, Boris Yeltsin was pushing for the breakup of that great corrupt Communist monolith. 'Grab as much sovereignty as you can swallow', Yeltsin famously urged the Soviet republics. The Chechens adored him. This was their version of the phenomenon taking place across the whole region – the search for *reabilitatsiya*.

The inspiration was Dzhokhar Dudayev. He was an odd figure for a nationalist, quasi-religious leader. Before taking up the job of leader of the anti-Communist National Congress of Chechen People in November 1990, he had been a major general in the Soviet airforce, commanding the nuclear bomber base in Tartu, a town in Soviet-held Estonia. The position alone meant he was a loyal Communist Party man, trusted by the KGB. He had served in Afghanistan, taking part in the merciless bombing of civilians and was, by his own admission, a somewhat lapsed Moslem. His wife was a Russian called Alla who painted and wrote poems, without much success.

There were other reasons to doubt Dudayev and where he would take Chechnya, doubts about his nose-thumbing at the Kremlin, his threats of holy war. Was he reckless, insane? 'I didn't like the fact he was a general. Generals have the mentality of war; they don't know how to rule, they know how to fight', a Chechen friend told me long after the fact, when it was already too late. 'I remember when Dudayev came to the hills and you know, he didn't say how beautiful it was, or what businesses could be set up, or anything like that. He said what grand territory this would be for a guerrilla war. Right then, I knew I didn't like him.'

But Dudayev was easy to sell to most Chechens. He was a general, the first Chechen who made it through the ranks to the top, a real fighter. Although he had served the Russians all his life, he was clearly not afraid of them. When this dashing pilot with a black pencil moustache invoked the Chechen independence heroes and Allah, his supporters – mostly the great mass of poor, rural Chechens – were thrilled. Even the contradictions of his background could be explained away by saying that Dzokhar had secretly plotted revenge against Russia his entire life, even as he reached the dizzy heights of nuclear bomber general, and that now his moment had come. Others pointed out that, while in the Baltics, he had shown his nationalist leanings by refusing to repress the Estonian independence movement. Besides, he had gone through the essential Chechen experience: a few days after he was born in Chechnya in 1944, the deportations took place and the first thing he knew was the cold and humiliation of the Kazakh steppe.

As the day of the USSR's final demise in December 1991 approached, Chechen nationalists could taste victory over the entrenched Communists and Dudayev was their prophet. 'A slave who does not try to free himself is twice a slave,' he said, words that would become part of his personality cult, the Dzhokhar canon.

In August 1991, a hardline Soviet junta in Moscow mounted a desperate bid to stop the tide and keep the Soviet Union together. Boris Yeltsin threw down the gauntlet and declared the Communist putsch illegal. His barricaded parliament building in Moscow became a symbol of the alternative to the putchists – freedom, democracy and national self-determination. He called for support from all democrats and prepared to fight off the tanks. One of the thousands who rallied to the barricades is said to have been none other than Shamil Basayev, the future warlord in Abkhazia, but then a student in Moscow. In all the regions and outlying republics, local leaders were called upon to stand and be counted. For most Communist *appartchiks*, like the Chechen Communist Party First Secretary Doku Zavgayev, it was a matter of guessing right – who would come out on top, the junta or Yeltsin? Slippery Zavgayev sat on the fence, but instead of going unnoticed, he became conspicuous by his silence and in stepped Dudayev, loudly condemning the junta and calling on all Chechens to support Yeltsin's democratic movement. It was the breakthrough Dudayev had needed.

Zavgayev's government, like the sickly junta in Moscow, tried to stop the inevitable, banning the nationalists, imprisoning some of the leaders and declaring a state of emergency. But the Dudayev faction had the numbers and the energy. Every day, large demonstrations against Soviet rule were held in the centre of Grozny. On 22 August, demonstrators seized the television tower and Dudayev went on air to proclaim a revolution. Two weeks later, on 6 September, Dudayev's paramilitary National Guard stormed the Supreme Soviet, or local Communist parliament. The Russian head of Grozny's *gorkom*, the town committee, was either flung or flung himself (depending on whom you talk to) out of a third-floor window and died. On 15 September, the Supreme Soviet held its last session. Surrounded by National Guard fighters, the parliament voted to dissolve itself and for the resignation of Doku Zavgayev. The revolution was almost complete.

There was still significant opposition to Dudayev, particularly among the educated. Some opposed the revolution because of its strident nationalism, others because the downfall of the old regime meant the end of their status as a pampered Soviet elite. But that initial violence had created an unstoppable momentum which would only be given further impulse by the increasingly high-handed reaction to events from Moscow.

Dubious elections were held on 27 October, 1991 which Dudayev won overwhelmingly, polling 90 per cent with a turnout of 72 per cent, according to the official, revolutionary figures. Unofficial estimates were that turnout was as low as 10 to 12 per cent. The truth was almost irrelevant. As in all revolutions, energy and myth are what count and Dudayev had both. Five days later he signed a decree affirming Chechnya's independence from the Soviet Union.

Although Moscow – particularly the parliament Speaker Ruslan Khasbulatov – had initially supported Dudayev in his battle against Zavgayev, relations deteriorated quickly. Vice President Alexander Rutskoi, also an airforce ex-general, blustered that the Chechens were getting out of hand and ordered them to lay down their weapons and behave like orderly Russian citizens. He claimed that Dudayev was supported by a gang of no more than 250 men. Dudayev hit back by declaring a state of war, which prompted Rutskoi to make yet another inflammatory speech about 'anarchy' in Chechnya. President Yeltsin ordered 'illegal armed groups' to hand in their weapons or face measures from the federal centre. Dudayev ignored the ultimatum and went ahead with his election, only to have the vote's legitimacy questioned by Khasbulatov.

The game of brinksmanship went one step further on 8 November when Yeltsin responded to Dudayev's declaration of independence by ordering a state of emergency – a suspension of constitutional rights – in Chechnya and Ingushetia. Hundreds of troops were dispatched to Grozny to 'restore order' and defend 'Russia's territorial integrity.'

Dudayev was ready. When the troops flew into the Khankala military airport in eastern Grozny they found themselves surrounded by the National Guard and faced with the choice of bitter fighting or a humiliating surrender. Simultaneously, Shamil Basayev gave a taste of the ruthlessness that would mark the Chechen–Russian conflict by hijacking an Aeroflot passenger jet with 178 people in. The plane was forced to fly to Ankara on 9 November and, after about five hours on the runway, turned around and flown to Grozny where the hostages were released unharmed. Basayev said his sole aim was to draw attention to the Russian troop deployment. Even the Turkish authorities were convinced, saying that Basayev hadn't carried out 'a terrorist act', but a 'protest act.' It was an explosive background to Dudayev's presidential inauguration that same day, 9 November, with tens of thousands of demonstrators gathering on Freedom Square outside the presidential palace.

On the edge of war, Moscow blinked. The Russian parliament refused to endorse Yeltsin's state of emergency and Yeltsin, as if realising how close he'd come to spilling blood, scrapped his own decree. The interior ministry troops in Grozny were put on buses and made to leave Chechnya. Dudayev had won his first showdown with Moscow and, out in the street, the nationalist crowds who propelled him to power were jubilant.

Bloodshed had been avoided, but the drama was full of warnings of what was to come. On the one hand, Moscow proved incapable both of taking decisive action and negotiating in good faith. On the other hand, Dudayev discovered that setting his countrymen against the Russian bogeyman was the key to his popularity. By standing up to the troops at the airport, he had also unmasked the physical weakness of the new Russian state. In essence, these factors would remain unchanged for three more years, taking Russian-Chechen relations through stages of paralysis, misunderstanding and finally total war. The dye was cast.

## 2. END OF INNOCENCE

*I wasn't looking for power, riches or duties. I've always had just one idea – to fight for the Chechen people's right to independence. That's my life's goal and I will not shy away from it. Not under any conditions, or any pressure.*

Dzhokhar Dudayev.

Dudayev's plans were printed up in a landslide of official books and pamphlets, like *Thorny Path to Freedom*, where Dzhokhar was shown on the hardback cover in a pilot's seat, smiling and giving a thumbs up. The president promised equal rights for the approximately 900,000 Chechens and the Russian minority of just under 300,000. Both languages were to be official. Although the republic would be independent and militarily neutral, it aimed for close economic ties to Russia. All religions were to have equal freedom and anyone arrested for political motives under the old regime would be set free.

There wasn't much wrong with the programme and, although the secession itself had been technically dubious, Chechnya's aspirations unquestionably had moral and historical force. The Chechen people had never willingly joined Russia; in fact they'd rebelled at every opportunity for generations, and the break-up of the Soviet Union was an especially good opportunity to effect a break from Moscow. On a moral level at least, there was no reason why Chechnya should not be allowed to go the way of only slightly larger Estonia, or any of the other ex-Soviet republics.

But those booklets with their high-minded titles and pedantic intro-
ductions had barely been printed before they began looking like museum
pieces. In less than a year since Dudayev changed the clocks, ethnic-
Russians in their thousands began fleeing Chechnya, the economy went
into terminal decline, and a new class of super-rich *biznesmen* took over
the government, while cut throats took over the streets. There was a
minister of economics, but no economy, a foreign minister, but no
diplomatic recognition, mountains of presidential decrees on law and
order, but only the rule of the gun.

All this served as rich material in 1994 when Russian politicians tried
to justify the war by calling Chechnya the 'first criminal state' But the
uncomfortable and much-ignored reality was that Russian politicians
and businessmen, if not actual Kremlin policy, were themselves present
at the birth of the Dudayev era. Most of what was happening in
Chechnya could have at least been curtailed by Russia, yet the situation
continued unchanged for three long years. As any Moscow businessman
paying protection money to the mafia knows, being left in peace costs
money. So it seems likely that Chechnya was left free to rob and swindle,
while Russia collected its cut. Independent Chechnya, in a sense, was
just another shady joint-venture.

Chechens wanting to run contraband had little trouble breaking the
blockade imposed by Yeltsin. On one side was the long rural border
with Dagestan, which did little to implement Moscow's directives; on
the other side was Ingushetia, where a formal border hadn't even been
demarcated since the split up of Chechnya-Ingushetia. What there was
in the way of a military blockade – manned by underpaid, unmotivated
Russian troops – soon became little more than a human cash till. For a
price any vehicle could get through and, if necessary, trucks could be
driven along dirt tracks where the Russian soldiers had no intention of
patrolling. All the blockade managed was to criminalise trade, cutting
off legitimate businessmen and boosting the role of black marketeers.

Trains which came up through Chechnya along the great trans-
Caucasus Rostov-Baku line were raided in Wild West style – 559 trains in
1993 alone, the Russians claimed. Since Grozny's Sheikh Mansur airport
remained open, unrestricted flights fed a first-rate arms market, and
Grozny became the gateway to Russia both for contraband and legal, but
wholly untaxed imported goods. The phenomena of 'shuttle traders' was
common all over the former Soviet Union, but tax-free Chechen goods
beat all competitors. Grozny's bazaar became an unlikely shopping haven
for the North Caucasus, with the biggest and cheapest range of goods:
Japanese televisions and videos from Hong Kong and the Arab Emirates,
French perfumes, western sports wear, Turkish woodwork and leather.
Perhaps the most famous section was the arms bazaar, against the wall of
the main telephone exchange. Here, tough-looking men in dark glasses,

leather jackets and short haircuts, could sell you anything from the Chechen-produced Borz (Wolf) sub-machine gun to an anti-tank rocket launcher, or heavier equipment. In a place where weapons were revered, this was Mecca.

The line between Russian officials turning a blind eye and actively working with the criminal regime for profit blurred on almost every front. Sergei Shakhrai, then Russia's nationalities minister – in charge of relations with ethnic minorities – said that 150 chartered flights a month were leaving Grozny, breaking Russian aviation laws. But there was a hollow ring to Moscow's complaints of the airport being a legal black hole. Without the cooperation of Russia's air traffic controllers it is unlikely the pilots would have taken off and landed in Grozny and they certainly couldn't have flown to the Baltics, Slovakia, or probably any of their other foreign destinations. Ultimately, diplomatic pressure could have been put on other countries not to accept Chechen planes, or the Russian air force could have simply enforced a no-fly zone.

Even though Chechnya had abandoned all Russian laws and declared itself independent, Moscow reportedly continued to pay federal funds for pensions and other social needs throughout 1992 and early 1993. How much of that money was stolen along the way and how much made it into pensioners' hands is another question. In another indication of how Moscow and Chechnya had decided to live with each other, Dudayev continued to enjoy semi-official status, listed in official publications as 'president' of Chechnya. In 1993 he even wrote warm letters to Yeltsin, wishing him luck in his struggle for power with the parliament. Phone links were not cut right up to the war, when planes blitzed the telephone exchange.

Perhaps the most convenient gift for a would-be independent micro state is an army, and that's exactly what the Chechens got in 1992. The ex-Soviet troops based in Grozny snuck out in a hurry, saying they were under threat from nationalist locals. By the Russian chief of staff's count, by June 1992, these troops had left behind 42 tanks, scores of other armoured vehicles, 145 mortars and other artillery pieces, and 40,000 firearms. There were mountains of heavy ammunition at the tank training base in Grozny, and exotic, but never substantiated rumours of nuclear materials at old military bases.

Again, the evidence is buried. The Russians' version that the arms were abandoned under duress is possibly correct. Between late 1991 and early 1992, there were continuous attacks by crowds of Chechens on the Grozny barracks, with the toughs who would grab the weapons hiding behind groups of civilians. Sometimes the raids led to bloodshed; 20 people were reportedly killed in one incident. According to Russian sources, the military believed that serious resistance would lead to a bloodbath. One army source said the Chechens were threatening the lives of the officers' families unless they left the republic. In Moscow, the consensus was that it was time to cut losses through negotiations and quit, and so the troops left – unarmed.

The man doing the negotiating (or dealing, depending on how you look at it) at this time, was the new minister of defence, Pavel Grachev. The Russian parliamentary enquiry into the Chechen war published a May 1992 telegram from Grachev, authorising the regional North Caucasus military headquarters to 'hand over' 50 per cent of the armour and other weaponry stationed in Chechnya to Dudayev, with the army evacuating the rest. Other reports say he was given 80 per cent. According to *Sevodnya* newspaper, Dudayev kept the lot. Even five years later, the question stood – how much of this arsenal was abandoned, how much of it sold, and if sold, by whom?

Big money was made in the oil bazaar. As part of the Soviet Union, Chechnya's small, but high-quality oil fields provided 90 per cent of the country's aviation oil, although only a fraction of the total petroleum output. By the 1990s, Chechnya's production was about 3.5 million tonnes a year, well below the republic's Soviet-era peak output. Easily recoverable reserves were increasingly limited and part of the oil reserves were now on the territory of Ingushetia.

The real cash cow, and the bulk of the Grozny installation's work, was refining crude from other regions, as well as charging for transit through Chechnya's section of the trans-Caucasus pipeline. The profits were Dudayev's best chance to overcome the debilitating poverty caused by a squeeze in Russian funding and his own government's corruption. By using oil funds for the economy and social needs, he might yet have saved his young republic. Instead, the money vanished.

Here the collusion of Russian and Chechen officials was undeniable. Blockade or not, oil arrived regularly from Siberia, then exited Grozny across to the Russian Black Sea terminal of Novorossiisk. According to a Russian parliamentary enquiry, in 1992 the prime minister Yegor Gaidar and his successor (then the deputy premier for energy) Viktor Chernomyrdin, were directly involved in this oil trade. The enquiry found that the Grozny refineries handled 15 million tonnes of oil in 1991, 9.7 million in 1992 and 3.5 million the next. Yusup Soslambyekov, who held various top posts in Chechnya before falling out with Dudayev, said that in 1992 four million tonnes of diesel, 1.6 million tonnes of petrol, 125,500 tonnes of kerosine and 36,600 tonnes of technical oil were shipped out from Chechnya. At world market prices, he estimated, these products were worth approximately $130 million.

'Of course, certain high-ranking circles of the Russian government were involved in this oil Eldorado, since Russian oil even in 1994 was going through Chechnya,' Soslambyekov said. 'There was no mention of any of this in the state budget. Meanwhile, transport of Russian-Chechen oil products to other parts of the Commonwealth of Independent States, and also to Novorossiisk and Tuapse en route to further markets, amounted to tens of millions of tonnes.' Soslambyekov became widely discredited in Chechnya – and had an axe to grind against Dudayev – but his charge was undeniable: 'Neither agricultural equipment, nor food, nor new technology to boost the Chechen economy, nor clothes were bought with the oil money.'

One of Dudayev's greatest financial coups was when newly independent Estonia switched to its own currency in 1992 and instead of returning its reserve of Soviet rubles to the Central Bank in Moscow, sent them to Chechnya. Planeloads of Soviet rubles – legal tender in Russia until the end of Moscow's transition to Russian rubles in the summer of 1993 – were flown in and deposited in Grozny. Later – during the war, in 1995 – I saw children playing in the street with armfuls of the by-then worthless banknotes near the ruins of the Central Bank, which, like the rest of the centre, had been bombed to the ground.

Amid this chaos, individual Chechen entrepreneurs used their republic as a launchpad for organised crime, knowing they could not be pursued by Russian police. In a particularly lurid case, two Chechen brothers sent to London to organise printing of Chechen currency were murdered in a Marylebone penthouse, sparking a vendetta in which a completely innocent British woman – the sister in law of the brothers' convicted murderer – was gunned down in Woking by mistake.

According to the 1995 book *The Criminal World in Russia*, Chechens in Moscow were heavily involved in prostitution rings, taxi firms, protection rackets, and auto markets. Chechens in Saint Petersburg organised transit of black market goods from the Baltics; a Chechen counterfeit money gang in Saint Petersburg was broken up in 1994. Luxury cars were a speciality. One common scam described starts in Germany, where the owner of a top-of-the-range Mercedes or BMW is forced to sell his car at a cut price or face having it stolen. By the time he reports the car stolen, after an agreed delay of several days, the vehicle is well on its way to Chechnya, helped along by corrupt customs agents. Fake documents are supplied in Grozny and the car is ready for the mafioso to use, resell, or even resell then steal a second time. Chechnya filled with foreign-made cars, often with their Swedish or German numberplates still attached.

But the most spectacular thieves were the *vosdushniky*, literally 'air men', who could create wealth out of nothing, either by printing fake money or through bank fraud. The most common method was for a ficticious company in the provinces to use a forged promissory note – or *aviso* in Russian – to show it was paying a second company, in Moscow, via bank transfer. Even though the first company had in reality paid nothing, the second company would collect its 'transferred' money in cash.

In June 1992, the Russian interior ministry said that mafia groups around Russia, particularly Chechen, had siphoned off 30 billion rubles from the Central Bank with fake *avisos*. The authorities said they had the situation under control, but that July, the interior ministry said that the missing monies actually amounted to several hundred billions of rubles. In a single fraud, the biggest bank robbery in Russian history, a Chechen gang was accused of siphoning off 60 billion rubles (then $700 million). Banking links with Chechnya were finally shut down.

Once again, the *aviso* scandal had the lingering whiff – although as yet unproven – of cooperation on the Russian side. Were the Central Bank functionaries regulating these huge money transfers really so incompetent that they could not institute thorough checks? Did the Central Bank have to take so long to shut down links with the Chechen banking system? Dudayev agreed that 'hundreds of billions' of rubles had been stolen and that some of the fake *avisos* originated from Chechnya; but he denied that his government had been involved.

It must be stressed that, to a large extent, the Chechen criminals simply mirrored what was happening around them. In the early 1990s Russia was in the grip of criminal organisations and, in many places, the authorities were part of the racket – that was the result of Soviet-era corruption and the general lack of law and order in democratic Russia. Few Moscow businesses were able to operate without paying protection in the early years. Neither were the Chechens the only ones committing bank fraud. Dudayev, however, proved particularly powerless to stem the rot. He admitted there was a problem, but then blamed everything on Russian plots, avoiding all responsibility, as one by one his tenets published in those hopeful booklets fell by the wayside.

There was an attempted coup against Dudayev in 1992, and the next year he entered a protracted battle with his parliament – which opposed his plans for greater presidential powers. Dudayev responded with a dubious opinion poll which claimed to show he had 97 per cent support. Then, when he still faced deadlock, in April 1993, Dudayev dissolved parliament, imposed a curfew and began rule by presidential decree. Again, Chechnya eerily mirrored the situation in Russia, where in October that same year President Yeltsin dissolved his parliament with tank fire and rewrote the constitution to give himself sweeping new powers.

Russians, who had been promised peace under the new Chechen republic, were leaving in their thousands for the southern Russian regions of Stavropol and Krasnodar. Many of those who stayed faced constant harassment, or were even forced from their apartments and robbed or killed. Again, Dudayev acknowledged the thuggery, but blamed it on Russian provocateurs – nothing to do with him.

Unlike Chechens, ethnic-Russians did not have the extended family network which guaranteed plenty to eat and places to stay in times of poverty or trouble. Likewise, they fell outside the vendetta system, making them soft targets for any criminal, who knew the Dudayev police would never intervene. One elderly Russian pensioner in Grozny, known by everyone as *tyotya*, or 'auntie' Natasha, was paid a visit by young Chechens at her tiny cottage in central Grozny. When the youths found nothing better to take, they ripped out her gold teeth.

'In the early 1990s, they could get away with anything as long as they knew you were Russian, not one of their own,' said Ludmilla, a half-Russian, half-Armenian woman who fled Grozny to live in Kabardino-Balkaria. 'I didn't dare walk around on my own. In the market one day, a guy just grabbed me and started to drag me away, but my sister was there and started screaming and we were both able to run away. After that, our parents told us to come here. They stayed behind. Our Chechen neighbours were good and they would defend us. But my father, who worked at the oil refinery, would be called a Russian pig. He's not even Russian, he's Armenian!'

Again, Chechnya was not an isolated case, rather an extreme version of events taking place in many newly independent republics of the collapsed Soviet Union – where an estimated 25 million ethnic-Russians became minorities and foreigners overnight. They left in droves from civil war and poverty in Tajikistan, they suffered political and linguistic discrimination in the Baltic republics. Of course, little did those Russians fleeing Chechnya know that they were only the first wave of refugees. The second would come in 1994 when Moscow sent the army in and the trapped ethnic-Russians suddenly found themselves being bombed by their so-called protectors. By the end of the war in 1996, the Russian community had almost vanished.

As elsewhere, the Russians had enjoyed a special status in Chechnya before the revolution, dominating the authorities and holding most of the skilled jobs, especially in the oil industry, where 90 per cent of the employees were Russian. Few Chechens were put through the oil institute and qualified. Chechens who did study at the institute were usually sent to other regions of the Soviet Union. Central policy was that Chechens were not to be allowed power or prestige. As a result the anti-Russian aggression was not only a tragedy for the ethnic-Russians, but left the Chechen economy debilitated.

None of this was what Dudayev promised in those first heady days. The general who wore pin-stripe suits rather than uniform so that people would not mistake him for a dictator became just that – a banana republic strongman. Unable to manage his own tiny country, he turned his attention to baiting Russia. He made the Confederation of Peoples of the Caucasus a vehicle for his futile and dangerous dream of uniting the nationalist forces in all the North Caucasus against Russia. The only diplomatic 'recognition' he won was from the toppled and discredited first Georgian president, Zviad Gamsakhurdia, who lived in exile in Grozny. Dudayev, like Gamsakhurdia before him, was becoming a megalomaniac. When he thought Russia was not big enough for his one million countrymen to take on, he flew to Iraq, Jordan and Sudan, declaring his support for a 'fight of Islam against Russia, the United States and the West in general.'

## 3. PHONY WAR

Negotiations to get Dudayev to sign the federation treaty, which would put Chechnya within the Russian Federation, collapsed every time. President Yeltsin was still refusing to meet with the renegade airforce general, who insisted on being treated as a head of state. Bluster had proved useless – Dudayev thrived on bluster and counter bluster – and by 1994 there was growing pressure for concrete measures. So, that summer, Moscow launched what looked like a textbook secret war, but in fact was the first step into the quagmire.

A Russian-backed coalition of anti-Dudayev figures based in the northwestern Nadterechny region of Chechnya formed an Interim Council and, in August 1994, announced that they held legitimate power in the republic. Immediately, the Interim Council began spending covert Russian funds to build an army and accentuate the dire economic situation in Dudayev-controlled areas. Opposition-held hospitals and schools were renovated, medicine was made available and teachers began receiving salaries. 'We need to win the hearts of the people', an opposition spokesman said at the main base in Znamenskoye. He told me his forces had just received two million dollars from Moscow. Along with the money came rifles, tanks, helicopters, and men. But as in any covert operation, setting up an opposition to Dudayev was considerably more complicated than imagined – and Moscow soon proved how poorly it understood this tiny republic it was trying to force under its control.

The first problem was the opposition leaders themselves. These warlords – called the 'healthy forces' of Chechnya by Yeltsin – were a dubious set of characters for the Kremlin's avowed fight to eradicate the Dudayev 'bandits'. Officially the opposition was led by a figure from the traditional pro-Russian north of Chechnya, Umar Avturkhanov, who flew to Moscow and met with Kremlin staff. But he did not have broad support, and few people wanted to join what was already suspected to be a Russian client army. Next to Avturkhanov was Beslan Gantemirov, a rich man in his thirties who as former mayor of Grozny had originally helped Dudayev, but then fallen out. And there was the infamous Ruslan Labazanov, an imposingly-built debt collector and convict, and another former associate who had turned against Dudayev.

The most popular anti-Dudayev leader was none other than former Russian parliament speaker Ruslan Khasbulatov. It was less than a year since the bloody anti-Yeltsin rebellion in Moscow and Khasbulatov was free again after being amnestied from jail by the new parliament. When he returned to his native Chechnya, he was given a hero's welcome, seen as a model of the successful yet rebellious Chechen, and a man with stature matching that of Dzhokhar Dudayev. But because the Kremlin could not countenance Khasbulatov in Chechnya's presidential palace, backing instead went to the other, far less credible anti-Dudayev figures.

Another underlying problem with manufacturing a civil war was that the Chechens did not want a bloodbath. The society has deep-rooted methods for resolving internal conflicts, and consensus is the traditional way to solve disputes. Chechens on both sides of the divide often repeated that there had never been large-scale civil war in their nation. During that hot summer, hatred between the pro- and anti-Dudayev sides boiled. Loyalties were divided along clan lines and there was little room for reasoned debate. This was tribal. But although the *Dudayevsky* and *oppositsy*, as they were known, each had a few hundred armed men swathed in grenades, camouflage and mirror sunglasses, there was little combat. It was a phony war.

For propaganda purposes at least, the situation suited both sides. What Moscow called the 'internal Chechen conflict' neatly confirmed Russians' worst suspicions about Chechens as a violent people whose independence revolution had led only to disorder. Meanwhile in Grozny, the spectre of Russian military assistance to the opposition played into Dudayev's hands. For three years, he'd been ranting about fighting another great Caucasian war and now he could finally say with some justification that Moscow was preparing to invade.

The sheer quantity of weapons, the Chechens' fascination with guns, the endless cycle of vendettas, and Moscow's interference guaranteed that fighting would eventually escalate. In late September I stumbled on one of the more deadly battles to date: 20 to 30 Chechens died fighting each other in the blazing sun on a scrubby hillside outside the village of Tolstoy Yurt. A tank and an armoured personnel carrier were blown up, and columns of black smoke snaked up into the fine, end-of-summer sky. This battle caused real shock. The next day in Tolstoy Yurt hundreds of *oppositsy* men in trilbys and Astrakhan *papakhas* gathered for funerals, standing in knots around the open graves of those killed. One man, a relative, tried not to cry as fresh earth flew off the shovel with a swish. Everyone prayed, their palms turned up to the sky.

'There was treachery there,' a peasant with a deeply tanned and lined face said to me, telling me about some relative shot in the back. 'That's never happened in Chechnya, we don't shoot in the back.' I asked to see Khasbulatov, but was told that one of his cousins had been killed and he was in mourning and would see no one. Back in Grozny, everyone I talked to, even Dudayev people, whose side had apparently come off better in the battle, felt the same shock. 'How many killed? 30? This is terrible', a restaurant owner and diehard Dudayev fan said. This was a civil war no one wanted.

One detail from that day stuck in my mind. It was how confident Gantemirov looked when I saw him at his base in Tolstoy Yurt at the end of the battle. He was stylishly unshaven, had his black hair slicked back and a pistol wedged into the band of his new blue jeans. His little army had just been battered, but Gantemirov was remarkably calm, as if he knew help, a lot of help, would be coming soon.

It did. On 26 November 1994, Russian regular army soldiers and tanks secretly joined the opposition forces for a concerted attempt to capture Grozny. Russia's secret services had finally leapt into the quagmire. Fifty tanks, all with Russian mercenaries, drove into the city centre and at first the assault seemed to go well. Within hours the Russian news agency ITAR-TASS, without mentioning the Russian troops, announced that Ruslan Labazanov had captured the presidential palace. Then the reality surfaced: Russia's secret army had indeed got to the centre, but only to be demolished in a series of well-planned ambushes. Labazanov and his men ran for the hills of Tolstoy Yurt, leaving behind them streets strewn with burnt-out Russian armour and a number of Russian soldiers taken prisoner. According to Dudayev's government, 300 Russian and opposition Chechen soldiers died. The Dudayev people always exaggerated enemy losses, but anyone who saw the hulks of ambushed Russian troop carriers lying in the streets knew how one-sided the battle had been.

At first the Russian authorities, notably Defence Minister Pavel Grachev, squirmed and bluffed, denying any involvement in the battle. Dudayev responded by parading some 20 Russian POWs before journalists and Russian parliamentary envoys. On 28 November the rebel government even threatened to execute the men. Despite Moscow's continued denials, the prisoners publicly confessed to having been hired by the FSK (the successor agency to the KGB, later renamed again as the FSB). What's more, many had been recruited from the elite, regular army Kantemirovskaya and Tamanskaya divisions. One of these unfortunate characters, Nikolai Potekhin, said he had been promised $600 for a hastily prepared operation to come to the aid of Russians endangered in Chechnya. Other reports spoke of these mercenaries being paid $1,600–1,900 – all this in an army where ordinary soldiers are virtually slave labour and thousands of officers live in dormitory conditions. Such is the price of secret wars: when they go wrong, they become horribly public.

Moscow's policy had collapsed. First the failure to negotiate and now the failure to mount a *coup d'etat*, were broadcast all over the nation. The time of reckoning was close. Although Dudayev had won his second direct confrontation with the Russians, the situation was spinning far from his control. Warplanes appeared over Grozny after the battle and bombed the airport, killing half a dozen people and destroying fleets of training aircraft and agricultural planes. The thunder of bomb explosions interrupted a press conference by Dudayev, and journalists who were present still remember diving onto the floor, only to look up and see the general remaining calmly in his seat. Moscow insisted these were Chechen 'opposition' planes, but trying to maintain the fiction at this point was almost grotesque.

On 29 November, three days after the Grozny debacle, Yeltsin and his inner circle of a dozen advisors sat down in the Kremlin to decide their next step. This was no ordinary government meeting, but a gathering of the secretive Security Council. Omnipotent, this tiny group of officials held the fate of Chechnya in its hands and the decision didn't take long to make: send the army in; go all out; invade. Invading was a historic blunder, but consider the situation at the time. For three years, Moscow had ignored Chechnya and now its options had run out. Either the Kremlin recognised the rebel state as having some legitimacy by opening high-level talks with Dudayev, or it went further down the interventionist path.Yeltsin felt that talks with Dudayev, who had repeatedly insulted him and Russia, were impossible. A quick, decisive war, on the other hand, was attractive. The Chechens would be punished, Yeltsin would look good and his entire entourage, for various reasons, would profit.

One specific factor that added pressure for Yeltsin to take action in Chechnya was the need for a solution to the problem of the trans-Caucasus oil pipeline. The big investment deal in the Azeri offshore oil fields had been signed just that September and the Russian oil industry was racing to ensure that its pipeline was chosen over rival routes. That meant bringing Chechnya under control. It is often said that a pipeline could have been built around Chechnya, but that plan had a fatal flaw – it would take time, maybe several years, and that meant calm, long-term policies.

However, the principal forces behind the war were political. That winter, Yeltsin was already laying the groundwork for his re-election in 1996, just a year and a half away, and he was deeply unpopular, with approval ratings of around 8 per cent. He was hated by nationalists for breaking up the Soviet Union and blamed by disillusioned democracy supporters for the chaos of free market and democratic reforms. So cracking down on this tiny, but enfuriating corner of the Federation could become the centre piece of a grand return to law and order, an end to the chaos, or *bardak*, sweeping the country. Yeltsin was superb at gauging political moods, and he couldn't fail to notice the country's nostalgia for Soviet empire and Russian grandeur. Forcing Chechnya into line would signal that the superstate was safe in Yeltsin's hands. Finally, he'd be remembered as Yeltsin the preserver.

Two factors allowed Yeltsin to enact his almost childishly ill-conceived plan. One was overwhelming personal power accumulated under the constitution he himself forced through in 1993. The presidency was almost unimpeachable, the new parliament little more than a debating hall, making Yeltsin, like the tsars and Communist Party first secretaries in the Kremlin before him, more a ruler than democratic president. The second factor was that, like any royal, Yeltsin was highly influenced by his court entourage, particularly since the onset of health and drinking problems. Whoever had Yeltsin's ear had power and for almost all major decisions, no outside consultation was necessary – truly the politics of smoke-filled rooms.

Yeltsin's post-Soviet circle of idealistic liberals, pro-westerners and free marketeers had faded away by 1994, and with them opponents of an authoritarian crackdown in Chechnya. Radical reformist prime minister Yegor Gaidar had been sacked; human rights advisor Sergei Kovalev was ignored; foreign minister Andrei Kozyrev saw the writing on the wall and changed his pro-western tune, before, eventually, he too was sacked. The relatively moderate figures still in the Kremlin, like deputy prime minister Sergei Shakhrai or presidential chief of staff Sergei Filatov, similarly believed in the advantages of a short, sharp restoration of order in Chechnya to relaunch Yeltsin's presidency. The ambitious Shakhrai was particularly active, hoping to hold Yeltsin's coat tails when this bold new policy propelled the president forward.

Beating the drums loudest was the so-called 'party of war' within Yeltsin's inner circle. This included security forces ministers, former KGB officers who'd become confidants and hardline politicians. Each had his own career interests and pet projects. There was also a shared view that a war would kill off the liberal agenda, leading to a restoration of internal control and a newly aggressive foreign policy, particularly in the ex-Soviet Union – in short neo-imperialism.

The hardline entourage's chief instrument of power was the Security Council, a gathering of ministers, including all the security forces chiefs. Under its secretary, Oleg Lobov, a jowly, oily-voiced man who came from Yeltsin's hometown of Sverdlovsk in the Urals, the Council expanded its advisory role to become a decision-making unit. The organisation, which met behind closed doors and had no role in the constitution, had become one of Yeltsin's key institutions for running the country.

Not all the members of the Security Council were anti-reform or in favour of going to war, Prime Minister Viktor Chernomyrdin being the most notable opponent. But it was people like the ministers of the interior and the secret services, Viktor Yerin and Sergei Stepashin, who controlled the debate. Yerin, and to a lesser degree Stepashin, had long been hawks on Chechnya and backers of the push for a newly assertive Russian state. To them, internal crises meant power and resources and an end to the hated liberal reformers. Ideologically, they were supported by the nationalities (ethnic minorities) minister, Nikolai Yegorov, who'd been governor of Krasnodar region, bordering the North Caucasus, and had developed a pronounced animosity towards Caucasians.

The interior ministry, in itself a remarkable organisation in a democratic country, was building a formidable army for use on domestic territory. The ministry had a force of 250,000 fully fledged soldiers and about 300,000 police officers across Russia by 1997, including heavy weapons like tanks and a proliferation of special forces units. This stood in stark contrast to the crumbling regular army, a phenomenon that became more marked when the Chechnya war got underway. Although regular army troops did most of the hard fighting, the interior ministry soldiers were far better supplied with uniforms, food and salaries.

The FSK (the revamped KGB) had initially been reduced after the collapse of the Soviet Union, but as Yeltsin's presidency went on, the trend was reversed, with the addition of its own detention centres and commando units. Chechnya was a natural place for the FSK (later the FSB) to flex its muscles. Its phony war that summer had not been a success. However, a major invasion, in which victory was certain, would, apart from any other benefits, ensure that people forgot about the embarrassing attempt to storm Grozny on 26 November.

Several officials, while not members of the Security Council, were at the heart of the party of war. A highly influential man in the Kremlin was the first deputy prime minister, Oleg Soskovets, who had close links to the military-industrial complex and wanted to restore internal state control, especially over the economy. During the war he would be responsible for the rebuilding of Grozny, a corruption-riddled project in which huge sums of federal money disappeared with almost no buildings being restored. Another figure from the financial world was Boris Berezovsky, one of the new Russia's industrial tycoons. After his LogoVAZ company bought into ORT, the national first television channel, at the end of 1994, Berezovsky exercised his influence over the rabidly anti-Chechen propaganda which fanned the early flames of the war.

Then there were Yeltsin's Kremlin security men – chief bodyguard Alexander Korzhakov and his ex-KGB colleague General Mikhail Barsukov, commander of the Kremlin's presidential guard. Neither were members of the Security Council, but both had much in common with the other party of war figures. Korzhakov in particular had enormous access to Yeltsin, whom he'd shadowed faithfully for a decade. It was Korzhakov, also an associate of Berezovsky, who reportedly set up a new intelligence centre made up of ex-KGB members, eclipsing the Kremlin analytical services as Yeltsin's window on the world. In the name of internal state security, a man like Korzhakov could get away with a lot. He was reported to have floated plans for yet another security force –

a small, but elite 'national guard' which would serve the Kremlin and Kremlin only.

Another pivotal figure at that Security Council meeting was the defence minister, Pavel Grachev. For Yeltsin to dive into Chechnya, Grachev needed to tell him that the army was ready. Grachev, desperate to keep his job, did just that.

Although a decorated Soviet-Afghan war veteran, Grachev was out of his depth when he made the extraordinary career leap to Russia's first defence minister at the age of 44. Until then, he'd never commanded more than a division, and it became evident that he was not up to the horrendously complex role of withdrawing from eastern Europe and reforming the armed forces before they crumbled of their own accord. Within the army Grachev had mixed respect, and within the Kremlin his pleas for budget increases fell on deaf ears. Before long the Russian media targeted Grachev by linking him to the corruption plague sweeping through every branch of the demoralised armed forces. It began with allegations of massive fraud during the withdrawal of the Western Group of Forces in eastern Europe. Then Grachev was accused of receiving a Mercedes bought with money from the budget for housing the withdrawing troops. The parliament was furious and set up an enquiry. Finally, in October 1994, Dimitry Kholodov, the young reporter for the newspaper *Moskovsky Komsomolets* who exposed the corruption story, was blown up in Moscow. The killer was never found.

After the 26 November battle for Grozny, Grachev blithely rejected the notion that regular Russian troops had taken part. 'If the Russian army had been fighting', he said 'then one parachute regiment would have resolved all problems in two hours'. Of course, that was bluff. Grachev knew the state of his army, and he knew how easily Chechen ambushers burnt the tanks borrowed from the army by the FSK when they discovered that the vehicles had no infantry cover. He knew this would all happen again. Yet Grachev was already so politically weak that he could not oppose his FSK and interior ministry colleagues and the rest of the party of war. It was easier to tell Yeltsin what Yeltsin wanted to hear.

The gamble paid off for Grachev, at least temporarily. As soon as the war started no one talked any more about army corruption, or the Mercedes, or Dmitri Kholodov; there was even talk of making Grachev a marshall. At the expense of thousands of his young soldiers' lives, the burly general with an infectious grin managed to keep his job and avoid prosecution.

Yeltsin's mind was made up. The only Security Council member who dared speak against military intervention, Justice Minister Yury Kalmykov, described later how Yeltsin asked for everyone to vote in favour before even debating the issue. This was the pseudo-democratic style of the Soviet Politburos and, showing old habits die hard, all 13 council members voted yes. Kalmykov's protests in the discussions afterwards fell on deaf ears. As Oleg Lobov famously said, what the Kremlin needed was 'a short, victorious war.'

The day after the Security Council meeting, Yeltsin signed a decree ordering 'restoration of the constitution and law and order on the territory of the Chechen republic', a throwback to Soviet phony legal language. The decree was kept secret from the nation and Grachev, given a week to prepare the invasion, immediately began massing troops on the borders of Chechnya.

The last reformers in Yeltsin's entourage dropped away or had their Kremlin phone links cut. One liberal parliamentarian later described the Council members as 'a collective maniac', while presidential advisor Emil Pain described the decision as 'conspiratorial adventurism'. Gaidar, the former prime minister, said 'if this button is pressed we will, with absolute certainty, see the collapse of democratic institutions in Russia.' Kalmykov – who incidentally was Cherkess, an ethnic-Adygei – resigned.

Over in Grozny, Dzhokhar Dudayev, with his macho fantasies and total disregard for democracy, bore a particular guilt for what was about to happen. When there were chances for negotiations, he baited the Russian bear; when compromise might have kept peace, he threatened war. He began his rule with a threat, in November 1992, to blow up Russian nuclear power stations and, on the eve of war, in December 1994, he threatened to kill prisoners and had his foreign minister repeat the threat about nuclear stations. A showdown, to Dudayev, was a self-fulfilling prophecy. But ultimate blame must be laid at the feet of Boris Yeltsin. While pretending to the role of great reformer, Yeltsin rejected *noblesse oblige* by failing to rise above Dudayev's insults. Had he invited the Chechen leader to the Kremlin in the early 1990s, or flown down himself to the Caucasus on the eve of war, and sat at the same table, it's quite possible a deal could have been reached. After all, Dudayev was a proud man and, with a degree of official pampering, might have agreed to some kind of compromise status for his republic. Yeltsin, equally vain, ruthless in his determination to keep power, and fed lies by his entourage, refused.

At the end of November, a letter was published from North Caucasus leaders asking Yeltsin, 'the guarantor of the Russian constitution, human and citizen rights and freedoms,' to 'take all measures to establish constitutional order and the defence of citizens' rights and lawful interests, especially the right to life and security.' The letter, a classic propaganda piece drafted in Moscow, was signed by the leaders of Adygea, Karachai-Cherkessia, Kabardino-Balkaria, North Ossetia, and the Stavropol, Krasnodar and Rostov regions. Only the signatures of Dagestan's Magomed Ali Magomedov and Ingushetia's Ruslan Aushev were missing. 'I understood that after the defeat of the Chechen opposition, the Kremlin powers had to do something quick', Aushev later said. 'This piece of paper showed what it would be. A great country had decided to punish little Chechnya.'

On 9 December – having already ordered the war in secret at the Security Council meeting – Yeltsin issued a public decree ordering troops to carry out the 'disarmament of all illegal armed units,' as the deadpan phrase put it. Grachev and Yerin flew down to the Chechen border to join Yegorov and Stepashin.

On 10 December, Yeltsin disappeared into hospital for what the Kremlin said was a 'nose operation'. The next day, an army of 30–40,000 under-trained conscript soldiers rolled in armoured columns across the flat, snowy borders of Chechnya. Many of them would not live to celebrate the Orthodox Christmas.

## Grozny

*September 1994. At reception in the Hotel Kavkaz on Grozny's main square, there are three silent old women, two men with rifles and a teenager with bloodshot eyes and a loaded anti-tank rocket launcher.*

*I'm the only guest and, for seven dollars, I take the 'luxe suite', with windows facing the presidential palace.*

*The Kavkaz has just undergone a big makeover and I'm one of the first guests. The facade is pinkish, with white arched balconies along the top floor. Inside, there's a standard Soviet lobby, something like an upmarket funeral parlour, with lots of marble and large mirrors rendered useless by the gloom.*

*The 'luxe suite' could be the set from a porn film. The vast bed has a pink satin cover and the bedstead is a mirror. On the floor are fancy carpets and the gold taps in the bathroom look as if they might produce champagne and bubble bath. I twist one and nothing: no champagne, no bubbles, no water. There's a terrible smell coming from the corner. I lift the toilet seat and realise the hotel's water cut has been cut off for a long time.*

*When I complain downstairs about the water, the gunmen laugh and one of the old women cries. 'I'm ashamed,' she says, 'If I could, I would have you stay at my house.' I feel terrible for making her cry and insist that the water really isn't a problem. One of the gunmen says 'luxe!' and the others laugh, the boy dropping his rocket launcher on the floor with a clatter.*

*That night I douse myself with half a dozen bottles of Russian mineral water still sold at kiosks, along with every kind of western chocolate and cigarette, despite the almost three-year blockade.*

*Sleep is impossible. Mosquitoes have chosen the 'luxe suite' for a breeding ground and I cower under the sheet, sweating. Outside, there's* the constant screech of tyres as young dudes race their cars. I kill a few mosquitoes, leaving splashes of blood on the beige walls, then go onto the balcony. An armoured personnel carrier crowded with men in headbands and bandoliers of ammunition rumbles by in the dark. Heated conversations in Chechen sound as if they'll lead to blows, but end in laughter.

Around midnight, I try again to sleep, but the television in the corridor is so loud that that the sound is distorted. I edge out of my room and find two Dudayev soldiers fast asleep in front of the set, Kalashnikovs on their laps. A maid is mopping the corridor. I'm surprised to see her at this time of night since I'm the only person staying. She approaches and asks if we can talk. 'Not here,' she adds, with a gesture towards the sleeping gunmen.

We go into my room. She's blonde, Russian, in her thirties and although lined with stress, her face has a wan beauty. 'I can't stand it when these soldiers come up here. These people scare me', she says.

'What are they doing?' I ask, something I haven't been able to figure out all day.

'They live here,' she says simply. Then, 'do you know what life is like? I haven't been paid my salary for months, but there is nothing I can do. I'm scared and I want to leave so badly.'

She asks if I could take her to Moscow. 'I have a little daughter, but we could work something out. Just if I could stay with you at first, find my feet.'

She takes my hand and I put my arms around her. But I'm too new in Chechnya to gauge the tragedy. It's like trying to comfort somebody who's crying but doesn't speak your language.

Only later will I understand the sadness of the Hotel Kavkaz, the Russian maid, the old women at reception, the sleepy guards, the empty rooms, the dread feeling that soon all this will be gone, blown apart and washed away in a sea of fire.

# PART 5

# The Fury

*... one would like to say that 'a battle is something which happens between two armies leading to the moral and then physical disintegration of one or the other of them' – and this is as near to a working definition of what a battle is that one is likely to get ...*

From *The Face of Battle*, by John Keegan.

## 1. NEW YEAR'S EVE

*Remember, our common goal is to help the Chechen people escape from the
misfortune into which they have fallen, to help restore a normal, peaceful and
calm life. ... Your specific task is to disarm bandits and get them to give in or
destroy their heavy weaponry. You are under the protection of the state and
the Russian constitution, under the personal protection of the president.*

President Boris Yeltsin in an address to the troops on 27 December, four days
before the storming of Grozny.

The first major daylight air raid on Grozny began a couple of hours
after I arrived. We'd driven in all night from Dagestan across rebel-held
roads, skirting the Russian guns, and got into the city at dawn. There'd
been an air raid on the city during that night and as soon as we arrived
we saw fresh rubble, downed power lines, smashed glass and intersections
flooded by broken water mains. Many people milled about the bomb
sites. A patch of blood in the snow outside the destroyed Okean
restaurant was a maze of frozen red footprints.

In the eastern Microrayon neighbourhood, bombs had flattened a row
of cottages at a crossroads. A crowd gathered at the remains of one of
the houses where an old woman was buried under her own rubble.
Pathetically personal wreckage – a cookery book, a broken suit case,
bedding, broken china, a dust-covered doll – lay on the street or poked
from the pile of bricks and stones. Journalists took pictures while
bystanders tried to find the corpse.

Air raids so far had been at night. At night the civilians of Grozny
hid, at daylight they resumed life. That was the unwritten pact and on
my first morning of covering the war for Agence France-Presse, 22
December, there were many pedestrians and cars in the streets. Despite
the night's bombings, there was an atmosphere of normality or at least
of people trying to recover normality.

At about 10:00 a.m. there was the sound of a plane. People looked up
into the cloud-covered sky. Then came another jet and another until it was
impossible to distinguish between the noise of different engines. The planes
flew high above the clouds, invisible, with only the sound switched on: the
gut-wrenching roar of aircraft circling, the grating scream as they went
into dives. Bombing began and people ran. Thunderclap explosions burst
out in every direction, echoing and magnifiying across the squares and broad
streets of Grozny. This was it, at last – an air raid in broad daylight.

I'd never been near a war before and, even now, what was happening
seemed unreal. I stared into the blank sky, wincing at the noise. Then
smoke began pouring out of the city in several places. Together with my
Associated Press colleague Chris Bird, I ran through the city centre
towards the nearest smoke plume. I had to see to make it real. Running

blocked out any sound except breathing, until a plane tore directly overhead, making me stumble and gasp with shock. Finally I felt fear.

The closer we got to the source of the smoke, the more people ran past us in the other direction. Everybody had the same expression – faces riven with tension, eyes almost wild. We kept going. A car and truck burned next to the bridge over the River Sunzha at the Oil Institute, black smoke billowing from red flames. To the side was a little park. Trees were shredded, the snow sooty. I almost stumbled over a body on the pavement, then saw the second and more trails of blood from the bushes. Both bodies were decapitated. No trace of their heads, just stumps of necks and gore in the snow. I felt sick and couldn't face looking at the burning vehicles to check for victims. We ran back. The war was real.

That was the day I met Paul Lowe, a Magnum agency photographer. I was back in my hostel room filing news about the air raid via our portable satellite telex when he ran in, his face covered in dirt, his eyes full of tears. 'Carnage, absolute carnage, bits of bodies everywhere', was all he said. It was too cruel: the Russians had again bombed that crossroads in Microrayon where they'd been looking for the woman's body from the night before. Exactly the same place. Shrapnel mowed down 15 to 20 people, including the bright-faced, 28-year-old American photographer Cynthia Elbaum, one of the first of 20 journalists to die in the war. She'd been out in the open when the plane fired its rockets. Some of the Chechens, Paul and another photographer, Steve Lehman, survived by sheltering behind a wall only a few metres away.

They were clearing away the corpses by the time I got there. Five randomly passing cars had been caught in the rocket blasts. A withered arm, its black, bony hand opened clawlike at the sky, stuck out of an incinerated Lada. In another, the driver, a middle-aged man, sat dead behind the wheel, slumped back, his face shredded with dozens of shrapnel punctures, little red tears in his already greying skin. A young woman stepped through puddles of car oil and blood in the snowy mud. 'This is a nightmare, a nightmare, a plague,' I heard her say.

That morning, almost the entire press corps left Grozny, throwing equipment into a special evacuation bus. The sky was filled with the noise of airplanes, the atmosphere one of barely repressed panic. It was an uncomfortable scene.

*Air strikes are only hitting military installations where shooting is coming from.*
Prime Minister Chernomyrdin.

*The Chechens 'are simulating explosions in residential areas.'*
Kremlin Security Council.

When the troops first rolled across Chechnya's western, northwestern and eastern borders in mid-December, I was watching on TV in Moscow. Columns of armoured personnel carriers and tanks, miles long, snaked across the snow-covered plains, escorted by helicopters skimming low over the telegraph poles. There were truck loads of soldiers, red-white-blue Russian tricolours flying from antennas. This was the biggest combat deployment by Russian troops since the Soviet war in Afghanistan and the sight of those armoured columns was mesmerising.

Of course I knew – everyone knew – that the former superpower army was in trouble. Every year there were thousands of non-combat deaths, some due to accidents, but most suicides and murders during bullying and hazing. For example 2,824 soldiers died in 1992 according to official figures, 4,000 according to non-official sources. Barely paid officers withdrawn from eastern Europe lived in railway carriages, tents, common halls, or ships. Teenaged conscripts on five dollars a day (if they were lucky) became virtual slaves, used to build civilian roads, pick cabbage and potato crops. There were teen-aged conscripts selling weapons or begging in order to buy food, soldiers close to starvation, catching frost bite, or going berserk and massacring their own comrades at isolated bases. There was the defence minister, Pavel Grachev, mired in sleaze. I knew all this.

There were other warning signs. Even after a week of operations, the three-pronged Russian advance on Grozny was only crawling forward. No effort was being made to blockade the southern end of the city, the hardest and most strategic end, because it linked up with the rebel-held countryside and villages of southern Chechnya. The Chechens certainly showed no signs of wavering. Everywhere in Grozny, the graffiti said 'freedom or death'. Dudayev was defiant and there seemed to be no shortage of volunteer fighters – *boyeviks*, or warriors in Russian.

Incredibly, some of the nation's top generals were refusing to take part. The deputy commander of Russian land forces, General Eduard Vorobyov, turned down the command of the war, saying the army wasn't ready. General Boris Gromov, who was highly respected and had commanded the Soviet withdrawal from Afghanistan, denounced the war. So did Grachev's paratrooper colleague General Alexander Lebed and deputy defence minister General Valery Mironov. Even the commander of one of the three columns advancing on Grozny, General Ivan Babichev, temporarily refused to go further because his road was blocked by civilians. 'It is forbidden to use the army against peaceful civilians. It is forbidden to shoot at the people,' he said.

But the odds looked laughable. The entire Chechen population numbered just under a million and the republic, at 15,000 square kilometres, was substantially smaller than Wales or Sicily; you could drive from one side to the other in just over two hours. Russia's armed forces officially had about 1.7 million men, as many as 2.4 million including the interior ministry troops and border guards. Besides, the propaganda from the Kremlin – that the aim was to restore 'constitutional order' and 'disarm illegally armed bands' – was repeated so often it began to sound at least half-true. Never did the Kremlin say the word 'war'. It didn't even declare a state of emergency, suspending constitutional rights. This was nothing more than a police raid on an unruly Moslem neighbourhood.

The Russian army had not been tested since Afghanistan. But to an outsider, those endless sleek, green guns on TV still looked invincible. The sheer quantity of men and machinery, if nothing else, looked overwhelming. I couldn't help feeling the slightly embarrassing thrill of the hunt – the Russian troops were going to 'restore order' in style. A news photographer who looked as if he had been near wars watched the TV with me and said: 'This isn't a place you should be when they really move in. Do you realise what those helicopters can do?'

Under President Yeltsin's bombs Grozny, founded in 1818 by a Russian general, disintegrated. The population, once 400,000, began to vanish. Columns of refugees poured out through the unblockaded south, taking only what they could carry or stuff into cars, their children sitting on top of each other in the back seats, serious-faced, pale. Along the exit route, abandoned dogs sat patiently waiting for their masters to return. Others became wild, formed packs and roamed the deserted streets, shell-shocked and savage. About 120,000 people could not leave. They had neither money, nor relatives to help them escape, nor the heart to abandon their homes. Most were ethnic-Russians who, unlike the Chechens, had no extended family networks in the countryside. The Russians whom Yeltsin was promising to save were the ones being killed by their own airforce.

Moving amazingly fast from disbelief to acceptance, the residents of Grozny learned to live like primitive humans, sleeping underground and thinking only about survival. Electricity and water supplies had halted, so people melted snow and huddled, freezing, around candles or oil lamps. People didn't go outside if they didn't have to. The broad avenues and warrens of side-streets were totally deserted and at night the city blacked out. The hospitals had been evacuated, but doctors still worked on emergency cases, with special rescue crews touring the bomb sites and bringing in torn bodies. Sometimes, operations took place by candle light.

I was with about half a dozen other journalists still living in Grozny in the days around the Western Christmas. The rest slept in Ingushetia or Dagestan, driving in and out during the day. We thought we could make a difference. It seemed simple: we had only to write what was happening in this 'restoration of constitutional order' and the world would act. At night we crowded around the radio to hear the BBC World Service, which sometimes quoted my reports for Agence France-Presse, confirming to me that there was a point to working. Sometimes we heard that Washington or London had condemned the bombings or urged Moscow to end the madness and we all felt good; one night, we even cheered. That was innocence. We hadn't yet understood how little real impact our reports made, and that the international community would never take concrete steps to pressure an end to the war.

One night the planes bombed a set of residential buildings just down the street from our hostel, called, curiously, the French House. The blasts blew out our windows and sent us scuttling into the cellar. In the morning I walked over and found that two apartment buildings had been demolished. In the middle of the rubble sat an old woman. She had a wooden chair and was wrapped in a yellow blanket, with two bodies at her feet. Her name was Anna Volkova, a Russian. The entire fourth floor, where her flat had been, was gone. Surrounded by piles of bricks and smashed furniture, she rocked backward and forwards on her little chair. The bodies were of her middle-aged son and his wife, lying next to each other as they might have done in life, hands almost touching, bloody faces turned up. Next to them lay a black book, maybe a Bible, and a child's sledge. There was nothing else.

'I was sitting on my sofa and my daughter in law asked me what the time was,' she said. 'Well, the clock was in the kitchen and there was no electricity, so she gave me a torch to go and look. As I went out of the room, a bomb exploded. When I woke up I was in the rubble.' Life and death. Pure chance.

At the hospitals, blood trails began out in the street and dotted through the snow, up the slippery steps and down the deserted, freezing corridors. Doctors had little medicine or anaesthetic. They knew the bombs would eventually hit their hospitals and they began sending the wounded out to the villages. Unpaid, badly fed, freezing and dealing with constant flows of torn bodies, these doctors were often close to gibberish when we found them in the morning. Their white coats were stained brown and red with blood, their eyes were black, and they stank of alcohol.

'How can they do this, how can they, bombing women and children every damned day, every damned day,' a doctor shouted at me, shaking with fury and fatigue. Out in the corridor, he lifted the blanket from the body of a small boy, his chest punctured by shrapnel. The child still wore the oversized anorak and ski hat he'd died in. 'They are pure fascists', the doctor said. Then, grabbing my arm and turning me to the boy, he ordered: 'Never, never forget what you have just seen. Promise me that.'

In a makeshift morgue, really just a tool shed, at the First Republican Hospital, the unidentified bodies literally piled up, preserved from rotting by the freezing cold. In the first room, maybe 50 corpses were stacked like wood, blackened, often naked and missing legs and arms like mannequins. I didn't look in the second. But for relatives searching for their dead, there was no choice. They came in trickles, already afraid of spending time out and being caught in an air raid. While I knew it would be what journalists call 'a good story', I didn't have the courage to talk to them.

Somehow, we kept thinking there had to be a limit, the madness would end. Innocence clung on because the reality was unacceptable. So when a doctor told Richard Beeston of *The Times* and me one morning that an orphanage had been badly bombed we looked at each other and thought the same thing: no way. Orphanages were beyond that limit.

But the doctor was right. A whole side of the five-storey orphanage in northern Grozny had been torn off, exposing the rooms inside like a doll house. The garden was scorched black, the play statues of animals beheaded, the swings burnt to a crust. An unexploded rocket lay embedded in what had been the playground. We were taken down into the cellar and saw that every one of the 40 orphans had survived. The teachers said that if the attack had come half an hour later all the children would have been outside playing in the garden. A massacre had been narrowly avoided. Apparently those over eight were terrified, but the toddlers laughed. They thought it was another playgroup game.

After a week or so, all this began to seem normal. Death became commonplace. When a bomb hit the parliament building, opposite the presidential palace, it was as if the Chechens there didn't think mere bodies were sufficient proof – they made us walk over the corpses sprawled on the steps and inspect the brains splattered on the walls and floor. We declined, but they insisted. We had to see the brains. 'That's brains. Now you see what they're doing to us'.

At the Republican Hospital, a wounded Russian woman lay in an unheated room, in agony, covered with her own vomit. 'They began to bomb and we didn't have time to run. I was hit by something in the back and I lost consciousness.' Eyes rolling, breathing irregular, she cried: 'This is not possible, it's the killing off of a people. I'm going to write to a newspaper.'

Up on Karpinsky Hill, near the oil refineries in the west of Grozny, Chechen *boyeviks* manned a few artillery guns dug in on a soaring hilltop overlooking an entire Russian column. This was one of the outposts of a defence system dotted around the city, holding off some 30,000 troops. Every day, Karpinsky was pounded by shelling and planes. The sky was black from the oil smoke pouring from the bombed oil refinery nearby, the snow on the summit was pockmarked with black craters and apart from trenches, there was no cover.

'Boom, boom, boom, everywhere, fire everywhere. Last night was a nightmare,' said Khizir Khachukayev, the hilltop's giant, bearded commander who referred to Russia as Satan. 'But if they think they can take this city without a fight, they've made a big mistake. I'll tell you why: Here, it doesn't matter whether you're for Dudayev or not. Here, we're fighting for freedom, here we fight for our families. I'm a Chechen and I simply want to have the right to speak the language of my birth.'

By late December it was clear that the Russian operation, under Grachev's personal command, had gone badly wrong. Troops advanced in three columns: one from Ingushetia, one from Dagestan and one from the north, where the town of Mozdok had become the main launch pad. The plan was to throw a noose around the city, but more than 10 days after the invasion, Russian troops were bogged down at villages outside Grozny and hesitant about trying to storm in. The blockade was still incomplete, with links to southern villages and mountains, all crucial for supplying the *boyeviks*, totally open.

Russian forces could call on impressive batteries of long-range heavy weapons, such as tanks, mortars, cannons, Grad (Hail) and Huragan (Hurricane) multiple rockets, and of course planes and helicopters. But all this firepower's effectiveness was undermined by the lack of motivation and training of the crews, including the airforce pilots, who according to some reports were getting only 19 hours a year of flying time, not the required 100. The bureaucracy and organisational problems of any major army were also magnified in the disillusioned, hastily called-up units sent to Chechnya.

Advancing against built-up areas, even villages, proved unexpectedly difficult. The Chechens would not flee under artillery fire, which meant sending in infantry – exactly where the Russian forces were weakest. Only out in the open or against immobile positions was the Russian military machine effective. Tanks and APCs covered by helicopters out in the open areas outside Grozny were irresistible, and slowly the ring around Grozny tightened. Every day, both sides prepared for the inevitable showdown.

The Chechens fought in mobile, self-sufficient groups and their sense of mission was so high that most of them seemed genuinely to have lost any fear of death. Wearing home-made smocks of white sheets and wrapping white ribbons around their weapons to hide in the snow, the Chechens operated in groups of between five and 20, rarely more. A well-armed group might have one machine-gun, one or two anti-tank rocket-propelled grenade launchers (RPG) and an automatic rifle for each man. Several men might go unarmed to carry ammunition or the wounded. Many units were made up of neighbours or even relatives from a single village who usually elected their own commanders. The ironic effect of President Yeltsin's war, particularly the savage aerial bombing, was that Dudayev's tawdry rebellion had become a people's uprising.

The star of the Chechen arsenal was undoubtedly the humble RPG, a hand-held rocket launcher which at close range can turn a lone man into a tank killer. Light enough to be carried all day and at a run, and accurate within a few hundred metres, the RPG is ideal for street combat. The

Chechens had several Russian-made types, ranging from the reusable bazooka model, to one-shot tubes the size of a poster case. There were also thin supplies of heavier, more powerful anti-tank rockets, including the wire-guided version, which were accurate at a range of several kilometres, most useful when defending the open country outside Grozny.

Chechen defensive tactics, simple, but requiring extreme coolness under fire, were concealment, destroying vehicles at close range with RPGs, shooting the crews if they survived, then changing position, or going into foxholes in time to avoid the inevitable heavy supporting fire called in by the enemy. Mobility was key. Fighters, who knew the neighbourhoods of Grozny back to front, travelled either on foot, or in the tough and inconspicuous Russian-made jeeps and Ladas, which became troop carriers and ambulances. Larger units got to the front in trucks or battered municipal buses. The Chechens also had heavy weapons amassed by Dudayev, including artillery pieces, Grad multiple rocket launchers and tanks. These guns were especially vulnerable to return fire or helicopter strikes, so the same tactic applied: fire and move. Grads could be mounted on the back of an ordinary truck, fired, then driven to cover.

Who were the *boyeviks*? The defence minister, Pavel Grachev, claimed that there were tens of thousands, including 6,000 'foreign mercenaries' and 1,200 'dangerous criminals'. But that was nothing more than propaganda. The core Chechen force, according to many sources in Chechnya, probably numbered little more than 3,000 men at the height of the war; some estimates were that only a few hundred combatants took part full time. The main force was bolstered by thousands more part-time fighters and an incalculable number of supporters and suppliers.

There were experienced soldiers among the Chechens, including volunteers from the Islamic world, Ukraine and the Baltics, Chechens who had been trained in Afghanistan, or who had fought in Abkhazia with the young warlord Shamil Basayev. There were also numerous ex-Soviet officers, including of course Dzhokhar Dudayev and his chief of staff, the former artillery colonel Aslan Maskhadov, who was now a Chechen general. Most were people with unexceptional pasts. Among Khizir's men on Karpinsky Hill, there were farmers, long-distance truck drivers and a teacher with spectacles under his helmet. But crucially, all except the very young Chechens had done military service in the Soviet army. This meant there was widespread familiarity both with the Russian-made weapons amassed by Dudayev and the weak points of the enemy's APCs and tanks.

The bulk of the *boyeviks* were inspired not by politics but by their national mythology of the warrior and defence of freedom. They might be Dudayev supporters, but they might also despise him and his team's robbery of Chechnya. 'Protecting my home', more often than not, was what a fighter answered if asked why he'd taken up arms. Chechens will also go to great lengths not to show fear and so, for many, joining the resistance was a matter of course. A guerrilla called Mussa recited to me one day a poem he had composed in honour of the fearless wolf, who even when trapped and wounded by a shepherd tries to kill his tormentor – a truly Chechen wolf.

> Hatred boils in the wolf,
> Agony grips his strong body.
> Then the shepherd sees the wolf's eyes in the darkness
> And for the first time feels mercy,
> Mercy for this grey-skinned thief who died so well.

Religion played a crucial supporting role to the resistance, although this was not by any means a religious war of Moslem versus Christian. Morale-boosting chants of 'Allah Akbar' (God is great) as they went into battle were standard, but many Chechens were only non-practising Moslems at the start of the war. Dudayev and Maskhadov, like any ex-Soviet military officers, were no strangers to the delights of vodka and even the most devout Chechens were often quite ignorant, in an academic sense, about their faith. Nevertheless their beliefs and the tradition of Sufi brotherhoods was one of the most important elements in maintaining morale and a sense of ethnic identity. Religious observance, not surprisingly, deepened the longer the war went on, helping bring discipline to the volunteer, sometimes highly informal armed units. Above all the Chechen combatants were united by an almost instinctive sense of self-defence, bred into them by the collective memory of the deportations and all the wars their people had fought. Their motto might have been 'never again'.

By late December, Freedom Square square, which you had to cross to get into the presidential palace, was a nerve-racking place. The area was frequently bombed, and the square was so wide that a plane could appear from nowhere and bomb before you had time to run for cover. We made a habit of jogging across that killing ground. Even the groups of old men who defied the planes to perform the *zikr*, whirling in the snow as they had done before the war, gradually ebbed away.

Curiously, however, one of the last buildings on the square to suffer a direct hit was the presidential palace – scarred and sandbagged, but intact. The survival of the palace and the Russians' failure to 'decapitate' the Chechen leadership was just one example of the bizarre way the Kremlin was conducting its 'short, victorious war'. It was no secret that Dudayev and his top people spent much of their time in that very building. Conversely, one of the first major buildings to be totally demolished in the bombings was the Chechen Central Bank, fuelling popular rumours that one of the reasons for the war was to cover up incriminating documents about the *avisos* scandals of the early 1990s.

To the Chechens, the presidential palace was a powerful symbol of defiance. The above-ground floors were abandoned, but down in the cavernous cellars and bunkers, business went on as usual. The cellars were crowded. Many corridors and rooms had only candle or oil-lamp light that flickered gently off the stacks of weapons, the ammunition and grenade webbings on the fighters, the green-red-white rebel Chechen flags. Above all, the place was warm and safe and there was a permanent cast of characters who, if nothing else, served to create an impression of continuity, that the Chechen revolt was not fizzling out.

A couple of unhelpful government spokesmen called themselves Chechen Press and sat in a smoke-filled room adorned with Arabic inscriptions and oil lamps. A Ukrainian who said he had come to fight for Chechen freedom but spent a lot of time in the bunker was another fixture, snaring new journalists with his romantic story, before they learned to keep at least a desk's length away. My favourite was a character who said he was Russian-American and represented something called Non-Violence International from Washington, DC. 'I don't have any hopes that my personal actions will make any difference,' he said, honestly enough, but in a DC bureaucratese that sounded hilarious in Grozny.

The last man to leave his above-ground office was Information Minister Movladi Udugov on the fourth floor. He wore the Chechen uniform of black jeans and jacket and put a metal sheet over his shattered window. On the table was expensive video equipment and a pistol. He'd never been helpful, but I had to admire him then.

Each day, the combat drew closer to Grozny. In late December Russian tanks pushed down to cut the main eastern road from the capital to Argun. Driving out to the battle, my elderly Chechen driver Usman and I left our car and took cover in a ditch by the road as soon as we saw smoke. Over the broad, snow-covered field beyond the ditch, four helicopter gunships circled low, rocketing a treeline to our right where the Chechens were dug in. Smoke poured from the field in two places – burning APCs or tanks. Suddenly we were spotted by the helicopters. One broke from the circle and strafed our ditch, sending the snow flicking up with a hiss. This was open country and the Chechens didn't stand a chance.

The road fell and the Russians moved one step further to fully encircling Grozny. On 29 December, Russian ground troops supported by helicopters and artillery fought a pitched battle with Chechens commanded by Shamil Basayev in Khankala, the airfield in the eastern outskirts of the city. The Russians were driven back, but it was the first time that fighting had taken place in Grozny's limits. That night we sat listening to the planes bomb unseen from the stars, the explosions flashing across the sky, and felt that time was running out. Even so, the Chechens had never been

further from giving in. On Sheikh Mansur square they erected a huge fir
tree, complete with decorations, to celebrate the New Year.

> '*The Russian commander has sent me: he will spare you if you surrender
> without fighting.*'
>     To this Khamzad answered: '*I came not here, oh Kagherman, for want
> of money. I came to win the death of the Ghazawat. And were I to surrender
> to thee, all the people of Ghikh would laugh me to scorn.*'
>     '*As a wolf tired and hungry longs to reach the forest, as a horse unfed
> and mettlesome the fresh clean meadow – so do my companions thirst for
> the fight unto death. Nor do I fear thee, oh Kagherman. I laugh at all thy
> force, for our hope is in God, the all-powerful.*'

From the 19th-century Chechen 'Song of the Death of Khamzad.'

New Year's Eve morning an air raid missed the cottage we were staying
in by a few streets, blowing our windows out, setting several houses and
parked cars on fire, and tearing a great hole in the side of an apartment
building. Dust-covered survivors crawled out into the street, dragging a
dead man. Then an old woman emerged and shook her walking stick at
the sky. Fearing a repeat raid, we evacuated the area and drove to an
abandoned hotel in the city centre next to the Dinamo stadium. There
was still electricity and we could write. But no sooner had we arrived
than artillery shells began hitting close by. The eruption of explosions
shook walls and floors, broke windows and sucked the breath away.
This was a first: artillery on the city centre. Chechens began firing back
with Grad rockets stationed just behind our hotel, another first. I felt the
ground would split open. Then the noise of helicopters, followed by the
distinct noise of machine-gun and rifle fire inside the city. People came
from the outskirts in a panic: Russian tanks were in the suburbs. The
storming of Grozny had begun.
    Aching with cold and nerves, I tapped out an urgent dispatch on our
satellite telex to give the news. Then my Agence France-Presse partner
Isabelle Astigarraga and I went outside to join our colleagues, Bill
Gasperini of CBS, Paul Lowe, and Carey Scott of *The Sunday Times*. We
had to think fast. Forget the earlier chaos: this time, thousands of troops
in tanks and APCs covered by planes and helicopters were attacking the
city from three sides. Personally, I didn't think the Chechens could last.
Now that the Russians were going all out, they'd take the city in hours.
Paul, an experienced war correspondent, said this was worse than
Sarajevo, this was 'insane'. He sounded convincing. There were rumours
of special Russian hit squads tasked with hunting down journalists.
'We've got to get out of here. It's going to be street fighting, absolute
hell', he said. Time to evacuate.

Keyed up, we drove in two cars, accelerating across open spaces away from the Dinamo, seeking side-streets, with the stench of cordite in the air and the feeling that the city was crumbling. Then just beyond the centre a strange thing happened. Isabelle and I looked out and saw Chechens – ordinary, unarmed Chechens – standing in the streets. They weren't running. All these people had a last chance to get out, but they were staying in their homes. Their defiance had not dropped. That was enough – Isabelle and I would stay too. We couldn't leave the city. Besides, as agency correspondents, we were filing news to radios and television stations around the world and for a few hours we would be one of the only independent sources of first hand information. We had an obligation and a scoop. We flagged down the others and said goodbye.

The pneumatic-drill hammering of machine-guns and steady thud of exploding shells never let up in the centre. Black smoke from bombed, burning oil refineries on the city edge gushed across the pale winter sky and by two in the afternoon the sun was blotted out. In the distance, refinery fires occasionally belched a silent mountain of flame, bathing the horizon in an orange glow. By night the brightest lights were the yellow flashes of explosions and streams of red tracer bullets, arcing like shooting stars over roof tops.

Moscow had made a terrible miscalculation. The Chechen bandits of Russian propaganda would have run, but not the real Chechens. As battle raged in the centre, Chechen reserves flooded in from the villages to the south, even men without weapons, who joked they were 'going to work.' In ski hats, anoraks or ordinary leather jackets, they looked strangely like crowds on their way to a football match. Groups of five often shared one rifle, but almost everyone could get his hands on something – a pistol, a shotgun, a handgrenade, a Molotov Cocktail. Few had commanders or any other plan than to support the resistance. Quite literally, men were walking towards the sound of fighting. They moved with studied nonchalance, almost a swagger.

'Each street defends itself. We all know each other that way. We do what we can, even if it is just making petrol bombs. We can't just sit at home,' said Issa, a 23-year-old shop clerk. His group of four shared a shotgun and an automatic rifle. Two boys – they looked about 12 and wore men's overcoats, collars up over their ears, sleeves rolled up – shifted from foot to foot, sucking in the energy of the men, pointing with envy at the Kalashnikov and whispering. 'Look at these two lads,' said Leche, a 39-year-old man who had once been a sailor in the Soviet navy. 'They're already helping us get weapons and ammunition. They're not scared of anything, not tanks, not rockets.' The group laughed. A machine-gun opened up somewhere down the street and we separated.

The *boyeviks* seemed relieved – at last, the battle was in territory suited to short-range weapons and guerrilla tactics. 'It's better for us in the dark and in the city. Here, they're our guests and we're the hosts. They have come in, but they won't leave', said the guerrilla, a 38-year-old man armed with an assault rifle, anti-tank stick-grenades and the conviction of a martyr. 'They're not fighting for anything, but we're fighting for our homeland – we're not afraid to die. They have planes and tanks and all we've got is Allah and the RPG. But we know what we're fighting for.'

Dirty Ladas bumped along in the dark streets, spilling out men, guns and ammunition; the pale light of Russian flares or burning buildings revealed ghostly figures of fighters in white smocks and green Islamic headbands; obscure piles of branches disguised a machine-gun post, its ammunition belt glinting against the snow; barricaded into the upper floors of apartment buildings, ambushers waited with their RPGs for the Russian armour to roll into the wide streets below.

A Chechen group snaked through the small houses behind the presidential palace, where the Russians were already being trapped. The group hugged the walls and stopped to consult with comrades lurking in the shadows. They had no commander and were simply feeling their way along to the forward positions. A tank rumbled past in the darkness, its long barrel silhouetted. We ducked against a wall and one man of the group ran into the dark street behind the tank. But it wasn't Russian – it was from the tiny Chechen tank force. 'Lucky for them, or they would have got this', the man grinned, pulling a hand-grenade out of his anorak.

Those Chechen Press characters who had been so unpopular with foreign correspondents suddenly came into their own, filming the fighting around the presidential palace. One of them would be killed. In an amazing piece of ingenuity, not to mention bravery, they left a night-vision camera running in one of the upper floor windows and relayed on local TV the fuzzy, greenish pictures of Russian APCs firing on the building. 'Tonight the fate of Chechnya is being decided' said Dudayev's vice president, Zelimkhan Yandarbiyev, in a ghostly voice over the pictures.

No ordinary person in Russia knew what was happening. Throughout the country, from Moscow to Vladivostok, families gathered in apartment kitchens to drink sweet Sovietskoye champagne and neat vodka before going out to light fireworks and celebrate the start of 1995. If they thought about Chechnya, it was only through the prism of official reports which said this was still a matter of 'restoring order'. Just before midnight, New Year's Eve, ITAR-TASS announced that Dudayev's presidential palace had been captured.

But the propaganda at last could not even hope to keep up with reality: the Russian force had been cut to pieces. Using a strategy uncannily similar to Shamil's destruction of Prince Vorontsov's army in the Dargo woods in 1845, the Chechens let the Russians storm deep, right to the city centre, then sprang a colosal ambush of mortars, RPGs and small arms from all sides. Russian soldiers had indeed reached Freedom Square outside the presidential palace, but only to realise they were trapped for the slaughter.

In his classic turn-of-the-century account of the Caucasian wars, J. F. Baddeley writes about the Vorontsov expedition, but he might have been describing Grozny 1994;

> The natural result followed. The centre became separated from the van, the rear from the centre and the enemy swarmed in between, firing from every point of vantage, from behind every tree trunk – even from the branches overhead, for, as in Grabbe's expedition, the giant beech trees gave shelter to numerous Chechen sharpshooters – and when wherever confusion ensued, rushed in to complete it with sword and *kinzhal*.

This time, the Chechens were in nine-storey apartment buildings and basements, not beech trees, and they were using machine-guns, not swords.

Tank crews got lost and were hunted down; infantry troops stuffed into APCs didn't dare get out and enter firefights, but were then killed by RPG rockets inside their vehicles; top commanders failed to coordinate and Russian heavy weapons fired on their own men. Within 24 hours, the assault had been broken and the presidential palace remained firmly in Chechen hands. It was one of the Russian army's worst single defeats – worse than battles in Afghanistan. One thousand soldiers were killed and about 3,000 wounded, an officer who kept track of figures in Moscow told me confidentially. Other non-official estimates have gone as high as 2,000 dead.

Sergei, a Russian conscript in the 81st Motor-Rifle Regiment from Samara – who said he was 20, but looked much younger – was one of the many soldiers taken prisoner that night. Considering the hundreds of soldiers who were shot dead as they tried to escape their ambushed APCs, he was lucky. When we met, the war had been going for several months and he was lying wounded in a cold Chechen hospital, hoping to be released or swapped back. As we talked, his airforce's planes kept screaming over the hospital, making him wince, and I couldn't help thinking he'd never get home.

Like so many conscript soldiers, Sergei had barely heard of Chechnya before being sent there to serve as the mechanic for an armoured personnel carrier during the assault.

> When we were first ordered to leave Samara, we didn't know where we were going. At first, we were based north of Grozny. On New Year's, they told us to form a column, but we still had no idea where we were going. Then they said it would be Grozny. They said there would be no fighting, that there were only armed criminals and no civilians. We got as far as a crossroads and they began shooting on us from fifth or sixth floor apartments. They were firing

from everywhere. I have no idea what they fired, but we were hit. We got out and hid in a small house. I was wounded. There was me and four others, including an officer. They were all wounded. We sat in there for four hours. We expected they would hit the house with an RPG. We were waiting for that. Then they shouted to us to come out, to give up, and they took us prisoner. I just want to go home now, it's all I want.

Of the 1,000 men of the Samara 81st, more than half were killed, wounded or taken prisoner, according to one estimate. Nearly all were 18 or 19, conscripts with no combat experience. The 131st Brigade, based in the Adygei capital Maikop, was virtually wiped out. It easily occupied its objective, the railway station in central Grozny, then found itself surrounded on all sides for 24 hours. A Russian report put the Maikop brigade's losses at 20 out of 26 tanks, 102 out of 120 armoured personnel carriers. Survivors talked of hundreds of soldiers dying.

Volodya, a professional special forces soldier, who had been wounded in the head by shrapnel after about 12 hours of fighting over New Year's, gave me the clinical verdict: 'Of course I understood what was going to happen. I think there should have been more infantry, they should not have driven straight into the centre, as if that was going to scare off the *boyeviks*. But I was following orders. Most of our men were not ready. I was, I knew that. It's not my business how they ran the attack, there are people who plan these things you know. That's why they have those big stars on their shoulders.'

'No one saw what it was like, no one will ever know. It was hell, our artillery fired on our own boys, there were dead everywhere. It was a disaster,' said Nikolai, another conscript, whom I met months later manning a checkpoint and wishing he would be sent home.

Grozny will go down as a historic defeat, not so much in terms of material and human losses, but because of the staggering failure of leadership and training at every level, from the conscript soldiers to the generals. Most to blame was Grachev, the Afghan war veteran. With personal command of the operation, he was in a better position than anyone to know what would happen when APCs and tanks moved in with no infantry cover into a warren of streets crawling with Chechen snipers and anti-tank-rocket crews. He'd said it himself before the war, that 'first, the infantry go. The tanks see nothing; they're good in fields, but in the city they're blind. There, it's absolutely necessary to have infantry to guard the tanks.' Grachev knew that the unreformed post-Soviet army didn't even have the sergeants and junior officers capable of leading small infantry units, the core of successful street fighting and the only way to protect the armoured columns. Yet still he went ahead, lying to the country. After showing such recklessness and inhumanity towards civilians during the first stage of the war, he now gave his own soldiers, mostly teenaged provincial boys, the same treatment.

The defeat also reflected the illusory numerical strength of the armed forces. Officially, there were about 1.7 million servicemen in the army, but actually there may have been as few as 1.2 million, according to one estimate, and of this still huge number remarkably few combat-ready units. Even the supposedly elite paras and tank formations were not at complete strength and included many raw conscripts. As a result, units sent to Chechnya were hastily created compilations of men who'd barely had time to learn each other's names, let alone train before they got into battle. The same confusion was rife at the highest levels between the various branches of the regular army, the interior ministry and the counter-intelligence services. As soon as the attack ran into such determined resistance, their coordination broke down, again undermining the effect of numerical superiority.

Another elementary error may have been that the storming of Grozny took place before reinforcements arrived. According to one Russian analysis, about 24,000 troops, with 80 tanks and 200 APCs were deployed in the initial invasion; reinforcements which arrived shortly after the attack on Grozny strengthened the overall force to 38,000 men, with 230 tanks and 450 APCs. In the storming of Grozny, the well-trained special forces of the Main Intelligence Directorate, or GRU, were reportedly not even used, an extraordinary ommission.

What could Grachev have done? If he had shared the principles of his insubordinate generals, he would have refused to carry out the attack, gone to Yeltsin and stated the real case. But Grachev was so sold-out by the time the troops went into Chechnya that he would do nothing but go along with the tide. He knew his future depended on Yeltsin and the Kremlin clique, not Grozny – and he was far beyond caring about his soldiers' lives, civilian lives, or the constitution. According to a well-placed military source, Grachev's decision to storm Grozny on New Year's Eve was taken, like much else of Russia's policy in Chechnya, on little more than a whim. This time it was a drunken whim during a party on December 30 at the base in Mozdok in honour of the defence minister's birthday on January 1. A 'birthday gift storming', the source called it.

Grachev was unapologetic. All the military dissidents were either sacked or edged aside, and Grachev said the conscripts 'died with smiles on their faces.' When the human rights activist Sergei Kovalev, who had spent weeks under Yeltsin's bombs, spoke out, Grachev called him 'an enemy of Russia, a traitor'. As for Kovalev's activist colleague Sergei Yushenkov, he was denounced as 'a vile little toad who defends the scoundrels who want to destroy Russia'.

Two weeks after the Grozny storming, the deputy defence minister, General Georgy Kondratyev, said what everybody who had been in Chechnya already knew, but the Kremlin, Grachev and the Russian parliament refused to accept: 'It's not just gangs which are fighting in

Chechnya. It's the Chechen people. The men have taken up arms. They are fighting for their homes and for their land and for the graves of their forefathers.'

### Grozny

*2 January, 1995. There's no doubt who won this battle. A green-red-white wolf flag flies over the roof of the presidential palace and the connecting streets, black from explosions, are dotted with mangled tanks, APCs and dead Russian soldiers.*

*Automatic rifle fire breaks out and I crouch by a wall just over the River Sunzha from the palace and wait. Just beyond, a couple metres away, is a dead Russian. He's very young, on his back, and his legs are bent the wrong way as if he couldn't decide which way to run. His eyes have half popped from their sockets, blue and white, like striped bar room pool balls. Even mutilated, he looks like any of the young conscripts you see all over Russia, with their oil-stained hands, yellowish skin and World War II-era uniforms. Death has not taken away the boyish, unquestioning conscript face. I wonder how many more like him will die today.*

*It's a sprint across Freedom Square to the presidential palace. Inside, crowds of filthy, tired Chechen fighters rest, smoke and clean weapons. Some eat quickly, tearing bread from flat, round loaves, reaching for pickled tomatoes in big, deep jars. Others talk quietly in their gutteral language. Others are silent and stare without moving.*

*The Chechen chief of staff, General Aslan Maskhadov, sits exhausted in a bunker, surrounded by maps, ammunition boxes, stacks of anti-tank rockets. At his elbow is a pile of red passports taken from dead or captured Russian soldiers. Maskhadov, soft-spoken, calm, with silver hair, is the most mild-mannered of the Chechen commanders. But his eyes are dark and hard.*

*The mastermind of the Chechen victory tries to look formal, forces himself to come up with an official statement that can capture the reality of what has happened. 'The Russian armed force that stormed the city two days ago is practically defeated. A Russian brigade commander was killed,' he starts stiffly. But his voice is breaking.*

*Maskhadov knows nothing is over, he knows that the planes will be back, that the heavy guns will one day drive his men out of the smoking city and into the villages, that this is only the beginning of the carnage in Chechnya.*

*But in that interlude between the bloodbaths, in the very first minutes after the New Year's battle for Grozny, with the stench of burning in the air, there is only one thing he can really say: 'Even I am amazed. I'm amazed by the courage of these people.'*

The presidential palace fell on 19 January, nearly three weeks after the storming of Grozny. Chechen resistance had become an embarrassment. Tanks, howitzers and planes bombarded the 11-storey concrete structure daily from close range. The city collapsed in every direction. The Hotel Kavkaz opposite broke up into a shell, the parliament burned, acres of houses and apartment buildings around the palace were either blown apart or caught fire. Yet the presidential palace remained standing, even when the entire back section – tonnes and tonnes of concrete, including huge portions of entire floors – broke off and the front section was polka-dotted with artillery holes. Astonishingly, the building's defenders, protected by deep bunkers, kept firing, even when Russian ground troops lay thick around.

Finally, the Russian air force, which had earned a reputation of such incompetence, successfully dropped two penetration bombs designed to break through every one of the 11 floors and into the bunker before going off. That night, the surviving Chechens crawled out and waded across the freezing River Sunzha to set up new positions on the far bank. The next day, Russian troops 'stormed' the ruins and raised a red-white-blue federal flag, Red-Army Reichstag style, an act that General Kondratyev branded 'blasphemy'.

The Russian government announced that the capture of the palace meant the defeat of Dzokhar Dudayev and the *boyeviks*. President Yeltsin said that 'the military stage of the restoration of the Russian constitution is effectively over' and Grachev announced that he was delegating command of the operation to the interior ministry. Even a week before the presidential palace was abandoned, *Sevodnya* daily columnist Pavel Felgenhauer, who consistently stated the Defence Ministry view, said the war was almost won. 'It seems likely that the desperate last stand of Dudayev's supporters in the bunker of the presidential palace is a sign that they themselves understand the game is up.'

Across the Sunzha River the game was not up. Chechen fighters regrouped, living in cellars and fighting from apartment block windows, while trapped civilians resigned themselves to death. The battle would continue for more than six weeks. The fighters had long since been battling not for Dudayev, but out of what can only be described as patriotism. For the Russians – to whom partisan resistance against the Nazi invaders in World War II is a proud memory – mistaking the durability of this resistance was yet another miscalculation.

Following the New Year's Eve battle, the Russians largely abandoned infantry and armoured assaults, instead resorting to the World War II strategy of systematic artillery and aerial bombardments, neighbourhood by neighbourhood to clear the city. Like the 'capture' of the presidential palace, but magnified a thousand times over – much of Grozny had to be destroyed to be liberated. Russian sources estimate that up to 100 122-mm and 152-mm howitzers and tanks were massed for the barrages, in addition to the Grad and Huragan rocket launchers, and the aerial bombers. The artillery helped keep Chechen moblity to a minimum and, as the city collapsed and burned, the Russian ground troops advanced, with reinforcements pouring into Chechnya all the time in columns hundreds of vehicles long.

The last weeks of the battle for Grozny were desperate. Periods where shells hit the city every few seconds for over an hour – that's three to four thousand shells an hour, compared to three thousand Serb shells a day on Sarajevo – were not uncommon. The shelling could hit any neighbourhood at any time, making lulls the most deceptive of luxuries. One second you were standing, talking or smoking, then you hit the ground like a whip as the first shell screamed in and you crawled for the cellar entrance or just hugged the ground, willing yourself into the tarmac. Incredibly, the southern exits of Grozny remained in Chechen hands, offering an escape and resupply route, but the artillery meant that they too were becoming more dangerous by the day.

In a cellar off the central Prospekt Lenina, where young blades had once done handbrake turns in their BMWs, a Chechen guerrilla commander carefully cleaned his group's sole RPG. About 20 men lay on mattresses in the dark, with a burning, broken gas pipe giving off an orange glow and much-needed heat. There were loaves of flat Chechen bread and some pickled vegetables. The men looked tired and dirty. In addition to the RPG, they only had 10 rifles among them, meaning they had to take it in turns to fight.

The commander – one of his men called him 'our legendary leader Dzhambula' – was 28. He had been in the police and he wore a Hawaiian shirt and dirty green tracksuit bottoms. There was an amulet around his neck. 'It protects me from bullets, shrapnel, APCs and tanks,' he said. 'My girl in the village gave it to me. There are prayers from the Koran inside.'

'We're just defending our land. They have planes, helicopters, multiple rockets, mortars and we have no weapons except our spirit', said another man in the cellar, who was 44. 'But we know why we're here. We're not fighting for Dudayev and we're not interested in politics – we're fighting for our land. We know what happened in 1944 and about the 19th century. All our history we've fought with the Russians and we just don't want them here.'

Even in February, units like this were scattered all over southern Grozny, and the commanders claimed to control a third of the city. But this was propaganda – in reality most of southern Grozny was little better than no-man's land. One Chechen tank remained in Grozny, I was told, firing its solitary rounds and then changing position. Moving about in the streets on foot was a lottery and the fighters were trying more to avoid being killed by artillery bombardments than engaging the enemy. In such conditions, and with almost no radio contact, coordination was particularly difficult. 'We're fighting, but there's not really control over us. We hardly have any commanders, it's just everyone who can get their hands on a weapon,' said Leche, a young volunteer.

However bad it got, you could still find the insane element – the Chechens who never flagged, who never believed they were losing. Dzhambula was one of them. 'It's not just that we think we'll win, we know,' he said. The Chechens lasted a month more in Grozny after I met Dzhambula, and I was never able to find out whether he survived.

Outside Grozny I found an old man resting by the side of the road. He and his wife had just walked out of the city with two sacks of belongings. I asked where they were going and the woman simply said 'there', pointing south, to the mountains. 'This isn't fighting or war,' said the old man. 'All they do is shell and mortar, methodically destroying the city, street by street. There were 15,000 people in our neighbourhood and when I left there were 100. Once an area is destroyed, they move on to the next. I'm leaving for a bit but I'll go home later. Ramadan starts tomorrow and I need to wash for it so I can prepare myself to die properly.'

The old man fumbled for words. 'These are the tactics of the Mongols. I don't understand what they're doing, or our fighters for that matter. No one is a winner here, they should all stop.' He paused, then: 'I was born in the mountains and was nine when I was deported to Kazakhstan. Since then I'd lived in Grozny. Who knows, maybe they're getting ready to send us away again. And they say men don't cry.' He turned away, weeping.

At the start of February Russian tanks broke through around the southeast of the city, closing one of the last big exits. The *boyeviks*, mostly from Shamil Basayev's battalion, held on until the end of the month, then, when the city was all but encircled, escaped into the countryside to the south. Grozny fell formally on 6 March with the occupation of the southern Chernoreche neighbourhood.

Official Russian figures at the end of February were 7,000 Chechen *boyeviks* killed to 1,146 Russian soldiers killed, 5,000 Russians wounded, and almost 400 missing, probably taken prisoner. The figure for the Chechen dead was without doubt exaggerated since it's unlikely that number was even on the frontlines. As for the Russians, unofficial reports put their losses at far higher. One secret service officer responsible for keeping the toll, who remained anonymous, said that 4,000 soldiers were dead. Certainly the families of the soldiers didn't believe the defence ministry. Dozens of Russian housewives risked their lives wandering around the Chechen side of the lines in search of their sons. Others combed the morgues and refrigerated train carriages at the big Russian camp in Mozdok. Others were told their sons had died and received human remains to bury, only to find out later that there had been a mix up – their son was alive and the remains sent to them belonged to another, unknown soldier.

Civilians were by far the hardest hit, but again, accurate numbers were impossible to gather. An estimated 120,000 people had remained in Grozny during the nine-week battle – mostly ethnic-Russians. The Russian human rights organisation, Memorial, conducted a survey among 400 refugees and extrapolated a civilian death toll for Grozny of 25,000. That seems too high, but the true figures will probably never be known.

Despite new predictions of the war ending, resistance raged on across Chechnya, eventually sucking in as many as 80,000 Russian troops at one time. Even in Grozny there was no victory for President Yeltsin. His 'restoration of constitutional order' left the city a wasteland of rubble, landmines, and hungry dogs searching for human bodies, which lay in the streets, preserved for a long time because of the cold.

The gaunt ruins of the presidential palace took on cult status and long after the Russian capture of Grozny, rebel green flags kept appearing on the walls. A year later, still no end to the war in sight, the exasperated Russians simply razed the building with controlled explosions. All that was left was a huge pile of concrete rubble. People still referred to it as the 'presidential palace'.

*Moscow*

*President Yeltsin publicly announces on two occasions that he has ordered the air force to stop bombing Grozny. The bombing continues.*

*On 5 January 1995, Sergei Kovalev, the former Soviet dissident and now the most outspoken Russian human rights defender, comes back to Moscow after three weeks in Grozny. Frail, tired, his thick glasses forward on his nose, Kovalev has one question: 'Who is lying?'*

*'I will put the question to the president: what did he have in mind when he addressed the people? Had he forgotten to give the order that he publicly declared, or perhaps the order was not fufilled? ... Perhaps he is not being lied to as brazenly as we are, because one has to be a very stupid person indeed to believe all these lies. Nazi propaganda at least tried to be more plausible.'*

## 2. MAN AGAINST MACHINE

*You see no people to fight out there, only machines.*

Chechen fighter retreating from Shali, the last town held in the plains.

Grozny had been a place where a guerrilla army could fight. It had cellars and walls, places to sleep, eat and hide, places to ambush and strategic points where a 20-man unit could hold up the might of Russia's tanks. But in the southern plains, where the Chechens retreated, there was none of that.

The plains are Holland-flat and mostly treeless. Along with Grozny, this area is where most Chechens live: rural market towns like Urus Martan and Shali, thriving villages like Germenchuk, and the only two real urban areas apart from Grozny – Argun and Gudermes. South of this layer lies the natural guerrilla territory of the Caucasus mountains. Their forested foothills rise steeply from the plains, with dozens of villages nestled in the valleys; higher up are the bare and rocky alpine slopes, which are little inhabited, followed eventually by the high peaks of perennial snows.

When the Chechens pulled out of Grozny, General Maskhadov was adamant. There would be no direct retreat to the mountains. Every inch of the flat lands must be contested. To Maskhadov, this was a point of honour, the key to a broader struggle to determine who was right – the Kremlin, which classed the Chechens separatist bandits, or the Chechens, who declared themselves a legitimate independent state?

'The Russians want to take Gudermes and then Shali and push us into the mountains. Then they will announce they have won the war and claim we are just bandits hiding in the hills', Maskhadov told me in Shali. 'I just want to show that I am ready to fight a real war, army against army, position against position.' It was an apocalyptic grudge, his vision of holding up the Russian mechanised army on flat, featureless ground with a few thousand unpaid, often untrained infantry.

Heavy guns were kings of the plains, not the close-range infantry weapons like RPGs and rifles, which had been so deadly in the city. During night-time battles, the sky shook and leapt. The Chechens still had Grads and the rockets streamed in red salvos, a dozen at a time, into the Russian lines, bursting with yellow flashes, one after the other. Then the reply, a barrage of spectacular, but sometimes blind suppressive fire: artillery and Grads, their explosions lighting up the night sky, automatic cannon fire and tracer bullets skidding red or yellow across the flat ground. There was beauty in the violence.

Helicopter gunships were more in their element than ever, flying fast and low so you only saw them as they appeared over roof tops or treelines; God forbid that they caught you on the road or in a field. Fighters could dig trenches, but spotter planes photographed their positions and guided in the artillery fire. If artillery was not enough, planes could bomb with impunity, their targets visible as if drawn on a piece of paper.

The Chechens' sole air defences were the fog and low clouds of the winter months and a small number of manual anti-aircraft guns, basically huge, mounted machine-guns firing intense bursts of explosive rounds. The only cover for ground battles was around or in the villages and towns themselves, but these could be encircled within hours by Russian armoured vehicles moving across fields, out of range of most infantry anti-tank weapons. Once a village was encircled, resistance by the *boyeviks* brought Russian firepower down on the trapped civilian population.

Worse still, the prospect of a long war highlighted one of the Chechens' main strategic weaknesses – the lack of easy access to a friendly cross-border power, such as the Vietnamese, Algerian or Afghan guerrillas had during their wars. The only foreign country bordering Chechnya is Georgia, but that is blocked by the Caucasus mountains. True, there were many sympathisers in Dagestan to the east and Ingushetia to the west; there was even a circuitous supply route from Turkey via Azerbaijan then Dagestan. But these border areas were far from full-fledged safe havens since they were at least partially under Russian control and rebel activity there had to remain underground. The Russians on the other hand had none of these problems. Bomber planes could fly from bases around southern Russia in minutes, helicopters were based at the airports in Grozny, and mechanised infantry could be poured in either by road or rail.

At the time, I thought Maskhadov insane. As promised, his forces were fighting position-versus-position against one of the world's most powerful armies, but the sacrifice looked empty. Every week they were driven further back, and it seemed only a matter of time before they would have to flee to the hills, leaving behind ruined villages.

As Maskhadov conferred with Shali commanders, squatting in the main square while one of them sketched a map in the dirt, a helicopter gunship suddenly opened up on the town and a Chechen returned fire with a machine-gun from the window above us. Artillery shelling was expected to follow any second and we started to take cover – Maskhadov's regular war was happening all around. Needless to say, he and his bodyguards left the main square in a hurry.

Yet the strategy had a ruthless logic – Dzhokhar Dudayev's government had scornfully insisted it was the legal equal of the Kremlin from the very beginning. The only acceptable peace talks would be talks between two independent countries, not Russia and some breakaway province. Now Maskhadov extended that rhetorical defiance to the battlefield. Russia claimed it was fighting Chechen bandits, but Maskhadov would force the Russian army to admit it was fighting a regular Chechen army, whatever the cost.

## Tsotsin Yurt

*Sayid, head down, runs along the winding, muddy trench outside Tsotsin Yurt village, then across a rough clearing and up a natural earth mound. He crawls to the top of the mound and tells me to follow. He hands me the binoculars. Russian tanks are dug in across a couple hundred metres of a flat field. Their long barrels point over our heads at the village behind us.*

*'I don't want to fight and I wish our Dudayev would simply get in a ring with Yeltsin – let them do the fighting,' Sayid says. 'But I'm defending my home. Grozny's gone, Argun's gone, Shali will probably soon be gone and if Allah doesn't help, Tsotsin Yurt will go too. You can't expect me to give up my weapons, that's ridiculous. During the negotiations, I talked with the Russian officers right there in the middle of this field. They're human, they absolutely don't want to fight, they want to go home. No one wants to fight.'*

*'We have this trench here, but it's nothing really. They could have rockets falling on it at any moment they want. They have all the equipment. They wouldn't try to storm us on the ground, they've stopped doing that since New Year's Eve in Grozny. They'd simply start shooting from a distance, it's all they know how to do. If we have to, we'll die.'*

The war in the plains filtered out the dedicated fighters from the men who'd joined up part-time in the hot-headed patriotism during the combat in Grozny. The shrapnel-scarred buses or trucks at the fronts in February and March were increasingly full of men who looked crazed from the strain. The pressure also showed in villages which, afraid of being bombed, declared themselves neutral, banning the *boyeviks*.

Urus Martan, whose leaders had a history of opposing Dudayev from the beginning, stayed firmly outside the war and, as a result, became a unique safe haven in the maelstrom, its population swelling to over 50,000 people. Outside the village of Goity, which lay right on the path of the Russian advance and had a strong anti-Dudayev contingent, the elders argued fiercely with a group of Chechen fighters and each other. They were one nation, but now separated for ever, the elders in their overcoats and trilbies, the young fighters in their dirty white smocks and muddy boots. To the *boyeviks* such villages were guilty of treason. But the Goity villagers and many others had seen Grozny demolished and knew that their rural communities were a thousand times more fragile. Knowing also that the Russians would stop at nothing, they pleaded for their villages not to be made war zones.

Many *boyeviks* quit at this time, either because they saw no hope in continuing, or because they were physically incapable. Others grew sick of the criminal elements threaded through the resistance forces, the petty warlords, the looting, the cut-throats with nothing better to do than to fight. Everywhere fighters were running short of weapons and ammunition.

Khassan, in his early thirties, decided to stop fighting in March and go back to his family. 'I said I'm not playing this game anymore. They have planes that bomb us and tanks that shoot at us and to this day I've not seen one plane or tank on our side.'

I spoke to him long after this all happened, but the bitterness and sadness immediately came into his voice. 'We were about the last people fighting in central Grozny. When we retreated we crossed the River Sunzha. You couldn't use the bridges and we waded across up to our necks in that freezing water. I was wounded twice by shrapnel and three of the 18 people in my group were killed. But I understand now that it's a farce. I could go out now and kill a Russian soldier but that's not fighting a war.

'I think Dudayev counted on our Caucasian neighbours coming to our help, but they never did. No one did. The first people to leave were all the businessmen, the *vosdushniky* and bandits. They all went off to big houses in safety and the poor people were left. The poor are the ones who took up arms and fought. It looks as if we made the wrong choice.'

But for every few waverers, the war had forged one suicide fighter, a hard core of combatants who had fought from the first day and would fight to the end. In the southern village of Stary Achkhoi, Ruslan, a tall, red-haired guerrilla who'd been on all the worst fronts, said he was just trying to hang in – it was his only aim.

Like Khassan, he knew he couldn't destroy the Russian army. 'We can ambush a column and even destroy it,' Ruslan said. 'But they have communications and within six seconds they can call in helicopters and airplanes. At the very start, we never imagined this – artillery and aerial bombardments. We thought there'd be close-quarter fighting, man-to-man. How could we have known this would happen? We thought we'd be fighting in the city, but then it went to the villages.'

Instead of quitting, Ruslan entered a personal war of attrition that would last to the end. 'Now we'll just keep going,' he said.

Then there were those tiny figures you sometimes encountered, standing rifle in hand, waist high among the *boyeviks*. These were children who had lost everything and become pitiless warriors. There was Magomed, a 13-year-old orphan, whom I met that March. He had a green headband around his camouflage cap and four hand-grenades hanging from the webbing of his tiny chest. His voice hadn't broken, but he'd killed and would kill again.

'I have no mother, my father disappeared before the war,' he began. 'I had six uncles when it began. Two of them were killed and now I have nothing left. That's why I went out to fight. My relatives stopped me going out twice and then they gave up. I found a group of fighters and they asked me why I wasn't at home. I explained and that was it – they gave me a rifle. Now I'll go on to the end.'

Magomed had been wounded twice. A sniper bullet went straight through his right leg and shrapnel had lightly cut his back and right foot.

'I'm amazed I'm still alive,' he said. Magomed was hard to talk to. He was only 13, but he had the eyes of a 20-year-old and when I saw him pick up the Kalashnikov rifle, almost as long as his body, it was comic, then amazing, then desperately sad. 'Before, I went to school. I was normal. Now my only dream is that the Russians leave here,' he said.

As from the first day of the war, many of the *boyeviks* had been driven to fight out of vengeance against the Russians' bombing of their relatives or friends. The sheer indiscriminate violence against civilians, especially by the air force, was doing the separatists' recruitment job. The bombs fell everywhere, without logic, without pattern, on roads, small houses, apartment blocks, woods, even in the middle of huge empty fields. An air raid on Shali at the start of January killed or wounded as many as 100 people gathered in the market place. The planes flew back and bombed the hospital the same day.

Because Chechnya is such a small place, no one could forget the war. One's village might not be bombed, but the sky was filled every day with the sound of warplanes and explosions. On rare occasions the grey skies cleared, or the planes flew extra low, scudding through the clouds, and Chechens could finally see their tormentors. Parents would hurry their children off the streets and even in anti-Dudayev villages, the men looked up and cursed. I read of a man who made a ritual with his young son of firing daily at a photograph of the commander of the Russian airforce, Pyotr Deinekin.

In February, one of those low-flying jets was shot down near Chechen Aul by *boyeviks* manning an anti-aircraft gun. 'No more flying for him,' laughed a Chechen fighter, posing for photographs the following day next to the tail of the plane, emblazoned with a Soviet red star. The rest of the wreckage was littered across the snowy field.

I asked about the pilot. 'He tried to eject, but his parachute failed,' said another fighter, called Sultan. 'He was still alive when he hit the ground, but his legs were smashed and his arms were torn. The only words he said were: 'I have a house and son.''

I asked what happened next and Sultan drew a finger across his throat and grinned, but another fighter quickly interrupted. 'No, no, he's joking. We took him to hospital but he was already dead.' Then, seeing I might have believed Sultan – I'd been told often that spies and pilots were beheaded – the second fighter added: 'his flight documents showed he had made 17 bombing runs over Grozny. Can you imagine?'

---

'Hearing that the Chechens, who had shut themselves in the three houses and refused quarter, were firing hard and had already killed a lieutenant-colonel and wounded several soldiers, Volkhovsky (chief of staff) set out with Colonel Brummer, commanding the artillery, Vsiovolovsky and Bogdanovich to settle the affair in person.

'... *A light gun was brought up and the shot ploughed through the three houses from end to end. After the second round, however, people ran to say that we were hitting our own people on the other side. If we cleared even one side of the sharpshooters and reserves it would open a way of escape to the enemy. And this was not to be thought of, so orders were given to cease firing and set fire to the houses.*

'... *Little by little, the fire extended to the remaining two (houses); there was nothing left for the enemy but to surrender or burn.*

'... *The firing ceased when Atarshchkoff went forward and called out in Chechen that he wanted to parley. The defenders listened to the proposal, conferred together for some minutes, and then a half-naked Chechen, black with smoke, came out, and made a short speech, followed by a volley from all the loopholes.*

'*What he said was to this effect: 'We want no quarter; the only grace we ask of the Russians is to let our families know that we died as we lived, refusing submission to any foreign yoke.'*

'*The Chechens, firmly resolved to die, set up their death-song, loud at first, but sinking lower and lower as their numbers diminished under the influence of fire and smoke. ... From the smoking ruins crawled six wounded Dagestanis, alive by some miracle; the soldiers lifted them up and carried them to the ambulance. Not one Chechen was taken alive; seventy-two men ended their lives in the flames!'*

The encirclement in 1832 of Chechens in the village of Germenchuk, described by Russian General Tornau.

Samashki, in the west of Chechnya, was a typical village of the plains – about 14,000 people living in a prosperous maze of brick houses surrounded by blue-green gates, courtyards, farm animals, grape vines and vegetable patches. But if Grozny was a latter-day Guernica, Samashki was Chechnya's My Lai – the unspecial, unheard-of village suddenly subjected to a whirlwind of violence so cruel and primitive that even those who had long ago switched off were shocked.

It all started at the end of January with one of those short, meaningless skirmishes erupting all over Chechnya, as the fighters gradually left Grozny and took up positions in their home villages. A column of about a dozen light tanks, armoured personnel carriers and a communications truck rolled into the northern side of Samashki at sunset on a freezing, foggy day. There was no prior warning, no artillery preparation, no air support. The column, travelling in close formation, simply rolled into what everybody knew was a hostile village. More than likely the Russians were lost, or their orders had been mixed up.

The Samashki men reacted the way villagers have always reacted in Chechnya to armed invasion: about 30 teenagers and men jumped into a truck with RPGs and rifles, shouting with excitement and telling us to stand back. They raced up to the edge of the village, hid, and when the column was at almost point-blank range, opened fire.

The next morning, the bodies of three young Russians still lay in the mud, staring up at the sky, dirt and blood in their open mouths. Around them were the twisted remains of their vehicles and the clothing of dead comrades. One RPG round had hit the ammunition magazine of a light tank and the turret lay 10 metres away from the rest of the machine. The communications truck lay off to the side of the road.

The clash had been without ideology or planning. To the Samashki villagers, this was not war – this was defending home. This was what the separatist leadership had been counting on when the war moved out of Grozny.

'This is what happens to the Russians when they come at us drunk!' shouted a furious man, pointing at the bodies. 'We have nowhere to go,' said another man, called Magomed. 'This is our home and I for one am not leaving. It's not because I'm braver than you that I'm staying, it's because of our spirit. We were born with it, I got it from my mother's milk.'

The response was equally simple: Russian soldiers in armoured vehicles surrounded Samashki then lobbed tank and mortar shells into the village. Then the helicopters came, strafing streets and houses. About 20 people were killed or wounded and there were injured people who died from blood loss because no one could get them out of the surrounded village. After five hours, the Russian armoured vehicles drove away.

The punishment raid was routine, but worse was to come. Russian troops, who were sweeping across eastern Chechnya, wanted to establish control in the west and for this they needed Samashki. Fearing the worst, the elders made the core army *boyeviks* leave the village, leaving only about 50 local men under arms. This was not enough for the Russians, who wanted the village to surrender entirely.

There were many minor clashes with troops trying to close in on the village and cases of local farmers running their tractors over landmines left by the Russians. Every week delegations of elders and religious leaders went out to negotiate with the Russian forces camped in the nearby fields, to plead with them not to storm the village, which they said posed no threat. But Samashki had got a name for itself and the devils of revenge and bloodlust were stirring.

On 6 April an ultimatum was delivered by the besieging Russian interior ministry troops: by 7:00 a.m. on 7 April, Samashki must allow Russian soldiers entry and also surrender 264 rifles, two machine-guns and an armoured personnel carrier.

The elders replied that there were not that many guns in the village and that they needed more time to try to defuse the stand off. But the ultimatum stood. A colonel told the elders that troops would enter the next morning and if there was shooting from a house, then that house would be destroyed by a tank. Those were the rules.

That night Russian artillery began firing on Samashki. Several hours before the ultimatum was to have ended, aerial bombardment began. In the early morning of 7 April, the village came under sustained automatic cannon fire. By afternoon, large groups of villagers tried to leave, but most had to turn back because of the shooting. A delegation of elders again met with Russian interior ministry officers and were again told: give up the guns.

The official version of what happened next was that the Russian troops proceeded to enter the village and were engaged in a fierce battle against more than 300 well-armed fighters from the core separatist army in which the attackers showed great heroism. In its report, ITAR-TASS wrote that 130 'Dudayevists' had been killed during combat.

The version of survivors, witnesses and human rights groups was that the 350 interior ministry troops, including elite units, faced limited opposition from up to 40 local men, not outsiders from the central army, then began systematically to pillage and massacre. More than 100 bodies were found after the fighting, many of them unarmed men, women, children and the elderly, not Chechen fighters, according to the report by the Memorial human rights group.

According to Memorial's study, many died in the preliminary mortar and artillery shelling. More died when the troops drove down streets in APCs, firing with heavy machine-guns and cannons at houses and anyone they saw moving. What the Russians officially called the 'mopping up' of Samashki began on the morning of the 8th. It was during this operation, when armed resistance had long ceased, that the Russian soldiers ran wild. Samashki residents said women were burnt alive and old men were gunned down in the street. Hand-grenades were thrown into basements sheltering families and people were summarily executed in their homes.

This was denied by the interior ministry and the government, of course, and the Memorial report was held up to ridicule in the Communist-dominated Russian parliament. But apologists were faced by a mountain of witness reports by survivors, burned and shot bodies of non-combatants, and destruction by arson, not combat.

Many houses were burned from the inside, not blown apart, as they would be by artillery. Interior walls were sprayed with bullet and grenade shrapnel marks when the exterior walls showed no sign of violence – these were houses where unresisting people were killed.

The human toll, documented by Memorial, was horrific: more than 100 dead, listed by name and address. Of these, only 45 were men between 19 and 45 years old, the active fighting age. The rest were 13 women, seven children under 18 years age, 19 men between 46 and 60, and 20 men over 61 years old. The youngest victim was 15, the oldest a 96-year-old man. Four ethnic-Russian residents were found shot in their own home. One of them survived and his tale was backed up by the physical evidence: an interior wall full of bullet holes and pools of blood underneath.

One of the survivors of Samashki who gave his account to Memorial was Yusup Sadulla, an elderly man living on Vygonaya Street. He had sent his family away before the original ultimatum had expired and stayed on himself, as is the Chechen custom, meaning to leave at the last minute. He waited too long and was forced to sit out the fighting in his empty house.

There was no fighting in his area during the night of the 7th to 8th. But at 10:00 a.m. on the 8th, soldiers ran up his street shouting 'bitches, get out', then firing their rifles into houses. Sadulla said he ran and hid in his small cellar, just as the soldiers reached his door.

> I moved up against the right wall. Where I sat I had put a small bed specially to rest when there was danger. He (a soldier) fired in right there. Then he started to leave, and his comrade said to him 'maybe there is someone left alive there.' He came back and threw a grenade in and then a little ring. It turns out that was some kind of lock. 'Well that's it,' I thought. 'I'm finished. I need to die quietly.' I was not even afraid. The grenade went off. The bed, which was of double planks, broke in two, and I was deafened. It had exploded under the bed. Something hit my shoulders, something hit my legs. I fell on my knees, totally deaf.
>
> ...They started to leave. I thought they had gone. I checked my legs, moving them here and there: my legs were OK, not broken. Something had hit them, what the hell. Some blood was coming out of my arms. I went out. They had taken the little safe, where the money and papers were kept. Two of them were trying to open it and a third was guarding, shooting into the house. God if they see me, they'll try to kill me again for a third time.

At the end of March the damn burst and Russian tanks poured through the last Chechen defences in the plains. Argun, Stary Atagi and Novy Atagi, Samashki and Achkhoi Martan – all the big villages or towns of the plains – were encircled, captured, or abandoned by the *boyeviks*. Now only Gudermes, strategically a lost cause for the separatists, and Shali, which the rebels made their capital after losing Grozny, were left. The retreat into the mountains commenced.

Fighters and civilians flooded south into the hills ahead of the Russian advance. Even at night thousands of people in columns of lorries, tractors, motorcycles and cars streamed up the narrow foothills valleys, forming chains of twinkling headlights. Almost 500,000 people – half the population of the republic – were estimated to be on the move, either fleeing to Ingushetia and Dagestan or shifting from village to village within Chechnya.

Thanks to Caucasian hospitality, the majority of this human tide didn't wash up in refugee camps, but found lodging with relatives, friends or often complete strangers. In mountain villages, like Vedeno and Dargo – both one-time headquarters of Imam Shamil a century before – many houses sheltered up to 20 people. The old summer camps and Pioneer Communist youth camps, built for the pleasure of far-flung Soviet holidaymakers, filled with refugees, one family per tiny room.

Doctors from the courageous aid group Medecins Sans Frontiers assigned two surgeons to the Vedeno hospital and prepared to evacuate totally from the plains. The hospital in Tsotsin Yurt, where the Russians were massing, was urgently transferred to a school house in a neighbouring village called Bachi Yurt, although the villagers at first resisted, fearing that they too would be bombed as a result.

Running could be as hard as staying. The military situation changed so rapidly towards the end of March that you never knew when you set out along a road whether you'd encounter a new Russian position or be attacked from the air. A school teacher fleeing the Russians at Mesker Yurt, just south of Argun, with eight small children crammed in his car, was strafed by a machine-gunner. 'The car was hit repeatedly and I was shot in the arms. Somehow, none of the children were hit,' said Sharpudin Abdulsalanovich. He was 57 and still in shock, his forearms swathed in bloody bandages. 'I've worked for 33 years. I've been a school director for 15 years and now I don't know whether my arms will ever function again.'

The ultimate goal in the swift Russian breakthrough was Shali, self-proclaimed new capital of the rebel republic. By the time the Russians were in position no one remained except a few fighters, civilians with nowhere to go, and the handful who stayed out of principle, like an old man with a red face and gold teeth I met who said: 'I'm defending my home.'

In the doomsday atmosphere the Chechens were left with two faiths: Allah and the escape route to the mountains, just six kilometres to the south. One night in Shali jets began circling during the *muezzin's* prayers, sung over a loudspeaker from the mosque minaret. The two sounds – the drone of the bombers and the sad, low voice of the priest – seemed so incompatible that I felt one must drown the other out. The prayers won, and even when bombs began falling on the edge of town, lighting up the sky with cheap yellow flashes, the *muezzin* kept singing. When the planes flew away, he was still singing.

My friend Mussa, who was driving me around the fronts in his Audi, pulled out of Shali at the last moment. We'd been caught in a Grad rocket strike, the closest of calls, when the world was a wash of red and black, the air pressure changed, and for a second I wondered whether I was alive. The splash of shrapnel from one rocket missed the front of our car by a metre – I checked the pockmarked wall later – a second rocket hit the house immediately to our left, another hit the bridge 20 metres ahead, another somewhere on the road behind. All this happened in a couple of slow motion seconds, with debris arcing over the street and our car, before everything vanished in a thick cloud of fire and smoke and we crashed into the pavement, my ears filled with the chilling sound of a woman's screams.

Escaping that was pure luck. I could only pray and give thanks. The miracle didn't seem likely to happen twice in a row, and Mussa made the decision to abandon his home and town. He set his Caucasian sheep dog, which was already half mad, loose and left him some food. As we drove out, Mussa began to weep. After dropping me off at Serzhen Yurt, the first village in the foothills of the Caucasus, he drove away to a quiet spot to be alone. It was hard for Chechen men to cry. 'Please don't tell anyone here', he said.

The Russians' final attack on Shali, beginning 29 March 1995, had the precise use of heavy weaponry I'd come to think only happened in films. The assault was the climax of the plains campaign and it made you wonder how the Chechens had held out at all those cold months. Planes came six at a time, circling, then diving out of the bright sun. They bombed and rocketed the outskirts of Shali and Serzhen Yurt, where I sat on a hillside watching. After the jets came helicopters, flying low, one covering the other, and rocketing the outskirts. There was still defiance in Shali and the helicopters were met with little yellow flashes of gunfire from the edge of the town. But most of the fighters had already pulled out to avoid encirclement, their usual tactic. Finally, the artillery began, firing patterns of shells which puffed up in neat black and brown clouds among the buildings where the defenders had been. Before the tanks began to move south, to complete the encirclement of the town, the artillery went to work on a trench cut through the field the armour would have to pass through. It wasn't a long trench, but it was hit a dozen times, each time a neat puff of smoke and mud going up next to the one before, perfectly accurate.

By 30 March Gudermes fell to the Russians and a day later Shali was formally taken. The last fighters who got out walked south into the hills. 'This automatic rifle is useless,' said Rustam, a 20-year-old member of Shamil Basayev's Abkhazia Battalion, who had just retreated from Shali. 'You see no people to fight out there, only machines. Just boom, boom and three or four of you are gone. Their clothes are half gone, their legs are gone. We have nothing to eat or drink. Look how thin I am. I was a karate champion once.'

Then: 'No problem, Allah is on our side. We'll go into the mountains. It will be much better there for us.'

### Shali

*At the mental hospital near Shali, the abandoned patients live like animals, surrounded by their own excrement, howling and giggling in the freezing cold. When war planes fly over, some go outside and laugh.*

By February 1995 only 24 patients remain at the hospital, which once held over 200 and was a model Soviet institution. Nina Ivanovna, a 75-year-old ethnic-Russian nurse, is their last and only hope for survival.

'When they started bombing around here, the other nurses ran away. I couldn't leave them. They're like children, but they're still people,' Ivanovna says.

The violent cases live behind a padlocked cage door. Two women huddle together on a mattress until one starts to scream and bite the other's legs. A third person – man or woman? – lies motionless under the blankets. 'There's nothing we can do for them,' Ivanovna says.

One man likes it outside. He wears a World War II great coat and waves at cars. If the area is shelled or bombed, he's sure to be killed, standing out in the open like that. 'Tell my mama to come and see me', he says.

Ivanovna whispers: 'His parents have never come and since the war began no one at all comes, not even when they die. We just bury them behind the hospital.'

Ivanovna has 100 lines on her face and when she tries to restrain her tears, another 20 appear. She shows me a batch of medicine someone has delivered. But she's barely trained and, anyway, the instructions are in English, incomprehensible to her.

'No sanitation, no blankets, no clothes, no bunker, nothing to do. If they bomb here, we'll die,' she says.

I return to the hospital several months later, when Shali and the whole area is under full Russian control. Only half the institute is still standing. I don't see poor old Ivanovna.

There are six patients. I recognise one – a woman with buck teeth and so skinny that her hip bones poke out like handles. She was one of the dangerous cases in the cage; now she scampers around the overgrown garden naked, screaming loudly.

'She screams to say she's hungry,' says a voice behind me. I turn around and find a Chechen woman who has taken charge. 'No human beings should live here. Pigs should not live here,' says the woman, Lila Muzáyeva.

Looking at the ruins of the building, I ask what happened. 'The boyeviks took up positions here during the battle for Shali. There were about 15 to 20 of them just for a day,' she says. 'Nearly all of them were killed. Helicopters were firing rockets at the building. We tried to get the ill into the basement, but they didn't understand a thing.'

Does she blame the fighters? After all, if they hadn't taken up positions here, fewer people would have died and the building would probably be whole. It's the dilemma of all fighting in Chechnya, especially in the plains, where the territory is so small that combatants rarely have anywhere to fight out of except buildings. They bring ruin on everything they touch.

'No. I don't blame the fighters,' Muzayeva says. 'They were with-drawing very quickly, holding out in the open fields against helicopters and planes. Until then, they were the only ones who'd bring food to these people. I don't blame them.'


## 3. FORTRESSES

*Freedom or death, the cry was heard again in the mountains,*
*Freedom or death, yes and Allah is on our side.*

From a 1995 Chechen war song by Imam Alisultanov.

Spring brought madness to the mountains. The *boyeviks* had imagined there would be an Afghan-style war of ambushes and close-quarter firefights. Instead, the Russians stayed camped down in the plains and the Chechens found themselves sucked into a mismatched battle of attrition with the enemy's long-range artillery. The mountain phase was not what the refugees had expected either. They'd gone to the mountains seeking safety and remote villages overflowed with civilians, especially children – I'd never seen so many children. But then the airplanes began bombing, the refugees discovered they were no safer than they had been in the plains and by summer they'd all fled back.

For the Chechen separatist leaders, up in the high hill villages of Dargo, Vedeno and Shatoi, the retreat to the mountains was a key test of political, as well as military strength. Now they had lost all their towns, the pressure was on to prove to the world that their unrecognised rebel republic still existed. So while the *boyeviks* dug into the first row of foothills villages – from Bamut in the west to Serzhen Yurt and Alleroi in the east – Dzhokhar Dudayev's team engaged the Russians in a ferocious propaganda war.

Symbols of statehood were especially important. All official statements referred to Chechnya-Ichkeria, Ichkeria being a traditional name for Chechnya, a phrase never used by the Russian government, or by the media, but insisted on by the separatists as part of their battle to maintain an identity. The green-red-white flag emblazoned with a sleeping wolf and full moon was everywhere, hanging from mountain houses and the back of rebel vehicles, or sewn in patches onto combat clothes. High-ranking leaders never gave interviews to journalists without the flag on the wall behind them, an image especially important on television.

Vestiges of a government structure were preserved long after they had vanished in practice. Rebel leaders loved talking about the constitution, which in their make-believe state still provided for a rebel parliament and a whole range of bureaucrats. As long as there was a constitution, the Chechens could argue they were not bandits, but a legal government temporarily forced to live in the mountains. Thus Dudayev was their elected president, and a series of rough-looking warlords or shady civilians turned out to be justice ministers, military prosecutors and ministers, while Aslan Maskhadov's grandiose title was 'Chief of Staff of the Armed Forces of Chechnya-Ichkeria'. There were an astonishing number of 'colonels' and 'brigadier generals'. The parliament supposedly held occasional secret meetings and Dudayev, president and commander in chief, continued to issue decrees published in the underground newspaper *Ichkeria*. My favourite was Decree Number 16, of 20 March 1995, on 'formation of special suicide battalions ... according to article 73 of the Chechen constitution'. It was clearly a meaningless decree that no one listened to – most active units were fairly close to suicide already – but it had all the necessary bluff and self-importance for the propaganda war.

Real power was held by a group of about a dozen leaders, headed by Dudayev, Maskhadov, the top field commanders and intelligence chiefs. The field commanders were essentially warlords, controlling their home regions with private armies. Including them fully in the decision making process was vital because they were the ones doing the fighting and making the day-to-day tactical decisions.

There were many lesser warlords, with correspondingly smaller units, but only a handful of key figures. In the southwest, the top field commanders were Sultan Geliskhanov, followed by Akhmed Zakayev, the handsome ex-actor who'd been Dudayev's culture minister. Over in the southeast, Khunkar Pasha Israpilov – a lithe, young commander with a cunning face – commanded from his home village of Alleroi. In the central and Vedeno areas – and often anywhere in Chechnya he chose to strike – commanded the unpredictable, ruthless Shamil Basayev.

All had unmistakeable charisma, whether it was due to their adoring entourage of fighters, their menace, or their carefuly cultivated personality cults. Geliskhanov boasted that 'when I go into battle, no one is scared around me. They follow me anywhere.' Basayev, the most talented and respected battlefield tactician, often showed his populist instincts by treating strangers and subordinates with a sense of humour and lack of formality

In some ways, the most dangerous man the Russians faced was Dudayev's minister of information, Movladi Udugov. He proved a mastermind in the behind-the-scenes war. Not only did he use propaganda with great persistence and skill, he was also a key ideological adviser to the other separatist leaders, a true believer in the political goal of the war – independence. Bearded, but never openly armed or even in camouflage, Udugov used a satellite telephone to keep the state of Chechnya-Ichkeria alive in the minds of foreigners and Russians who might otherwise have thought the whole crazy separatist dream had gone up in smoke.

Udugov's media battle was almost as epic as the military war. Against him was the combined propaganda machine of the Russian government and its loyal media, especially the state television channel ORT and the news agencies ITAR-TASS and Interfax, which, at least in the first year of war, broadcasted whatever Moscow said and little else. When Russian television told lies – no civilians killed, Chechen fighters panicking, airplanes not being used – Udugov countered with his own – 500 civilans killed in one bombing raid, 800 Russian soldiers killed in one attack. Regularly, he rang up foreign or Russian news agencies, radios, TV channels and newspapers to give the separatists' side of the story. To the outside world it all sounded perfectly real when Udugov announced that 'the president and chief of staff of Chechnya-Ichkeria' took some decision or another. His language was always appropriately official and bureaucratic. No one was told that the meeting had taken place in a wood. Sometimes it wasn't Udugov calling, but his man in Istanbul, who faxed 'Chechen Press' news bulletins around the world thanks to the Turkish government's policy of turning a blind eye to pro-Chechen activists on its soil.

The Chechens also waged the propaganda war in the most simple but effective way: journalists had an almost free hand to travel where they wanted, to stay with frontline fighters, interview leaders and see the effects of Russia's war, which generally spoke for themselves. The Chechen openness, barring the ever-present spy paranoia, contrasted sharply with the lack of access on the Russian side of the lines. Like most formal armies, the Russian forces largely banned independent and foreign reporters from bases or front lines, and the only information given by the military came from official spokesmen, whom no self-respecting journalist believed.

The Russian side suffered further blows from its own media. ORT channel one and the news agencies rarely broke from the official line, putting out official lies verbatim. But newspapers like *Izvestia*, *Sevodnya* and *Moskovsky Komsomolets*, the private NTV television channel and, to a lesser extent, the national RTR channel two, savaged the handling of the war. Interfax, and to a lesser extent ITAR-TASS, began publishing reports quoting separatist officials. The highly critical shortwave broadcasts by Andrei Babitsky, one of the correspondents for the Russian service of the US government's Radio Liberty, became an institution in Chechen homes. The Russian media's independent streak lasted for much of the first year of the war, only bending back towards the Kremlin, particularly on television, as President Yeltsin's 1996 re-election battle approached. These reports, while not as critical as foreign journalists' work, were enough to ridicule the government's insistence that there was no major war, only the rounding up of scattered bandits. And although most Russians had no particular sympathy for the Chechens' suffering, the pictures of their own scared, disillusioned conscript soldiers caused fury.

Unprotected by foreign passports, Russian journalists faced double danger. They were regularly accused of spying in Chechen territory and subject to the wrath of the FSB Russian secret services and other minders. Of the 20 journalists known to have died in the war, two were westerners, nine were Russian and nine were Chechens, who also risked run-ins with the FSB or angry Russian soldiers. Two Russians, including an ORT correspondent, were shot dead by Russian troops in broad daylight at checkpoints. A young woman, Nadezhda Chaikova – who had written stories about Russian human rights abuses for the *Obshaya Gazyeta* weekly – was found murdered outside a village in March 1996. Three more Russian journalists disappeared, as did three Ukrainians, a young American and a Chechen. Their fates were never cleared up, but they could have been killed by either side and for almost any reason.

While Udugov dealt with the outside world, an underground television station, the *presidentsky kanal,* or presidential channel, beamed into Chechen homes from a secret transmitter carted over the mountains. The channel operated sporadically, with abysmal quality and limited range, but huge morale-boosting effect.

The channel's sheer audacity was what most pleased Chechens, many of whom sat up late into the night trying to tune in. Like a true electronic pirate, the *presidentsky kanal* would cut into regular local programming put out by the Russian authorities. It played interviews with field commanders, gave speeches by Dudayev and showed footage taken by the channel's woman camera team, headed by a remarkable 34-year-old called Khazman Umarova, who filmed several of the heaviest battles of the war. Unlike men, these women could move freely across Russian-held territory since women were not checked at roadblocks. Often, the television simply showed fighters singing to the guitar or talking confidently about the war – to show that not all was gloom at the front.

Under Stalin, or his successors, there would, of course, have been no press. Now, although the state kept churning out lies, Moscow did not even try to impose real censorship on the domestic reporters or throw out foreign journalists. This was partly due to technology. Like Udugov, any journalist with a satellite telex or telephone and car battery or portable generator could freely file reports, even from the most remote spot. But the uneven control over the media also highlighted Moscow's general problem in the war – the confusion between imperial reflexes and democratic aspirations, while having neither the physical capacity nor the willpower to properly fulfil either.

Where the Russians did show utter ruthlessness was in their campaign to empty the mountains of refugees, thereby depriving the *boyeviks* of social support and undermining their attempt to maintain a separate state. The first refugee centre to be bombed was the Pioneer camp in the village of Serzhen Yurt on 27 March, just when the mountain villages between Shali and Vedeno were overflowing with civilians. Four people were killed, 10 were wounded. One of the dead was a man who had invited me in for tea the night before. He had asked me about Manchester United and, when I admitted I knew nothing about football, told me everything he knew. The Mancunians lost one of their most far-flung fans. His wife was horribly injured, but survived. Another bomb at the camp failed to explode and went straight through the roof, the floor and deep into the ground below. The family were still in the room, trying to tidy up around the crater when I arrived. They'd escaped injury but were so scared they looked more fragile than glass. Outside, a Soviet lifesize scuplture of a model boy and girl, dressed in neat regulation Pioneer shorts and shirts, escaped the blast and continued to look innocently onto the woods. Down the road, bombing snapped big trees like straws and killed a man as he sat in his car.

At the refugee centre up in Elistanzhi, a village perched in the high foothills, I counted 20 craters. Eight buildings, again at a former holiday camp, had been hit. A cow had been cut in two, the separate halves lying several yards apart. After bombing, the jets strafed the area, shredding walls with cannon fire. Here, five people were killed and 12 wounded. At another camp along the main Shali–Vedeno road, where refugees had been living in an old barn, everyone managed to get out as soon as the planes circled the area. But no one was going to live there anymore. The building had collapsed, surrounded by craters several metres across and two metres deep.

Those were just the camps I was able to visit. There were similar camps dotted all over the Vedeno region and the stories filtering out that day were the same. There were more than 1,000 refugees living in these camps; none that I visited housed combatants.

The stress of the air raids could be unbearable. Good weather brought fear because pilots could see targets more easily. People never stood around in large groups. Your sense of hearing became acute. Conversations froze as everyone in a room heard the warning noise of approaching jets. People would suddenly stop in the street, say 'shush,' and cock their heads, then strain their eyes to find the tiny triangles of death. If you were in a car, your best hope was to watch pedestrians closely. If they were scanning the sky, you knew why, and a chill passed through your body.

There was method, and some mercy, in the bombing. The Russians could have killed a lot more people by making the raids at night, when all those buildings would have been full of sleeping refugees. Instead, they attacked in mid-afternoon, when nearly everyone was away or outside, always aware of the danger. The air raids were repeated the next day and then the next. Between raids, there were lulls, enough time to load up lorries with children, animals and furniture, and leave. Everybody did and, by summer, those once-overcrowded villages were ghostly quiet.

In Serzhen Yurt, the first stop for refugees before they moved higher up into the hills towards Vedeno, Yeragi, a 54-year-old man, buried his son with an eye on the sky at all times. The outskirts of the village had been bombed that morning and every few seconds, Yeragi, or one of his relatives, looked up from his cupped hands, paused in his prayers, and glanced nervously around. Only the corpse, wrapped in a white sheet, was at rest. Yeragi and his son had come under fire while fleeing Shali, just before it was captured. The son, who had been driving, was hit by a bullet and killed. 'I got us out. Then they fired a shell and the car caught fire', Yeragi said. 'I lay there with my dead son in a ditch for six hours. There was no way to get out until dark. Then I escaped and during the night, we went back and fetched his body. There was shooting everywhere. I suppose I was simply not fated to die.'

'It's those bastards fault,' Yeragi said, as a few *boyeviks* walked single file into the woods above Serzhen Yurt. 'We didn't need this war. So many funerals, so many old people killed or made to run.' Hatred of the Russians had become instinctive, but some people were also angry at the fighters – they attracted bombing. Many dreaded the day that combatants came into their villages, set up local command posts, raised rebel flags, and fired machine-guns at airplanes, more in brazen defiance than with any hope of hitting them. Everyone understood that this brought retribution.

---

*A Frenchman would be appalled by what a Russian soldier has to endure in this mountain warfare, living on sodden black bread, sleeping in the snow, dragging himself and his equipment over trackless wastes of granite crags. And what a war! A war with no quarter, no prisoners; where a wounded man is left for dead, and where his fiercest enemies collect human heads. (The mildest of them cut off their victims' hands.)*

*Our men have had something of the sort in Algeria, apart from the differences of the terrain, but they were well paid, well fed, well clad, and they had some hope of advancement, slight though it might be.*

Alexander Dumas, 1858.

As the ferocious war for control of the foothills dragged on, the Russian soldiers' awkward, old-fashioned Soviet army uniforms disappeared piece by piece, replaced by salads of camouflage, sports wear and ski hats. Hair fell long, rose in Mohicans or simply vanished in the practical skinhead. Gradually, the weather improved and the troops got tans, grew beards and wore mirror sunglasses under piratical bandannas.

The troops holding Grozny charged down potholed roads in their APCs, scattering civilian traffic onto the verges like a wake. Their vehicles flew red flags and Lenin portraits from the long rear antennas in an unintentionally absurd reenactment of the Red Army glory. At the ruins of the presidential palace Chechen street urchins took polaroids for two dollars and young Russian soldiers posed bare-chested, bayonets fixed to their Kalashnikovs. Once I saw two huge soldiers staggering around with rifles and body armour like something from a science fiction film – great helmets and pads of camouflaged, bullet proof material over their shoulders and torsos – while a friend filmed them on video.

At first I thought these were the fashion experiments of young men who felt good and powerful – victors. 'I have a gun and strength and youth ... and the mountains!' as Tolstoy's Olenin says on his way to Chechnya in the 19th century. But all that playing the conqueror was a facade. These were demoralised, not victorious men, soldiers fighting a politicians' war, unable even to maintain discipline within their own ranks. Already damaged by the collapse of the Soviet idea, huge budget cuts and the sudden withdrawal of troops from all over Europe and the ex-Soviet republics, the Chechnya war was finishing off the Russian armed forces as an effective military organisation. Privates deserting, officers unable to feed their troops, generals ordering attacks on civilians – every rank was caught in the collapse. The lack of discipline invaded even at a structural level, with the divide between the relatively well looked after interior ministry forces and the crumbling, resentful regular army widening every day.

With no breakthrough along the hilly frontline, the Russian propaganda machine had to concoct fantastic explanations for the delay. They said Bamut was impregnable because of a disused Soviet nuclear missile base that Russia's artillery and airforce could not destroy; they said nearby Orekhovo had hundreds of foreign mercenaries; they said thousands of fighters were swarming around, armed better than the Russian army. Villages in the first line of foothills were even described on television as 'high-mountain' settlements.

There was an old missile bunker in Bamut, but it wasn't the cure-all the Russians claimed. The Chechens couldn't concentrate themselves in one defensive position to hold the entire valley of Bamut, they had to be spread out, and anyway, the bunker was well outside the village. The hordes of foreign mercenaries were pure fabrication, and the so-called high mountains were foothills between 500 and 1,000 metres above sea level. The dirty secret was that no more than 200 men in each village – the numbers actually fighting may often have been as low as 40 – had halted the Russian advance.

The claim that the Chechens were better armed was particularly shocking to the Russian public, but ridiculous. Their best weapons were the RPG, longer-range, wire-guided anti-tank rockets, and a few captured heavy guns. Many fighters had Kalashnikov rifles so beaten up that they looked as if they'd fall apart at the next shot. In Bamut, the pride of their armament was a tank captured from the Russians during one of the attempts to storm the village and what they called 'the Chechen arms industry'. These home-made arms were certainly powerful, but hardly ideal. One was a black market helicopter rocket rigged up to a do-it-yourself firing tube and turned into an RPG. Another was a heavy machine-gun stripped from a captured APC and welded to a tripod for shooting at aircraft.

The basic Chechen arsenal had been amassed by Dudayev, all of it either ex-Soviet, or Russian. According to a Russian military source who opposed the war from the start, new supplies of weapons and ammunition, such as Grad rockets and RPGs, were smuggled in from Azerbaijan and Turkey through the Caucasus mountains. Sometimes the weapons were brought by stealth, other times with the collusion of paid-off Russian border guards in Dagestan. There was also at least one reported air drop from Azerbaijan. However, despite frequent accusations, the Russians never proved that the *boyeviks* had a regular foreign supply of weapons.

The real scandal – and perhaps the darkest symptom of how far army discipline had fallen – was that the Russians themselves were selling arms to the Chechens. The combination of low morale, low sense of mission, real poverty and hunger made this ultimate act of corruption inevitable. Many regular troops were reduced to desperation. Even a captain's salary was only about $700 a month – that's $22 a day for combat – and payments were usually late by several months. Conscripts were on five dollars a day. Almost any road checkpoint served as a black market where the soldiers sold their armoured vehicles' petrol to passing cars in exchange for vodka and food. Sometimes the soldiers actually begged from the people whose documents they were meant to be checking. Once I saw a scrawny young conscript soldier fill his shirt with onions from the back of a delivery truck being inspected at a checkpoint in Argun. In these conditions, it was only a short step to selling the hottest commodity of all – weapons and ammunition.

In one case a unit of Russian soldiers was publicly accused of selling off its APC. The Chechens said, and all the evidence corroborated, that this arms sale had been far from an isolated incident. Some weapons, particularly tanks and APCs, were genuinely abandonded by their crews and captured in battle. But there was also a racket in which the Russians simulated battles, pretended to lose weapons in action and sold them to the Chechens. A Russian officer told me of tanks sold for $6,000, as well as Grad rockets.

The military's failure on the battlefield extended behind the lines, where almost no attempt was made to win over the local population. As a result the troops remained hated occupiers, not the respected authority. Once territory was taken, soldiers sat inside heavily barricaded posts at strategic crossroads and bridges, only emerging to inspect passing cars and check documents. Then they disappeared again behind their sandbags, trenches, and the haze of vodka binges and rock music. These often isolated checkpoints became the focus of the Chechen hatred and regularly came under attack. In turn, the soldiers became more aggressive with the civilian traffic, refusing to let people through, shooting over the heads of people on foot, or shooting out the tyres of cars which didn't wait in line. Aggression and alcoholism – these were the Russian soldier's only pressure valves.

Even in Grozny, Russian rule never evolved from a state of military occupation. Improvements in ordinary people's living conditions were negligible. Electricity and partial water supplies resumed and a couple of hospitals were somewhat refurbished, but that made little difference when tens of thousands of houses and apartments had been destroyed over the last few months. The most visible piece of reconstruction was at the headquarters of a puppet government set up by the Russians and led by Salambek Khadzhiyev, a former Soviet petroleum minister. The buildings smelt of fresh paint and buzzed with the sound of chatting Russian secretaries, Russian officials and their Chechen allies. The sense of normality in there was shocking, as if you'd just been beamed to Moscow. Outside, the only reality was anger, revenge and mistrust.

At night in Grozny, snipers hid in the ruins and picked away at the troops behind their concrete barriers and bunkers, and the Russians blazed back. By day – every Russian knew – those snipers walked the streets in civilian clothes, indistinguishable from the next man. Unable to root out the combatants, the Russians got rid of their cover, bulldozing block after block of destroyed houses and apartment buildings around the presidential palace until the city centre was absolutely flat. The foreignness of the place and the people meant the hostility was inescapable until the soldiers returned to their checkpoints and bases. A soldier could spend hours in the city and not understand a word of what was being said around him in Chechen. The men on the corner might be talking about food prices, cars or fixing their ruined houses. Or they might be partisans discussing killing and sabotage. The soldier never knew. To him, Chechens looked alike. No sensible Russian soldier entered the labyrinthine main market in the centre, where you could still buy anything from firearms to fur coats and spices. There were incidents of soldiers gunned down there in broad daylight, the assailants vanishing into the colourful crowds. Sometimes soldiers went missing in Grozny until their decapitated heads were found in the street.

Even at Khadzhiyev's government building, you couldn't tell what the people really thought. Anti-Dudayev Chechens enlisted as guards wore Russian uniforms, but one of them asked me, 'so, what do you think of the *boyeviks?*' I thought he was about to curse Dudayev and the rebels, but instead he said quietly, 'they're showing these Russian swine how to fight, aren't they?' Then: 'If you go up to the mountains and see them, please, tell them they have our support.' Khadzhiyev himself, despite being Moscow's straw man, begged the Russians to curtail the abuses and called them an 'occupying army'.

It wasn't just the men whom the Russians learned to hate. Children had taken part in the war from the first days, helping carry the wounded or ammunition, and hoping for the day they could fight beside their elder brothers or fathers. They too were the enemy. Likewise the women. How did a soldier know whether the woman selling him cigarettes was not the mother or daughter of a fighter, or even an active member of the partisan network? Once I was on a bus full of chattering women who fell into a poisonous silence as soon as a soldier stepped on to conduct a search. The red-faced young soldier spent less than 10 seconds conducting his 'search' before leaving.

Nothing the Russians or their Chechen clients did could bridge the gap of hatred. In Grozny propaganda officers sometimes used to drive through the centre in APCs fitted with loudspeakers advising the populace to abandon support for the rebels; helicopters were used to scatter leaflets with the same message in areas under rebel control. But no one was fooled.

Once an APC parked by the bazaar and an officer began handing out newspapers full of anti-Dudayev articles and information about the benefits of Russian rule. At first a curious crowd gathered, then came hecklers, and before long the APC and its nervous crew was surrounded by angry men and women. The officer, who seemed educated and good natured, tried to argue back, but there was so little he could say. 'That's all you've brought us!' shouted a man, pointing around him at the landscape of gutted ruins. The officer dropped back down his hatch and the APC left, loudspeakers blaring. 'Do not help the bandits. The bandits are using you. The bandits are hiding behind the people's backs to shoot at the federal forces who are restoring order. Do not help the bandits …'

Further from Grozny, and closer to the frontline, the fear and misunderstanding multiplied. In Shali the Russian soldiers began low key street patrols, but they were not a success. A soldier who went out with no shirt was harangued by several unarmed men. 'You're breaking your own military code and insulting our customs' a Chechen shouted. And as the mob grew, the soldier moved off quickly. During a patrol I went on with interior ministry soldiers in an APC in March, the atmosphere changed as soon as the outskirts south of Grozny turned to farmland. Down went the hatches, the machine-gunner took up his seat and the soldiers sitting on the outside put on their thick special forces helmets.

There were no people or vehicles along the road, and that intensified the sense of isolation. At a water plant station that had to be checked, we found the remains of a woman in a bombed-out hut. She'd been dead a long time, probably killed in an air raid at the start of the war, and she looked mahogany. The place was silent and spooky. The APC commander, a lieutenant called Nikolai, posted sentries and said what everyone was thinking: 'Let's pay attention now. We check this place and then we leave. My time is almost up here and I want to make it home.' His nervousness was infectious, and peering through the tiny slit windows of the APC, I began to anticipate the blast of an RPG round, fired from those hostile, alien woods. It felt good to get back to the ruins of Grozny.

As morale dropped, so did the troops' respect for human life – both Chechen and their own. The general culture of brutality within the Russian armed forces had long been known, but the war illustrated the often inhuman attitude of the army as an institution. There was the perpetual chaos over casualty figures, the refusal to tell mothers the fate of their sons, rumours of mass graves that hid real losses. At the end of the war RTR national television filmed a remarkable case of soldiers living in a tent alongside corpses in body bags. The only reason this had come to light was because the tent caught fire and burned down.

The situation only worsened as the troops in Chechnya shifted from young conscripts to older soldiers on relatively well-paid contracts – *kontraktniks*. The widespread use of *kontraktniks* was meant to introduce tougher, more mature men into the ranks – volunteers, not ex-schoolboys forced to fight. But these were not necessarily professional soldiers in the Western sense; they were often men on contracts lasting a few months, often with no previous military experience beyond national service. And like classic mercenaries, the *kontraktniks* were asked few questions by recruiters. Even the army admitted that many of these volunteers were convicts, drunks and even homeless people looking for an escape. Some said they had volunteered out of patriotism or a sense of adventure, but there were more who simply had no other place in society, and those, perhaps even sadder, who said they had come to Chechnya to make a bit of money. 'I'm going to buy a refrigerator', one near Shali told me.

The contradictions in age and pay served further to demoralise the armed forces. These newcomers were often in their 30s, paid about $360 a month, and lorded it over fellow privates who were virtually unpaid conscripts and 10 years younger. There could also be tension between short-term *kontraktniks* and the professional career officers they were meant to serve under, but who were often much the same age.

*Kontraktniks* were especially hated by the Chechens. Conscripts could be forgiven because they were not fighting of their own will, but volunteers – volunteers fighting for money – were hated and hunted. *Kontraktniks*, it was said, fought especially hard in battles because they knew if they were taken prisoner they'd be executed.

The *kontraktniks* played a leading role in the search for suspected combatants and the reprisals, the dirty side of almost all wars against partisans. Chechen men particularly feared checkpoints manned by *kontraktniks*, where they were often checked for bruises on their right shoulders, or other signs of having used firearms. Men could be detained on the slightest suspicion and this meant entering into the system of secret, extra-judicial 'filtration camps' behind Russian lines. Men of fighting age had been disappearing to camps in Grozny and on the edges of Chechnya in Russian military bases since the start of the war. Many never came back. By the summer of 1995 there were more than 1,000 Chechen men listed missing. Human rights organisations and journalists were barred from filtration camps, but the men who came out were often scarred and bruised. They told stories of being kept in pits, being beaten, burnt with cigarettes, pelted with stones and scalded with hot water.

Among the professional officers, many seemed almost embarrassed by the war and kept trying to square their training and their memories of the Soviet army with the fiasco around them. 'We need to end this and begin negotiations,' said an officer outside Samashki at the start of the summer of 1995. He pointed at Samashki and admitted that the village was still not under his control despite having been 'cleansed' in the infamous spring attack. 'Every night they come through the woods and fire at us with machine-guns and rifles.' When he talked about Bamut, it was without any of the official propaganda. His honesty was almost a shock. 'There're about 100 fighters in there, but it's a hard place for us to storm. We shell it, but they take low casualties in their bunkers. Every day we shell and rocket Bamut and every now and then our planes bomb it, but that's not very effective. We should talk. As for me, I want to go home. I'm tired, I've been here six months.'

Most lost were the conscripts, products of a society which didn't back the war and an army which couldn't fight it. 'I don't know if I've killed. I've shot every day. Now, I want to go home. I don't think anyone needs this. We all want to go home. A lot of us are dying. A friend of mine from kindergarten died in Grozny,' said Leonid, a 20-year-old conscript. Hundreds like him were taken prisoner, often giving themselves up as soon as they fell under attack. Once made captive, some Russians died under their own shelling, some were released or exchanged, and an unlucky minority were kept long after the war, forgotten almost entirely by their government. But to understand the deep despair of the conscript army, you had to meet the deserters – boys who fled one of the world's largest armies and went over to an enemy they had been told executed all prisoners.

Deserters were all over southern Chechnya, tidying up and cooking for guerrilla units, helping with the animals, and even fighting alongside the *boyeviks*. In a bizarre extension of the hospitality tradition, conscript prisoners and deserters were told they could join the fighters if they converted to Islam, or be kept prisoner until they could be exchanged.

For many there was probably little choice – staying with the Chechens, however strange, was probably better than going back to face court martial and a prison sentence for desertion.

In some cases, the conscripts' parents were contacted and helped to smuggle their sons back into Russia, but those were the lucky few. Many, maybe hundreds, of POWs were kept and sold between Chechen families as collateral against the eventual return of their own sons held by the Russians. In the same way Russians would sell Chechens their sons, or the bodies of their sons, for hundreds, sometimes thousands of dollars. This was the barter in human lives which Alexander Dumas had described more than a century before.

Up in a mountain camp, a 20-year-old Russian called Konstantin said he walked out on his regiment because 'we were like animals. An officer beat me with a shovel in the legs, damaging them so it took two months to heal after I managed to desert. Lots of people thought about deserting. No one wanted to fight.' Konstantin had taken up Islam, changed his name to Kazbek and joined a guerrilla unit fighting his countrymen.

Another deserter who joined the Chechen fighters was Sasha, a gangly 20-year-old from southern Russia. He had deserted because his officers made him live in a pit in the mountains and after his conscription period ended, when he should have been released from the army, they kept him on for another three months. Sasha was sure he'd never be allowed free and that he wouldn't survive. So in the early summer he dropped his rifle and sneaked into the forest, where the Chechens found him, gave him civilian clothes, and took him to Shamil Basayev's camp. When I met him again by chance two months later, he'd changed his name to Serazhdi and was holding prayer beads. 'I'm staying here with the Chechen lads,' he said.

————

*Your heart stopped beating,*
*The cry 'Allah!' froze in your mouth.*
*You won't see the sun again,*
*Allah's taken you away.*
*As we say farewell before your final journey,*
*We swear to you we'll give our lives*
*So the Caucasus may be free.*

*You could have stayed at home*
*And looked on evil from the sidelines,*
*But you came to this land*
*For the freedom of this little country.*
*You came to this land, you came to save*
*Chechnya from its enemies,*
*And today, you've died for freedom.*

Sung by a Chechen fighter in Bamut, April 1995.

To the Chechens, Bamut had become one of the legends of the war, alongside the defence of the presidential palace and the rout of Russian troops on New Year's. With a typical sense of theatre, Dudayev officially dubbed it 'Fortress Bamut.' For 18 months, until the rubble of its 1,300 houses was captured in June 1996, it was just that – impregnable.

Like several other frontline villages, Bamut was nestled in a valley bordered by steep, wooded hills that were perfect for defence. Equally important, the rear of the village backed up into the border of Ingushetia. If the Russians could have attacked Bamut from this side, they would have soon encircled it. But because Moscow feared dragging the Ingush, or even other areas of the North Caucasus into the war, the frustrated generals were highly restricted in what they could do on Ingush territory. Troops could move through, but launching active operations on (or even from) Ingush territory was impossible.

With their rear secure, the *boyeviks* of Bamut could discreetly use the village of Arshty, just inside Ingushetia, for resting and supplies. Many of the refugees from Bamut lived in Arshty, making the village a natural rear base. Moves to cut the link between Bamut and Arshty, both with air raids and an attempt to send ground troops, were called off after furious protests from Ingush President Ruslan Aushev.

From the front side of Bamut, looking out onto the plains, you could see the Russian positions 700 metres away. You saw a block house, dug-in armoured vehicles and the occasional careless soldier wandering above ground. Twenty four hours a day, rotating shifts of *boyeviks* patrolled the outskirts, while their snipers picked off Russians from hiding places in the ruins. From the hill top on the right flank, Chechen mortars and other artillery fired into the Russian camps.

In response, night and day, the Russian artillery rained down on Bamut, setting fire to already ruined buildings, tearing more craters out. The mosque was in ruins and the graveyard had been hit by shell fire. The stench of dead, rotting animals, savaged by crazed stray dogs, spread throughout the village. The woods and hilltops around Bamut were bombed and shelled so badly the earth was churned up into powder on dry days. Patches of woodland lay in splintered piles. But after every bombardment the Chechens, who were scattered in small groups and always stayed close to cover, emerged and fired back. By April 1995, they'd driven back four Russian attempts to storm in with tanks and APCs.

Knowing they would be there for a long time, the fighters adapted to the rubble, scratching out a mock normality. Most of the defenders came from Bamut itself. They could show you where their houses had been, where they grew up. Even during the apocalypse, it was home. One of their favourite phrases was *'humma a dats'* – Chechen for 'no problem.'

The headquarters was on the edge of a river gully in a street of broken houses, craters and splintered trees. Nearby was a working sauna. The two-storey house next to it had taken a direct hit, but the bath house in the garden, heated by a small wood stove, stood unscathed. A darkly bearded *boyevik* called Magomed and I steamed, then doused ourselves with a bucket of cold water, standing in our underpants amid the rubble, cooled by the evening breeze, and looking out onto the distant snow-capped peaks of the Caucasus. It was hard to remember where we were until a Russian artillery shell screamed through the air. I hit the ground, but the shell had been high over our heads on a trajectory to the positions up the wooded hill. Magomed laughed and told me to get back into the sauna.

Because I was a guest, the commander, Khanzad Batayev, always brought me into the surviving room of the otherwise ruined headquarters house and had Raisa, the cook-nurse, make me tea. At dinner Raisa cooked a soup of meat and potatoes and served it up on china bowls for me, Khanzad and a few favoured fighters. It was like eating in a theatre set. The room looked real, but the one next to it, separated by a curtain hung over the door, was a roofless pile of rubble. How long our room would last was just a guess. Shelling started during dinner, rattling the walls and tea cups. 'Don't worry', Khanzad said. 'Nothing will happen to you in here – you're surrounded by believers'. I thought he was joking, but Chechens actually believed things like that.

Khanzad's unit slept and stored ammunition in heavy concrete cellars, fully clothed, their rifles and grenade launchers on the shelf over their heads. For an hour or so one night, a 17-year-old called Movladi, with twinkling eyes, khaki trousers, tennis shoes and a Russian-army helmet, sang to his guitar inside the cellars.

'What do wolves care about Grachev?' and 'What do eagles care about Yermolov?' were the refrains to one song and everybody cheered and shouted 'Allah Akbar!' wiping tears of laughter from their eyes. Movladi didn't have a particularly good voice, but everyone enjoyed this hint of their former lives. Some of the fighters began dozing like children.

Bamut's people belong to the Melkhy *teip*, or clan, one of the most closed and ultra-traditional in Chechnya, and for them Sufism plays an important role. During an evening lull in April, eight or nine of the fighters gathered in the courtyard of the headquarters and performed the *zikr*. At first the singing was out of tune and rhythm, but as so often happens, the *zikr* took on a life of its own. The rhythm came with the stamping and the clapping, and with the rhythm came the special breathing, the hyper-ventilation which lightens the mind. Soon, the young fighters were whooping and sweating, oblivious to the occasional crack of gunfire on the perimeter of the village and the first Russian signal flares floating up, red and green, through the dusk.

Boots crunching broken tiling and glass, the dancing fighters became one, a writhing, animal entity. Stamping, spinning and clapping, they sang the verses and refrain 'there is no God but Allah!' Their faces were transfigured. When they stamped, their ammunition clips and knives slapped and clanked. At full pitch, the fighters were frenzied, spell-bound, and, I thought, ready to kill and die. They had transported themselves from this world. At the end of the *zikr*, with one man quietly saying prayers and the rest responding, you could sense the fighters gently return to earth. They were returning different men, as if they'd seen the other side and knew that if they were killed during the night they'd go to paradise. I often wondered whether the Russians in their trenches ever heard snatches of the *zikr*. It would have been terrifying.

Bamut was a dark place, defended by hard, unforgiving, and sometimes vicious people. When *kontraktniks* were captured they were liable to be executed. Captured conscripts were kept alive, but to survive their own army's bombardments they too had to become cockroaches and live in the cellars and dug-outs. Any outsider was considered a potential spy and, because survival depended so much on the Russian planes and tanks not knowing exactly where their positions were, the Chechens greatly feared fifth columns. Fred Cuny, an American aid expert, who was sent by the New York-based Soros Foundation to study the humanitarian situation, disappeared in the spring of 1995. Bamut was one of the last places he'd been seen and he was probably killed there or in the neighbouring frontline village of Stary Achkhoi, the victim of spy mania. Cuny's family spent dangerous months in Chechnya, but never was able to find his body – a strong indication that his killers were anxious to remain unknown at any cost.

When I made a trip in the depths of winter, some eight months after my first visit, I hardly recognised the *boyeviks*. Young men had become old, suspicious, brutal. They no longer bothered asking me about the outside world. The hospitality had become a formality and more people seemed to suspect I was some kind of spy or traitor than a guest. The nurse and cook Raisa had left and the fighters were often hungry. Their bunkers were damp and cold.

The night was terrifying. Grad missiles slammed into the streets, one after the other, so close that the sky and earth seemed to turn over, and we ran for the cellar. The already ruined roof of the house where we were based caught fire and two young Russian conscript prisoners, broken young men themselves, were made to fetch water in buckets and put out the flames. Yellow illumination flares shot up from the Russian positions, bathing the rubble in sickly light. A 17-year-old *boyevik*, who'd been caught in the street outside when the Grads struck, entered the bunker, flushed with adrenalin and relief, his eyes shining, his skin marble white. Minutes later, he and another 17-year-old went out to do their shift at the defensive positions on the outskirts. They had a rifle each, ill-fitting anoraks and ski hats. I couldn't wait to leave.

*Bamut*

For the 50th anniversary of Victory in Europe day on 9 May 1995, President Yeltsin orders a truce in Chechnya. The Chechens know it's a lie, the Russian forces know it's a lie. But when the Western leaders flock to Moscow to meet with Yeltsin and celebrate world peace, they pretend it's true. The truce is set from the end of April to 11 May – when all the western leaders will have gone home and the war can officially start again.

The Western leaders mark their indignation by insisting that no Chechnya veterans take part in the military parade on Red Square. This, the press secretaries explain, indicates the West's firm stand on Chechnya.

Then, to emphasise their principles, the Western leaders – John Major, Helmut Kohl, Bill Clinton – turn down an invitation to a second, even bigger military parade. They are 'anxious to avoid being seen as giving an endorsement to military excesses in the breakaway region', the news announces.

At a press conference on 10 May with President Clinton, Yeltsin tells a plain lie: 'There are no military operations now in Chechnya. What is going on is mostly constructive work.' Clinton does not flinch. Pressed, he says: 'The civilian casualties and the prolongation of the fighting have troubled the rest of the world greatly.'

At exactly the same time as the two stand in front of the world's press, live on TV, helicopter gunships are rocketing Serzhen Yurt.

Just at the start of Yeltsin's phony truce, diplomats from the Organisation for Security and Cooperation in Europe, the OSCE, visit Bamut for the first time. They've been expected for days and the refugees outside Bamut and the fighters inside are impatient. Once these foreigners see for themselves what has happened, their powerful governments will understand, the scales will fall from their eyes.

The five OSCE delegates come in a yellow bus from Ingushetia. The Chechen fighters act self-important and give the OSCE a tour of Bamut. It's a sunny day, there's no shooting and the atmosphere is relaxed. I can't help feeling happy for the Chechens.

But something is wrong. Something is wrong with the OSCE people, with their blazers and safari gear, the way they snap instamatic pictures of the wrecked streets, looking more like tourists than documentalists. There's the impression that they're talking to each other instead of to the Chechens.

I ask one, a suave, well-spoken, Franco–Anglo called Olivier Pelen, why the ceasefire seems to have made little difference to the fighting. He speaks for 10 minutes without a pause and I have no idea what he is talking about. Something about how complex the situation is, with 'levels within levels,' 'modalities' and a lecture on how this is a 'moratorium,' *not a 'ceasefire'. I open my mouth, then quickly shut it, dreading another dose of stuff I can't understand.*

*Near the edge of the village, the frontline, we're spotted and come under direct fire. Nothing too heavy, mind you, but we're forced to sit and wait under a broken wall, a few yards from the incinerated remains of a Russian tank. Sniper bullets whack into the earth a few metres beyond the wall and there's the whirring sound of mortar shells passing overhead into the village, far beyond their mark. The OSCE fish out matching flack jackets.*

*'We hope to get the parties to use this period to get talks started on a ceasefire,' says the head delegate, a Hungarian called Sandor Meszaros. 'However, the military machine is still in motion as we saw today', he adds. The Chechen fighters, ragged and wild, look at this man with a mixture of humour and despair.*

*The OSCE's next stop is Arshty, where the population of Bamut is now living on the floor of the school house, in barns and overcrowded homes. The civilians, more naive than the fighters, immediately surround the delegates, as if trying to touch their robes.*

*A man called Movladi is trying to tell them that he has lost everything; someone else is shouting the old refrain 'why won't the West do something?'*

*At first the diplomats nod gravely, then someone actually begins writing things down on a notebook. But it starts to drizzle and I can tell the officials are not listening. They get on a bus and leave the Chechens to their moratorium. I ask Movladi whether his hopes have been fulfilled.*

*'They are good people, but this was useless,' he says. 'They came, took a quick look and left. They'll have gone home, had some vodka and relaxed. Then they'll tell their bosses whatever seems best at the time. They don't really care about us. They need to stay here and see that people are dying, people are running out of things to eat, that my family is now living in a farm with the animals because they have nowhere to go. Then they would have an idea.'*

*That night, I stay in Arshty. Bamut is four kilometres away but when the shelling there begins, the ground trembles under my feet, the windows rattle and the refugees around me shake their heads in silence.*

By mid-May, 1995, the Russians finally looked poised to break the resistance and punch up into the mountains. The walls of the 'mighty fortress', as they were described in the 19th century, were getting ragged. After all, hill tops and remote villages which had been impregnable strongpoints a century before, were now the easiest of targets for a Sukhoi-25 dive bomber. General Mikhail Yegorov, commander of the operation, said he was ready to finish the offensive on the mountains, using 'all units and available means'.

The big prize was Vedeno, a place heavy with history, the hometown of Shamil Basayev and semi-official capital of Chechnya-Ichkeria. With summer starting, the skies were clear every day and the planes circled like cats around a fishbowl. Driving through the green, rolling hills, lookouts hung out of the car windows, scanning the clear skies for the tiny triangles of high-flying jets. Chechens sat in shifts on the hilltops watching for paratroopers and firing their rifles in pathetic, angry bursts at the aircraft.

Anatol Lieven of *The Times* and I stayed in Hadji Yurt, a village across the valley from Vedeno. It too had been bombed and, like every village, was almost deserted. As we slept in a cellar with Islam, one of the half dozen men who'd stayed, we could hear the planes hit Vedeno during the night. In the morning they came back and we watched as they circled and dived gracefully, fired their streams of rockets, then peeled back up into formation to circle and rocket again.

In Vedeno itself, Dudayev's state endured. People even kept their watches on Dudayev time, one hour ahead of Moscow. The local leadership sat in the administration buildings in the village centre, a rather obvious target for an air raid, but all part of the attempt to keep up appearances. A dull administrator made us register to indulge his fervour for bureaucracy, but, rather embarrassingly for him, the process was cut short by the third air strike of that day.

The Russian airforce denied using any exotic bombs, but we saw the shrapnel on the ground and the Chechens studiously collected fragments. There were cluster bombs which scattered a series of shrapnel-filled smaller charges, ball-bearing bombs and bombs which spewed small spiked diskettes. Down in the plains, doctors had treated victims of the 'needle bomb', which sprayed thousands of red-hot barbed darts. Of course the Russians denied this too, but they denied they'd bombed orphanages, civilian cars and old people's homes. Often they even denied their planes had flown at all.

Much of the time, they dropped what the Chechens called 'depth bombs.' These left craters the size of a reasonable swimming pool, causing houses to be not just demolished, but to disappear altogether. Recently, one of these had severed the asphalt main road from Vedeno to the frontline at Serzhen Yurt. Another had hit Shamil Basayev's family house, reducing it, literally, to knee-high rubble. He wasn't there, but eleven of his relatives were killed. 'That was nothing', Basayev said without hesitation when we asked him about the bombing. A hard man.

During the air raid which interrupted our registration, the planes attacked the centre of the village with depth bombs, annihilating several houses, and rocketed a farm on the outskirts, killing a 57-year-old man tending cattle. The only reason more people weren't killed is that so few were left. After the planes flew away, the cattle herder was brought in for burial. His head and right leg were missing, but they still laid him out in the main room and washed the remains, according to Moslem custom. Outside, about 20 old men with skull caps, beards and carved walking sticks stood in a circle and prayed.

During the retreat from the plains into the mountains in March, there'd been the claustrophobia that cattle must feel when they're herded through a gate. Now in Vedeno, the atmosphere was rarified, unreal – this was not a retreat, but more a last stand and the very fact that time was running out seemed to make time pause. Apart from the occasional journalist or doctor from Médecins Sans Frontières (MSF), there were no people from the outside world. The long, empty streets made you feel self-aware rather than lonely and the weirder the people you met the more normal they seemed.

Strange rumours circulated of a troupe of men in skirts, who for all the world sounded like Scottish dancers, and although we never saw any kilts, there were all the trapped freaks and heroes who gather at last stands. Imam Alisultanov, a handsome singer whose songs about the war had become anthems for the fighters, was said to be somewhere in the village.

There was a figure who introduced himself as a 'Dutch journalist colleague', but carried a Kalashnikov rifle and spoke almost no Russian. There was a woman fighter, with rifle and pony tail walking down the central street. There were the usual half dozen fighters who claimed to have personally shot down a plane whose wreckage lay all over the road below Vedeno. There was the boring administrator's Soviet-era *apparatchik* black Volga saloon with a telephone which had clearly not worked for years but was his pride. There was Khassan Bachayev, the tired, brave doctor, now working all alone in a school building because his hospital had been bombed.

Dzhokhar Dudayev stopped by, then disappeared back into the mountains. Then Maskhadov came to talk strategy with Basayev, looking for all the world as if the war was going his way. 'They thought this would be a stroll against a few bandits and it would all be over in a few hours. They didn't study Chechen character and our history. If we can hold out a month it's a victory; against such a huge army, six months is a supreme victory. ... Russia can't win here. It's like Afghanistan or Vietnam – defeat awaits them, I guarantee you.'

When Anatol and I walked down to the front at Serzhen Yurt, the fighters couldn't disguise how bad the scene was. They seemed half drunk from the violence, tension and fatigue. One, who said he was called '.545' after the automatic rifle calibre, looked on the point of tears. 'Our leaders are all rats. They sit up in Vedeno and hide from the real fighting. We're not fighting for them, we are fighting for Allah and our dead relatives and comrades. We need no one, not Dudayev, not Maskhadov, only Allah.' He prayed briefly. I asked him why he wore a red headband, not the Moslem green headband most others wore. 'It's for my brother's blood. He was killed in Grozny. This war is for his blood now.'

In the central street of Serzhen Yurt, where every house was in ruins and fires still smouldered from the last air raid, a 27-year-old called Beslan Yerkiyev, with two RPGs over his back and a rifle in his hands, looked up with his red eyes and said: 'Let them destroy everything. We'll still keep fighting.'

At the rear base for Serzhen Yurt, about a kilometre from the village, they had half a dozen APCs and artillery guns hidden in the trees. The king of the Serzhen Yurt heavy weapons was an almost grotesquely beaten up APC, carrying of all things a Russian airplane's multiple rocket launcher, either salvaged from a downed plane or bought on the black market. 'It's our champion – we've driven back a whole attack with that thing', one of the Chechens grinned. One of the howitzers at the camp had been worn out by over firing, one of the APCs had flat tyres and another's engine had broken down irreparably. 'We even have to be careful with our rifle ammunition now', said a *boyevik* called Sidik.

As we talked, there came the sickening sound of jet engines high in the sky. There was no bombing, just the noise of the planes circling repeatedly. Everyone sat under the trees in silence, drinking black tea brewed on a small wood fire, or moved into the dug-out. 'They're looking for us' said Sidik, 'they're looking for this base.' We were being hunted.

Back up in Vedeno, Maskhadov was clean-shaven, freshly washed and wearing a brand new camouflage uniform. We pressed him. He'd retreated from Grozny to the plains to the foothills. Now where? Look at the map: beyond the foothills, there was nowhere to go, just the tortured topographical squiggles of 15,000-foot mountains.

But he didn't look or sound like a general about to go down. His conditions for peace talks were the same they had been every time I talked to him – end the war, get the troops out and then talk about independence. First, stop the war. 'Do we need a referendum? Do we need elections? Do we need talks, or other types of mutual relations with Russia? What status? Let the people decide. We're ready for everything. But only after the stopping of aggression and withdrawal of troops.'

He spoke quietly as always, but sounded dangerous. 'If Russia doesn't accept this, then the war will take a different character. The people who slept will wake. Then it will be a religious war.' No surrender.

Exactly six days later, on 3 June, Russian armour and helicopter-borne paratroopers burst through Chechen defences to the west of Vedeno, part of a sudden offensive across the central and eastern fronts, from Shatoi to Nozhai Yurt.

Instead of the usual frontal assault, the operation was a sophisticated blend of rapid deployment by helicopter and a push on Vedeno from the flank and rear. Surprised, the Chechens transformed their last stand into yet another lightening retreat, abandoning Serzhen Yurt and Vedeno before they could be encircled. Russian troops entered Vedeno almost without a fight. On Wednesday, 14 June, in similar circumstances, they captured the key mountain centre of Shatoi.

Chechen combatants had now either died or disappeared into deep mountain woods and a half dozen remote villages. Bamut, Orekhovo and Stary Achkhoi were still holding out in the southwest, but that was a mini-war unto itself with limited strategic importance for the whole republic. The fact was that with the capture of Shatoi, Russian troops stood at every major crossroads in the republic, and the Russian tricolour hung on administration buildings from Grozny to the mountains. In Moscow, where excited preparations were being made for a visit by Princess Diana, the war was considered as good as over.

That same day, 14 June, a strange report came out over Russian news agencies. Shooting had broken out in a sleepy Russian town called Budennovsk. The police headquarters was under attack. Men were on the roof of the town hospital with a machine-gun. There were unconfirmed sightings of a green-red-white flag.

Like a photographic print developing in liquid solution, the full, impossible horror emerged. Somehow, Shamil Basayev and 150 suicide fighters had sneaked into a Russian town 240 kilometres from Vedeno. They had run amok. Now they were in the hospital with 1,500 hostages and a pile of explosives. Basayev had one demand: stop the war.

## 4. VENGEANCE

*They say we're cowards – let them. We won't just sit here in Chechnya and be exterminated. I warned that we would fight in Russia and there are a lot more targets. We have radioactive elements, biological weapons that Russia left us. We could put biological weapons in Yekaterinburg and let them all get sick. To put uranium in Moscow would require one person. One of our people gets killed and a city dies with him. ... If someone spits at you in the face for half a year, wouldn't you spit back just once? That's what we did and we'll do it again.*

Shamil Basayev in his mountain hideout after raiding Budennovsk.

The Chechen attack on Budennovsk was the old *nabeg* – the cross-border raid aimed at capturing hostages and inflicting maximum damage as quickly as possible – sharpened by the 20th-century horrors of machine-guns and RPGs.

The ruthlessness of the 100 to 150 *boyeviks* under Shamil was shocking. Hiding in the back of closed lorries, they infiltrated all the way from the besieged mountains, across the plains, then into the Stavropol district town of Budennovsk, a quiet place known only for its bankrupt plastics factory and an air base used by planes bombing Chechnya.

Basayev claims he got through one Russian checkpoint after the other by paying thousands of dollars in bribes. This may be partly true. Most likely the Chechens infiltrated using a mixture of bribes and simple evasion. The area between Chechnya and Budennovsk is little inhabited and, with careful reconnaissance, it seems the Chechens could have first swung east through Dagestan, then north, easily skirting troops and police posts. One of the truck drivers whom I later met was a blonde Chechen who on first sight could pass off as a Russian. Yet the feat, at a time when Chechnya had been all but reconquered by the Russians, remains astonishing.

Outside Budennovsk, the group was finally confronted by suspicious police. Where the Chechens were heading remains unclear; some say the plastics factory. According to Basayev he intended to go further but, now that their cover was about to be blown, decided to spring an attack in Budennovsk itself. Alternatively, the Chechens may have planned the centre of Budennovsk as their target all along and later confused the story to cover their strategy. The trucks drove into the centre and, to the terror of the inhabitants, out spilled the *boyeviks*. Within a few hours, they had stormed the police station and administration building, shot down several civilians in the streets and rounded up hundreds of people, sometimes forcing them right out of their homes, then herded them up to the hospital. Between their captives seized in the town and the staff and patients already in the hospital, the Chechens had at least 1,500 hostages; some said 5,000. It was one of the largest hostage takings in history.

Long before Russian security forces could react in strength, Shamil Basayev mined the hospital entrances, put his fighters with machine-guns and RPGs in defensive positions and executed several airmen found among the hostages, adding to a car load of pilots shot to pieces during the rampage through the town. His assault was sickening. Whatever their later excuses, fighters were hiding behind the backs of women, the sick, the pregnant, doctors and children. But the single demand he put to the shocked authorities never wavered: to begin peace talks in Chechnya.

President Yeltsin, abroad in Halifax with the Group of Seven world leaders, fiddled while Budennovsk burned – sneering about 'bandits in black headbands' and vowing no mercy, apparently with no inkling of how dangerous the situation was. Both he and Pavel Grachev indicated, in their usual hedge-betting way, that storming the hospital to free the hostages would be the best response.

It was obvious attacking would be a disaster: the Russian forces who had performed so poorly throughout the war in Chechnya were ill equipped to storm a hostage-packed building defended by 150 heavily armed suicide fighters. But the attack went ahead. To the amazement of millions of television viewers who had never seen or cared too much about the bloodbath in Chechnya, the crack Alpha commandos went in covered by tank shelling and APCs blindly spraying cannon fire at the windows of the hospital. In minutes, the main building caught fire, with thick smoke billowing out of the roof. Anyone watching thought the main goal was to kill the Chechens, not save the captives. When the hostages were forced by the Chechens to stand in the windows and wave white sheets and scream, the attack stopped. Shortly after, a second commando assault began and, again, the Chechens held it off.

The whole action was a miniature version of the last six months of war in Chechnya: *boyeviks* take up positions surrounded by civilians; the Russian army makes no attempt to avoid civilian casualties and, despite an obscene level of violence, still fails to dislodge its enemy. What made Budennovsk very different was that this was taking place in southern Russia, in a Russian town and on Russian television. For Russians, the Budennovsk hospital storming was humiliating, but eye opening. Here was a concentrated display of the pain of war, the incompetence of their government, and the desperation of these fighters from the mountains. After the second storming failed, Prime Minister Viktor Chernomyrdin, in Yeltsin's absence, did the unthinkable: he personally began to negotiate.

When Chernomyrdin, filmed by national television, first picked up the phone and called Basayev, it was almost as much a surprise to the Russian public as the hostage taking itself. Their leader was negotiating to save lives, even if this meant abandoning state ideology, the ideology of eradicating Chechen 'bandits' at any cost. Not only that, but someone was actually taking public responsibility for a crisis, something every general and politician had managed to avoid throughout the war. Chernomyrdin later said it was 'the first time in Russian history that saving lives has been put above the interests of the state'.

Basayev's demand for peace talks was unbending and he refused offers of a plane, money, safe passage abroad. On the sixth day after the crisis began, the Russians caved in: there would be a full ceasefire in Chechnya and Basayev's men could escape. Basayev released all the hostages except for 150 volunteer human shields and drove back with his men to Chechnya in a convoy of buses and one refrigerated truck carrying the bodies of 16 *boyeviks* killed in the fighting. The convoy was shadowed every kilometre by the furious Russian military, but once in the southeastern corner of Chechnya, the last captives were let free and the *boyeviks*, given a hero's welcome by villagers, melted away. True to their word, the Russians signed a ceasefire accord on 21 June and stopped the war. The hard-pressed fighters and separatist leaders in the wooded mountains were given a desperately needed breather and, in the ruins of Grozny, preparations began for full-fledged peace talks. Basayev had saved the Chechens from defeat.

Russians were dazed by the Budennovsk events – alternately amazed by Basayev's coolness, ashamed by Yeltsin's handling of the crisis and their own troops' performance, full of hate that Russian civilians had been taken hostage, and stunned by Chernomyrdin's intervention. There was loathing and a new understanding of the war.

In Budennovsk, this confusion was even more marked. A total of 142 local people died in the raid, some of them when the Chechens initially burst out onto the streets, but most during the Russian artillery and commando attacks on the hospital; another 198 were wounded. Although people were quite used to the sound of planes taking off for bombing missions, Budennovsk had seemed far away from Chechnya, divided by the vast, empty steppe. To many residents, in what was a typically conservative southern Russian town, the raid confirmed the view of Chechens as born bandits. Who could fail to be shocked by the Chechens' deliberate, carefully executed plan of engulfing a large hospital in bloodshed? But to these Budennovsk residents' incomprehension, many of the locals held captive came out actually praising the Chechens, or at least placing equal blame on the Russian authorities.

The Chechens, they said, had not abused their hostages, telling everyone that they were only doing this to save their homeland. Basayev had said, 'for seven months, we've been fighting on our own land. Every bullet hits a Chechen or part of Chechnya. We've had enough and now we'll continue to fight, but on Russian land, so that the bullets hit Russia, not Chechnya.' Finally, the indiscriminate violence used in trying to storm the hospital convinced many terrified hostages that their defenders were the *boyeviks*, not the government troops.

'They didn't need to try and storm us. They were talking about the fate of 5,000 people and they didn't seem to care,' said Valentina Vasilyeva, a doctor who was taken hostage. 'If they had actually got in here and captured the place, I don't think any of us would have lived through it. The Chechens had laid mines all over the floor and our side knew that. There was a Chechen with orders to blow up the whole building, he told me so. And they'd also warned the troops about that.'

'When the building started to burn, we could barely breathe and we wore wet towels around our faces. The Chechens were hardly firing back, just their RPGs. There was almost no infantry out there, only armoured troop carriers, so their rifles were useless. They were panicking too. I guess they didn't expect this would happen.

'The first time they stormed, the Chechens made us stand at the windows and scream for it to stop. The second time, when tanks started firing on us, they told us we could hide,' she said.

Valentina's husband was killed by a bullet in the crossfire. She didn't know which side was responsible. She didn't know where her hatred lay. 'Of course, there's hate for the Chechens. They came here and attacked peaceful people. But they also demonstrated to us what was happening in their land. They didn't abuse us. If it wasn't for this war, there wouldn't have been the hospital taking, there wouldn't have been the Chechen syndrome, none of that.'

---

*Q: Why did you meet with Dzhokhar Dudayev?*

*A: I offered him a comfortable way out: a plane, money, security guarantees and no investigation by Interpol.*

*Q: The deal didn't work?*

*A: As you see, no. He's still sitting in Chechnya.*

From an interview in July, 1995 by *Komsomolskaya Pravda* newspaper with Arkady Volsky, one of the Russian peace negotiators in Grozny.

In the wake of Budennovsk, Yeltsin fired Interior Minister Viktor Yerin, FSB secret services chief Sergei Stepashin and Nationalities Minister Nikolai Yegorov. All three were party of war stalwarts but, on closer inspection, the upheaval did not augur well for Chechnya – the replacements, if anything, left the hawks strengthened.

General Anatoly Kulikov, the hard-headed commander of forces in Chechnya, became interior minister. Ex-KGB general and party of war fixture Mikhail Barsukov took over the FSB, while Stepashin was shunted over to a government commission on peace negotiations. Vyacheslav Mikhailov, a grey Soviet-style conservative, replaced Yegorov. Defence Minister Pavel Grachev, incredibly, remained at his post. Oleg Soskovets, one of the key authors of the war, was still in charge of rebuilding Chechnya and given a budget of billions of dollars, much of which was disappearing. Oleg Lobov, the Kremlin Security Council secretary who'd also backed the war from the start, was made President Yeltsin's personal representative to Chechnya, truly a cat among the pigeons.

Nevertheless, the Grozny talks were the first serious attempt to end the bloodshed. They took place at the OSCE headquarters, a small house shut off from the street by traditional blue metal gates. Outside, journalists, bodyguards from both sides and crowds of wailing women hoping for news of their disappeared relatives, spent the long, hot summer days waiting for some result. Russian APCs and beaten-up rebel jeeps with green flags parked together, with soldiers from both sides examining each other's weapons and chatting. In the countryside skirmishes and shelling continued, but the war was in lowest possible gear. There was hope.

The Chechen delegation, which came down from the mountains in a convoy of jeeps flying rebel flags and packed with bodyguards, was headed by Dudayev's justice minister Usman Imayev. The Russian side was headed by Mikhailov, with purely military talks taking place between the new overall Russian commander, General Anatoly Romanov, and Aslan

Maskhadov. On 30 July, after six weeks of often marathon sessions, the two sides signed an accord agreeing to voluntary Chechen disarmament and a gradual Russian military withdrawal. The accord was billed as the demilitarisation of Chechnya, the end of the war. But there was no political deal, not a word on the underlying issue of Chechen independence. Even after six months of fighting, neither side was ready for the inevitable compromises necessary to hold political talks. The Russians, who had come so close to winning, were not going to give in now; the Chechens, emboldened by Budennovsk, also felt they could hold out longer. In reality, the war had merely been put on hold

To keep the theatre of disarmament alive, the Chechens grudgingly began handing in a trickle of weapons to the Russians. There were comic scenes as old men – rarely men of fighting age – came forward to special collection points and offered rusty Kalashnikovs rifles, broken RPGs and even antique hunting guns. The Russians, as if trying to believe that demilitarisation really was taking place, paid compensation on the spot – $190 for a Kalashnikov, $220 for a machine-gun. Behind their white beards and peasant poker faces, you could sense the old Chechens laughing like crazy. In the market places of the big villages in the plains, where the nearby Russian soldiers would not dare set foot, dealers openly sold weapons. It was a merry-go-round. 'We hand over the old .762 calibre Kalashnikovs to the Russians, then we take their money and we come to the market and buy the new one, the .545 calibre AK-74,' a Chechen fighter said to me, grinning.

Up in Vedeno, *boyeviks* and Russian soldiers lolled on the grass on an idyllic summer's day, as a tank methodically crushed the rifles handed in by local people. It looked like an impressive haul – 135 RPGs of various models and 26 Kalashnikovs – but nearly all the rifles were old AK-47 or AKM models and broken, as were the two big wire-guided rockets. Among the 31 shot guns handed in ($30 each), there were some which wouldn't have looked out of place in a museum. In return for this, the Russian 506th motorized rifle regiment was to leave its hilltop positions around Vedeno and withdraw.

'We have to believe people are approaching this the right way,' said Colonel Vyacheslav Miroshnichenko, of the 506th. 'The more weapons there are, the more chance of war, as they say.'

'I'm hoping that in a week or so when this is all over, we'll shake hands, have a kebab and escort them to the border, live in peace, hold elections and all that,' smiled Shervani Basayev, Shamil's brother, and organiser of the demilitarisation in the Vedeno region.

Perhaps substantive political discussions could have been held, giving the demilitarisation a chance. But militants on both sides, fearing too much would be given away at the negotiating table, gave no indication of being ready to compromise, and even manoeuvred to undermine the process.

Dudayev, hiding in the mountains, knew he had nothing to lose by pressing for his all-or-nothing goal of independence and Russian troops out. If he compromised, he would go down as the leader who plunged his tiny nation into a bloodbath for nothing. Offered money to step down and disappear, the old general, ever the master of baiting the Russian bear, turned the offer around: he would step down, but first they had to recognise Chechen independence. He abruptly fired his chief negotiator, Imayev, and continuously made statements undercutting the fragile sense of optimism among the delegates in Grozny.

Meanwhile, Basayev, who like Dudayev made it clear he had little faith in the peace talks, kept up a string of shocking threats, including his warning of biological and nuclear terrorism when I interviewed him just after Budennovsk. No one seriously believed Basayev had the technical capability to carry out such threats, particularly the nuclear ones, but his words frightened ordinary Russians and made the peace talks that much harder. I knew he was essentially using me as an outlet to put force on the peace talks, but it wasn't my job to censor him. Ordinary *boyeviks* watched the talks with scepticism. Budennovsk had been a huge morale booster and they were able to put behind them the losses of every town in the last six months from Grozny to Vedeno. Basayev was widely seen as a national hero, not a terrorist, and a farcical promise by the Chechen negotiators to help the Russians hunt him down highlighted the emptiness of the entire peace deal.

Moscow, of course, was equally, if not more culpable for the failure to hold meaningful negotiations. President Yeltsin had little idea how to end the disastrous adventure he'd entered so enthusiastically half a year before. Moreover, his health was collapsing – he was hospitalised twice for heart trouble, once during the summer, and again in the autumn – and the subsequent power vacuum only strengthened the party of war. Humiliated by Budennovsk and the order to hold talks, the security forces ministers, elements within the military, and quite possibly Yeltsin himself, wanted revenge. They were infuriated by the way the Chechens were recouping, and patience for Chernomyrdin's 'lives before the state' approach had worn thin. Like some of the Chechens, the party of war figures were consumed by the war which had become their *raison d'être*. Unlike the Chechens, they were not fighting for their homeland. They needed to avoid being remembered as butchers, or worse, failures.

Kulikov, just before his promotion to minister, greeted the ceasefire by threatening to launch a new offensive if Basayev wasn't handed over, and had to be given a public dressing down by Chernomyrdin. Grachev also thought peace talks were a waste of time. He claimed that Basayev could have been captured in Budennovsk – he could have been, with the loss of hundreds of civilians' lives – and made it clear the Chechens were not worth talking to. 'There is on one side Russia's federal forces. On the other side there are only scattered bands waging sabotage and terrorist warfare,' he said.

Adding to the tension, Yeltsin signed a decree creating a new army, the 58th, to be based permanently in the North Caucasus 'to defend the state and the territorial integrity of the Russian Federation.' Troops were to be stationed permanently in Chechnya. That left little doubt that even if there were political negotiations, Chechen independence would not be on the agenda. Then at the end of July, to no one's surprise, the constitutional court ruled that Yeltsin had been within his rights to launch the war. No one questioned his right to continue.

Meanwhile, the Chechens used the truce to reorganise their scattered forces and infiltrate weapons and fighters in civilian guise to villages in the plains where the Russians had long since established control. The Russian troops, who kept up artillery shelling of rebel areas but called off any offensives, also had military reasons for a summer break: winter, when the Chechens would no longer be able to live in the open, was better suited for offensives. As the summer days grew shorter, tension mounted and a carefully placed match was all that was needed for the entire peace process to go up in flames.

In July, masked men massacred a Chechen family on the outskirts of Grozny – the culprits were never discovered – and the talks were briefly suspended. In August, a loose-cannon Chechen field commander, Alaudi Khamzatov, grossly violated the ceasefire by charging into Argun and taking over the town centre, sparking a Russian assault. But the talks survived. On 20 September, Lobov narrowly escaped assassination during a trip to Grozny; responsibility for the attack was never claimed, but the implication was that the separatists were to blame. Then in October, the puppet Chechen government installed by the Russian authorities began harassing the OSCE quarters, accusing the diplomats of being pro-Dudayev. Each incident shortened the wick.

An assassination attempt against General Romanov was the final spark. It could not have been a more brazen attack – a remote-controlled bomb going off as the Russian commander's convoy drove in full daylight through the Minutka traffic tunnel in central Grozny. The huge explosion gauged a large crater out of the solid concrete wall in the tunnel and ripped through the convoy, killing four people. Romanov went into a profound coma, from which he still had not recovered two years later. Although no one claimed responsibility, and the ceasefire was not officially broken, talks were suspended and the last vestiges of hope for peace disintegrated. In Moscow, Grachev forecast 'active military operations' in the near future and, in the Chechen villages, the newly reinfiltrated *boyeviks* prepared to fight.

Who bombed Romanov and restarted the war may never be proved conclusively. There were certainly elements in the Chechen separatist camp unhappy with the slow pace of the peace talks. Romanov may also have been held responsible for the Samashki massacre or any number of other bloody episodes in the war. The bombing could simply have been the work of Chechens working for a bounty on the heads of Russian generals. But Maskhadov, who established a solid working relationship and a considerable rapport with Romanov during the talks, has repeatedly denied ordering his men to carry out the attack. The separatist leadership certainly had little to gain from an end to the truce – after all, they were winning back strength and political legitimacy.

Among the Russians, the bulk of the army would have welcomed a political solution and a way out of the quagmire. Although the Chechens had been on the run before Budennovsk, their rapid recovery over the summer made it clear that a total military victory remained far off. On the other hand, the top generals and Kremlin politicians whose careers were now entwined with the war actively opposed the peace process. A political deal with Dudayev would underline the failure of their 'short, victorious war'.

The puppet Chechen government installed to rule over Russian-controlled territory also stood to lose from political deals with the separatists. Led by Salambek Khadzhiyev and Umar Avturkhanov, these were essentially the same Chechens hired in 1994 to try and topple Dudayev from the inside. Now they were out of exile in Moscow and had power and above all money, since they had access to the huge sums being sent for reconstruction. A man like Beslan Gantemirov, the pre-war mayor of Grozny before he fell out with Dudayev, was now deputy prime minister of the puppet government and running Grozny with his fat budget and private army. A deal leading to the return of the separatists would mean the end: Dudayev's people considered the puppet government guilty of treason.

Movladi Udugov blamed the party of war in Moscow for the collapse of the peace process, but refused to name names. According to him, a possible meeting between Dudayev and Yeltsin, something the separatists had always hoped for, was sabotaged within the Kremlin. Udugov also accused Russian officials 'fairly close' to Yeltsin of trying 'to blackmail the Chechen side. ... They demanded money'. Udugov would not say what the blackmailers proposed. They could have been offering the Chechens a good peace deal, or direct talks with Yeltsin, in return for money. What they threatened to do if the Chechens didn't pay, Udugov also never said. But killing Romanov may have topped the list.

### Grozny

*The masked gunmen come to the Chapanova family's small house in the Grozny suburbs at dawn 7 July. They shoot dead the father, grandfather,* uncle, two children and a two-year old baby girl; the aunt is fatally wounded. The mother survives, because she was out at the time tending the cows.

No one heard the shooting – silencers must have been used – and witnesses can only say that the men came in what looked like a Russian APC with Russian uniforms. But there's no proof. As the Russians say, anyone can put on their uniform. Yet the motive of the massacre, a few hours before another day of peace talks begins in the city centre, is clear.

The bodies of the Chapanova family are laid out on white sheets on an open truck and brought to the central square of Grozny, next to the carcass of the presidential palace. Waxy hands and feet stick out from the bloodstained sheets. When the gory cargo stops in the square, a crowd of thousands gathers, praying, weeping and staring in anger. 'If this is peace, then there may as well be war,' a woman shouts.

Russian soldiers deploy around the square, encircling the crowd with APCs. Soldiers sit alertly on the vehicles, seared by the sun and the hatred of the crowd. The crowd wants to march to the OSCE building and exhibit the bodies. The troops are adamant: no one is to move. The bodies warm in the sun. The crowd sways around the truck, chanting 'Chechnya! Chechnya!' As always, small groups perform the zikr.

When the Chechen leaders at the OSCE hear that the procession has been blockaded, they storm out of the negotiating room. Civilian airs vanish and the negotiators suddenly revert to guerrilla fighters. Within seconds, Usman Imayev, Aslan Maskhadov and the culture minister Akhmed Zakayev are loading into their jeeps with a dozen bodyguards, rifles, a machine-gun and RPGs. They drive at speed to the main square.

As soon as they reach the rear of the Russian line, the Chechen leaders jump out and simply walk through the gaps in the APCs, eyes forward, weapons cocked in the air. The Russian soldiers look down from their APCs in silent fury. One shot from either side and there will be a bloodbath.

'Allah Akbar!' the crowd cries triumphantly as Maskhadov and the others push their way through to the truck and climb up by the bodies. For that moment, Grozny's main square is again in Chechen hands.

Imayev, trembling, picks up the body of the infant in his arms and looks over the square. Everyone cups his hands in prayer. The mother sits on the side of the truck next to her dead family and sobs. 'Talks will be suspended until the culprits are found', Imayev tells the crowd. 'You see, this is their work. This outrage will continue as long as the people don't prevent it. It will come to all your houses.'

The leaders order the bodies to be brought to the OSCE. This time, the Russians know better than to stand in the way. All the troops have melted away with their APCs, and the procession, led by Maskhadov on foot, flows unhindered to the OSCE building.

*As the crowd stands with the bodies in front of the OSCE building chanting 'Chechnya! Chechnya!', a member of the puppet government is spotted trying to slip into the building. The crowd goes berserk, beating their fellow countryman with sticks and fists. Olivier Pelen, the OSCE diplomat, wades into the frenzy, grabs the grey-suited official and drags him to safety.*

*After a brief suspension, the Chechens agree to continue negotiating. The culprits haven't been found and everyone knows they never will be.*

*Three days later, a severed head, green from decomposition and swarming with flies, is found lying outside the house where the Chapanovas were massacred. No one knows whom it belonged to, but its message is clear – terror will continue. 'Whom do you blame? That's a hard question', says Sharani Yakhiyev, a neighbour. 'All we want is peace.'*

## 5. PARTISANS

The Kremlin, which had once dreamt of a 'short, victorious war,' was reduced to a single, desperate aim in the winter of 1995: somehow to finish the conflict before the June 1996 elections and save President Yeltsin from defeat by Communist Party leader Gennady Zyuganov.

Russian strategy in this new round came in two parts. The army would go back into all those villages that had been quietly reinfiltrated over the summer, again pushing the rebels into the hills. Then, correcting one of the fatal errors of the first year, a new puppet government would establish firm political control. Wherever the troops went, the pro-Russian Chechens would follow, bringing reconquered villages into 'zones of peace and accord' – areas which were to be spared Russian bombardments, but in return had to bar *boyeviks*. This was to be pacification, not war; this was the long awaited hearts and minds campaign.

The lead role fell to none other than Doku Zavgayev, the last Soviet boss of Chechnya, overthrown by Dudayev in 1991. Flown in from Moscow, he was appointed head of the puppet government in October, then elected in a highly questionable vote in December. To the Kremlin Zavgayev was seen not only as more effective than his predecessor, Salambek Khadzhiyev, but more ideologically sound, given the latter's increasingly outspoken criticism of the armed forces' behaviour.

The Russian strategy aimed at the keystone of the separatists' partisan army – the support of the people. The longer the war, the more the *boyeviks* relied on the logistical and moral support of non-combatants. The 'zones of peace and accord', if they worked, would be like choking the rebel army's air supply. Zavgayev was not popular, but it was hoped that his promises of peace and reconstruction would appeal to exhausted civilians. He also had a certain following among those nostalgic for the stability of the Soviet era. To the hardliners in Moscow, Zavgayev was also a perfect tool for preventing further peace talks. Because he was 'elected', he could be presented as the legitimate power in Chechnya, and the separatists nothing more than a marginalised 'anti-Zavgayev opposition' group, hardly worthy of attention.

For the separatists, a swift response was vital. They had to demonstrate their strength, embarrass the Russians and make Zavgayev look helpless. Maskhadov chose Gudermes, the second town in the republic, lying on the main east-west road and railway. On 14 December, coinciding with the opening of voting in the election, in which Zavgayev was effectively the only candidate, hundreds of guerrillas attacked the Russian garrison in Gudermes and seized control of the town. After the Chechens beat back a counterattack by infantry and tanks, the Russians sealed the town and settled down to artillery and helicopter bombardments, finally driving the Chechens out on 25 December.

This opening shot in what people already called 'the second war' did not bode well for the demoralised Russian military. Although Gudermes had been recaptured, the propaganda victory went to the Chechens: not only were they making the Russian army fight for a major town it had already captured the previous spring, they also managed to escape. Before the Russians and Zavgayev had recovered from Gudermes, the Chechens struck again, this time across the border in Dagestan. The ensuing drama was one of cruellest and, for the Russians, most humiliating, since the war began.

Salman Raduyev, a 28-year-old nephew of Dudayev, with a long pointy beard and shining eyes in a thin face, had been a commander in the battle for Gudermes but was otherwise not well known. On January 9, he and Khunkar Pasha Israpilov led a commando force of about 200 men up to a Russian helicopter base at Kizlyar, in northern Dagestan. The attack was unsuccessful. Russian troops rapidly responded in strength and there were unexpectedly few helicopters to destroy. Cut-off, Raduyev's men charged into the Kizlyar hospital, where there were about 2,000 innocent people, and took the entire place hostage. Nine soldiers or policemen, several *boyeviks* and as many as 24 civilians were killed in the shoot-out.

This was Budennovsk mark II, but with none of the earnestness and desperation which accompanied Shamil Basayev's operation. After an agreement with the Dagestani authorities that would let Raduyev's men escape in buses with about 150 hostages as human shields, the Budennovsk scenario again appeared to be repeating itself. But this time Moscow was not going to let the Chechens get away.

Just before the convoy carrying the terrorists and hostages reached the Chechen border, where Raduyev was to have released everyone and escaped with his men, a helicopter gunship opened fire on the road ahead.

The buses stopped, but the Chechens still had their human shields, so they couldn't be attacked out in the open at once. Moving fast, Raduyev's men drove back to the nearby Dagestani village of Pervomaiskoye. A police checkpoint there was surrounded and the police taken prisoner without a fight. Next the *boyeviks* took their hostages into Pervomaiskoye, by now deserted by all its inhabitants, and immediately set up defensive positions. Negotiations on freeing the hostages from Pervomaiskoye lasted five days, during which the Chechens made every preparation for battle. Although surrounded, they had plenty of food, water and buildings in which to set up defences, plus the arsenal from the police checkpoint – reportedly seven RPGs, 35 assault rifles, three sniper rifles and 10,000 rounds of ammunition. Hostages were made to dig trenches.

There was no hope of a negotiated solution. The Kremlin could not under any circumstances allow the Chechens to bargain their way out. The presidential elections were just five months away, and the ill, feeble Yeltsin desperately needed to show who was in charge. Besides, this time the Chechens were trapped and could not claim to be anything but terrorists. To make the most of it, Interior Minister Anatoly Kulikov and the FSB secret services chief Mikhail Barsukov flew down and took personal charge of the operation. For moral cover, Moscow announced that Raduyev had begun shooting captives – as it turned out later, a complete lie.

The attack started on 15 January with a barrage of tank fire, followed by units of commandos. I had just caught the plane from Moscow to Dagestan that morning and expected to arrive in time only for the bodycount. About 2,000 soldiers were positioned around the village. Alpha, SOBR, all the elite units which, despite their record in Chechnya, still had that undying movie-star quality, were there in their impressive helmets and black ski masks. The Kremlin talked about triple rings of troops and President Yeltsin, in his slurred, sick voice, made a clown of himself by promising on national television that 38 snipers were following every movement through telescopic sights.

But when I got to the area later that day, the distant sound of shooting made it clear the battle was still in progress. The interior ministry talked about 'cleaning last points of resistance' and said that the Chechens were in panic and 'had lost contact with each other'. But the truth was that the crack troops had gone in and only some of them had come back. The Chechens were still resisting.

For the next two days, my colleagues and I stood at a checkpoint four kilometres from Pervomaiskoye – as near as we were allowed to get – and tried to follow the operation. There was little to see, but the boom of artillery and helicopter rocket explosions in the village almost never stopped. Smoke rose into the grey sky. We were kept back by a savage black dog and several cold, bad tempered soldiers. Sometimes the guards let the dog loose to bite people; sometimes a column of a dozen ambulances or ammunition trucks rumbled past on its way to the Russian lines; once a local shepherd, oblivious of the media circus, wandered through the television cameras, parked jeeps and satellite telephones with his shaggy-fleeced sheep and long-horned rams. There wasn't much to write down, except one crucial fact: the Chechens were still shooting back. You could hear it. Who was liquidating whom?

The longer the Chechens survived, the heavier the army shelled and the more blatantly the spokesmen lied. The FSB man said everything was going just right: six Russian soldiers had died and 60 Chechens. Then the reason for launching the storm: the Chechens had executed eight policemen and threatened to kill the rest of the hostages. Just to spice up the story, especially with the local audience in mind, they put out that six Dagestani elders, who'd gone to negotiate with the Chechens, had been shot. On state television, this stuff might play. Day three, the Chechens were still resisting. What could the Russians say now? Would they still claim everything was going to plan? The FSB spokesman, General Alexander Mikhailov, had something new:

'Today the operation will be completed.'

How?

'I won't say exactly how, you'll see. The most severe action possible.'

What about the hostages? Wasn't the idea at the start to save them? Wasn't this a hostage rescue operation?

'Now, it's no longer about hostages.'

We looked at him in disbelief.

'I want everybody to understand that now we have a situation which is not about liberating hostages. If you're following military rules, the task here is to capture a military fortress held by a battalion strength unit in urban conditions. This is about liberating a city.'

Liberating a city? Pervomaiskoye? But the hostages, what about the lives of hostages?

'Our information' the general said, 'is that there are very few left alive.'

I ran over my tape once, twice, three times, before I knew I'd heard him right. The Russians had cracked. Their public relations dream of smiling hostages hugging handsome commandos, Chechen bandits strewn over the ground, was never going to happen. They'd even given up pretending this would happen. Now they were moving to plan two: a village, which was too small to appear on most maps, was about to be annihilated.

That afternoon, the few journalists who'd been allowed closer to Pervomaiskoye were rounded up and delivered to our checkpoint with the black dog. The 'most severe action possible' began. Grad rockets opened up at a range of a couple of kilometres, blowing the village apart and setting the ruins ablaze. Helicopter gunships, half a dozen at a time, circled and fired in a systematic way for hours, until it became monotonous to watch: the plumes of black smoke from rockets, the puffs of fire and smoke as they exploded among the houses. Even where I stood, the earth and air shuddered under the thump of explosions. Unbelievably, the Chechen rifles and machine-guns still hammered back. Standing in the snow, I just hoped that those hostages were lucky enough to die quickly. As for the Chechen fighters, they'd taken over a hospital, they'd kept human shields, they'd gone bad, even evil. But you had to admire the way they went down.

The rumour was out by the time we woke up the next morning. Local Chechens living in that area of Dagestan said they'd sat up all night tuning into *boyevik* radio frequencies and that this was the news: Raduyev and Israpilov had broken th e siege and made it back to Chechnya. They said Raduyev had escaped the inferno and even managed to keep some of his hostages. We laughed, but the story snowballed. Then, one or two at a time, hostages who'd managed to escape altogether during the flight surfaced like shipwreck survivors and confirmed everything. The rumour was true.

Later, it emerged that the breakout had been aided by a simultaneous diversion launched from inside Chechnya on the Russian rear around the village of Sovietskoye, which neighboured Pervomaiskoye. Aslan Maskhadov said about 400 fighters took part in the diversion, giving Raduyev and Israpilov a crucial chance to fight out. 'Moscow intended to kill everyone alive, so we undertook a major, planned operation to break the seige of Raduyev's men and save the hostages from the rockets, artillery and bombs. We undertook this and succeeded'. It was one of his force's most dramatic recoveries from total defeat.

As the truth emerged that first day, the Russian government, so keyed up for victory, was agonised. At first the interior ministry spokesman said a breakout had happened, but had been repulsed. Then the government admitted the truth, but produced revisionists and military experts to declare there hadn't been enough troops, or they'd been underfed, or even that the Chechens had built a huge military base in Pervomaiskoye. Adding to the embarrassment, commandos later revealed that they had been fired on by their own helicopters during the first day of the battle. The confusion extended to the death toll – some said 80 hostages died, others 24, others even fewer – although it should have been easy to count the bodies littering the village and the escape route. One of the independent tolls for military deaths was 100 Chechen fighters and 70 Russian or local Dagestani troops.

After this, there was still one hope: that Raduyev had been killed. You could feel the Kremlin praying that it be allowed just one happy result: let Raduyev be dead.

He wasn't. With a Chechen guide from one of the Dagestani villages, Carlotta Gall of *The Moscow Times* and I slipped across the border into Chechnya the night after the break out. Walking over frozen fields, around a Russian position, and down deep-rutted cart tracks we took about two hours to get to Engel Yurt, just over the border. The spokesmen and the TV maps claimed this plains village was well under Russian control, but at night everywhere belonged to the partisans. At Engel Yurt, a van load of fighters waited in the darkness. They were looking for stragglers from Pervomaiskoye and instead found us, me lugging my satellite telex equipment and coated in a film of frozen sweat. Had the hostages escaped? Yes. Was Salman Raduyev alive? Yes. Two hours later, we were taken to him.

The last hostages were released a few days later and the Kremlin did its best to bury the episode. Pervomaiskoye, where every single house had been damaged or destroyed, was rebuilt and its residents were given money and cars. Kulikov and Barsukov received no reprimand. In fact the operation was declared successful. Asked why the 'rescuers' used Grad rockets, one of the most destructive artillery pieces, Barsukov gave the surreal answer that they were 'a psychological tactic'. When the hostages stated unanimously that the pretext for the Russian decision to use force was false – neither hostages, nor Dagestani elders had ever been executed – they were ignored and even slandered as 'collaborators'.

President Yeltsin, showing how terribly far he had sunk, covered his humiliation with bluster. 'Mad dogs must be shot,' he said, threatening that 'federal forces will start destroying the strongholds' of Dzhokhar Dudayev. 'The bases discovered by our special services threaten all Chechnya with an explosion.' But the Chechen partisans were full of confidence now. 'They wanted to destroy the Chechen army fighters and the hostages, but great Allah did it all the other way', Maskhadov said. 'The Russian forces showed their complete helplessness.'

An unexpected sideshow to the Pervomaiskoye drama only exacerbated the humiliation. During the battle for the village pro-Chechen Turks, several of them part of the Abkhaz diaspora, seized a ferry with 200 people aboard, mostly Russians, in the Turkish Black Sea port of Trabzon and demanded an end to the war in Chechnya. Many in Moslem Turkey, with its large population of North Caucasians, already felt a kinship with the Chechen rebellion; now supporters of the ferry hijackers lined the shore with the Chechen flag and a Russian flag was burnt.

Yeltsin criticised the Turkish authorities as being too 'slow' and suggested Russian help, an offer verging on black humour given the bloodbath in Pervomaiskoye. But on the third day, the gunmen gave themselves up without a fight and all hostages were freed.

It was an open secret that the Chechens had supporters in Turkey. Chechen separatist officials were sheltered and even able to set up offices in Istanbul. Some Russian analysts accused the Turkish government itself of aiding the Chechens, partly to jeopardize Russia's export oil pipeline from the Caspian Sea. But this was unlikely, since Istanbul, fighting its own dirty secret war against the Kurdish minority in the southeast of the country, probably needed good trade relations with Russia more than it needed Chechnya. Still, after the ferry crisis ended the prime minister, Tansu Ciller, had this to say: 'A human tragedy is continuing in the Caucasus with mothers and children being massacred. The attention of the world must be drawn to what is happening there.'

## Novogrozny

*When Raduyev enters the cellar in the town of Novogrozny, the hostages sprawled on mattresses get up and greet him like an old friend. 'Hello Salman,' they chorus. 'How are you all,' he grins from behind his pointy beard, then shakes hands with or hugs the captives one by one.*

*Some of the hostages are wounded, all are deadly tired and bathed in that deep calm which comes over people who've just cheated death.*

*To them, Raduyev is no longer the terrorist, the hostage taker, the man who hid in a hospital to save his life when a mission went wrong. He's Salman the saviour, the man who led the hostages to safety.*

*'I just want to remind you that you are now safe,' he says, his eyes twinkling, and the hostages murmur approval and gratitude.*

*The hostages say they heard on the radio that they were all presumed dead in Pervomaiskoye and that executions had begun. They realised this meant carte blanche for an assault to wipe out the village. The Chechen commanders there also understood after the Grad strikes that planes would start bombing and that then even their trenches were not going to keep them alive.*

*During the break out fighters went first, followed by the hostages carrying ammunition and the wounded on stretchers. No one was left behind. The group crossed a minefield, and hostages describe explosions going off in all directions, cutting people down. It was here, the Chechens say, they lost dozens of men. Boyeviks, not hostages, cleared the way.*

*The fighting was wild. 'There was total panic, every man for himself, and no one thought he'd live,' says hostage Dima. 'The Chechens were firing everything they had – machine-guns, RPGs, rifles – and we were being shot at from three directions. They destroyed several Russian positions. We walked in ditches and in a river because the illumination flares made it seem like day and there was nowhere to hide.'*

*After the fighting stopped, they had to race across the frozen landscape, lugging the wounded, to reach safety before dawn. 'We knew the*

*helicopters would start hunting us when there was light, but we were not
quick enough,' says Arkady, a maths teacher. 'At about 6:00 a.m. they
came, three of them firing machine-guns at us. We had our faces in the
ground most of the time and it took us three hours to go two kilometres.'*

*'Do you know what a lamb feels like when the wolf is near? That's
how we felt, and here the wolf was all Russia,' says a hostage called
Magomed.*

Putting the Pervomaiskoye fiasco behind, the Russian offensive went into
high gear. The mid-winter months have been the best for the Russian
armies in Chechnya for centuries – the rivers are low, heavy equipment
and vehicles can travel easily across the frozen ground and the Chechens
are deprived of much cover and have difficulty camping in the woods. The
Russian military machine steamrolled across the plains, from one point of
resistance to the next, once again gradually advancing on the mountains.
Moving on from Gudermes in December, they captured Novogrozny –
which lay just down the strategic east-west road from Grozny to Dagestan
– in February. In March, a Russian offensive began in the west of
Chechnya, first against the town of Sernovodsk, then against Samashki,
and with increasing pressure on the area around Bamut.

Defence Minister Pavel Grachev talked confidently in March about
how he would pursue the *boeviks* into the hills. Well-known Moscow
columnist Pavel Felgenhauer wrote off the rebels, saying the spring
offensive

> is now in full swing. The fighting is happening in the same places as last year.
> However the Chechens are much worse off. Last year they had dozens of
> tanks and guns. Now they have mostly handguns and grenade launchers. But
> what is even more damaging is the almost complete collapse of the Chechen
> medical system.

On the map, it did look yet again as if the Chechens were being
cornered. Russian soldiers occupied southern centres from Vedeno to
Shatoi, and Gudermes to Achkhoi Martan. But close up, the rout proved
an illusion, because although the Chechens ran, they were never caught
and annihilated. They picked their fight, made a tactical retreat when it
got too hot, then reappeared in another village to fight again. This was
war without frontlines, partisan war. Only in the southwestern cluster of
Bamut, Stary Achkhoi and Orekhovo did the grinding brutality of trench
warfare in fixed positions continue.

Aiding mobility, communications had greatly improved, a far cry from
the early days of the war when poor radio links were one of the *boeviks'*
main problems. Even mid-level commanders now carried Motorola
walkie-talkies. It was as if the separatist force had grown up, transformed
from the almost spontaneous resistance of the early days into a well-

organised partisan army. Their hit-and-run strategy required careful coordination and was hard on the string of villages sucked into the fighting, but the separatists believed they'd found their pace and could outlast the Russians, whatever happened. 'Every village is a fortress', Aslan Maskhadov told me in January. 'If necessary, every village and town can be held to the end. All that Yeltsin and his armed forces can do, they've done. There's nothing apart from nuclear weapons they haven't used. In the end, they'll have no choice but to leave.'

Take Samashki. There was savage fighting, including close-quarter infantry combat after heavy artillery and aerial bombardments. The 300 to 400 Chechen defenders lost at least 40 men killed and many wounded, a relatively heavy toll by the guerrillas' standards for one battle. Yet even in these dire straits, after five days of siege, the fighters were able to escape through Russian lines. My Agence France-Presse colleague Boris Bachorz, who was with the *boyeviks*, said that at one point they were within 100 metres of Russian positions and must have been heard. But troops with low morale do not leap at opportunities to engage an enemy of unknown size in the dark; letting the guerrillas sneak by without a fight was human – and it happened often in Chechnya, leaving the *boyeviks* to fight another day.

In March the Chechens gave the Russians one of their biggest shocks to date, attacking the entire southern half of Grozny at dawn, knocking out checkpoints and firing on the Zavgayev and Russian administration buildings for three days, before disappearing. To dislodge the 1,000 or so Chechens, the Russian forces used helicopter gunships and Grad rockets. Some 100 Russian soldiers died, according to official figures, and as many as 400 according to officers who fought. There was another embarrassing Chechen success in April, when an armoured column was ambushed on the road to Shatoi, in the central foothills. The ambush – a textbook piece of mountain warfare, in which the terrain gave the attacking infantry total domination over a much stronger armoured force – was recorded on a grainy cassette tape for posterity. The ambushers, waiting in foxholes, were dug in on high ground overlooking a narrow road whose other side was an almost sheer drop. When the long convoy of trucks and APCs rolled into range, the Chechens demolished it with RPG and machine-gun fire. For the Russians, there was almost no way to turn around, and nowhere to escape or even to set up defensive positions. It was a shooting gallery – the official figures were that 73 out of 199 soldiers were killed.

The commander behind the ambush was a fundamentalist Islamic volunteer called Khatab. He only identified himself as coming from the Arab world; the Russian security services said he was Jordanian. Fighting under Shamil Basayev, Khatab, who said he had experience from the wars in Afghanistan and Tajikistan, claimed several other ambushes.

Khatab was now only one of a string of young Chechen commanders who'd emerged from a year of warfare, adding crucial expertise to the partisan army which, in its early days, had had only a handful of trained leaders.

The speed that packed villages and towns were transformed into battlefields gave few people the chance to escape and civilians suffered terribly that spring. According to witnesses, during the fighting in Gudermes hundreds of people were killed or wounded in the bombardments of residential areas by mortars, Grad and helicopter rockets. Russian General Anatoly Shkirko was reported as saying that 267 civilians were killed, but then claimed he'd been misquoted. In Sernovodsk, civilian areas were shelled until they burned. In Samashki, going through its second agony in a year, large areas were bombed flat and scores of civilians died.

In each of these battles, the encircling Russians shot at refugees as they tried to escape, while aid agencies and journalists were not allowed near, provoking even the rigorously neutral International Committee of the Red Cross to lodge an angry protest in Geneva. The news that did leak out was horrible. Russian television broadcast footage filmed secretly in Sernovodsk showed streets of burnt-out houses, incinerated vehicles and the charred remains of bodies in the still-smoking ruins of the town mosque. Survivors spoke of troops following up their capture of Sernovodsk with looting, summary executions and rape. In Samashki, an estimated 5,000 people were trapped in their cellars during the battle; there were accusations of civilians being made to sit on top of APCs as human shields to prevent the *boyeviks* from opening fire.

Despite subjecting civilians to the horrors of Russian bombardments and the interior ministry's subsequent 'mopping up' operations, the *boyeviks* retained widespread support. Indeed, without it, they couldn't have successfully fought a partisan war. Fighters were seeded all over the plains, including Grozny. More than ever there was a need for food and places to store weapons and simply to live in civilian guise. These *boyeviks* lived in ordinary houses, and didn't carry weapons in the street until called out on an operation. Basayev said his men had heavily infiltrated even the Zavgayev police force, and this was no empty boast. When the separatists launched their three-day assault on Grozny in March there were cases of Zavgayev police going over to their side, or surrendering their weapons with mysteriously little resistance. 'The police escorted my reconaissance chief into Grozny', Basayev said.

An example of the way the separatist network intertwined with the civilian world was the moonshine petrol business. In addition to the support from abroad – Turkey, Jordan and Saudi Arabia, according to Chechen and Russian sources – a chunk of the fighters' financing was believed to come from sales of this petrol. Crude oil was stolen from installations across the republic, then distilled in homemade factories and sold by rebel supporters in glass jars by the side of the roads. This ingeniously made, but not always reliable petrol was often the only source of car fuel during the war, when there were no such thing as formal petrol stations, and deliveries of legally produced petrol from outside Chechnya were scarce. The Russians could hardly stop sales of petrol, and so the *boyeviks'* coffers kept filling.

The partisan structure of the Chechen forces made it difficult to know their numbers. Only a few thousand men, at the most, were actually fighting. But for every *boyevik* there were his friends and family members, even children, lending active support; for every active supporter there was another group of sympathisers who gave occasional, or just moral, support. The *boyeviks* were the tip of an iceberg.

Deepest under cover was Dzhokhar Dudayev. Throughout the early months of 1996 Dudayev remained at large, moving from safe house to safe house in the foothills, never spending two nights in the same place, but more brazenly defiant than ever. Like a brilliant mad man, the old nuclear bomber pilot seemed part out of touch, part visionary. His rhetoric and propaganda was extreme to the point of comedy.

'Now the leaders and the people of Dagestan and all the Caucasus will be united in their stand against Russianism – that humanity-hating ideology and policy which comes out of the Satanic Russian centre', Dudayev told Voice of America radio over his satellite telephone in the woods of the foothills in January, just after the Pervomaiskoye battle. In February, in an interview with the Turkish newspaper Sabah, Dudayev was even more apocalyptic. 'The Chechen war will first spread to the whole of the Caucasus, ... then to Turkey and then to Europe and eventually it will lead to the Third World War. In Chechnya, our war will continue for decades, until the last Chechen is killed.'

At the same time Dudayev remained what he had always been – a military man, a talented general. Thanks to his lifelong ties with colleagues in the Russian military and the uncanny effectiveness of Chechen intelligence, he was also able to prove repeatedly that he had an unusually clear idea of what his enemy was up to. In March, he spat out more of the same purple language at a press conference, but he also said that the three-day attack on Grozny that month had been just a 'dress rehearsal'. The statement was widely dismissed, but in fact it was prophetic.

### Vedeno region

*The partisans come for us deep in Russian-held territory one May night. They drive a captured police jeep, complete with blue lights on the roof, and the initials of the Russian State Road Inspectorate – GAI – in big letters on the door. At about 1:00 a.m., we drive south from Grozny*

*without headlights down unguarded roads under a strong moon. There
are glimpses of other fighters moving on foot. 'Night is the time of the
wolves,' Askhab the commander says.*

Across the plains as far as Stary Atagi on the Argun river. All the
bridges are in Russian hands, so we begin to drive through the fast-
flowing, grey current. Water seeps through the doors, but we've almost
got across, when the jeep lurches into a deep hole and suddenly there is
silence – the engine is flooded. We abandon the jeep, pushing open the
doors and struggling, chest high in cold water, to the bank. The Russians
are about a kilometre away, straight down the river. A few flares and
we'd be seen. But the Chechens laugh, light cigarettes and plug into the
partisan network, that invisible, vital base of support. Within minutes,
a man with a truck is fetched from Stary Atagi to tow the jeep clear
from the river. At 4:00 a.m. we reach the next village, Chiri Yurt, and
stop at a house to repair the engine and have a hot meal.

Because of the delay, the sun is already rising as we leave the plains
and enter the mountains. From now on aircraft, not ground troops are
the danger. Askhab takes the jeep off the road onto a shallow river bed
which snakes up through the forest into the hills, a partisan corridor. No
one knows how long this nine-kilometre stretch of water pools, cliffs
and rocks will remain open before the Russians discover it, but no one
seems worried. 'We'll find another way,' Askhab says. Partisans fight
flexibly, searching for options, and, like flowing water, always finding
the point of least resistance.

We live in a camp high up painfully steep hills near Vedeno. A unit
of about a dozen 'woodsmen', as Askhab calls them, camp out in a small
shack and in defensive positions. They're guarding a weapons dump
hidden further up the hills, and do their best to remain unnoticed. When
planes fly over, everyone shrinks into the shadow of trees. The anti-
aircraft gun is screened with branches and you could almost fall into the
foxholes and trenches before noticing them. The GAI jeep is hidden
under branches. At the time of the namaz, a line of fighters kneel on
army blankets, boots off, and sing 'Allah Akhbar,' each verse echoing
around the hills.

When Askhab is away, the younger fighters get restless. Living
outdoors and outlawed has left them wild. No one's been told that rule
about never pointing guns. They're forever sticking Kalashnikov barrels
in each other's chests, pointing pistols, slipping off safety catches to add
an edge. A 16-year-old called Alikhan, overflowing with teenage energy,
is bound to shoot someone by mistake before long. When a helicopter
flies hesitatingly towards our hill top, he whoops and drags out a heavy
machine-gun from a shed, long belts of ammunition draped around his
shoulders, before the others tell him to cool it and get out of sight.

'We're a stupid bunch aren't we?' says one. 'Chechens are dumb. But *if we weren't we probably wouldn't still be fighting the Russians for the second year running.'*

Shamil Basayev roams the Vedeno region, and it takes two days to arrange an interview. We meet at a small farmhouse. It's 2:00 a.m.

Only 31, Basayev has been wounded many times, a living war museum. Shrapnel in both legs, a bullet in an arm. Sixteen of his relatives have died. But he survives – he even survived Budennovsk – and that's part of his aura, the reason his fighters follow him anywhere. 'The thing about Shamil,' one of them tells me, 'is he never gets surrounded. He always gets out'. His eyes are shockingly dark. Even in the sunlight, with his face at ease, the eyes remain menacing. Tonight, they're ringed black with fatigue, under a black wool hat which is wrapped around the base with a green band and Islamic prayers written in white, in Arabic.

Basayev explains the new war, what the separatists call 'fighting clever'.

'The Russians only control the bit of land they sit on. It's easy for me to move about. I don't have to hold trenches. Before we had a lot of soldiers sitting in trenches with nothing to do. Now I have two or three good bases in the mountains guarded by small units since tanks could never get up there. That frees up three or four battalions of mine and I use them down in the plains.'

A few days later we travel back down the river. We hear that a jeep full of fighters has just run into a Russian APC on this stretch and, in the firefight, three Chechens were killed, two wounded and only one came out unscathed.

This time, Askhab's got some hard men travelling, not the youngsters from the camp. There are four of them up front in the GAI jeep with rifles and two in the back section, where prisoners are meant to sit, with RPG anti-tank rockets. No one speaks of the tension, Chechens rarely do. 'Humma a dats' – 'no problem' – they say.

Askhab jokes that the two in the prisoner compartment are going to be jailed for life. They're always laughing about the quirks of their stolen vehicle: the nail bent in the ignition instead of a key, the way the horn never works when they try to toot girls, how they've driven past Russian soldiers in daylight, pretending to be the police. Then there's the lefthand back door which no one can open, lethal when exiting a vehicle fast can save your life, but still a joke.

We set off in the dark and the fighter next to me begins mumbling prayers. The duo in the prisoner section sing softly from the zikr. Down where we'll leave the river bed and take a dirt track back out onto the plains – the danger zone – there's silence except for the snap of rounds being loaded into Kalashnikovs. The fighter next to me lowers his rifle so it points right down the middle of the car into the front window. Somewhere up ahead, a red Russian signal flare sails into the night. Of course, I'm the one sitting against the jammed door this time. 'Want to

*die first do you, Sebastian?' a voice in the dark says and everybody
giggles.*

Even before the spring of 1996, it was clear, yet again, that Moscow's
policy was near collapse. Unable to win the war, unwilling to negotiate
with Dudayev and faced with the prospect of a Communist winning the
presidency, the Kremlin was paralysed. Boris Nemtsov – the young,
reformist governor of Nizhny Novgorod region – presented Yeltsin in
February with a petition to stop the war signed by one million people,
but he was ignored. To stop fighting and negotiate would mean admitting
the truth – that the war was unwinnable and had been a horrendous
mistake. It would mean personal humiliation for Yeltsin, already
physically ill and politically feeble, and political death for the entire
party of war clique. By ending the war, Yeltsin 'would win over the
civilian electorate,' said Konstantin Borovoi, a liberal parliament member
who was in frequent satellite telephone contact with Dudayev. 'But he
would lose the army because it would again feel like the loser. With
untrustworthy ministers like Grachev that is very dangerous.'

With the army clearly unable to wipe out resistance in the near future
and Zavgayev unable to establish authority, the Kremlin was left with
one fall back plan: to turn the propaganda machine onto overdrive, to
don the emperor's clothes. First, pretend there was no war, then announce
victory before the June elections, whatever the reality.

According to Moscow and its servants in the ITAR-TASS news agency
and ORT national television, there were no military offensives, only
'special operations'. That meant there were no bombardments of civilians,
so when villages were rocketed or bombed by aircraft, the propaganda
merchants either blamed 'unmarked aircraft' or actually claimed that
Dudayev was using a secret airforce to bomb his own people. Villages
were not forced to surrender at the point of tank barrels, they signed
'peace and accord' documents. After a heavy bombing of the
southwestern village of Shalazhi, airforce commander in chief General
Pyotr Deinekin told a press conference that the villagers who talked
about three planes circling and rocketing were 'provocateurs' and
'emotional'. The truth, he said, was that the Chechens were blowing
themselves up, putting huge charges under peoples houses and exploding
them when the planes flew over on their missions to 'hit bandit
formations' positions, camps, dumps and bases'.

Official casualty statistics were almost surreal. Rebel casualties announced by the Russian military were so high that you often wondered
where all the fighters could be coming from. Russian casualties were
reported, but at suspiciously low rates, given the almost constant
skirmishing and, in several places, heavy fighting. In mid-May, the
commander of defence ministry troops, General Vladimir Shamanov,

confidently announced that 80 per cent of Chechen territory was under federal control and there were only 500 to 700 fighters active, 20 per cent of whom were trying to flee the republic. Confronted with a set-back as devastating as the April ambush on the armoured column near Shatoi, the military and government reassured the public by rationalising it as a one-of-a-kind disaster. President Yeltsin spoke of a national tragedy, the Chechen ambushers were called cowards and someone even said the column had been carrying humanitarian aid. A special commission was set up to investigate how such a terrible slip up could have happened. It was made to sound like the first military catastrophe of the war, not a sign of the Chechens' real strength.

The jewel in the emperor's clothes was a peace plan announced by Yeltsin himself on 31 March 1996, less than three months before election day. For weeks, it had been called the 'secret plan' and both sides waited in anticipation. When Yeltsin unveiled the plan – it called for a ceasefire, negotiations, and phased withdrawal of Russian troops from 'quiet' areas – he was applauded in the West. In Chechnya, the plan had no effect. There, the war continued, either because Yeltsin hadn't meant his orders to be obeyed, or because Grachev, Kulikov and the other hardliners didn't bother obeying him. The overall commander of troops in Chechnya, General Vyacheslav Tikhomirov, said bluntly that he would respect the plan but still carry out 'special operations against armed bands and terrorists' – in other words, keep fighting.

There were voices in the dark. The human rights champion Sergei Kovalev called the peace plan 'hypocritical from beginning to end' and said the offensive under the mask of peace and accord zones was 'the cruelest and most abhorrent. This repugnant strategy continues and the president is perfectly aware of it. Villages are destroyed without anyone looking to see whether there are civilians or not'. Kovalev knew his words would have little effect. Even at the very start of the war, when his bravery under the bombs in Grozny grabbed the world's attention, he told me outside the presidential palace: 'I'll go back to the Kremlin and I'll tell them everything I've seen. But I have a feeling they may not want to listen.' Nothing had changed.

Médecins Sans Frontières, whose doctors had been working in all the most dangerous areas of Chechnya since the start of the war, also tried to save Chechnya from the obscurity of being an 'internal affair', as apologists in the West called it. An MSF report in April, which was timed to coincide with the meeting of the Group of Seven states in Moscow, said what all the Western leaders couldn't bring themselves to mention for fear of undermining President Yeltsin's re-election bid. 'Civilians are killed, hospitals, schools, mosques are targetted. It's a flagrant violation of the Geneva convention and the international accords signed by Russia.'

According to MSF, villages being encircled and shelled under the 'peace and accord' system were forced by the Russian soldiers to pay up to 10,000 dollars for the opening of humanitarian corridors. When civilians then tried to flee, they were often fired on and men were rooted out and taken to the notorious extra-judicial 'filtration camps'. There were cases of women being herded by Russian soldiers as human shields, and villages captured by troops were systematically looted. Doctor Eric Goemaere, head of MSF, said the West had to demand 'an end to the massacre,' while Doctor Mario Goethals, head of operations, said 'our governments know what is going on and they do nothing. Now is the time to react'. The same point was made by the International Helsinki Federation for Human Rights in May – that the West could not in good conscience ignore Chechnya. 'Thousands of civilians die – not as casualties of warfare per se, but as victims of needless and ruthless slaughter. The Chechnya conflict is no 'internal affair' of Russia, but a threat to European security.'

But the international community had long since put Chechnya on the back burner. Foreign news organisations sent fewer correspondents, instead writing their stories in Moscow where, inevitably, the lies told by ministers, television and press secretaries got bigger play than they deserved. Much of the time there were probably ten stories from Moscow for every eyewitness account from Chechnya.

Even reports from Chechnya were swamped by worldwide indifference. In May we happened to drive into Urus Martan just after one of those particularly cruel incidents in which helicopter gunships had fired rockets at a busy crossroads and then at a market place, the biggest in Chechnya. Three young boys were killed and 20 people were wounded – a toll considered miraculously low given the crowds.

While female relatives stood in the courtyard wailing like the chorus in a Greek tragedy, the father of the 16-year-old boy took me into to see the body, lain out on a white cloth in the main room of their house in preparation for burial. The boy had been sitting in a petrol truck by the side of the road when it was hit by a rocket. The truck burst into flames and all that was left were stunted, charred human sticks. The room stank of roast flesh. The skull was baked hard and black, with the top missing like an opened boiled egg. Unrecognisable pieces lay in a bucket at the boy's feet. 'Grief has come', the father said. 'Today it came to me, tomorrow it will come to all of us. This is genocide.'

Again, the propaganda drug took its numbing effect and Moscow's inquiry into whose 'unmarked helicopters' could have carried out the massacre was forgotten by everyone except the people of Urus Martan. This was a town that started the conflict as a bastion of anti-Dudayev opposition but had increasingly joined the resistance. Its hospital was crucial for treating wounded *boyeviks* in the southwest sector. Maybe the helicopter attack was meant as a warning or a punishment, or maybe it meant nothing. The only certainty was that it happened and very few people outside Chechnya cared. That wasn't the first or the last attack from the air on Urus Martan or several other places where there was no active resistance and the Russians had promised to leave people in peace.

There were squeaks and hand wringing abroad – like German Foreign Minister Klaus Kinkel's comments in April that a 'savage war' was underway and that President Yeltsin had to 'assert himself' against his apparently mutinous military – but no one really pressured the Kremlin. In fact support for Yeltsin's re-election fight against Zyuganov was so strong abroad that it became almost a liability for him among anti-Western voters.

At the G7 summit in April, US President Bill Clinton not only failed to mention the human rights abuses, he compared the hammering of the tiny Chechen minority to America's North-South civil war 130 years ago. When Clinton held a separate summit with Yeltsin, Chechnya didn't even come up. 'I wouldn't draw great inferences from the fact that you didn't get paragraphs of data about exchanges on human rights between the president of the United States and President Yeltsin,' a US State Department spokeswoman said afterwards, hiding behind the wall of diplomatic non-language.

Perhaps the most hypocritical act was the vote by the Council of Europe – a pan-European organisation which is meant to promote respect for human rights – to admit Russia as a member in January 1996. The decision had been frozen after the start of the war, but somehow the diplomats persuaded themselves that the Russian 'internal affair' was now sufficiently stale so as not to be an obstacle to Russia joining their cosy club. Membership compels governments to prosecute human rights abusers, respect minority populations, abolish the death penalty and end torture. Was Moscow going to comply with any of this? Certainly not in Chechnya, as Council members were perfectly aware. They didn't even have to leave Strasbourg to find out – there was always the MSF report. When President Yeltsin told the Russian delegation to the Council in March to 'block all attempts to put pressure on Russia, to get involved in internal affairs', there should have been an outcry. Instead there was more 'understanding' about the fact that Yeltsin was in an election campaign and trying to pander to nationalists. But Yeltsin, the butcher of Chechnya for the last 16 months, was fooling them all – he was the nationalists.

At the heart of Moscow's inability to face up to the truth and stop the war lay Doku Zavgayev. An expert at self-preservation, Zavgayev was from the same mold as the former local Communist Party first secretaries running republics across the North Caucasus in the 1990s. He had no ideology except working hand in hand with the centre, whether Communist or democrat, and receiving his share of the pie. A short man with eyebrows fixed in a permanent arch of irony, Zavgayev appeared almost daily on Russian state television talking about 'peace and accord' zones and disarray among the ranks of his 'armed opposition'. He could be highly persuasive.

Zavgayev was well known to the Kremlin. After being kicked out by Dudayev in 1991, he had gone on to find work as head of the presidency's department on problems within the Russian Federation's republics. At the start of the war he opposed sending the army into Chechnya, but never spoke out once hostilities began. His desire to avenge himself on Dudayev was obvious. Now he used his charm to tell his masters in the Kremlin exactly what they wanted to hear – that the war was being won and the rebels were crumbling. In return, Zavgayev and his cronies got houses, status, big cars and millions of dollars in funds from the Russian budget.

Zavgayev spent most of his time in Moscow and, when in Chechnya, lived at the northern Grozny airport or at the eastern Khankala airport, both transformed into fortresses by the Russians. RTR national television at the end of the war reported that the house in Khankala included a swimming pool. Zavgayev could not count how many men had declared vendettas against him and Chechens, nicknaming him 'the stewardess,' joked his plane was always on standby.

As under the previous puppet government run by Salambek Khadzhiyev, Zavgayev's administration was apparently most busy defrauding the Russian budget on a grand scale. Money was sent for humanitarian aid, but no aid appeared; money was sent to reconstruct the ruins of Grozny, but after a half dozen government buildings in the very centre were done up, nothing was rebuilt.

Exactly who was pocketing the money, and at what end, Moscow or Grozny, remains secret. What's sure is that Chechnya had become as much of a financial black hole as during the Dudayev years. In 1995, 2.5 billion dollars worth of funds for reconstruction alone disappeared, including – according to Russian reports – a sudden rush in November and December, just as Zavgayev arrived on the scene.

Food, clothing, blankets and other aid left Moscow, but never got further than the big military base at Mozdok north of Chechnya where it was sold off, Russian news reports said. Likewise, millions of dollars of medicines and vaccines left Moscow but never arrived in Chechnya. The federal audit chamber found that by February 1996 only 1,082 out of tens of thousands of eligible families had received promised aid to rebuild their houses, while more than four million dollars were still sitting in the state bank and millions more were in other banks, not in Chechen war victims' hands.

By May 1996, half a year since Zavgayev's election, the Russian government said it had handed out 40 million dollars for pensions and other social benefits. But in Grozny one had a hard time finding a single person who had received his miserly pension or compensation for his ruined house, or any road where the craters had been repaired. Prime Minister Chernomyrdin announced that 1.3 million square metres of apartment blocks had been rebuilt in Grozny, but they were nowhere to be seen and Chernomyrdin himself never visited.

That same month, Zavgayev's deputy, the former mayor of Grozny under Dudayev, Beslan Gantemirov, was arrested by Russian authorities and charged with corruption. He was clearly just a scapegoat, a victim of internecine greed – Zavgayev and the rest of his team stayed on, untouched. The Kremlin couldn't get rid of Zavgayev. Whatever the reality, he represented stability and his freshly painted government building in Grozny represented success, the Potemkin village of the propaganda war.

## Vedeno

*Up over Vedeno, where the Russians maintain a tenuous hold, the wooded hills are black and mist hangs over the summits. When the rains begin the hills disappear behind a curtain of water. It's a lonely place for a unit of Russian soldiers for whom every patch of wood and every house is enemy territory.*

*'The boyeviks are up there,' an officer says, pointing at the black mountains.'They shoot at us, but we can't see them. It will be hard to get them out of there.'*

*Inside the hut, Alexander, the unit's 35-year-old kontraktnik holds court. He's tall, with a shaved head and has muscular arms sticking out from a blue-and-white striped army vest.*

*Alexander says he's happy 'fighting for our constitution, for Russia', and especially happy about the hundreds of dollars he claims to make a month, and even more happy about the chance to use all these weapons. The officer, who's young, cleancut and blond, looks on uneasily. The conscripts sit in silence.*

*'Our weapons are the best in the world. Take the Kalashnikov, you can even drop it in water and nothing happens,' Alexander says. Bored, he trains a sniper rifle on some villagers walking outside Vedeno, then puts it down, picks up a handgrenade and throws it behind some cattle walking in the field in front of the post. They lurch away in panic and the explosion echoes around the rain-soaked hills.*

*I ask the officer if there can be a military victory in Chechnya. He says, 'no, I don't think so'.*

*Alexander cuts in and at once the officer falls silent, catching my eye for one second across the table, with a half-apologetic, half-frightened look. 'Take out any Chechens who aren't against Russia and drop an atomic bomb on the rest', Alexander says. 'It was Stalin's fault. He didn't do it properly. They're terrible people.'* I ask Alexander about the local ethnic-Russians who have suffered so terribly. *'They're dogs. Why did they come to live here? Is Russia not good enough for them? I'd have them all shot.'*

The rain stops. We drive through Vedeno, down towards Shali in the plains. Every few kilometres there are more posts, with their mixture of kontraktniks, officers and conscripts. All are dressed like tramps, filthy and thin.

At one stop a conscript asks for a cigarette and I give him a whole pack. He doesn't understand and looks back at me. I nod and there's light in his eyes for the first time. *'We get a pack each a week,'* he says. What about letters? *'They should come every 20 to 40 days. We never know if the ones we send arrive.'*

At the checkpoint above Serzhen Yurt, the soldiers are so drunk they can barely walk up to the car. A tiny, tanned young conscript with his shirt off and helmet hanging lopsided, staggers up. With him is an older man, one of the kontraktniks, also smashed.

I ask the kontraktnik why he volunteered to fight. He's been wounded by shrapnel. He looks at me with the theatrical seriousness of a drunk who wants to share a secret and says *'I've got personal problems at home. But now I want to get out of here.'*

We come out of the hills and forests and onto the plains. There's one more checkpoint before Shali, where we'll spend the night, if they let us through. The soldiers are too drunk to approach the car. I get out and go over to the APC, where they sit in the shade, paralytic.

*'Of course we'll let you through,'* says Nikolai. Then he has an idea. *'I shouldn't let you. But I will if you take me to where I can buy vodka for my boys.'*

We tell him we'll take him into Shali, buy the vodka and then take him back. Nikolai slumps into the front passenger seat with his rifle and excitedly explains that his unit had saved up together to buy a tape recorder and that *'some idiot set fire to it today.'*

*'We could listen to music at our post. We needed that. We don't need Chechnya, we need our tape recorder,'* he says, and, to my amazement, begins to cry in great drunken sobs.

Poor, lucky Nikolai. In Shali, some Chechens get him his two bottles of vodka and he's driven back to his checkpoint to drink the night away. He tells us he's 20 and comes from Siberia.

What Nikolai will never know is that the men in Shali almost imprisoned him. They could have got away with it – who would know what happened? *'We should have kept him, put him down in the cellar for a while, and made a slave out of him,'* a Chechen says. *'We let him go.'*

## 6. RESURRECTION

*The main plan is to kill Dudayev.*

Dzhokhar Dudayev in his last press conference in March 1996, one month before his death in the woods of southern Chechnya.

General Dzhokhar Dudayev, hunted by the Russian army and airforce, always on the move, and tirelessly directing his mad rebellion, still managed to look dapper. With his neat moustache and pressed Soviet uniform, the ex-pilot's appearance seemed to represent the Chechens' incredible durability. This man, who'd dominated Chechnya for five years, had pushed his nation into the fire but never been singed himself. Like anyone at the centre of a personality cult, Dudayev had the aura of immortality. His was well-earned.

Russian journalists and politicians quite rightly asked why the FSB and the multitude of commando groups had not managed to kill Dudayev. After all, he managed to meet regularly with journalists and appear on Russian television. The failure even prompted conspiracy theories that Defence Minister Grachev – or other high-ranking Moscow officials – had struck some kind of deal with Public Enemy Number One.

Experience shows that it would have been difficult for even elite ground troops to kill Dudayev. The American Rangers' attempt to 'arrest' Somali warlord Mohammed Farah Aidid in Mogadishu turned to a bloody fiasco when the high-tech helicopter gunships and commandos became enmeshed in Aidid's defensive net. Getting near Dudayev meant entering rebel territory, where every ordinary looking man, woman and child was a potential intelligence gatherer or fighter. Strangers would not get far, and the idea of elite soldiers blazing around in search of one man in such circumstances only works in films.

Another approach would be to throw a net around Dudayev with a massive, lightening troop deployment as soon as his rough location could be fixed. But the Russian troops were not sufficiently well-trained for such operations, as one humiliating escape by Chechen fighters after the other had shown. More subtle approaches, such as undercover Chechen assassins, still came up against the security screen of Dudayev's bodyguard. It is true that journalists could see him, yet they first had to go on wild goose chases lasting 24 hours, from village to village and house to house, before finally they were admitted into the leader's well-guarded presence.

The surest way to kill Dudayev was from the air, and this was something he, an airforce general, understood clearly. The Russians knew he lived in the strip of villages from Roshni Chu to Gekhi Chu, and they could follow his movements with the help of spies and sophisticated surveillance aircraft. However, although Dudayev was careful he didn't sit in bunkers or trenches. He was a proud, scornful man and could hardly violate his own image by showing fear. Several attempts were made, including an air raid on the village of Roshni Chu which killed as many as 27 people (one of them Dudayev's bodyguard) but missed Dudayev only because he had not been present as expected.

Dudayev, always the master of confrontation, seemed almost to relish the fact that his fate was sealed. He'd taken on the Communists, then the Russian army, and now he was taking on doomsday. In what was to be his last press conference, he said he had intelligence information that President Yeltsin had personally ordered his assassination.

A month later, the separatist leadership announced that Dudayev was dead – killed by a Russian airforce rocket. The news stunned both sides. Could Moscow, groping for some way either to win the war or to extricate itself ahead of the June elections, have finally struck a knock-out blow?

Immediately the rebel defence council – gathering the top field commanders and political leaders – held a top-secret meeting and named vice president Zelimkhan Yandarbiyev as successor. Moscow predicted and obviously hoped that the relatively little known Yandarbiyev would never be able to hold together the separatist movement. Doku Zavgayev said 'Yandarbiyev has no authority whatsoever. He's not worth talking to.' False reports were issued that Yandarbiyev had been killed in a shoot-out with his own men.

Again the Russians were to be disappointed. One by one, the major warlords and commanders – like Shamil Basayev and Aslan Maskhadov – came forward and swore allegiance to the new president. The commanders weren't doing this for personal reasons, but for the simple fact that under the constitution of Chechnya-Ichkeria the vice president automatically replaced a dead president and commander in chief. It was that almost eccentric love of bureaucracy again. It was the rebels' way of telling the world that they were not the bandits of Russian propaganda, but what Dudayev had always claimed they were – a legitimate, organised force fighting for independence. What could have been the Chechen separatists' deepest crisis turned into a defining display of political strength.

'Of course this is a big loss', said Khunkar Pasha Israpilov, the eastern sector commander. 'Dzhokhar was our symbol of freedom and he'll remain that. But people who think that after the death of the president we'll give up are mistaken. If our new president is named according to the constitution, then he is my commander in chief and I'll strictly follow his orders. We don't care if outsiders don't recognise our state. After all, we refuse to recognise several ourselves, including Russia.'

Yandarbiyev's background contrasted sharply with Dudayev's. Wearing a red tie and grey *papakha* hat with his camouflage suit, he was an ex-writer and veteran separatist ideologue, not a *boyevik* or a military commander. During the war he hadn't fought, but he stayed in the presidential palace in Grozny to the bitter end and never fled the republic along with other less-than-warlike government members. He was remembered most as one of the first people to agitate against Zavgayev's Soviet government and to be imprisoned.

Yandarbiyev had the reputation of being a hardline nationalist. In his poem 'Russia,' he wrote of 'the sword of slaves, of unclean forces, the rootless mass of many tongues, spread like the plague.' But in his first press conference as president Yandarbiyev surprised people by showing himself more flexible, and certainly more diplomatic, than his fiery predecessor.

Talks on independence for Chechnya could be set aside 'until a later date', Yandarbiyev said and, despite the assassination of Dudayev, he was ready for immediate negotiations. 'I am ready to talk with their top leaders – the president and prime minister. For their ordinary ministers, we have our ordinary ministers.'

Four weeks later, to everyone's amazement, that is exactly what happened – Yandarbiyev, president of Chechnya-Ichkeria, flew to Moscow and met with President Yeltsin and Prime Minister Chernomyrdin at the Kremlin. For the first time since the start of the Chechen crisis in 1991, Yeltsin had agreed to direct talks.

---

*In our minds, Dudayev didn't die, he went straight to Paradise. We are proud to have had a president like that who never retreated. It's a big loss, but nothing more. Everybody's time comes up. It's not important when you die, but how.*

Shamil Basayev reacting to the death of Dzohkhar Dudayev.

Many people refused to believe the news. Loved or hated, Dudayev had seemed invincible and the public saw no body, no grave, no photographs. Initially, there was only the word of a handful of top commanders. Some supporters went into a kind of hysteria, an end-of-millennium fever, entangled in political conspiracy theories and religious legends, as they tried to explain the impossible. 'You're being fooled. He's not dead. He's safe,' said Ruslan, a young fighter in the hills, with a broad, cunning smile across his face.

If the Dudayev disappearance was part of a conspiracy, then the leadership showed an almost inhuman ability to keep the story straight and not reveal secrets. The official, rebel government version never varied. During the night of 21–22 April, Dudayev went out to make a satellite phone call. He drove in his Niva jeep with aides and bodyguards into the woods just above Gekhi Chu and parked in a narrow gulley, set up the phone and called his friend in Moscow, the parliamentary deputy Konstantin Borovoi, to discuss the chance of setting up peace talks.

Homing in on the antenna signal, a Russian warplane then fired a specially targeted air-to-ground missile that scored a direct hit. The rocket attack wasn't a chance air raid, but an assassination, using 'a satellite guidance system in which not only Russian means were used but satellites from several Western countries,' stressed the terse, official statement in the underground newspaper *Ichkeria*. Dudayev was fatally wounded, and his longtime representative in Moscow Khamad Kurbanov and military procuror Magomed Dzhanayev were killed instantly.

A young Chechen rebel in Gekhi Chu, who refused to give his name, said he went to the scene immediately after the air raid took place and saw everything. 'The president had had a long discussion. He was standing together with Kurbanov and the procuror. The others, the guards, were standing further away in a circle. Only one of them was wounded, not seriously. When the rocket exploded, the car was thrown 15 metres. The president was hit in the head, the left arm and right leg. He was still alive for a bit, long enough to say some words. 'Carry on this fight to the end,' is what he said. The other two, I picked them up with my own hands.'

Shamil Basayev swore on the Koran that it was true and that was enough to convince his fellow commanders, but not ordinary people. There was no body and the grave site was declared top secret to prevent it from being defiled by the Russians. Even Dudayev's brother, Baskhan, was in the dark about the funeral. 'Some people came down from the mountains into Grozny and told me Dzhokhar had died and had been buried', he said at his house in Grozny as mourners performed a *zikr*.

That something happened out in the woods near Gekhi Chu is sure. A large crater was left in the gulley. Pieces of a Niva, a burnt tire and bits of dashboard, were scattered dozens of metres away. At the hospital in nearby Urus Martan the records showed that one of Dudayev's body-guards was admitted for light shrapnel wounds the day of the explosion. So the crater was no montage – an explosion had gone off and if the bodyguards were there, then so, probably, was Dudayev.

But who set off the explosion and how?

The story that Dudayev was betrayed by his satellite phone was fantastic, but feasible. An Ilyushin-76 aircraft with radars could pinpoint the signals from a satellite telephone and direct a Sukhoi-25 jet fighter to the target. Yet the Russians' initial reaction to the death of their nemesis was curiously muted and confused, as if they hadn't been expecting it. The military refused to confirm it had targeted Dudayev, only saying that its aircraft bombed the area that night, hitting 'fighters' bases'. President Yeltsin just said 'we're checking the information' and his Chechnya advisor Emil Pain said 'Russian leaders did not and could not have given' the order.

Another twist came from the US State Department, which, rather oddly, issued one of the first confirmations. An anonymous official in Washington said he was 'certain' about Dudayev's death. Earlier that year President Clinton had talked about helping Russia deal with the Chechen crisis, but never explained what he meant. This prompted theories that Washington provided Moscow with its pinpoint-accurate spy satellite technology.

What had happened? Had Dudayev been assassinated by the Russians or his own men? Killed in a chance air raid? Had he fled Chechnya, or had he been wounded and spirited to Turkey while his men put out that he was dead to wrong-foot the Russian spies? The mystery only deepened when Dudayev's Russian-born wife Alla left Chechnya for 'an Islamic country', an exile apparently arranged by Moscow in return for her sensational appearance on Russian TV calling for voters to back Yeltsin in the June presidential elections. Would Dudayev, declared dead, be coming back the way Imam Shamil had reappeared after everyone thought he had fallen in battle at Gimry?

Even a year after the war, question marks lingered. A monument – a plain stone marker – was erected on the spot of the bomb site, but the grave had still not been publicly identified. The reason given, both by the government and relatives, was the same: that internal or external enemies might violate the grave. Some Chechens continued to suspect foul play or that Dudayev had been spirited out of the country. The fact that the brother had not been invited to the funeral scandalised many ordinary Chechens. On this, Basayev gave me a harsh but convincing answer. The funeral took place secretly on 23 April, 'so the Russian swine wouldn't stick their noses in'. The brother, who lived in Grozny and had not taken up arms, was simply ignored. 'We are more Dzhokhar's relatives than his brother is. We are the ones who fought alongside', Basayev said angrily. But the controversy kept nagging.

Almost all Chechens say it would have been impossible for Dudayev to be assassinated by his own people – that kind of murder would go against all tradition and belief. But it can not be excluded. Everyone knew in the spring of 1996, with elections approaching, that the Russians were looking for ways to end the war, but that the Kremlin would never agree to direct talks with Dudayev. That March, he'd threatened terrorism within Russia and scorned Yeltsin's admittedly floundering attempts to rein in the hawks and establish a peace process. Chechnya was ready to keep fighting because it had nothing to lose, he said. 'We are much more interested in continuing the war than Russia, because what is left for us? A destroyed economy, no industry, no production.' The Chechens' only chance for a meeting with Yeltsin – and they'd long believed that this would be enough to pull the wool from his eyes – was a change in the leadership. This reality was rubbed in by the announcement, so soon after Yandarbiyev took over, that the long-awaited Kremlin talks would take place.

In the end, the official version – that Dudayev was bombed by the Russians, then buried in a secret place – was just as likely, if not more so than any of the alternatives. The other versions would have meant a half dozen people like Shamil Basayev, and a few relatives, lying grievously to their comrades in arms, including many high-ranking commanders; it would have meant a sacrilegious hoax on the ordinary people across southern Chechnya who observed the three-day mourning period.

But the conspiracy theorists will never be satisified until a body is produced. In Chechnya, predictions of Dudayev's reappearance became part of the war's mythology. On 1 August 1996, a Grozny newspaper reported that Dudayev was about to reappear in Chechnya. He didn't, but that didn't put anyone off – the announcement was repeated every few weeks, often with an exact date supplied. The new Russian FSB director Nikolai Kovalev insisted Dudayev was dead, but he too was sucked into the conspiracy game. The Chechens, he warned, were preparing a Dudayev double.

Maybe the weirdest episode in the immediate aftermath of Dudayev's disappearance was a press conference given by his wife several days later at a house in Gehki Chu. Alla was quirky, as befitted a Russian woman married to a Chechen liberation leader, a Russian surrounded for the last year and a half by young Chechen men killing young Russian men. She rarely met with outsiders and was known only as the creator of some pretty awful paintings and poems. But to journalists Alla was the ultimate source, the wife who could clear up the mystery and tell us once and for all how Dudayev died. Surrounded by fighters in the presidential guard uniform of black jeans and jackets, Alla sat down in a chair, a Chechen flag on the wall behind her. At once, she launched into one of her poems. Not many journalists – only foreigners were allowed – understood it until we'd played back the tape later.

> When I am deceased, betrayed by a friend,
> Again, don't judge me – I believe in love.
> When I fail to see the treachery and evil
> Don't judge me – my heart is clean.
> When my eyes are shut by a layer of earth,
> Then God will judge you – and you may judge me.

Making the poem even harder to follow, Alla clutched dramatically at her face and sobbed, barely able to talk in her tiny, reedy voice. This was the picture of a woman in severe distress.

After her reading Alla announced that she wanted to undertake a peace mission to Prime Minister Chernomyrdin. She said she would be the woman of Caucasian legend who stops fights by throwing a white scarf between the combatants. The journalists looked around the room at each other with a mixture of disbelief and impatience.

Finally, a guard announced we could ask questions. 'No political questions,' he growled.

'Were you present when Dzhokhar died?'

Everyone waited, pens poised. This would be the eyewitness account. Groan. Another poem. Except, this one didn't last long. A couple lines and Alla threw her hands over her face and dashed from the room, leaving us in a stunned silence, our notebooks almost empty.

Before anyone had said a word, the door of the next room burst open and out came Alla, surrounded by guards; she rushed out into the courtyard and disappeared in a grey Volga down the dusty village road.

I felt as if I'd been at the theatre of the absurd. One detail nagged more than anything else that week – for all her wailing and clutching, Alla hadn't cried. I'd been sitting two metres away and could see clearly. Not a single tear.

## Moscow

*Salman Raduyev is attacked in a road ambush by other Chechens in March 1995 – reported killed. The story is they got him for messing up the raid on Dagestan. The Russians are relieved. That's one less futile man hunt for them to carry out.*

*Then in July a man in large sunglasses and a beard appears on Russian television. He says he's Salman Raduyev. At first the Russians say it can't be true. True, the face isn't quite right – it's messed-up, post-surgery. But there's no mistaking that thin voice. Salman is indeed back from the dead, or at least back from multiple operations which he somehow was able to receive abroad.*

*There's a bigger shock: Dzohkar Dudayev, Raduyev says, is alive. He survived the rocket attack and is being treated abroad. Raduyev swears this on the Koran.*

*Raduyev is an eerie character, no doubt. They say the Pervomaiskoye battle unhinged him. He gave me the chills when we ended up staying in the same safe house after his breakout and he kept repeating one joke every time he saw me. 'Sebastian Bach, Sebastian Bach.' Only later I discovered that it might have been 'Sebastian bah' – 'bah' being the word children use in Russian when they pretend to fire guns.*

*The assassination attempt and the surgery have made him even freakier. His face is messy, but not his clothes. Before, he wore ordinary combat gear; now he dresses up in special tailored military uniforms with medals, like something from Versace, and travels with a bodyguard of some 40 of the toughest-looking people you've seen. He's too weird for most people. But there are some who always will believe what he says. He'll always be Raduyev, the man who came back from the dead, the man who says he knows about Dzhokhar.*

On 27 May, three weeks before the Russian presidential elections, Zelim-khan Yandarbiyev, Movladi Udugov, and the actor-turned-commander Akhmed Zakayev, left for the Kremlin. This was what the Chechens had always wanted. There was even a naive feeling that Yeltsin didn't know the truth and that if only he would meet with them, he'd understand.

On paper at least the Chechens were not negotiating from strength. Just on the eve of the Kremlin talks the Russians finally captured Stary Achkhoi, Orekhovo and even Bamut, that great symbol of resistance. The week of bombardments on Bamut by Tupolev and Sukhoi bomber planes was so heavy that windows broke in a town 10 kilometres away and the wooded foothills were enveloped in smoke. As always, the Chechens, who had run out of ammunition, retreated into the woods with most of their men alive, but the capture of Bamut was a big psychological blow. Stary Achkhoi, once a tiny village, was bombed so heavily that the rubble rose to waist level in most streets. Orekhovo was left unrecognisable. Movladi Chadayev, one of the surviving Stary Achkhoi *boyeviks*, told me later that just 40 men were defending the village at the time of the final Russian storm. Eighteen of them were killed.

The Chechens had one strong card: Yeltsin, desperate to end the war before the 16 June election day, would be ready to bargain. He himself had described the war as his biggest mistake and said he couldn't win re-election if it didn't end.

Among ordinary people, there was real hope. Excited crowds lined the roads as Yandarbiyev's convoy swept down from the mountains to the airport in Ingushetia. Improbably and typically Chechen, Yandarbiyev rode across the republic in a long black Zil limousine, a relic of the Dudayev heyday, covered in dust but otherwise undamaged. The rest of the convoy was a circus of blaring horns, cries of 'Allah Akbar!' and fighters triumphantly leaning out of their jeeps waving the rebel flag. Russian troops stationed along the route watched in silence. Here was the target of all their assaults, motoring past on his way to meet with Yeltsin.

After brief talks, Yandarbiyev and Prime Minister Chernomyrdin signed a document announcing a ceasefire in a week's time. Yeltsin declared 'the main question of peace in Chechnya is solved.' But as television footage of the Kremlin meeting made clear, there were only thin hopes for real peace.

Yeltsin greeted Yandarbiyev with disdain, berating him for turning up 'two and a half hours late' and saying 'no one has ever dared be late to meet the president, even by five minutes.' Then the Russian president took the head of a long table, insisting that Yandarbiyev's delegation sit to his left, and Chernomyrdin's delegation, which included Doku Zavgayev, to the right. What Yeltsin wanted was to portray himself as the mediator in an internal Russian affair.

Yandarbiyev objected, threatening to walk out. 'Sit down, sit down,' Yeltsin repeated several times in an angry, school master's voice. In the end, Yandarbiyev got his way and Yeltsin sat opposite him, as if with an equal partner. Zavgayev was made to sit at the end of the line of Russian officials. Chechen separatist pride had been satisified, but the atmosphere was poisoned.

Looking at the Chechens in their camouflage gear, Akhmed Zakayev in a piratical black head dress, on one side of the table, and the besuited Russians on the other side, you felt they'd never been further apart. There was no dialogue, just pre-election machismo by Yeltsin and hostility from the Chechens. Yeltsin and Yandarbiyev talked over each other. Udugov even interrupted Yeltsin to ask bluntly, 'do you know what's going on?' then offered to supply video tapes of the horrors.

But the session was above all a classy propaganda gimmick for Yeltsin. He was talking to the bandits, but he was talking tough. And he had one more trick. The day after the Kremlin talks, while the Chechen leaders were still in Moscow as unwitting hostages, Yeltsin secretly went to Chechnya, his first visit since the war began.

Flying in one of a string of military helicopters, Yeltsin went to Pravoberezhnaya a village in the north of Chechnya that had seen no fighting and was populated almost entirely by either Cossacks or anti-independence Chechens. He then hopped down to one of the military bases in Grozny and told soldiers: 'The war is over, you've won'. Within four hours Yeltsin was on his way home. He hadn't met a single war victim, or even a resident of Grozny, and it's quite possible that on his helicopter route he didn't see a ruined building. But none of that was mentioned on national television. All viewers saw were pictures of Yeltsin in Chechnya and that meant, as he said, that 'Chechnya is part of the Russian Federation and nowhere outside it'. Now Yeltsin could say he hadn't heard 'a single shot' and that meant the war must be over. 'Peace has come, not just on paper, but in reality.'

Even so, the Chechens had some hope. Full negotiations between the two sides to follow up on the Kremlin talks were held in Nazran, Ingushetia and, on 10 June – six days from Yeltsin's election showdown against Communist challenger Gennady Zyuganov – a new accord on demilitarisation and withdrawal of troops was signed. Backed by the OSCE, the accord was seen as having a better chance than the 1995 deal.

The first round of the election was a tight contest. Yeltsin only polled three per cent more than Zyuganov, forcing a second round run-off for 3 July. Still having to fight for re-election, Yeltsin maintained the peace process. One of the most outspoken critics of the whole war, retired general Alexander Lebed, had placed an impressive third in the first round, so Yeltsin, desperate to expand his electorate, promptly made him his high-profile national security adviser. Several of the main backers of the war – Defence Minister Pavel Grachev, shady chief Kremlin bodyguard Alexander Korzhakov, FSB secret service chief Mikhail Barsukov, the anti-reforms first deputy prime minister Oleg Soskovets, and Security Council Secretary Oleg Lobov – were finally sacked.

But no sooner had Yeltsin defeated Zyuganov and won a second term on 3 July, than it became evident that the peace process was on the thinest of ice. Although the party of war stalwarts had been fired, there was still no one who could or would undo their legacy. As from the beginning, the Kremlin had either to keep fighting the Chechens or say it had made a disastrous mistake and stop – in other words, admit defeat. The logic of war ground on, even more so now that Yeltsin's re-election had lifted any pressure to negotiate. In addition, the 65-year-old president had suffered a heart attack between the two rounds of the election and he began his second term an invalid, once again plunging the Kremlin into a policy vacuum. The hawks' last chance had come.

'All the bandits' remaining strongholds of resistance will be destroyed,' said General Vladimir Shamanov, commander of defence ministry troops in Chechnya, on 11 July, one week after Yeltsin's victory, a month after the Ingushetia peace accord. 'We have to wage a cruel campaign against those bastards in every field – military, political, economic and in the media.' As an example of the 'banditry' sweeping Russia, Shamanov cited several recent bomb explosions in Moscow, even though there was never any evidence that they were the work of Chechens.

The military machine geared up for another great push. Wave after wave of planes and helicopters flew south to rocket and bomb mountain villages. Ground troops with tanks and artillery moved fast up the valleys, gradually capturing or blockading every village from Dargo to Vedeno, and forcing the Chechens to beat several retreats. In the plains, the large village of Gekhi was stormed after heavy artillery destroyed an estimated one in ten houses. The commander was killed and his body held by the Russian troops for ransom.

The new air raids on the mountains were perhaps the heaviest yet against villages where there were still many civilians. The entire rebel leadership, including Yandarbiyev and Maskhadov, came within a hair of being wiped out when Mekhkety, near Vedeno, was surrounded by ground troops then bombed from the air. Ironically, the Chechens had been meeting there with a representative sent by Lebed to talk about new peace negotiations. The representative, Russian reports said, was filmed screaming during the air raids: 'Lebed doesn't know about this! This is a nightmare! Give us three days and we can stop this war.' No one was listening.

Even Chernomyrdin, who had previously advocated a negotiated solution, blamed the Chechens for starting the new round of war. So, to the surprise of many, did Lebed, who met with the tough commander-in-chief of forces in Chechnya, his old colleague General Vyacheslav Tikhomirov, on the eve of the new offensive. According to Lebed, Tikhomirov was taking 'appropriate action'.

The offensive was spectacular and, despite all the past corruption and incompetence, I began wondering whether this time the Russians wouldn't finally achieve their task. The Chechens issued a statement that said 'sadly we have to note that Russia, which claims to be a world power and whose people call themselves great, does not keep its word.' The rebels vowed to resist, saying 'the Chechen side is obliged to organise resistance', but, at the mercy of aviation and thousands of suddenly advancing troops, there seemed little they could do.

Zavgayev reacted to the end of the ceasefire in true form, coming to Moscow and insisting there actually was no offensive in his homeland. 'I can authoritatively declare that in the last eight days not one bomb has been dropped and not one shot has been fired in Chechnya,' Zavgayev told a meeting of the Chechen diaspora in the Russian capital.

At the time I thought this was just another chapter in the great cover up conducted over the last 20 months, the propaganda delirium which had helped keep Zavgayev in his post and the war going. But later I realised I'd attended a historic moment – the last appearance of the emperor with no clothes.

Unknown to Zavgayev, the troops who propped him up and all the phony peace negotiators, the Chechens were at that very moment cleaning weapons and saying their prayers in preparation for the final and most astonishing event of the war – the recapture of Grozny.

### 7. COMING HOME

*A year and a half ago we were forced to retreat. Now it's the counter-offensive. We're liberating our city from Russian occupation.*

Akhmed Zubarayev, a Chechen fighter in Grozny, August 1996.

At the Russian position near the old canning factory, on the northern edge of Grozny, the interior ministry officer was about to crack. The post was a mess – trenches zig-zagging through the long grass, an untidy pile of concrete bollards, sandbags, a pill box. The place looked deserted, until we realised that the soldiers were sitting so deep in their safe holes that they'd almost become part of the earth. On one side lay empty fields, on the other the city, raging with the din of battle.

The lieutenant came out with a walkie-talkie in one hand, a Kalashnikov in the other. He was tanned and dirty, wearing tracksuit bottoms and a cut-off camouflage T-shirt, and he was in a bad way.

'Get out of here,' he told me and colleagues from WTN television,

EFE news agency and Radio Liberty as we cautiously emerged from our white armour-plated Landrover. 'There's fighting here, can't you see. Get out and don't film or I'll break the camera.' We tried to argue, to sweeten the officer, but we'd only just arrived in Grozny and he'd already lived through the first two days of the Chechen assault to recapture the city. The more we tried to reason, the tighter wound the lieutenant became until he was a single, dangerous, twitching muscle attached to a rifle.

He'd experienced things which made him act this way. This was more than fear, or battle fever. This was a one-man reflection of the melt down taking place in the entire Russian armed forces in Chechnya.

At dawn August 6 – just three days before President Yeltsin's inauguration at the Kremlin for a second term in office – 2,000 to 3,000 Chechen *boyeviks* snaked into Grozny and emerged from pre-prepared hiding places, Trojan Horse style, inside the city. Within a day, they'd engaged every Russian position in and around the city and established neighbourhood command structures. The second and third biggest towns, Gudermes and Argun, had been seized almost without a shot being fired.

At first, the Russian first deputy interior minister, Pavel Golubets, said nothing serious was underway. 'This is a *nabeg* by *abregs* coming to steal. The fighters have no aims,' he said. 'Grozny stood and will stand. Any talk about the city being captured is complete rubbish.'

This brave talk withered quickly. The Chechens knew where the Russians were, they surrounded them, wiped out relief units, and were already laying seige to the central administrative buildings. The Chechens' speed and the Russians' flat-footedness was shocking. In the climax of the long-running breakdown of coordination between the interior and defence ministries, it took 36 hours for regular army armoured columns to come from the bases on the outskirts and aid the besieged interior ministry units inside the city. The situation, admitted the army, was 'totally out of control.'

Movladi Udugov, the propaganda man, gave President Yeltsin a jab in the guts, calling Russian state television on his satellite telephone and wrily announcing that the rebels were 'restoring constitutional order'. 6 August was the day everybody feared, but the generals said could never happen.

Now it was 8 August, the third day of the offensive, and things were not any better. The whole landscape jumped with war. Troops sealed off all roads approaching the city. Near the northern canning factory Russia's big guns were at work. Artillery pummelled a row of houses, sending up a rosary of black smoke puffs, one after the other a couple of hundred metres from where we stood. Overhead two war planes circled in the bright, blue sky. But the lieutenant knew that was all show – the situation was a disaster and his own forces were shooting at each other in the chaos.

'Get out of here', he shouted. 'They're sending helicopters, Crocodiles, any minute and they'll take out your vehicle. They don't like cars.' The lieutenant was clearly frightened. 'It doesn't matter if you leave the car next to our post – they'll still take it out. Four cars have been shot at like that on this road and I'm getting sick of seeing bodies. I've got four men wounded by one of our own helicopter strikes. Get out!'

On cue, two Crocodile gunships clattered low over the trees, right over the post as the lieutenant talked. His face twisted with anger. One of the choppers lurched from side to side as it passed directly over our heads, then gave two bursts of machine-gun fire into the field of long grass to our right. A warning.

We'd find another way of getting into Grozny. But that meant traversing back over several kilometres of open ground between Grozny and the hilly moorlands to the north. It meant passing back by another Russian position which earlier in the day had opened Kalashnikov fire at our Landrover. From where we were, the position was just visible across the fields, a tricolour flag flying over its blockhouse. Could the lieutenant signal to them that we were friendly? No. 'Different unit. We have no radio links with each other.' Chaos.

As soon as we ran parallel with the second Russian position, at a range of 500–800 metres, they opened fire with automatic rifles, some of the bullets smacking harmlessly into the armoured side of the Landrover, making us laugh and shout 'bastards' at the same time. Then an explosion went off on the dirt road just behind us kicking up a twist of black smoke – RPG or light cannon. Much more serious. Vakho, WTN's big Georgian driver, put his foot down and careered around a corner, ramming the vehicle through ruts and holes until we were behind the lee of the first hill. The Russians were out of control; thank God they were also bad shots.

We tried another road, this time approaching Grozny from the east. The sky here buzzed with helicopters, each equipped with rockets, cannon and machine-gun, circling over the flat woods, fields and scrublands. They flew nose down, five of them, staggered like steps, one just above the other to watch for ground fire. Suddenly their precision blipped and one left the dance to take a new course – towards our road, towards us. Although our Landrover was the only vehicle on the road, it was civilian enough and we were driving well outside the battle zone. But in the nightmare of having Grozny snatched from under their noses, the Russians were flailing at anything, anywhere, and the battle zone lost any definition. The enemy was everywhere. We were the enemy.

'Faster!' we shouted. Just visible in the distance were the red brick farm houses of Novy Tsenteroi, seven kilometres from Grozny. The helicopter closed in and we knew it would fire. If we could only get in the village, ditch the car and take shelter. Just not here, not on this pan-flat, treeless road. But then the shocking blast of machine-gun bullets slamming into the road and against the armoured side of the car. Not at all like the smack of rifle bullets, but full-blown punches with a percussion effect that suddenly made this armoured box on wheels feel like a coffin. 'Faster!' 'Stop!' 'Faster!' 'Stop!' contradictory shouts rang out and Vakho, face contorted, lifted his foot, then slammed it back down, hurtling the coffin towards Novy Tsenteroi. It was no good stopping. Innocence wouldn't save us, only cover.

A hundred metres further a second burst of machine-gun, ear-splitting, then the whirr of the helicopter as it flew past, readying to turn. The village was still 500 metres away; we'd never make it before the helicopter turned for a third pass. A tiny copse of trees appeared by the side of the road. 'Stop! Stop!' A chance to go to earth. Jerking to a halt, throwing open the Landrover doors, we spilled out, six journalists and a young Chechen who'd been unlucky enough to ask for a lift to Novy Tsenteroi.

Only one instinct drove me: get out of sight. I took the first cover, under a single thick thorn tree by the side of the road. The others ran into the copse 25 metres away. I picked wrong. The Crocodile whirred back and, terrified, I understood he'd seen me dive under the tree. Machine-gun bullets ripped through the branches and the dry earth spat a dozen mini-fountains behind my feet. I tried to sink into the ground, I gripped the dirt with my fingers, flattened myself, forced myself further in under the thorn tree until trickles of blood began running down my forehead and arms. My entire body was saturated with energy and I prayed. A second burst. God knows where – I had my face hard against the dirt this time. My ears rang and my nostrils filled with the hot scent of live fire. That tree was a target. As soon as the helicopter passed over, I sprinted to the copse, not looking, crashing through the cool darkness of the trees. There, to my amazement, were the others, crouching in an old dug-out, an abandoned Russian position from earlier in the war. A dug-out. Pure, life-saving chance.

The helicopter pilots didn't give up easily. They knew we were all somewhere in the copse – our Landrover, doors open, lay abandoned on the road and there was no other cover – and for 25 minutes they passed back and forth, strafing with machine-gun and cannon fire until leaves and pieces of branches cut down by bullets fell like confetti. They tried so hard to kill us, but the shelter was too good.

Even when the helicopters were no longer audible, we were frozen, not daring to leave our dug-out. Suddenly men from the village arrived. Two of them, waiting till the Crocodiles broke away, ran across the open ground to the copse, appeared like angels above our hole and ordered us to get out and follow. Salvation, because the helicopters had only moved away temporarily; minutes later they were back over the copse. By then we were already inside the village.

A crazy, Mistral-like wind blew across the hot, dusty, deserted streets. Women gave us black tea and we sat at a table in the courtyard of a house with an old man wearing a gold sequined prayer cap over his white hair. 'We thought you were all dead', one of the women said. The Crocodile pilots must have realised we'd escaped and now they searched, some skimming over Novy Tsenteroi, some circling high and slow. One fired a rocket at an empty house on the outskirts of the village. But all this held no fears now. The charms of Chechnya took over as they always did. They fooled you and at the same time made the war bearable and kept you coming back: the sudden sight of a valley full of cherry blossoms; glimpses of the eternal snows; the pride in hospitality when there was nothing left to give; the soothing rhythms of village life defying the madhouse of war.

Wind blew through the courtyard. The old man drank tea and said nothing. The young men squatted in the sunlight, vicariously enjoying the pilots' failure to kill us. A tiny boy with a shaved head demonstrated his high karate kicks and his father Salamu, one of the men who had rescued us, laughed. The helicopters droned on and on, ignored. Salamu, a big, bearded man with red hair, informed us that, the next day, volunteers were going into Grozny through the woods to join others from the village already fighting. They could take us.

### Grozny

*The first commander I see inside Grozny is none other than Khizir Khachukayev, the giant I met on the outer defences of Grozny at Karpinski Hill at the very start of the war, some 20 months ago.*

*Khizir's unit is now deployed deep inside Grozny, between the 9th City Hospital and the Red Hammer factory, close to a couple of big strategic avenues. Khizir , who comes from western Chechnya and is very religious, holds green prayer beads. Under his camouflage jacket he's got an Islamic dark green collarless shirt. A camouflaged Russian special forces helmet is wrapped around his huge head, with a black, bushy beard sticking out the bottom. He's ferocious.*

*I ask him whether the guerrillas really aim to hold Grozny or to do what they did during that three-day attack in March – hit and run. 'We've come home. March was to show how fast we could capture the city. Now we're going to show how we can hold the city. We're fighting to the end, to victory. We're not leaving.'*

Andrei Babitsky, from Radio Liberty, and I walked in from the outskirts where the guerrillas left us to the dead zone in the centre. At first we moved against a tide of tired, frightened people fleeing on foot, in tractors, cars and trucks, with bundles of clothing, carpets and white flags ripped from sheets and attached to broom sticks and small branches. We were the only ones going in.

A Russian position surrounded by sandbags and concrete blocks appeared to have surrendered. A white flag flew and the soldiers did not even signal to us. We hurried on. Then came no-man's land – zones with no civilians, no fighters, no Russians, just abandoned houses and empty, menacing streets.

Then the final layer of war – the contested inner zone. We'd been walking down a narrow side-street, with the racket of battle getting louder. Side-streets were comforting, somehow less threatening, but we hit the side of a broad avenue. Still sheltered in the side-street we could see a burnt-out APC in the middle of the asphalt, downed telephone lines, smashed glass, bricks. This was the frontier. Here, emptiness was a deception because any building or corner could be a sniper position, any street could be shelled or mortared, any open space could be a killing zone. Babitsky and I had to cross that avenue. We counted together to three, put our heads down and sprinted. Bursting across into the next side-street, we froze. Someone had whistled. I looked around slowly and saw figures emerge from the shadows. A Chechen who appeared hardly older than 14 sat in a fourth-floor window with a shotgun, some tough fighters with Kalashnikovs emerged from doorways, and one beckoned us with his finger to come forward. We'd arrived in what the *boyeviks* were already calling 'liberated Grozny.'

To the *boyeviks* in Grozny there was the exhaltation of a battle royal. Everything was being thrown into this operation. Hardened commanders were deployed sector by sector, with Shamil Basayev in the very centre, where Zavgayev and the Russian administrators once had their refurbished office buildings. Most of the core army – perhaps 2,000 to 3,000 men – which had fought throughout the war was in action, but now joined by waves of volunteers and part-time fighters, a phenomenon which hadn't been seen in Chechnya for months.

'A lot of us are combatants who have fought throughout, but others are taking up arms for the first time,' said Ramzan Madzhayev, a 21-year-old in Microrayon, a key neighbourhood on the outskirts, next to the Russian base of Khankala. 'When the city was captured by the Russians and the fighting moved into the countryside, a lot of people put down their weapons. Now they're digging them up again,' he said.

It had been a long time since I'd seen so many *boyeviks*, with their cast-off uniforms, jeans, Kalashnikovs and RPGs, in one place. It reminded me of the almost boyish enthusiasm at the very start of the war. One crucial difference: this time there was no naivety. The volunteers knew exactly the effect of shrapnel and bullets on the human body, they knew how many soldiers, planes and tanks the Russians had, they knew the risks – and still they came forward.

The strategy of the assault was two pronged. With lighter weaponry and far smaller numbers, the Chechens knew they could never sustain a frontal attack on every Russian position for long. So, rather than trying to wipe out their enemies within the city, the *boyeviks* concentrated on surrounding them and keeping them pinned down. There were an estimated 12,000 Russian soldiers dotted around the city. But because the troops were caught off guard, this powerful garrison was soon neutralised into pockets of trapped troops desperately waiting for help. Having corralled the troops inside the city, the *boyeviks* implemented the second half of the strategy: facing outwards and preventing the arrival of reinforcements from Russian bases on the outskirts.

This completely turned the tables, transforming the Chechens from attackers into the easier role of defenders. The Russians, who had lorded it over Grozny for a year and a half, were forced to act as invaders to try and rescue their blockaded troops. Again, the Russians had the brutal task of sending mechanised troops into an urban setting crawling with RPG teams and snipers. Columns of APCs and tanks sent in from the big bases at Sheikh Mansur Airport – the Russians called this Severny, or Northern Airport – in the north and Khankala in the east ran into ambushes and suffered horrific losses. At the cinema in the Microrayon area, where the last apartment buildings faced out onto Khankala, they'd destroyed a tank and an APC. The bodies of the crew still lay in the sun. 'A dog ran into our building carrying a severed hand from the field,' a woman there said matter-of-factly. Even official figures admitted that 27 APCs or tanks and six helicopters were lost in the first two days of fighting. The Chechens also captured several APCs and a couple tanks, which they immediately turned on the Russians.

Just as in the first battle for Grozny at the start of the war, the Russians could call on their long-range artillery, helicopters and airplanes to bombard the Chechen defenders at little risk. But the kind of saturation shelling and heavy aerial bombing which had won in 1994–1995 was ruled out now, because thousands of Russian soldiers, not to mention civilians, were trapped in there with the *boyeviks*. Ultimately, the Chechens could only be engaged in the most costly way – on the ground. On 6 August the Russians were like a man who discovers he has cancer when, just a day before, he considered himself healthy. Over the next few days, the cancer spread and the Russians realised that removing every tumour would mean killing the patient.

## Novy Tsenteroi – Grozny

*How did the boyeviks get in? That's what really angers Russians. What about all those checkpoints, the secret services, the helicopters and aerial reconaissance? How did the boyeviks penetrate the most heavily defended region in Russian-held Chechnya? The men of Novy Tsenteroi show us that the answer couldn't be more straightforward, even now, with the battle raging for several days and all efforts being taken to plug the leaks.*

*Unarmed and in civilian clothes, the villagers tell us to walk down to the edge of the village. The helicopters are flying, circling over the fields, woods and rooftops, as they have done for 48 hours now, even at night. So as not to attract attention we split into ones and twos and try to walk casually – just strolling – never even looking up at the choppers. Behind us ride two men on a beaten-up motorbike with a sidecar.*

*At the bottom of the village, the woods begin. There's a small path. We duck in, one after the other. Someone pulls back the tarpaulin on the sidecar: it's full of ammunition webbing, one-shot RPGs and rifles. Six Chechens gear up quickly, now a mixture of civilian clothing and weapons – the typical part-time boyeviks. Two are just teenagers.*

*The motorbike returns and at once we set off deeper into the woods. We walk fast with few rests. Often there is no path and the undergrowth is jungle thick, hot and full of thorns. I ask our guides how they know where we're going and am told they played here as children, then they hunted, now they fight.*

*Almost at once you understand the helicopters can't see through the canopy. We're invisible, even though the choppers are flying, sometimes with a great rush, directly overhead. They're searching for infiltrating boyeviks, but they won't find this group. All that technology cheated by the cover of leaves. It seems too easy.*

*We reach an open field. Time to run. We go in pairs, as far as an isolated tree, kneeling, checking for helicopters, then running across the bareness again.*

*The pause is vital. Running, you only see the rough ground under your feet; all you hear is pounding breath. You'd never even know the helicopter was coming.*

*The next field is much wider. We can hear a helicopter, but none is in sight, and we run. The risk is that they arrive before we reach the other side. Mid-way, we pause again at the only available cover – waist-high wild flowers – and check the sky. There are still 100 metres to go. Suddenly a green chopper clatters right over the tree line. We're done for. Everyone falls, flattens himself in the high flowers and grass. Incredibly, the helicopter fails to see us and flies right by. No commands are needed: as soon as we're out of the pilot's line of vision, we rise as one and sprint across the rest of the field into the woods.*

*One final alarm: Russians shouting and shooting single rifle shots in the woods ahead. Our scout hadn't expected this – a Russian patrol or some new position. If they hadn't been shouting and shooting we'd have walked right into the fireworks. Instead, we're warned, and a long detour begins. Several hours later, we come across a shepherd with a flock of*

*curly horned goats, then wasteland, then buildings, cars, streets.*
*'Welcome to Grozny', someone says.*

It was easy to see the new battle for Grozny as glorious. Surviving each
day felt good, and seeing the Chechens win, after so many defeats and
so much suffering, felt good. But for the civilians, there was no glory,
just another chapter in the persistent policy by both the *boyeviks* and
the Russians to force non-combatants into the firing line.

All year the Chechen *boyeviks* had been moving suddenly into
supposedly Russian-held settlements no matter what the cost to the
civilians trapped there. Now that strategy took on a grand scale, with
an estimated 250,000 civilians stuck inside Grozny. And unlike at
Samashki, Gekhi or countless other village battles, the urban conditions
meant that this one could last not days, but weeks, whatever the result.
The *boyeviks* were fighting for their own city, but undeniably they
benefited from the shield of all those captive civilians. The *boyeviks*
claimed to protect civilians, but sometimes the opposite was true.

Equally to blame were the Russians, this army of demoralised, demoral-
ising soldiers, armed drunks, make-believe Rambos and thousands upon
thousands of blameless, browbeaten conscripts pushed into a war supported
by no one. They were experiencing the threat of a major defeat, the kind
of panic and desperation the Chechens had faced time and time again.
Their response was predictable: civilians became as much the enemy as
*boyeviks*, refugee columns were shot up, the 4th City Hospital was rocketed
by a plane, roads were bombed and strafed miles from any sign of *boyeviks*
and civilians were taken hostage by stranded units.

The closer to the centre, the more the streets looked deserted. Paradoxically, however, there were actually more people there than elsewhere,
but they were hidden away under cover. There had been rumours of the
offensive several days before in the main bazaar, the nerve centre of Grozny
life, and some had got out in time. But the fighting erupted so fiercely and
suddenly on 6 August, with the Chechen *boyeviks* immediately seizing the
centre, that there was little chance for most non-combatants to escape.
Only from the outer rings of the city could people leave safely.

For the first week of the battle, civilians in bad zones cowered in their
cellars, if they were lucky enough to have them. There was no electricity
or running water, food supplies dwindled and fetching water from outdoor
taps was dangerous. Often people were killed or wounded by snipers or
mortar shells on these trips. Ruslan, an ambulance crewman living in the
very centre, told me how he sheltered seven mothers with new-born babies
during the fighting. They'd been at a maternity hospital with infants just
a day or two old when the fighting broke out. The first outsiders they saw
were Russian soldiers who burst in looking for food. But there was no
food, no water, nothing, and even the mothers' milk risked drying up. So

the women had to go out into the street, where the bullets were flying and shells exploding, in a desperate search for safety.

Near the 9th City Hospital, where Babitsky and I found Khizir and linked up with other colleagues, I talked with Nikolai, an ethnic-Russian living in fear on the second floor of an apartment building. 'We're going to die here. We've no food. That sack of flour is all we have left,' he said. Hundreds of others in Nikolai's building were in the cellar, living by candle light. I was the first outsider Nikolai had seen since the fighting started, but he was so nervous he didn't even seem to register that I, a foreigner, had somehow dropped into his life. When I said I'd managed to walk in that morning and that perhaps he could try walking out, he simply ignored me. He was resigned to his fate: death.

The Chechens had a captured tank and a mortar gun in the neighbourhood and at night I lay in the dark in a second-floor apartment, unable to sleep, visualising the action. First the thunder of an outgoing shell and four or five seconds later the faint sound of the explosion several kilometres to the east, probably where the Russians were trying to establish a bridgehead between Khankala and the strategic Minutka traffic circle.

Then the Russians' return fire. The firing, usually four rounds, one after the other, was faint, but each incoming shell flew in with a loud whistle. Even when the round landed at a safe distance, the explosion and night-time lightening flash were heart stopping. Sometimes shrapnel smacked with a sickening tinkle into walls across our courtyard. The Russians also regularly fired illumination and marker flares. You heard the boom and the whistle of the incoming, but then, instead of an explosion, just a silent wash of yellow light came in through the windows. If the light was really strong, that meant the marker flare was overhead and your neighbourhood was pinpointed for the next salvo of real shells. If it was off to the side, someone else would be getting it, leaving you relieved and a little ashamed.

There was no cellar, so I smoked, prayed, tried to fight the sickness of fear and waited for dawn. Best of all, there was the law of averages: of all the apartments in the city, ours was unlikely to suffer a direct hit and if it wasn't a direct hit we had a damned good chance of coming out unscathed.

After a few days of the battle, fed up with the imprisonment of fear, people got bolder and used lulls to go out for fresh air. Suddenly, there were scenes of utter normality: dogs playing, young women talking to the fighters as they rested in the sun, old folks chatting. Once I heard a steady rhythm and leaned out my window to see four Chechen women in a circle clapping and one dancing in the middle, rotating, arms out horizontally in the graceful Lezginka dance. She should have been waving handkerchiefs, but instead she gripped two pieces of scrap paper. 'If we're going to die, let's die with music,' the dancer cried, throwing her head back and laughing. There was no electricity, but people rigged up televisions to car batteries to hear a snatch of news or one of them would listen on a portable radio, then slip around to his friends to relay information. The satellite telephone we used to file our reports also ran off a car battery. When that died out, we walked to a nearby municipal garage during a lull and stole the battery from a parked truck. We were looters.

Then, without warning, explosions, the crackle of gunfire, or the grinding noise of a helicopter gunship wheeling over, and the normality dissolved back into deserted, hostile streets. Even stray dogs sprinted to find cover, tails between their legs.

The International Committee of the Red Cross said 1,500 civilians were wounded in the city. God knows how many more went uncounted. During lulls ICRC ambulance drivers, local Chechens, made suicidal missions to pick up casualties. They drove rickety minivans, many of them riddled with shrapnel, doors and windows missing, and some which had to be jump-started. For the wounded in the centre, there was only first aid, with hospitals running out of medicine and electricity, then falling into the crossfire, and finally being abandoned.

To reach the ICRC compound during a lull we had to traverse no-man's land, jamming a battered Lada through the deserted streets in a succession of violent accelerations across intersections, only to brake hard at corners, where we'd check for the sound of shooting. Always, we drove with one eye out for helicopters and prayed we wouldn't run into a Russian unit or APC. You never knew in no-man's land. No sooner had we reached the compound than a firefight erupted just beyond the perimeter trees and the nurses, ambulance drivers and civilians gathered outside scattered like leaves in the wind.

Inside, Fery Aalan, the ICRC director, stunned me by offering coffee and biscuits, something I had only dreamed about during a week that felt like a month.

Two artillery shells had fallen within the compound, terrifying people but causing no casualties, and four people had been wounded by snipers just down the street, he said. The compound was almost totally blockaded and aid convoys were being detained by Russian soldiers 15 kilometres outside the city. 'Please give us two hours to bring in a convoy of much needed supplies and then begin killing each other,' Aalan said, to no one in particular, since he said the Russian military refused to answer radio calls and his contact with the Chechens was 'none, zero'.

### Grozny

*The refugees flow out from the nightmare of inner Grozny to the edges, thousands at a time. Slow moving crowds of people on foot accompanied by lorries, tractors and cars waving white flags and loaded with children, carpets, bundles of clothing. One black Volga has a body tied to the roof rack.*

*In the eastern neighbourhood of Staraya Sunzha, there's no fighting and the Russians retain control. But instead of letting the refugees out into the country, they're bottling them up, about 40,000 of them in the streets, local houses and in an ever-growing queue of overpacked cars. Back in the centre, the noise of explosions and machine-gun fire blurs into a uniform thunder.*

*At last the APCs blocking the exit pull back and the soldiers announce that women and children will be allowed to leave the city – but on foot and without their menfolk. Males over the age of 11 are considered suspect boyeviks and must remain in Grozny. Few women accept the offer. It's seven kilometres to the next village and the heat is great.*

*Zaryema Sultanova asks an exception be made for her husband. He's not a boyevik, she says – he's 84 and paralysed. There he is, sitting motionless in the passenger seat of the family Lada. Request refused. Orders are orders. No males over 11.*

*Zaryema begins to cry. Away from the troops, the family begins talking quietly with several young men. It's agreed. They'll take the old man on a stretcher; they'll take the partisan paths through the woods, around the checkpoint, through the Russian lines.*

*You can't tell if the old man understands. He's motionless, staring blankly through the windscreen.*

*Zaryema leans down to say goodbye. Unexpectedly in a place where people are so used to hiding tenderness, she runs a hand over his old face, rough with several days' white stubble.*

*The man's head doesn't move. His entire body remains still. But tears begin streaming down his leathery skin. He understands.*

The 9th City Hospital, one of Grozny's biggest, came to symbolise the double death sentence imposed by the *boyeviks* and Russian forces on civilians. On the first day of the battle, Khizir's men took up positions, not in the hospital, but nearby. Obviously, they expected to have their wounded treated there. So immediately, the staff tried to evacuate their worst cases and then themselves. They'd seen this all before.

For Doctor Saipudin Mamayev, it was the third time he had to flee his workplace during the war. 'I worked at the main Republican Hospital at the start in 1994. That was bombed flat. Then I worked for several months from my home and then I went to the 9th City Hospital. Now this time our *boyeviks* came into the hospital and fought around there. That's not right. But then what the Russian forces are doing – well, what do they think they're up to? Does Russian democracy mean anything?'

Mamayev was lucky to get out at all. When the hospital staff tried to reach the haven of Staraya Sunzha in a column of buses with white flags, they came under fire from a Russian helicopter and turned back. On the second attempt, the medical staff tried to walk out, wearing their white coats and waving white flags, but along the way they came under mortar fire and three doctors were wounded by shrapnel. After that, the evacuation disintegrated. Only the fit were able to escape and the worst cases were left behind, along with a few medical staff who refused to leave.

On 9 August Russian soldiers entered the hospital, clashed with the *boyeviks* around the building, then left. The next day some 25 infantry soldiers stormed into the hospital and began searching for wounded guerrillas. According to Memorial human rights group, one of the officers was shot by a sniper and badly wounded as they left, prompting the whole unit to go back inside the hospital. Another version is that stranded Russian troops ran into the hospital after their armoured column was ambushed nearby.

As soon as the Russians deployed in the hospital windows, the building was surrounded by Khizir's fighters. According to the medical staff, the Russians radioed their base and were told to take up positions and prepare to hold out. This was the tactic patented by Shamil Basayev and Salman Raduyev: when cut off in enemy territory with wounded comrades, take over a hospital and negotiate your way out. The 'order restorers' had become the bandits.

The role reversal put the Chechen fighters in a spin. Should they condemn the Russian hostage takers or boast about how their side did it better? The hypocrisy was almost comical. 'That's Russians for you, taking hostages, you see! They're all drunk, they looted the vodka shop. Their officer, he wants to be a second Shamil Basayev, but he'll never manage,' a Chechen fighter said as he sheltered in the stairwell of an apartment building with half a dozen other fighters. Khizir said: 'We're waiting for orders and so far we've been told not to storm the hospital to avoid having the patients killed. But if we get the order, we'll show them how to storm a building, not the way they tried against Shamil in Budennovsk. We'll clear that place out in 15 minutes.'

On the 11th, the Russians did become second Shamil Basayevs, emerging from the hospital on foot with about 100 patients and medical staff and walking straight by the furious Chechens and disappearing down a side-street towards their own base. The people forming the human shield were released later as promised and some of them walked back to the hospital. No sooner did they arrive than the Russians began dropping mortar bombs.

Of course, shelling. With their own troops safely out, the Russians could shell us at leisure. They had the local coordinates and they wanted revenge. Until now, the presence of those Russian soldiers in the hospital had actually protected all of us in the neighbourhood, both Khizir's men and civilians. The Russian soldiers used doctors and patients as a human shield, while the Chechens effectively used the soldiers as a human shield. Now the game was back to zero.

Khizir had come to our apartment just before the shelling began. There was total, tense silence, broken only by the regular thunderclap of mortar shells in the hot afternoon air. I lay on the floor and smoked. Khizir adjusted his special forces helmet, sat back and picked up his prayer beads. 'The bastards, I knew they'd do that after we let them go', he muttered. 'Never mind. The most important thing is to stay alive so we can keep fighting.' Outside, a nurse who'd lived through the entire hostage drama and just made it back after being released by the Russian soldiers was killed in a mortar blast. Two doctors, two more nurses and a patient were wounded.

The last 22 patients of the 9th City Hospital were evacuated after that, and the big building sat empty for the rest of the battle. These patients were all serious cases, too injured or sick to move far, so they were carried into the cellar of a shop next to the hospital. Oil lamp light flickered over damp walls. The floor was covered in a mixture of mud and indefinable garbage. In chambers leading off a central passage, the wounded lay in their own blood. One man had a deep headwound, a woman had a leg missing. A couple who were so old and sick that they'd shrivelled like raisins approached, thinking perhaps that I was some kind of aid worker. 'Write us down on your list too will you', said the old woman. 'Look at me, look at my husband.' I couldn't.

A barely trained paramedic was the only person looking after this human debris. Natasha Papova, a 26-year-old woman with a strange intensity and calm, maybe due to shock, had come to Chechnya from Russia as a volunteer a few months before, never imagining what would happen. 'Yesterday they shelled while we were in the hospital, so during the night everyone was carried down here. All yesterday, we couldn't go out for water so there was nothing to eat or drink for these people except a bit of cocoa. We have only a few bandages, nothing to fight infection, no anaesthetic.'

### Grozny

*Andrei Babitsky and I move quickly across a courtyard, leaving the boyeviks and the hospital to our rear. Suddenly, 150 metres ahead on the main road, there appear three or four Russian APCs. We freeze and crouch.*

*For a few seconds the machines disappear behind some trees, camouflaged and silent. I feel a second's relief: they're heading away. Then a jolt of adrenalin: they've turned around, they're moving down the road, towards us. They're attacking.*

*'APCs! APCs!' Babitsky and I begin yelling together. Pure chance, but*

we're the first to spot the attack – the boyeviks are around the corner and screened. It feels weird to be warning the boyeviks, to get sucked into the war. But if they're taken by surprise, we could all die.

'Where?' a Chechen shouts back. 'On the main road, heading towards us now!' we reply.

We soon hear the engines of the APCs, closer, closer. The Chechens scramble into position.

'Come on, come on!' a Chechen commander cries out to his men and the column comes into full view at a range of about 25 metres.

A Chechen fighter swings round the corner of his building, drops to his right knee, an RPG on the shoulder and fires. The first APC erupts into a ball of yellow flames.

Rifle and machine-gun fire thunder out as the Chechens spring their ambush and the Russians fight back. There's a second RPG explosion.

Scrambling across open space, Babitsky and I race to take cover in an abandoned building, then across to our apartment. A minute after we get inside, four Russians who've escaped their knocked-out APC charge across our courtyard and take cover in the first apartment building they see – the doorway next to ours. The Chechens are close behind, but too late: the Russians are inside and they've taken an apartment hostage. Human shields again. Anything to survive.

'Don't shoot, or I'll kill them', a soldier screams from the building.

'Whoever's in charge, come out unarmed and talk', a thin Chechen commander with a balding head shouts back, leaning around the corner of the courtyard.

Voices are strained. If one shot is fired, the whole place will explode.

Unexpectedly, heroically, the Chechen commander puts his rifle down and simply walks across the courtyard and straight into the apartment building.

A minute later the Chechen reappears, with the four terrified soldiers, one of them wounded, behind him in a line. The Russians clearly had no choice but to surrender or die fighting, along with their hostages, and they didn't take long to persuade. The rarest of all things in Chechnya has just happened – a massacre has been avoided, innocents have survived.

Afterwards, it's so easy to condemn. The Russian soldiers shouldn't have taken that apartment hostage and we journalists shouldn't have involved ourselves in a battle, however small the role. There's condemnation, there's guilt, but only after. In the clutch there is no condemnation, no guilt – only survival.

Between 11–13 August, one week since launching their offensive, the Chechen *boyeviks* had captured or set on fire every strategic building in the city centre. Doku Zavgayev's administration building was a blackened, gutted hulk. Burned-out APCs and tanks lay discarded in street after street.

With the Russian troops inside the city pinned down and the troops outside the city barred, the Chechen fighters were able to move freely around much of the city. The besieged Russian positions were in desperate condition, full of wounded, lacking ammunition and food. Russian reinforcements were unable to enter the city in decisive numbers and even the two fortress bases of Severny Airport and Khankala had come under attack. Zavgayev took refuge in Khankala, while his last representatives in Grozny waited anxiously, powerless in the Staraya Sunzha neighbourhood.

Official figures indicated 400 Russian soldiers killed and 1,200 wounded in the battle. Another 130 were missing, either dead or taken prisoner. Shamil Basayev, himself wounded by a bullet in the foot, claimed the Russian losses were 2,000 dead. Chechen losses were heavy by guerrilla standards, but because of the tactics, nothing approaching those of the Russians.

Basayev told journalists that the Russians could still recapture Grozny. But 'it would take half a year and they would have to destroy the city. They could even take it in a month, but it would cost them 10,000 to 15,000 men.' Allowing for exaggeration, Basayev was right. Not only did the Chechens have most of the capital under their control, the trapped Russians units were effectively their prisoners, and the situation could only be reversed at enormous cost. Check mate.

On the night of 11 August, Alexander Lebed, the Kremlin Security Council secretary who had just been given full responsibility for Chechnya by President Yeltsin, secretly entered the republic to meet Aslan Maskhadov. Driving in from Dagestan in the dark, Lebed travelled by jeep with none of the usual retinue of bodyguards and APCs. Once in Novy Atagi, a prosperous village just south of Grozny, he went to his *rendez-vous* – the huge house of a Chechen millionaire where Maskhadov was waiting. By 4:00 a.m. they had the outlines of a ceasefire agreement and Lebed was spirited back to Dagestan.

On the 13th, Maskhadov and General Konstantin Pulikovsky, who was acting overall Russian commander in the temporary absence of Tikhomirov, met outside Novy Atagi. They met again on the 17th. The setting was spartan and tense. Maskhadov came in a convoy of battered jeeps, Pulikovsky in a fleet of helicopter gunships. The two generals then sat across a folding table in a simple kakhi tent by the road. Russian tanks ringed the site and the gunships circled overhead, sometimes so low and loud that I wondered if Maskhadov and Pulikovsky could hear each other. But it was there that they agreed to a preliminary ceasefire. Although it would take weeks more for this to become clear, the war was ending.

Lebed's peace negotiations were ferociously opposed by the government party of war lobby and the Communist and nationalist elements dominating parliament. A key enemy of Lebed and the peace plan was the interior minister, Anatoly Kulikov, a politician who had invested his career in the war, but whose troops had been humiliated in the battle for Grozny. Pulikovsky, apparently in league with hardliners in Moscow, almost managed to reverse the process when he suddenly threatened on 19 August to recapture Grozny in an all-out blitz. It was to be the military's final madness. Not only the *boyeviks*, but tens of thousands of civilians and all the Russian soldiers still encircled inside the city, faced a firestorm. Pulikovsky gave civilians 48 hours to leave and thousands fled in panic, only to be attacked by artillery and helicopters – long before the ultimatum expired – as they poured into the countryside. The *boyeviks*, nervous, but resolute, dug more trenches and braced for the end.

It never came. At the last moment, Lebed and the new defence minister, Igor Rodionov, stepped in, reasserting their authority and finally putting the generals under control. The episode had illustrated a crucial, but bitter truth: if the war was going to be ended, Moscow would either have to capitulate or take the Pulikovsky route – the wholesale massacre of a city, and, eventually, genocide.

Lebed, an ex-paratrooper and Afghanistan veteran, like so many of the officers who'd fought in Chechnya, was free to choose. Unlike previous negotiators, he wasn't tied up in the start or the prolongation of the war. He wasn't part of the great cover up, and he broke a taboo by openly admitting that the army was not engaged against bandits or terrorists, but 'fighting a people'. Besides, he wanted badly to become president one day and had no reason to try and protect his boss Yeltsin from humiliation. So Lebed chose capitulation. 'We will no longer talk in the language of ultimatums,' he said.

On 22 August the Russians agreed to withdraw from Grozny and the mountains and go to their bases at Khankala and Severny. The Chechens were to be given back their republic. Then, on 31 August, Lebed and Maskhadov met in Khasavyurt, on the Chechen-Dagestani border, to cut the Gordion Knot of Chechnya's claim to independence. Their accord allowed for the whole debate to be dropped until both sides were ready to talk. They gave themselves five years – 'until cool heads prevail', Lebed said. The formula was so simple it seemed obvious. The war was over.

In parliament in Moscow, the deputies greeted Lebed with cries of 'shame' and 'traitor'. Lebed entered a vitriolic slanging match with Kulikov, both accusing each other of everything from mafia dealings to treason. Lebed, so bold in Chechnya, was unequipped for the intricate business of political infighting and his reckless, arrogant counterattacks only earned him, and the peace plan, more foes.

In the chaos everyone waited for President Yeltsin to intervene. Only he could say whether the peace plan stood, and with it the end of the war. Still incapacitated by heart trouble, and wary of Lebed's popularity among ordinary people, the president said nothing. On 17 October he went on television and announced he was firing Lebed for insubordination. But the momentum of war had been definitively broken, the emperor shown to have no clothes. Moscow had proved itself 'corrupt, helpless, stupid and indifferent', as Alexander Solzhenitsyn put it, and Lebed had done the right thing 'given the total defeat'. There was no turning back. Finally, grudgingly, Yeltsin accepted the plan; he would make peace with the Chechens. On 23 November, almost two years to the day since that first bungled covert tank attack on Dzhokhar Dudayev's Grozny, the president did the unthinkable: he ordered the complete withdrawal of all troops from Chechnya.

The Chechens had won.

## Budennovsk

*When the battle for Grozny is over, the Russian soldiers leave the city and mountains in columns of hundreds of trucks and APCs flying white flags and escorted for their own safety by jeeps of Chechen boyeviks. The Chechens go back to their villages in buses, jeeps, trucks and captured armoured vehicles packed with cheering men and flying the rebel flag.*

*Across Chechnya, Russian checkpoints and defensive positions, once full of dangerous, brave, frightened, drunk, merciful, angry men, empty out. Corrugated iron which used to roof foxholes flaps in the wind. Barbed wire fences sag and trenches begin slowly to cave in. Grafitti on the concrete pill boxes tells where the soldiers came from and went back to – Samara, Moscow, Leningrad.*

*For the 205th and 101st brigades, the humiliation of loading up troop trains out of Chechnya is far from the end. These were the brigades specially formed to maintain a permanent Russian presence in Chechnya – they have nowhere to retreat to. For them, there will be no anxious relatives on station platforms, no brass bands or familiar home comforts to cushion their fall. They're simply given empty fields in the Stavropol region and told to do the best they can.*

*The 205th gets Budennovsk: an empty field covered in tents on one side of the town, an unfinished building site on the other. When the soldiers first arrive in mid-winter, local people meet them with donations of fresh food and warm clothing. But the welcome soon wears off. The soldiers have lost their discipline and the retreat only magnifies the decline. Within weeks, the local joke, based on a pun in Russian, is to rename the 205th Brigade the 200th Drunken Brigade.*

*'They're a bunch of hooligans,' says a farmer called Viktor. 'A drunken*

soldier came up to us once with a grenade and we all ran off. Their officers have taken over the town's hotel and a girl I know who works there says she's found landmines and grenades on the floor and doesn't know what to do. Every night they're smashed.'

At the building site, meant to become a large garage until taken over by the army, there are not only no guards at the main gate, but no one to tell me where I can find the officers. Entering the first building I come to, I meet a young major on the stairs. Surprised by how instantly friendly he seems, I realise he's sodden drunk.

He takes me down the corridor, past some conscript soldiers who don't look old enough to shave and whose World War II style greatcoats are either too long or short in the sleeves. 'In here,' the major says. A cloud of cigarette smoke hits me as soon as he opens the door. A dozen officers sit at a table covered in plates of half-eaten food, bottles and glasses. Some are in their jackets, some in jumpers, some in the blue-and-white sleeveless vests of the army. My arrival causes excitement. 'I've brought you a guest from France,' the major says, as if making a report.

A colonel tries to get up to make room for me at his side, then staggers and has to hold on to a television for support, only to knock it over. All the officers begin talking to me at once, competing to see who can pour me the most drink.

'Have more vodka. Come on, come on, just a little more. Just out of custom', the colonel says.

'Give him some wine', another officer says from across the table. 'Has he tried the wine? Have you tried our wine?'

'Maybe he doesn't like wine. There, have some of our beer', someone else says.

A handsome, robust lieutenant colonel opposite me is the only person carrying a weapon – a pistol in a shoulder holster. 'I see you're looking at my pistol. It was presented to me specially by the minister of defence,' he says proudly. 'Look,' and he pulls out the loaded gun and hands it over to me. The other lieutenant colonel abruptly intercepts it and removes the ammunition clip.

It doesn't take long for everyone to lose interest in me. One leaves to sleep, another enters an emotional conversation with his neighbour. The colonel suddenly gets suspicious and demands to see my papers, declares me in violation of security, then just as suddenly seems to suffer amnesia, gently hands back my ID and fills another tin mug of vodka.

At last, I can talk to one of them at a time. What, I ask, went wrong?

'This was an active, tested brigade,' says the lieutenant colonel with the pistol. 'Now it's a discarded brigade. Not one officer has an apartment. We live in rooms like this, 72 officers and their families. It's the paradox of Russia that the boys who defended the state's interests in Chechnya are now not wanted. We'll never understand.'

## 8. THE PRICE OF PEACE

*Grozny*

*The withdrawal of troops means freedom of movement. No more checkpoints, no columns of APCs and tanks thundering down the broken roads, no twisting your neck to check the skies for aircraft. No more filtration camps, no disappearances, no nocturnal gunfights in the streets of Grozny. Drive where you like, when you like.*

*Amid the euphoria and relief, all the marriages held up by the war take place in a rush. Wedding convoys, the cars decorated with flowers and carpets, speed through villages. Parties thunder with celebratory gunfire. In the past, rifles or shotguns were enough, but now guests fire machine-guns in the air. 'People must have thought the war had started again,' a friend says after a wedding in Gudermes, where an RPG was fired to explode high in the sky. Inevitably, there are injuries, even cases of a wedding being held one day, a funeral the next. But Chechens love the sound of shooting, and now they can waste all that ammunition without worrying: they've won. They're delirious.*

*'I remember you once said it wasn't worth going on with the war, that the price was too high,' chides my friend Makhsharip. 'Now we can breath freely again – this is what we were fighting for and it was worth it.'*

On 27 January 1997, elections supervised by the Organisation for Security and Cooperation in Europe were held in Chechnya and Aslan Maskhadov was overwhelmingly elected president, beating Shamil Basayev and Zelimkhan Yandarbiyev.

Now that the last Russian soldiers were out, Chechens could freely choose their fate for the first time since the chaos of 1991 and the election turned into a national celebration. Polling stations everywhere were jammed, queues of voters stretching far out into the snow, and the polling time had to be extended by two hours to accommodate the numbers. 'People hope for something better. They're tired of all this and they want to build their state,' Asudin, a 40-year-old man, said as he prepared to vote for Basayev in Mekhkety, one of the last villages to be bombed before the Grozny recapture. Experienced OSCE election observers – led by the courageous, tireless head of the OSCE mission in Grozny, Tim Guldimann – were amazed by the Chechens' enthusiasm and the way they defied predictions of vote rigging and violence.

In the afterglow of his victory, Maskhadov declared that 'Chechnya is an independent state. ... Only this remains: that the rest of the world, including Russia, recognise this independence.' Indeed, this 45-year-old man who had withstood the Russian military, won a free election among his own people, and now sat in front of journalists from around the globe, did look a lot like the president of a tiny, battered, but independent republic.

Yet the Chechens had not won real independence and that was the bitter caveat to the end of their war. They now had *de facto* independence, able to pick their own leaders, keep their own army, make their own laws. But full *de jure* independence, with a UN seat, embassies and the internationally recognised right of self-defence, remained as far off as ever. Under the Khasavyurt peace accord, Maskhadov had up to five years to negotiate, but ironically, the switch from war to talks had left him no less vulnerable. Although Chechnya had the potential of rich agriculture, the oil refining business and a people with famous trading skills, it could only be a viable independent state if Russia cooperated economically. Ruined Chechnya would be all the more dependent, needing Russian trading, Russian aid, Russian rail, air and road links. Moscow offered such help, but with the qualifier of Chechnya joining the Russian Federation. Moscow failed to crush the Chechen independence movement, but it could afford to try and bleed it to death.

Maskhadov also faced the intense problem of maintaining order and combating the heavily armed criminal bands left in the wake of five years of instability and war. In December 1996 six employees from the International Committee of the Red Cross were murdered in their sleep at the hospital they'd opened in Novy Atagi, and all winter there were high-profile kidnappings of Russian journalists. The perpetrators were never identified. Many Chechens claimed the Red Cross killings and other acts, which undermined the standing of Maskhadov and the republic around the world, were carried out by the FSB Russian secret services. Blaming the FSB was too easy. Even without Russian meddling, Maskhadov was unable to control groups of gunmen who, like the *abregs*, were apparently beyond any law. Kidnapping, particularly of journalists, became big business. Nevertheless, fears that the FSB was attempting to destablise post-war Chechnya were far from groundless. Preventing the separatist authorities from fully controlling their republic would be an obvious way to weaken their position at the negotiating table.

Any Chechen sense of triumph was especially muted by the colossal physical cost of the war. That first winter of peace brought remembrance ceremonies for the dead, snow falling through smashed roofs, cold winds funneling across the jagged walls, and ice over fields which no one crossed for fear of landmines.

No one really knows how many of Chechnya's approximately one million people were killed and wounded in 21 months of fighting. As far back as April 1996, Médecins Sans Frontières estimated that 40,000 civilians had died. Alexander Lebed, in his typically haphazard way, announced after the war that between 80,000 and 100,000 people perished, a figure the Chechen authorities – again, with no scientific proof – also used. You had only to look at the rows and rows of fresh graves, including warriors' graves identified by a tall pole, in nearly every village cemetery to get a feel. How many *boyeviks* died can only be guessed at, but because of the nature of the fighting, their losses were certainly lower than among the non-combatant population. An OSCE diplomat estimated the human and physical toll for such a small place proportionally equivalent to the ghastly Soviet losses during World War II. Everybody knew someone who'd died and about 1,300 people remained missing, nearly all of them believed to be dead or to have disappeared in the 'filtration camp' system.

Losses among the Russian army and interior ministry should be accurately known, but given the contradictory and often incomplete information released during the war, there were doubts about the authenticity of figures given once it was over. Lebed said in late 1996 that 3,826 soldiers died, 17,892 were wounded and 1,906 were missing, either dead or still prisoner. A list compiled by Memorial human rights activists in early 1997 said that 4,379 soldiers, all of them identified by name, died. Another 1,408 were missing in action, held prisoner, or listed as having deserted, the report said. Only a few hundred of the missing were believed to be still alive.

The human rights group Soldiers' Mothers put the figure of dead at around 7,000, while a defence ministry source, who was in a position to know the truth, told me just under 10,000 soldiers perished. He said 5,620 men from the army died and roughly three times that number were wounded; the interior ministry lost between 1,800 and 2,500 men; the FSB, border guards and other branches of the security forces lost a few hundred more, he said.

The full story may never come out. Long after the Chechnya peace accord, military refrigerators in Rostov-on-Don, southern Russia, were still full of unidentified soldiers' bodies and new ones from recently discovered mass graves in Chechnya kept coming in. Even a decade after the end of the 10-year Soviet war in Afghanistan, many believed the real casualty toll – officially about 15,000 dead – has yet to be published.

The material ruin was much easier to document. The oil refinery complexes were badly damaged, although reparable; public utilities installations were in many places bombed so badly that only makeshift services could be provided; the huge concrete products factory in the south had been bombed to pieces; the Red Hammer metallurgy factory in Grozny worked at minimum capacity; large parts of agricultural land were untended or abandoned because of landmines. In Grozny, block after block of apartment buildings had been gutted with fire, leaving just the empty outer walls. The city centre had been bulldozed away. Entire neighbourhoods of small houses with courtyards disappeared, as did whole villages in the south. Lebed put the number of homes destroyed at

46,000 and even at the end of the war, an estimated 300,000 to 400,000 people remained refugees, including the many Russians who left under the pre-war Dudayev regime.

In some places the ruins were restored astonishingly fast. Along the river bank of Argun, where houses were demolished in their hundreds in early 1995, the town was almost entirely rebuilt by the end of the war. Only the mutilated trees, stubby branches sticking out like thumbs, recalled the disaster. But Argun was lucky in that the fighting there only lasted a few months early in the war. In more remote places, or villages where the fighting continued to the end, there was despair.

By the time of Maskhadov's election, just 10 families had moved back to Bamut. The rest of the village, once home to about 6,500 people, lay in twisted, burnt ruins and, because of landmines, no one dared try to rebuild. Every few weeks, another person was killed or mutilated. Down the slope in one of the streets of Bamut where the *boyeviks* used to keep their bases, Ayup Khanzatov, 64, showed me the remains of his house. Only the foundations were left and, curiously, the delicate blackened remains of the grapevines which once grew like a roof over the courtyard. In a courtyard just down the street, fighters sat around chatting as a miserable-looking Russian prisoner, one of the many abandoned by their army, did chores. 'We built this over 40 years. Now I'm 64 and won't be able to start again', Ayup said. The Bamut commander, Khanzad Batayev, looked more depressed than when I'd seen him during the war. 'Our mosque, our most holy place, built by village donations, has been knocked to the ground. Our graveyard has been bombed. We can forgive them for what happened to the living, but the graveyard is desecrated. Twenty percent of the graves are ruined, or the bodies have been blown up. People here are exhausted – financially, physically and morally.'

Orekhovo, Stary Achkhoi and Zony were likewise uninhabitable, as were chunks of Samashki and several other once-prosperous villages. In Stary Achkhoi, Leche, a 40-year-old man, worked with relatives in the rubble of what had been his home. There was no one else in the entire village, which I'd been in several times during the war, but now couldn't recognise. 'Two rooms are left. If we can rebuild the roof then some of us can live here', Leche said. 'The problem is the landmines. We don't know where they are or what to do with them. Winter's coming. It's getting cold. Our people are dispersed all over the place, in dormitories, barns, tents, friends' floors. Worst of all is the amount of people we lost, our young men who died defending against this barbarity. What for? What was strategic about this village?'

'We must have optimism,' he concluded. 'We have good land. Anyway, how can we not return to our homes? This is where my father lived, my grandfather too. Our ancestors are buried here.'

Many of the *boyeviks* found it hard to adapt to peace time given that there was little to adapt to – no jobs, often no houses. Older ex-combatants had their families, but the young unmarried warriors, who long ago had cut themselves off entirely from mundane responsibilities, were especially adrift. A few became bodyguards to the warlords or the ministers in the new ruling elite. Others turned to crime or sought more war to fill the gap. Some fighters hoped to get to Tajikistan in Central Asia to join the outlawed Islamic opposition movement in its battle against the neo-Communist government and the Russian troops backing it up.

Magomed, a 17-year-old who had fought in Bamut, said he wanted 'to go and help our Moslem brothers who came here to help us, like the Arabs. I've got used to war over two years and there are so many places to fight.' His two friends, Vakha, 18, and Islam, 16, nodded in approval. All three were physically slight and didn't yet shave. They were likeable, and you had to keep reminding yourself that these were not average teenagers. The only clue was in their eyes, which stayed hard even when the mouth smiled. You could tell by the way they held their cigarettes and concentrated deeply as they inhaled that they'd learnt to smoke in times of great stress.

Vakha, who had also fought in Bamut, described the burning down of the government building in Grozny during the August battle as if it had been a fun outing. 'All it took was pouring petrol in and then firing an RPG off to light it up,' he said happily. Magomed could top that – his own atrocity. 'We captured this Cossack outside Bamut. He was loaded with weapons but when we caught him he tried to tell us that he'd been hunting and got lost and didn't even think he was in Chechnya,' he said, laughing at such an idiotic excuse. 'Obviously he was a *kontraktnik* and we decided to behead him. Everyone wanted to do it, but they picked me because I was the youngest and because it was me who captured him.' He still had a long knife taken from the Cossack as a 'trophy'.

A doctor in Grozny described the effect of war on children. 'They have become more aggressive, nervous, cruel, impolite. They don't respect elders. They're dangerous to be around. They have psychological illnesses, terrible emotions', the doctor said. 'The younger they are, the less they understand and the more they forget. Starting at about 10, they see and know everything and they'll remember it for life.'

I asked about Magomed, the head cutter.

'He's no longer a person. He can only solve problems with a gun. As long as he lives he'll be like that – he can't be saved.' I noticed the hands of the doctor, a Russian, were shaking uncontrollably. 'Please don't put down my name,' he said. 'I'm afraid'.

For ethnic-Russians, the withdrawal of troops was the final blow to their community and any hopes of being protected by Moscow. Ethnic-

Russians once numbered about 300,000 in Soviet Chechnya-Ingushetia. They held most of the skilled jobs and almost all the power posts, and considered Grozny a historic Russian city. Now they were a dying breed, maybe as few as 30,000 in the city, and in the old Cossack villages along the River Terek, nearly all of them too poor or old to leave. Certainly, Doku Zavgayev, the last vestige of the Soviet regime, would not be coming back. Shortly after the war, he was made Russian ambassador to Tanzania, an almost theatrically fit ending to his story, and, more importantly, far from the *kinzhals* of his vengeful countrymen.

Next to the burned-out ruins of the Orthodox church on Leninsky Prospekt in central Grozny, a few slightly crazed old women looked after their priest and kept the refurbished residence and chapel shiny clean. Once, while I happened to be there, two thuggish Chechens in black silk shirts appeared at the gate and demanded to see a certain Sasha. One of the old ladies, Maria, tried to make them go away, but they kept insisting. 'Don't worry, we're not going to hurt you. If we wanted trouble, we'd just walk in anyway', one laughed rudely. Maria was close to tears by the time she caved in and went to get Sasha. He turned out to be a young Russian living inside the church compound. He gave the Chechens a wad of money and they left. I couldn't tell what had been going on, but Sasha walked off looking worried. 'God forgive them, God save us', Maria said, crossing herself repeatedly in front of where the altar would have been if the church still stood.

The landmark for me was when tyotya, or 'Auntie' Natasha finally quit and moved to Russia just weeks after the end of the war. This cackling old Cossack woman had often looked after me and many other journalists in her tiny cottage on Griboyedova Street, behind the main bazaar, where she'd lived her entire life. Miraculously, she survived the war unscathed. But the Chechens' aggression and sense of revenge which followed the war were too much: she wanted to spend her last years in real peace. She made the right choice. A few days after Natasha departed I heard that a 72-year-old Russian woman had been shot dead nearby. No one knew why, but one neighbour's feeling was that she had a 'sharp tongue' and had injured the pride of someone with a gun. That was all it took – Russian lives meant nothing to some Chechens.

Chechens said that they meant the local Russians no harm, and insisted that the aggression was neither organised nor widespread. Given what had happened, some Chechen hostility was understandable, but whatever the apologists said, more than hostility was at work – innocent people were being killed and robbed and, worst of all, no one was intervening to stop it.

In a Russian refugee centre near Stavropol, Tatyana Ivanovna sat in a room just big enough for a cupboard and bed, which she shared with her eight-year-old son. She'd fled Grozny at the start of the war and, now it was over, knew she'd never return. 'I've already found out that Chechens have moved into my house. I wouldn't dare show my face.' A descendant of Cossacks, with a good job at Grozny University, Tatyana had been a typical Russian resident. Equally typically, she couldn't understand why the Chechens had rebelled. To her, the Soviet Union had been a success and everything had made sense in the days that she taught the Chechens Russian literature. 'It was fine before. I used to go up to Vedeno and Shatoi to inspect the schools. Until 1985 or 1987, they were very nice to us, the Chechens. They were nice because there were proper authorities and they were afraid of us.'

For months Moscow refused to drop its hardline negotiating approach – effectively, that aid depended on Grozny dropping its independence claim – and Chechnya, in a dangerous limbo, looked abroad for help. Russian Foreign Minister Yevgeny Primakov had warned on the eve of Maskhadov's election that Moscow would sever ties with any country recognising the republic. Nevertheless, Maskhadov's first post-war trip was to make the *hadj* pilgrimage in April 1997 at the invitation of Saudi Arabia's King Fahd. Discouraged by the West's washing of hands, Maskhadov made no secret about the fact that he tried to win political and material help during his meetings with the king and other Moslem leaders. The Saudis paid the plane tickets of another 1,000 Chechens, an act of generosity which stood in sharp contrast to the stubbornness of Russian negotiators.

Chechnya was being pushed into a corner and that, as experience showed, was potentially lethal. Even simply giving up on Chechnya and leaving it as an outlawed, semi-independent republic was dangerous. An isolated Chechnya would certainly become a breeding ground for armed political and religious radicals. 'Liberation' of the entire North Caucasus was a favourite theme of Dzhokhar Dudayev, and it was no coincidence that one of Shamil Basayev's role models was Fidel Castro. Basayev's Arab friend, the Wahhabist fundamentalist and guerrilla warfare expert Khatab, not only stayed after the war, but married, bought a house and set up a training camp. In the right conditions – continued confrontation, poverty and hopelessness – Khatab could prove the thin end of a wedge pushing the more tolerant Sufi Chechens into extremist, infidel-hating Islam.

As ever, the fate of the game lay in Moscow. President Yeltsin, finally recovering from eight solid months of illness and political isolation, bounced back in February, 1997, and that spring appointed two young reformers – Anatoly Chubais and the longtime anti-war governor of Nizhny Novgorod region Boris Nemtsov – his first deputy prime ministers. Here was a sea change. These were men interested in economics, not ideology, men with the age and background which allowed them to shed the Soviet, neo-imperial mentality. The liberal shift throughout government gave impulse to the dovish Security Council Secretary Ivan Rybkin, who had replaced Lebed and was in favour of a new, economically-orientated *Realpolitik*. Ironically, Rybkin's right-hand man was none other than Boris Berezovsky, the canny industrialist whose ORT television had helped stir up the war at the start.

One of the last obstacles to real negotiations was the bulldog-like interior minister, Anatoly Kulikov, now the final representative of the old party of war. Kulikov snarled and did what he could to disparage Maskhadov's troubled rule and prevent further talks. When terrorist bombs went off in the rail stations of Armavir and Pyatigorsk in April 1997, he was quick to blame the Chechens, but there was growing suspicion that the violence had been orchestrated by the secret services in Moscow, not Grozny. Berezovsky openly suggested that Kulikov had 'not had enough of war' and Rybkin told the interior minister to keep his hands off the peace process. 'However many stars they have on their shoulders, people should not choke on their ambitions,' he said.

Boris Yeltsin, as usual watching his squabbling ministers from above, swallowed his pride and came down on the side of the doves – not in the old hedge-betting manner, but irreversibly, dramatically. On 12 May, a smiling Yeltsin greeted Maskhadov at the Kremlin, their first ever meeting, and signed a generously worded peace accord promising to 'give up the use of force and the threat of force'. Fittingly, Kulikov was sent away on an urgent trip to the far east of Russia.

Yeltsin and Maskhadov decided that relations were to be based, from that day, on 'international law'. This was a peace declaration between two equal presidents – a first in the history of the Russian Caucasus. 'Right now, with the president of the Chechen Republic of Ichkeria, we signed a peace agreement, an agreement which is destined to have historical importance because it puts a full stop to 400 years in which there has always been some sort of war and uncertainty for a whole people,' Yeltsin said. Finally, the president, who now regularly referred to Ichkeria, was atoning for his terrible mistakes.

The peace accord – which neatly sidestepped the still impossible issue of Chechnya's political status – also opened the way for the money men to talk about financing Chechnya's reconstruction. The Russian Central Bank signed a deal with Chechnya's National Bank which virtually conceded the republic's economic independence, allowing it to set its own cash circulation policy and oversee the activities of its own local commercial banks. A novel plan was proposed for Chechnya's recovery, in which Russian regions and possibly former Soviet republics would bring investments and, in return, Moscow would write off part of their debts. Ironically, another potential economic olive branch proved to be the Azeri oil pipeline, one of the immediate causes of the war. As final preparations were made for the early oil to flow from the Caspian in late 1997, the powerful new economists in the Kremlin understood that the best way to secure the route would be to cut a deal with the Chechens. The stakes were huge. Although transit fees for the early oil were relatively insignificant, the decision on how to send the lucrative main oil in the next century – via Georgia or via Chechnya and southern Russia – would likely depend heavily on the experience of the routes used in these initial stages. At last, Chechnya and its northern neighbour had common cause.

Of course, the desire to fence in the Chechens never vanished altogether. Plans were announced by Moscow to build a bypass pipeline around Chechnya and Kulikov said he would establish a military cordon on the borders. But although these measures were seen as a badly needed insurance policy, they risked alienating the Chechens and were unlikely to have much effect on stemming terrorism.

Following up on the Kremlin treaty was another milestone when representatives of Russia, Chechnya and the other North Caucasus republics met in the southern Russian spa town of Kislovodsk on May 31 to sign a regional declaration of peace. The meeting reflected Moscow's belated realisation that the North Caucasus' problems could no longer be treated in isolation, but had to be put within the context of a common regional policy. There was even a favourable reaction to the Chechens' idea of creating a collective Caucasus security organisation. Chechnya, at horrific cost to both sides, had forced Russia to treat the region's peoples with respect.

Moscow's *noblesse oblige* went far from unrewarded. Aggression and table-thumping had only pushed Chechnya away, whereas economic links were pulling the republic in. 'Russia is a great power', Maskhadov said in May. 'She is close to us and today we are linked economically in every way. That is why I am committed to Russia, much more so than to the West and the Moslem world.'

### Moscow

*November 1996. Aslan Maskhadov, now wearing a dark suit and tie instead of camouflage gear, holds a press conference in his former enemy's capital for the first time. I'm thinking about where I've interviewed this man before – in the presidential palace bunker, in the mountains, in the woods, in safehouses where they asked you to identify the place only as 'a village in southern Chechnya'. Here he is now in Moscow's Hotel Arbat, just behind the Stalinist-Gothic tower of the foreign ministry, flanked by Movladi Udugov and Akhmed Zakayev. For me, the war has ended.*

*'Aslan Maskhadov', one of the journalists asks. 'Do you feel that you won?'*

*Maskhadov, cautious as always, pauses for several seconds before speaking. Then, in his quiet voice, he says: 'Our goal was not to defeat the Russian army. We know the Russian army is big and has nuclear weapons.'*

*'We fought with what forces we had so that there would not be a single Russian soldier on our territory and our citizens would not be killed. I think we achieved that.'*

# PART 6

# Chasing Paradise

*The Caucasus mountains are sacred to me. And so early! At ten! Oh that mystery, that lost paradise will claw at my mind until the grave!*

Lermontov.

## Karachayevsk

*The Karachai elders ask to see me in the mosque. There are about 30, kneeling on carpets where they've just completed the namaz and they want to hear about Chechnya. The official version seen on television is all they know.*

*'Why is the government sending planes to bomb its own people in Chechnya?' an old man in a prayer cap asks.*

*'Who is right – just tell us, who is right?'*

*'Is what they say on the television true? We sometimes think they're not telling us half of what happens over there?'*

*'Is it true that the Chechen fighters have foreign mercenaries? Did you see any?'*

*'Tell your Clinton that innocent people are being murdered there!'*

*Venting anger has become more important for these men than hearing my answers, and I feel I could slip from the dais where I'm sitting with the mufti and go out into the street almost unnoticed.*

*Suddenly, an old man, some kind of Islamic authority in a high Astrakhan hat, interrupts to ask: 'How do we know you're not FSB, spying or something? Who sent you?'*

*I think he's joking and laugh. But there's silence.*

*'Show him your papers,' the mufti next to me says. My pink press card is passed around the kneeling men until they're satisfied. The questions start again. 'Why does Russia always try to crush its minorities?'*

How to pin down the North Caucasus? You can't. You change worlds and centuries in an hour. In a single day you meet patriarchs and brigands, swaggering mafiosi and shepherd boys; there are faces from ancient Greek pottery and strains of music from Turkey. None of it can or should be pinned down. The North Caucasus is a hall of a thousand distorting mirrors, each showing a different reflection, and people have long forgotten which are straight, which crooked.

I close my eyes and watch the images in whatever order they come. I think of driving through the mountains of Dagestan, breathing in the sweet smell of evening among the poplars and apricot groves, trying at each stone village, with its winding streets, to guess which nation lives there, and rarely getting it right.

I think of Alec, living in Cherkessk with a household which looked as if it was picked at random from a bowl of ethnic groups. He was Cherkess, his ex-wife was Abaza, and his new wife was Nogai, a descendant of the Mongol hordes; his son was Cherkess-Abaza but about to marry a Russian. They spoke several languages and dialects each, but when together, their only common tongue was Russian.

I think of how even the centuries get disordered and history taps you on the shoulder when least expected. Take Alec again. Alec was a taxi driver. He looked like Bluebeard, a cut throat with a crooked row of yellow, gold and missing teeth, but he told me his family name was Pshiun, 'which means house of the king'. Long before the Russians came, his family had been royal Circassian.

Because of history's grip, the North Caucasus is also about war – wars past and present, wars yet to be fought, and wars which have already been fought but need to be fought again. For me, there will always be the leaden feeling of fear at the sound of jets; the Chechen defending Shali with a shotgun and his ecstatic shouts of 'Allah Akbar!' as artillery shells fell around us; the thrill of survival; the wild, wrenching sound of the *zikr* in a bunker in Stary Achkhoi; the broken presence of Russian prisoners in a dark, underground cell; the way all human corpses look the same, the horror when you realise your body would look no different.

Some say the wars are over. At Vladikavkaz football club, the best in Russia when I visited in 1996, there were players from 14 ethnic groups in the top squad, and the manager, Batrak Bitarov, talked about peace. Bitarov, an Ossetian, was one of those oil-smooth characters who coexist with the toughs in the Caucasus. Plenty of gold on his wrists, a long camel-coloured overcoat and a silk scarf. Look, he said – Kabards, Greeks, Georgians, Jews, Ossetians, Russians, and all in the same strip. Fourteen nationalities and all happy. 'Let's forget these distinctions, Caucasian and Russian. Lets just call each other Russian citizens. There's no such thing as a good people or a bad people – we're all the same.'

But Bitarov was wrong, because in the North Caucasus, especially in North Ossetia, not everyone is the same, and the wars make sure people remember that. Prigorodny region was less than an hour's drive from Bitarov's stadium and there, the weeds grew thick in the ruins of Ingush houses. Four years after the war ended, there were certainly no Ingush on Bitarov's multinational team.

Nor was everyone the same in northern Chechnya. There, the last Cossacks not to flee endured, poor and frightened, along the left bank of the River Terek where their ancestors built forts, never expecting that one day the Chechens would take over. Not everyone was the same in Adygea. An Adygei man explained the untideness of an ethnic-Russian village near Maikop saying, 'they don't take care, the Russians, because they know in their hearts that these lands aren't really theirs. They don't feel at home.' The Russians had lived in that village for over a century, but Adygei memories went back further.

The North Caucasus will also be about many things that are not war. Drinking homemade apricot juice in the sun after a hot walk. Making a toast to the pagan gods of North Ossetia. The Chechen who gave me a trick pen which had a nib at one end and a lighter at the other, purely to give me pleasure, and when he'd known me for 10 minutes. Ruslan Kirimov, who lived in central Grozny all the war and still had enough humour to try and fail to teach me the Lezghinka dance. Aslanbek, the 10-year-old refugee boy from Bamut who galloped his horse bareback in the dust, forced to grow up before his time, but full of childish life all the same. The sudden sight of the sun, falling huge and bloody over the Caucasus. Mountain Jew children singing Hebrew songs in Nalchik. Buying a lamb kebab at a place in the hills, where they put the chunks of meat with chopped up raw onions in an empty cigarette carton, and which tasted better than anything imaginable.

To the imperial Russians, the North Caucasus was paradise – rich, abundant and strategic lands, washed by a sea on each side – and the arrival of the tsars was inevitable. But then the curse of the Caucasus: how to rule such a region? How could Britain be ruled if each county were inhabited by a separate nation speaking a different language? How to rule the unruleable? Since the collapse of the Soviet Union, most Russians have seen little but trouble and banditry in the Caucasus, but there is no escaping the region now. Not only is the North Caucasus linked to the export of Caspian Sea oil, the future of the Russian democratic state will depend in part on how Moscow's relations develop with the highlanders.

There is some hope. In Chechnya, the neo-imperialists may have had their last hurrah, handing Russia a chance to emerge from the past. Russian voters whose sons were taken away to die are unlikely to be fooled again by politicians claiming to 'restore constitutional order'. Most important, the war, shocking as it was, did have its limits. Movladi Udugov said 'this was a great victory for the truly democratic part of Russia. Russia declined to wipe out a people. That may be Russia's greatest victory in the Caucasus in history.'

Of course Chechnya may prove only a temporary shock. Without a change to the political structure crafted by President Yeltsin, in which a tsar-like president can take huge decisions free of checks and balances, the door will remain open to more political adventures like the 'short, victorious war'. Yeltsin was not a tyrant *per se*, but when his thirst to remain in power led him to an act of tyranny, there was nothing in the system to stop him.

Then there are the unknowns, sown like the landmines in Chechnya's fields. At some point – 2001 according to the Khasavyurt accord –

Moscow and Grozny will have to make up their minds on the republic's
political status; even with the cooling-off period, that decision is likely
to remain explosive. Many of the Chechens who fought and suffered
will never put up with anything less than full independence. If Chechnya
does become independent, what will be the knock-on effect? While a
wave of independence declarations would be unlikely, there would
certainly be new impetus to demands for autonomy from groups such as
the Balkars. Militant Islam, a new Ingush-Ossetian war, the break-up of
Dagestan, Cossack paramilitary units functioning as state security forces
– these are only some of the other potential devils. Perhaps the bold
Kremlin declarations of peace in 1997 will sound empty in a decade and
the Russian army, having undergone major reform, will again fight for
the Caucasus.

In the 19th century Leo Tolstoy compared the Avar hero Hadji Murat
to a thistle which, alone in an entire field, had survived the plough,
refusing to 'surrender to man who had destroyed all its brethren around'.
That toughness, above all, is the fascination of the mountains and their
people. All the world admires survivors, and everyone backs David
against Goliath. But this admiration masks the fragility and the ultimate
tragedy of the North Caucasus. The mountain nations may be small and
hardy, but they are also small enough to be persecuted *en masse*, small
enough to disappear. In a warning to all highlanders, the last Ubykh
speaker died in Turkey in 1992, a century after his people were pushed
out of the North Caucasus by the Russians. The Ubykhs, who are related
to the Adgygei-Circassian tribes, made the mistake of over-assimilating
to their place of exile and, finally, suffered this quiet linguistic extinction.
In the same way that the most rugged countryside eventually erodes
under the weight of tourists, the highlanders' strength is great, but finite.

### *Prokhladnoye, Kabardino-Balkaria*

*I walk out of Bamut through the woods. Twenty four hours later I've
left Chechnya altogether and reach Prokhladnoye, an ethnic-Russian
town in Kabardino-Balkaria, where snow falls gently over the big Lenin
statue on the main square. I'm invited to a drink by the deputy rail
station manager, an important man in this junction town. Two of his
friends come. They all bear a striking resemblance to Communist Party
leader Gennady Zyuganov – hearty, provincial, congenial and bigotted.
I'm not surprised to hear they'll be voting Communist in the upcoming
parliamentary elections.*

*'Everyone's sick of disorder. They want discipline', Valentin says. 'The
Russian people have been sold out', Boris adds. 'Everywhere they're
giving people independence, when what we need is to unite. Strictness is
what we need.'*

'That's right, you have to fight fire with fire down here', says Nikolai, the deputy station manager. 'I like what they did in America. The blacks rose up, a few hundred were burned, then very quickly it all went quiet again.'

Each of us has two glasses – one for locally made Prokhladnoye brandy, which we drink in large shots, and one for soft drink to recover. There are long toasts. My head spins and we all smile at each other. Chechnya seems far away, but occasionally between the spins, like slight electric shocks, I see darkness and fire. Then someone pours another brandy, half a glass full.

When it's my turn to give a toast, I say: 'to peace in Chechnya'. They like that, even though they've just finished telling me that Chechens are bandits, that only the Communists could keep such a people in line. More brandy. More toasts. To peace between all peoples of the world. To our friendship. It all sounds so *convincing*.

# Select Bibliography

## Ancient History

Abayev, V. I., *Isbrannye trudy*. (Selected works)Ir. Vladikavkaz, 1990.

Ascherson, Neal, *Black Sea*. Jonathan Cape, London, 1995.

Burney, Charles and Lang, David, *The Peoples of the Hills – Ancient Ararat and Caucasus*. Ebenezer Baylis and son, Ltd, The Trinity Press, 1971.

Gadagatl, Asker M., *Mifologiya i Adygsky epos Nartkher. (Mythology and the Adygei Nart epos.)* Caucasologie et mythologie comparée, *Actes du Colloque international du C.N.R.S.* Paris, PEETERS, 1992, pp. 53–67.

Gamzatov, Gadji G., 'On the Problem of Mythology in the Daghestanian Epos: the problem of the general and the particular'. Caucasologie et mythologie comparée, *Actes du Colloque international du C.N.R.S.* Paris, PEETERS, 1992, pp. 69–82.

Herodotus, *The histories*. Penguin, London, 1954.

Isaenko, Anatoly, *Ancient Metallurgy in the Caucasus as Reflected in Ossetian Epic Poetry*. North Ossetia University, Vladikavkaz.

Sergent, Bernard, *Caucasiens de Grèce*. (Caucasians of Greece.), Caucasologie et mythologie comparée, *Actes du Colloque International du C.N.R.S.* Paris, PEETERS, 1992, pp. 37–50.

Traho, Ramazan, 'Circassians', *Central Asian Survey*, vol. 10, no 1/2, pp, 1–63, 1991.

## Russian Conquest

Baddeley, John F., *The Russian Conquest of the Caucasus,* Longmans, Green and Co, 1908.

Bell, James, *Residence in Circassia* (during the years 1837, 1838 and 1839), London, 1840.

Blanch, Lesley, *The Sabres of Paradise,* Quartet Books. London, 1978.

Broxup, Marie Bennigsen et al., *The North Caucasus Barrier. The Russian advance towards the Muslim world,* Hurst, London, 1992.

Gammer, Moshe, *Muslim Resistance to the Tsar. Shamil and the conquest of Chechnya and Dagestan,* Frank Cass, London, 1994.

Gammer, Moshe, 'Vorontsov's 1845 Expedition Against Shamil: A British report.' *Central Asian Survey*, vol. 4, no. 4, pp. 13–33, 1985.

Hadjetlache, Mohammed Beg, 'Aul Yulan: An episode of the Caucasian war', *Central Asian Survey*, vol. 4, pp. 47–9, 1985.

Henze, Paul B., 'Fire and Sword in the Caucasus: The 19th Century resistance of the North Caucasian mountaineers', *Central Asian Survey*, vol. 2, no. 1, pp. 5–41, 1983.

Isaenko, Anatoly and Petschauer, Peter, 'The Long Arm of the dead: Traumas and conflicts in the Caucasus', *Mind and Human Interaction*. vol. 6, no. 3. University of Virginia School of Medicine, 1995.

Kelly, Laurence, *Lermontov. Tragedy in the Caucasus*, Robin Clark, 1983.

Layton, Susan, 'Primitive despot and noble savage: the two faces of Shamil in Russian literature.' *Central Asian Survey*, vol. 10, no. 4, pp. 31–45, 1991.

Lermontov, Mikhail, *A Hero of our Time*, Penguin, London, 1966.

Luxenburg, Norman, 'Russian Expansion into the Caucasus and the English relationship thereto', University of Michigan dissertation, 1956.

NART, 'The Life of Mansur. Great independence fighter of the Caucasian mountain people', *Central Asian Survey*, vol. 10, no. 1/2, pp. 81–92, 1991.

Tolstoy, Leo, *Master and Man and Other Stories (for Hadji Murat)*, Penguin. London, 1977.

Tolstoy, Leo, *The Death of Ivan Ilyich and Other Stories (for The Cossacks)*, Penguin, London, 1960.


## Soviet Period and Deportations

Bammate, Haidar, 'The Caucasus and the Russian Revolution (from a historical viewpoint)', *Central Asian Survey*, vol. 10, no. 4, pp. 1–29, 1991.

Bennigsen, Alexandre, 'Muslim guerrilla warfare in the Caucasus (1918–1928)', *Central Asian Survey*, vol. 2, no. 1, pp. 45–56, 1983.

Conquest, Robert, *The Nation Killers: the Soviet deportation of nationalities*. Macmillan, 1970.

Jabagi, Vassan-Giray, 'Revolution and Civil War in the North Caucasus: End of the 19th – beginning of the 20th Century', *Central Asian Survey*, vol. 10, no. 1/2, pp. 119–32, 1991.

Murad, Sultan, 'The Jihad of Said Shamil and Sultan Murad for the Liberation of the Caucasus', *Central Asian Survey*, vol. 10, no. 1/2, pp. 181–7, 1991.

Tak eto bylo. (That is how it was.) Vols I–III. Insan. Moscow, 1993.

Tutaeff, David, *The Soviet Caucasus*, George Harrapp, 1942.


## Soviet and Post-Soviet History

Chervonnaya, Svetlana, *Conflict in the Caucasus. Georgia, Abkhazia and the Russian shadow*, Gothic Image Publications, Glastonbury, Somerset, 1994.

Clarke, Bruce, *An Empire's New Clothes*: The end of Russia's liberal dream. Vintage, 1995, London.

Coppieters, Bruno, ed., *Contested Borders in the Caucasus*, Zed Books. London and New Jersey, 1994.

Galeotti, Mark, *Afghanistan. The Soviet Union's last war*, Frank Cass, 1995.

Goldenberg, Suzanne, *Pride of Small Nations. The Caucasus and post-Soviet disorder*, Vubpress-VUB University Press, Brussels, 1996.

Henze, Paul B., 'The Demography of the Caucasus According to 1989 Soviet Census Data', *Central Asian Survey*, vol. 10, no. 1/2, pp. 147–70, 1991.

Hewitt, B. G., 'Abkhazia: a problem of identity and ownership', *Central Asian Survey*, vol. 12 (3), 267–323, 1993.

Krag, Helen and Funch, Lars, *The North Caucasus: Minorities at a crossroads,* Minority Rights Group, UK, 1994.

Murray, Brian, 'Peace in the Caucasus: multi-ethnic stability in Dagestan', *Central Asian Survey*, vol. 13 (4), 507–23, 1994.

Ro'i, Yaacov, ed., *Muslim Eurasia: Conflicting legacies*, Frank Cass, London, 1995.

*Severny Kavkaz: vybor puti natsionalnovo razvitiya.* (The North Caucasus: the choice of path for national development.) Meoty. Maikop, 1994.

Vasilyeva, Olga and Muzaev, Timur, *Severny Kavkaz ve poiskakh regionalnoi ideology.* (The North Caucasus in search of regional ideology.) Progress. Moscow, 1994.


## Religion

Bennigsen, Alexandre and Wimbush, S. Enders, *Moslems of the Soviet Empire,* London: Hurst, 1985.

—— *Mystics and Commissars. Sufism in the Soviet Union,* University of California Press, Berkeley and Los Angeles, 1985.

Bryan, Fanny E., 'Anti-religious Activity in the Chechen-Ingush Republic of the USSR and the Survival of Islam', *Central Asian Survey*, vol. 3, no. 2, pp. 99–116, 1984.

Lemercier-Quelquejay, Chantal, 'Sufi Brotherhoods in the USSR: A historical survey', *Central Asian Survey*, vol. 2, no. 4, pp. 1–36, 1983.

Panarin, Sergei, 'Muslims of the Former USSR: Dynamics of survival', *Central Asian Survey*, vol. 12 (2), 137–49, 1993.

Popov, K., *Svyashchennaya Roshcha Khetaga,* (The holy grove of Hetag.) Ir. Vladikavkaz, 1995.

Tarran, Michel, 'The Orthodox Mission in the North Caucasus: End of the 18th – beginning of the 19th Century', *Central Asian Survey*, vol. 10, no. 1/2, pp. 103–17, 1991.


## Chechen Conflict

Baev, Pavel K., *The Russian Army in a Time of Troubles,* Sage Publications, London, 1996.

Dixelius, Malcolm and Konstantinov, Andrei, *Prestupny Mir Rossy.* (The criminal world in Russia) Bibliopolis, 1995, Saint Petersburg.

Dudayev, Dzhokhar, *Ternisty put k svobodye,* (Thorny path to freedom) Vilnius, 1993.

Express Data, *Rossyskie vooruzhennye sily ve Chechenskom konflikte,* (Russian armed forces in the Chechen conflict), Moscow, 1996.

Iskandaryan, Aleksandr, *Chechensky krizis: Proval Rossyskoi politiki na kavkaze.* (The Chechen crisis: the collapse of Russian policy in the Caucasus) Carnegie Endowment for International Peace. Moscow, 1995.

Marchenko, Veronika, *Takaya armiya ...* (Such an army ...), Norma, Saint Petersburg, 1995.

Soslambekov, Yusup, *Chechnya (Nokhchicho) - Vzglyad Iznutri.* (Chechnya – a view from within), Moscow, 1995.

*Belaya kniga.* (The white book.) FSK public relations centre. Moscow, 1995.

*Komissiya Govorukhina.* (The Govorukhin commission) Laventa. Moscow, 1995.

*Neizvestny soldat Kavkazskoi voiny.* (The unknown soldier in the Caucasus war.) Memorial. Moscow, 1997.

*Vsemi imeyushchimisya sredstvami.* (With all available means.) Memorial. Moscow, 1995.

*Za spinami mirnykh zhitelei.* (Behind the backs of civilians) Memorial. Moscow, 1996.


## Travel Writing and Ethnography

Abercromby, Hon. John, *A Trip through the Eastern Caucasus,* Edward Stanford, 1889.

Babich, Irina, *Narodny traditsy v obshchestvennom bytu Kabardintsev.* (Popular traditions in Kabardinos' way of life), Rossyskaya Akademiya Nauk, Moscow, 1995.

Cunynghame, Sir Arthur Thurlow, *Travels in the Eastern Caucasus on the Caspian and Black Seas, especially in Dagestan, and on the Frontiers of Persia and Turkey during the Summer of 1871,* John Murray, London, 1872.

Dumas, Alexander, *Adventures in the Caucasus.* Peter Owen, 1962.

*Chechentsy. Obychai. Traditsy. Nravy.* (Chechens: Customs, traditions, temperament) Kniga. Grozny, 1992.

Farson, Negley, *Caucasian Journey.* Evans Brothers Ltd. London 1951.

Grove, F. C., *The Frosty Caucasus.* Longman's, Green and Co, 1875.

Henze, Mary L., 'Thirty Cows for an Eye: the traditional economy of the central Caucasus: An analysis from 19th Century travellers' accounts.' *Central Asian Survey,* vol. 4, no. 3, p 115–29, 1985.

Wanderer, *Notes on the Caucasus,* Macmillan. London, 1883.


## General

Gilbert, Martin, *Atlas of Russian History. From 800 BC to the present day,* Orion Publishing Group, London, 1993.

Lawrence, John, *A History of Russia,* Meridian, 1993.

# Index

parliamentary inquiry into, 131;
Western loss of interest in, 225; Western
view of, 224; Yeltsin orders truce, 195);
Yermolov's attempt to pacify, 42
Chechnya-Ichkeria, 122, 179, 180, 181, 197,
231
Chechnya-Ingushetia, 57, 58, 62
checkpoints on roads, 186, 187; passing of,
201
Cherkess, 88, 89, 92, 94, 100
Chernomyrdin, Viktor, 131, 139, 147, 202,
203, 206, 228, 232, 235, 237, 239
Chervonnaya, Svetlana, *Conflict in the
Caucasus*, 103
Chomayev, Kazbek, 89, 91
Christianity, 8, 14, 32, 35, 36, 37, 48, 79,
81, 100, 104, 106, 107, 112, 154
Chubais, Anatoly, 265
Circassia, 42, 98
Circassians, 36, 43, 48, 49, 50, 51, 53, 271;
as soldiers, 36
civilians, forced into the firing line, 248;
sufferings of, 219, 239
Clinton, Bill, 195, 234, 270; summit with
Boris Yeltsin, 226
collectivisation, 58
Commonwealth of Independent States
(CIS), 71, 103
*Communist Manifesto*, 54
Confederation of Peoples of the Caucasus,
100, 116, 134
Conquest, Robert, *The Nation Killers*, 59,
60, 62, 77
Cossacks, 36, 37, 38, 39, 42, 46, 50, 53, 54,
55, 89, 90, 94, 95, 96, 97, 98, 102, 271,
273; living situation of, 37; role of, in
colonisation, 96
Council of Europe, admission of Russia,
226
Crimean War, 50, 51
criminal bands, activities of, 260
Cuny, Fred, 194
Cunynghame, Arthur Thurlowe, 19

Dagestan, 2, 3, 7, 9, 22, 23, 27, 32, 40, 41–
54, 55, 57, 76, 83, 84, 85, 86, 101, 105,
116, 129, 142, 146, 149, 152, 168, 175,
186, 201, 211, 212, 217, 220, 236, 270,
273
Dagestanis, 53, 102
Dargo village, 24, 175, 179; battle of, 47, 49
Degoyev, Vladimir, 116

Deinekin, Pyotr, 171, 223
Denikin, Anton, 55, 56
deportation of populations, 1, 3, 58, 59,
60, 61, 63, 64, 65, 67, 75, 77, 78, 80, 84,
85, 88, 89, 90, 91, 107, 108, 111, 112,
126, 165; figures for, 58–9
deserters, from the Russian army, 190, 191
Dima, a hostage, 216
*dolmens*, 32
drinking alcohol *see* alcohol, consumption
of
Dudayev, Alla, 234, 235–6
Dudayev, Baskhan, 233
Dudayev, Dzhokhar, 10, 12, 15, 89, 103,
104, 115, 116, 122, 123, 125, 126, 127,
128, 130, 131, 132, 133, 134, 135, 136,
137, 138, 142, 148, 151, 152, 153, 154,
158, 163, 164, 168, 169, 170, 179, 180,
182, 186, 192, 197, 198, 204, 206, 210,
215, 220, 223, 227, 265; death of, 230–6
Dumanov, Khassan, 114, 115
Dumas, Alexander, 43, 47, 88, 184, 191;
*Adventures in the Caucasus*, 37
Dzhagamat movement, 88, 89
Dzhamal, Kazir, 66
Dzhambula, a commander, 164, 165
Dzhanayev, Magomed, 233

Elbaum, Cynthia, 147
Elbrus, a North Ossetian, 112–13
Elbrus, Mount, 8, 13
Elchibey, Abulfaz, 71
elders, respect for, 23, 25
Engel Yurt, 215
Estonia, 132

Fahd of Saudi Arabia, King, 265
family structures, 22, 23
Felgenhauer, Pavel, 163, 217
Filatov, Sergei, 139
filtration camps, 190, 225, 261
forests, Russian destruction of, 49, 51
FSB secret services, 28, 137, 182, 204, 212,
213, 230, 235, 239, 260, 261, 270

Gaidar, Yegor, 131, 139, 142
Gaisultan, Dakha, 14
Gall, Carlotta, 215
Gamidov, Gamid, 87
Gamsakhurdia, Zviad, 103, 135
Gantemirov, Beslan, 135, 137, 208, 228
Gasperini, Bill, 156